# SPORTSMARKETING

MELISSA JOHNSON MORGAN & JANE SUMMERS

THOMSON
SOCIAL SCIENCE PRESS

Australia · Canada · Mexico · Singapore · Spain · United Kingdom · United States

THOMSON™

102 Dodds Street
Southbank Victoria 3006

Email: highereducation@thomsonlearning.com.au
Website: www.thomsonlearning.com.au

First published in 2005
10 9 8 7 6 5 4 3 2 1
08 07 06 05



National Library of Australia
Cataloguing-in-Publication data

Morgan, Melissa Jane Johnson.
Sports marketing.

Includes index.
For tertiary students.

ISBN 0 17 012859 8.

1. Sports – Marketing – Textbooks. 2. Sports sponsorship – Textbooks. 3. Sports – Economic aspects. I. Summers, Jane, 1962– . II. Title.

796.0698

Editor: Liz Filleul
Project editor: Chris Wyness
Publishing editor: Elizabeth Vella
Publishing manager: Michael Tully
Indexer: Julie King
Text designer: Chris Ryan
Cover design by: Olga Lavecchia
Photo researcher: Michelle Cottrill
Typeset in Gill Sans, Melior and New Aster by Linotype
Production controller: Jodie Van Teylingen
Printed in Australia by Ligare

This title is published under the imprint of Thomson.
Nelson Australia Pty Limited ACN 058 280 149 (incorporated in Victoria)
trading as Thomson Learning Australia.

The URLs contained in this publication were checked for currency during the production process. Note, however, that the publisher cannot vouch for the ongoing currency of URLs.

# Contents

# List of figures

# List of tables

# Dedication

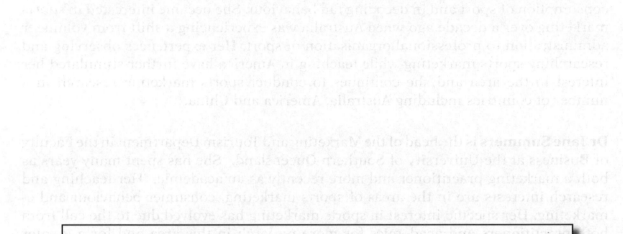

To our families for their love, encouragement and support –

J. Dale, Scarlett, Isabella and Buckley Morgan

Des, Jessica and Ben Summers

# About the authors

**Dr Melissa Johnson Morgan** is a Senior Lecturer at the University of Southern Queensland and an adjunct Professor of Marketing at Tulane University in New Orleans, USA. Her research interests lie predominantly in explaining the experiential consumption of sport and in decoding fan behaviour. She became interested in sports marketing over a decade ago when Australia was experiencing a shift from volunteer administration to professional organisation of sport. Her experiences observing and researching sports marketing while teaching in America have further stimulated her interest in the area and she continues to conduct sports marketing research in a number of countries including Australia, America and China.

**Dr Jane Summers** is the head of the Marketing and Tourism Department in the Faculty of Business at the University of Southern Queensland. She has spent many years as both a marketing practitioner and more recently as an academic. Her teaching and research interests are in the areas of sports marketing, consumer behaviour and e-marketing. Her specific interest in sports marketing has evolved due to the call from both practitioners and academics for more research in this area and for a greater understanding particularly of consumer behaviour and attitudes in relation to sports consumption. The international applicability of some of these consumption-related issues is an area that Jane is pursuing for future research.

# Acknowledgements

We would like to thank all those people who have spoken to us about sports marketing and the sports industry over the last few years. We would particularly thank those sports marketing and management professionals who gave so willingly of their time and experiences at many different professional sports conferences and events in Australia and overseas.

Many people contributed to the book and in particular we would like to thank Michael Volkov, Bridget Marcou and Amy Boyle for their case studies. Thanks to Marty Hirons from Sweeney Research for his ideas and access to information about the sports market in Australia. Special thanks to Dr Meredith Lawley for her advice about Chapter 5. We would also like to thank Rae Jones for her excellent administrative support with this and so many other projects.

The authors wish to thank the reviewers and editors for their many suggestions and constructive comments about the book. In particular we would like to thank the team at Thomson including editor Liz Filleul, Michael Tully, Publishing Manager – Higher Education, Chris Wyness, Managing Editor, and Anne-Marie Scoones, Educational Representative for Higher Education.

Thank you linesmen, thank you ball boys ...

# Preface

This book takes a strategic perspective of sports marketing and is organised into five parts. Part 1, 'Introducing sports marketing' offers students a broad strategic perspective on sports marketing, beginning with an introduction and a general discussion about some of the issues and concepts (Chapter 1) that will be addressed later in the book. Chapter 2 provides a more detailed examination of the elements of sport that are common to both marketers of sport and marketers using sport and also provides discussion relating to the development of a strategic framework for sports marketing.

Part 2, 'The sports environment' begins with an examination of the role of sport in society (Chapter 3), dealing specifically with issues of socialisation, violence, ethics and sport and business, moving through a discussion of sports consumers. Also in this part, Chapter 4 provides students with a focused discussion of the individual consumer-related issues that need to be considered in sports marketing. This is followed by a review of the sports marketing environments and an explanation of how to understand and gather information about them (Chapter 5).

The third part, 'Marketing of sport' begins with an examination of the four Ps in relation to strategic sports marketing. Specifically, issues involved in developing and managing sports products is dealt with in Chapter 6, Chapter 7 deals with promotion and IMC decisions by examining how to create and communicate value in sport through mining of the sports value chain, and finally pricing and distribution elements are addressed in Chapter 8.

Part 4, 'Marketing using sport', examines the use of sport as a strategic marketing tool in non-sport organisations (Chapter 9) and the subsequent leveraging of sport in the overall marketing strategy (Chapter 10).

The fifth and final part of the book examines contemporary issues in sports marketing and looks at global issues (Chapter 11) before concluding with a preview of the future of sport and sports marketing (Chapter 12).

# Part 1

# Introducing sports marketing

# Chapter 1

# Understanding the sports industry

## Learning objectives

After reading the chapter you should be able to:

- discuss the pervasive nature of sport
- define sports marketing and outline how it differs from mainstream marketing
- describe the evolution of the modern sports industry
- discuss the global size and economic importance of sport
- define experiential consumption and its role in understanding sports consumption.

## Scene setter

### Sport is a winner for corporations trying to reach 15–24 year olds

Latest research on sports marketing effectiveness from the United Kingdom suggests that sports sponsorship has the most impact on 15–24 year olds. Forty per cent of this age group indicated that they would feel more confident about brands that were sponsors for high-profile sporting events, such as the Olympics, the Soccer World Cup or the Rugby World Cup. The impact levels drop, however, for older groups. Only 19 per cent of 25–34 year olds, 18 per cent of 35–44 year olds, 13 per cent of 45–54 year olds, 6 per cent of 55–64 year olds and 11 per cent of the over 65s say they would feel more confidence in such brands.

These results suggest that sponsorship of high-profile sporting events should be an important part of the marketing mix for many organisations, particularly those targeting 15–24 year olds. High-profile, global sporting events such as the Olympics and the Soccer and Rugby World Cups represent a rare opportunity to reach large global audiences. Interestingly, it appears that only truly global brands are likely to achieve high success rates with such high-profile sporting events, as regional or national brands run the risk of irrelevance with global audiences. In spite of this however, regional and local brands can achieve similar results with their local markets by involving themselves in sport at the community level. There are many cases where small companies have managed to build positive profiles in their local markets through their involvement in school-based, regional or local sporting events and teams. For example BankWest in Western Australia with their support of regional netball, AFL and rugby league, Country Energy in NSW with their support of surf lifesaving and rugby league, and Port Nelson in New Zealand with their support of the Sportsperson of the Year awards and other local events.

In spite of the potential for increased awareness and positive consumer attitude building, organisations should also investigate whether or not sponsoring sporting events could have a negative effect on existing consumer perceptions and the company's profitability before deciding on sponsorship deals. The risky element in associating with a sport or sporting team occurs when sports people misbehave or act in a way that is in conflict with the sponsoring organisation's values – for example, the highly publicised behaviour of a number of footballers from various codes in Australia in 2004 and the resulting impact on women's groups and companies with female markets.

An alternative could be to align the organisation with a particular sport at a strategic time, without actual commercial agreements – 'ambush marketing'. For example, Pepsi ran ads featuring David Beckham during the 2002 World Cup. In some surveyed countries, Pepsi's recognition as an 'official' sponsor was nearly as high as that of the real official sponsor, Coca-Cola. What specific brands do you think would most benefit from this type of approach and why?

Source: Daily Research News Online 2002a, 2002b

# Introduction

Sports consumption (either participating in sport or watching it) is one of the most pervasive leisure roles in modern society. It pervades all aspects of human life and has worldwide appeal. Indeed, sport speaks to people of all ages across all cultural and national boundaries. The global trends of increased personal wealth, more sedentary lifestyles, and increased mechanisation have resulted in an increased reliance and relevance of leisure activities in everyday life (Arnaudon 1993; Pitts & Stotlar 1996; Shoham & Kahle 1996).

Indeed the current generation of baby boomers (most of whom are now in their 40s and 50s – born between 1946 and 1964) are still one of the largest population segments in the world and their focus on hedonic self-gratification means that participation in sport and attending sporting events are popular attractions for them. Interestingly there is also increasing information available for this segment on how to prevent sport-related injuries (there has been an increase in injuries by about 33 per cent per year in this group since 1998) as this group have taken to heart the message of staying healthy through sport (Sentara.com 2002).

Sport is seen by many as an integral part of not only their daily life, but also their heritage and history. The increase in both direct (attendance at sports events) and indirect (watching/listening/reading about sport) sports consumption is evidenced by the millions of dollars spent annually on new, improved and larger sporting facilities and sporting teams and players. Changes in lifestyles and attitudes to health and fitness have also brought about changes in recreation preferences towards newer, more varied activities over a greater range of time-frames. This in turn has given rise to development of new facilities better attuned to people's needs.

In particular, this decade has seen the construction of an increasing number of multi-functional recreation complexes, combining in the one location facilities for indoor sports, weight and machine-based fitness activities, swimming and other community recreations. In addition there is also an increase in creative and entrepreneurial activity in the sports industry worldwide with considerable funds going into sports entertainment. Corporate sponsorship of sport and recreation, in particular, has been growing at a phenomenal rate as business attempts to capitalise on the profile that sport and recreation can establish for their company and their products (Sport.vic.gov.au 2004).

Sports facilities are increasingly multi-functional

This chapter will provide an overview of the sports industry globally, and will introduce the key concepts involved in sports marketing, which will be expanded in later chapters. The chapter will commence with a historical review of the sports industry and of sports marketing, before examining the size and scope of the industry globally. Finally, the chapter will introduce the major players in sports marketing and highlight some of the key elements that make this discipline unique.

## What is sports marketing?

Sport, as a product, has a unique bundling of qualities, processes and capabilities that has resulted in standard marketing applications being largely unsuccessful for early sports marketers. Basically it is the unpredictability of sport as a product combined with the largely intangible and experiential nature of sport that has resulted in early sports marketers struggling to understand how to apply marketing principles to maximum effect. It is relatively easy to see how to apply many of the principles of promotion to sport, but when it comes to the other marketing mix elements, it becomes far more challenging as we will see in future chapters. This is why the study and research of sports marketing is now accepted as a discipline area in its own right.

So what is **sports marketing**? Many people see it as promotions or sports agents like the famous 'Jerry Maguire' screaming 'Show me the money!' But sports marketing is more complex and dynamic than merely a single sporting event, a sports star making a celebrity appearance or sponsorship spend. Specifically, sports marketing is 'the specific application of marketing principles and processes to sports products and to the marketing of non-sports products through association with sport' (Shank 2002, p.2).

As you can see this definition is based on the same principles as the marketing concept that suggests that **marketing** in general terms is:

> the process of planning and executing the conception, pricing, promotion and distribution of ideas, goods and services to create exchanges that satisfy individual and organisational goals.
>
> Summers, Gardiner, Lamb, Hair & McDaniel 2003

As you can see by this definition, successful organisations adopting the marketing concept are market driven. That is, they take time to find out the customers' needs and wants, they incorporate the needs of customers in their planning and decision-making and they take into account the activities of the competition when developing marketing strategies. The benefits of this approach are that the organisation is generally able to be innovative and responsive, it is able to keep abreast of the competition and it will usually also have high levels of customer involvement. In sporting organisations these benefits can translate into loyal patrons or members, and a relevant and dynamic organisational approach. The costs of adopting a marketing approach are that it takes considerable time, and sometimes additional skills (particularly in the area of market research) to stay in touch with your market. A sporting organisation that is not market focused will also be one that is slow to change, and possibly seen as irrelevant to its stakeholders.

Therefore, sports marketing is the application of the four Ps (pricing, product, promotion and place) specifically in a sports context all designed to meet the needs of the sports customer whether they be individual consumers, sports participants or players and corporate investors.

See Figure 1.1. We will explore each of these dimensions in detail in later chapters.

**Figure 1.1:** The sports marketing mix

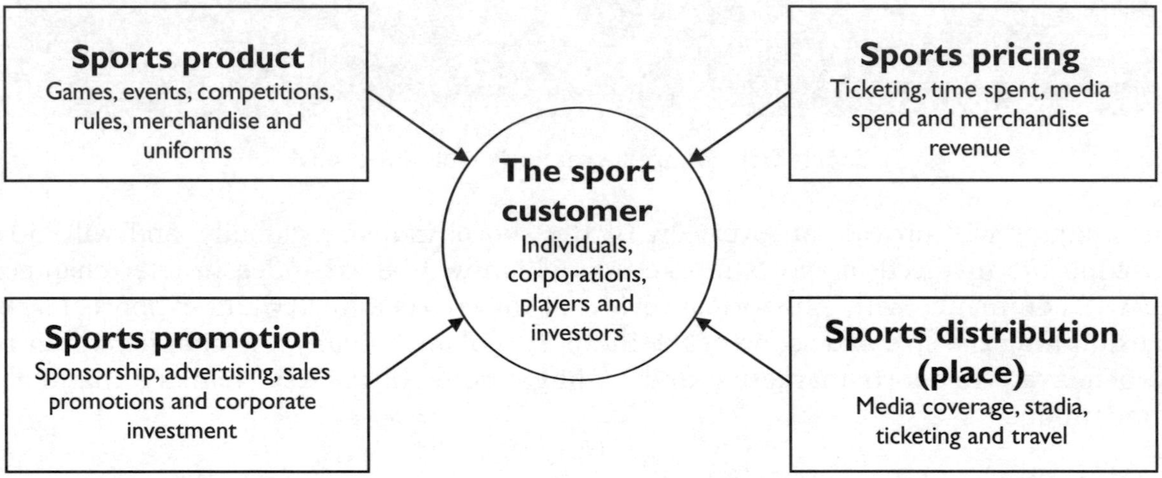


As mentioned earlier, one of the reasons that we deal with sports marketing separately is that it is quite a complex area. Sport has many of the characteristics of a service, such as: *intangibility* – most sporting encounters and experiences are not physical and tangible in nature; *separability* – sporting encounters and experiences are produced and consumed simultaneously; *perishability* – it is not possible to keep an inventory of sporting events or sports product and if tickets for a sports event are not sold then that future revenue is lost forever; and *heterogeneity* – every sporting experience or encounter is unique for every sports customer. However it also has some of the more tangible elements of a good – things like merchandise, videos of games, sports memorabilia – and it is this dichotomy that provides unique challenges for marketers who need to combine strategies of both services and goods marketing to sport (Summers 2003).

Similar to service encounters in other industries, consumers' satisfaction with sporting events is largely determined by the quality of their experiences. Further, these experiences are impacted by other consumers, the physical surroundings (servicescape) and by the consumer's moods or feelings. As sports marketers cannot control nor predict either a consumer's emotions (moods and feelings), or the interaction of others in the consumer's consumption experience, they are only able to exert limited control over the physical surroundings. Thus, sports marketers must make marketing decisions in an environment where the outcomes of those decisions are unpredictable.

However, this issue does not seem to discourage companies from utilising sport as part of their marketing strategy. Indeed, there are no limits to the sorts of organisations that get involved with sport as part of their marketing strategy. Even Lego, the Danish toy building-block company, recently joined the move to sports marketing with the signing of a one-year deal with Major League Soccer to launch a new range of soccer themed products.

Finally, as with all marketing applications, the concept of exchange has important implications in the sports marketing context. When marketers use the term 'exchange', they refer to the idea that people willingly give up something of value to receive something they would rather have (Summers et al. 2003). In sport, customers give up time, money, physical effort and emotional energy to watch, participate and be involved in sport in some form or another. It is the intangible elements of this exchange process that can cause problems for sports marketers particularly as the expectations and perceptions of the value being exchanged for both parties often is not clear. It is almost impossible to reach agreement on how much your emotional energy and team loyalty is worth to a sporting team – although this is exactly what sports marketers strive to achieve (we will discuss this further in Chapter 9).

## Evolution of sports marketing

One view of the origins of sports marketing dates back to Ancient Rome and Greece where wealthy citizens supported athletic festivals and aristocrats sponsored gladiators in the Ancient Roman Coliseum all in an attempt to win public esteem (Ukman 1984). Obviously this approach did not necessarily consider the marketing concept (appealing to consumers' needs and wants within the capacity of the organisation), but then the marketing concept is also a relatively new approach with early marketers also being more internally focused on either their production capability or their sales and revenue forecasts.

Perhaps the first more recognisable form of sports marketing following a customer focused marketing concept approach, was the very first Olympic Games in 1896, which were privately funded by stamps, ticket sales, commemorative medals and program advertising (Berich 1995). Sports sponsorship wasn't seen as a marketing tool until the 1950s when US President Eisenhower asked Union Oil to help fund a presidential fitness program in the US in return for national coverage and presidential endorsement (Lazarus 1984).

In early times sports marketing activity was primarily confined to major sporting events, such as the Olympics, until the late 1960s and early 1970s. It was at this time that sporting organisations began to recognise that more efficient and traditional business practices were needed to be successful, with marketing being one of these business functions. In addition at this time many governments in Europe, the USA and Australia banned cigarette advertising on television and radio (Cornwell 1997), which forced these companies to look to the sporting arena for exposure to their markets. This provided a substantial boost in investment for sports in many countries as sponsorship of sporting events, particularly tennis, cricket and motor racing, offered a means to keep cigarette brands in front of spectators and media viewers. More recently, this option has been removed for cigarette companies in Australia (1995), New Zealand (1990) and the UK (2002) when governments banned all sponsorship of sporting events by cigarette companies.

The 1984 Los Angeles Olympics provided the next big boost for sports marketing and is generally credited with starting the trend of sports marketing on a more formal basis – turning athletics into a sponsored business and employing market-based pricing concepts, merchandising efforts and even product modifications with athletes' uniforms and television coverage of events determined by their 'marketability in terms of attracting audiences and attendances' (Schlosberg 1987). This was the first Olympics to depend entirely on private money – mainly sponsorship – and was the first Olympics to generate a profit. After this, Olympic sport was truly recognised for its commercial value (Shannon 1999).

Sport has continued to be big business with multi-million dollar payrolls, newer and more extravagant facilities and the costs of sports franchises escalating into the hundreds of millions of dollars in the USA. Even television contracts for professional sports now run into the millions of dollars in Australia and New Zealand and into the billions of dollars in the USA (Shannon 1999).

This use of sport in the marketing efforts of firms is termed *marketing using sport*. This is where strategic decisions are made to incorporate sport as a vehicle into the marketing strategy of the firm in order to gain attention, develop a particular brand or corporate image or perhaps to communicate specific benefits of the product or service to a particular target group.

*Marketing of sport*, in contrast, is just one element of the sports management process. Thus, just as the management of a company such as Coca-Cola involves elements such as staffing, production, accounting and marketing, so too does the management of a sporting club or association, regardless of its size or profile. In this context, marketing activities are used to help sporting bodies achieve their corporate goals and objectives and to communicate with their various publics. These different aspects of sports marketing will be explored in more detail in Chapters 6 to 8 with the strategic marketing of sport covered in Chapter 2. Before we can examine the techniques required for effective sports marketing, we need to have a better understanding of the size, structure and importance of the sports industry globally.

# Defining the sports industry globally

Sport itself is generally defined as a source of diversion or a physical activity engaged in for pleasure (Shank 2002). It takes us away from our everyday life and entertains us in a way that is usually more involving and more social than other forms of pleasurable diversion (watching movies or reading a book). This definition of sport suggests the close link that emotion and feelings have with sports consumption. In addition, sport is seen as a pleasurable activity in that it is not work – a position that many professional athletes would probably question! But even they participate in sport because of a strong emotional connection and because of the adrenaline rush of competing and (hopefully) winning.

There is probably no better example of the extremes of emotion in sport than the annual state-of-origin rugby league football games played between Queensland and NSW each year. It becomes a matter of state pride – quite akin to national pride for many spectators – to win this series and so far in the history of the matches the scores are relatively even. See the 'Sport spotlight' below for the full story.

## Sport spotlight

### The rugby league 'state-of-origin' series

The first NSW v QLD rugby league match was played on 11 August 1908 in Sydney with NSW winning the game 43–0, a trend that was to stay until the 1920s when Queensland finally defeated NSW (rl1908.com/Origin/States 2003). However there was one small difference with these earlier games to those played post 1980 and that was the rule that players could only play for the state where they played their first game of first grade football. Prior to this ruling, Queensland players regularly played for NSW due to their contractual arrangements with southern clubs. This immediately stemmed the tide of Queensland players who regularly played the NSW v QLD game in a blue NSW jersey.

This seemingly small rule change was met with indifference by the rugby league community of NSW, but was received with electric anticipation by Queenslanders (rl1908.com/Origin/States 2003). The first sign that this annual event would become one of the premier events in the Australian sporting calendar was the size of the crowd at the first Queensland game – 35 000 people. In 1980 this crowd represented a sevenfold increase on normal interstate audiences. Modern state-of-origin games attract close to a million television viewers and more than 50 000 live spectators where stadia allow – not bad considering the games really only have relevancy in two of mainland Australia's states.

There is even up-to-the-minute coverage of games in newspapers and other media in New Zealand, Taipei (*Taipei Times*), New Guinea and Singapore.

Players for each state are treated like royalty (particularly when they win) (TVNZ 2003) and efforts in the game were often described using highly emotional terms such as 'right up there with everything I have ever achieved!'; 'the one mountain left to climb…'; 'sporting dynasties being created…'; '… it was worse than heartbreak…'; and 'gladiatorial conquests'. Legends of the game are still revered by fans both new and old and performances are constantly compared to great games past. State premiers have been known to wager with their counterparts on the outcomes of the series with losers having to fly the wining state's flag over their city hall and so on and victory celebrations can take days to end.

All this emotion, passion and pride for a football game – quite amazing really!

Sources: Kent 2003; Bawden 2001; Rugby League History 2003; NRL News; http://tvnz.co.nz 2003

This earlier definition of sport also suggests that sport is essentially an amateur or informal activity and while this may have been true largely of sport in Australia and New Zealand particularly 10 years ago, there is now a growing trend for both professional and amateur sporting bodies in many countries around the world to improve and professionalise their operations and their competitions. For many this means including marketing personnel and practices in key operational areas of their sports management practices and decision-making.

In spite of this increasing awareness of the need to adopt more professional business (and therefore marketing) practices, sports sponsorship is still seen as the most prevalent form of sports marketing. However, those of you who have completed any introductory marketing studies would realise that marketing is about much more than just promotional activity. Those who have not taken an introductory marketing course, will find that the information in Chapters 4 to 8 will reinforce that product, pricing and distribution (or placement) decisions are also critical to the success of a marketing plan. In Chapter 2 we will investigate the strategic implications for sports marketers of all the elements of the marketing mix.

The business of sport in Australia and New Zealand is booming with the sports industry in Australia in 2003 worth about A$10 billion in revenue, television rights, sponsorship, gate takings and corporate hospitality (Stensholt 2003) and in New Zealand worth about NZ$300 million (SPARC 2003). This trend is being followed by many other countries with the USA leading the field in terms of investment and revenue.

Most Commonwealth countries (Britain, Australia, New Zealand and Canada) have similar sports industry structures with a high reliance on government investment and infrastructure. In these countries, sports commissions (or other government bodies) are established to take on board the task of developing sports participation at grassroots and club level and of fostering and nurturing elite athletic performers. In Australia, the Australian Institute of Sport caters for the elite athlete in a range of predetermined sports, while in New Zealand the same task is handled by the New Zealand Academy of Sport. Figure 1.2 illustrates the structure of the sports industry in Australia and Figure 1.3 illustrates the same structure in New Zealand.

As these diagrams show, both countries have a heavy reliance on government funds and administrative assistance, resulting in sport being largely non-professional in these countries. In contrast, the American system is essentially corporate based and funded, which has resulted in sport in that country embracing professional systems and practices much earlier. Australian and New Zealand sporting bodies are only just coming to terms with the demand for a more professional approach.

As mentioned earlier, many people consider the main economic impact of the sports industry in terms of sponsorship investment. However, sport also provides jobs for many people and for many companies that are both indirectly and directly involved in the provision of sport. Sport

**Figure 1.2:** Structure of the sport and recreation industry in Australia

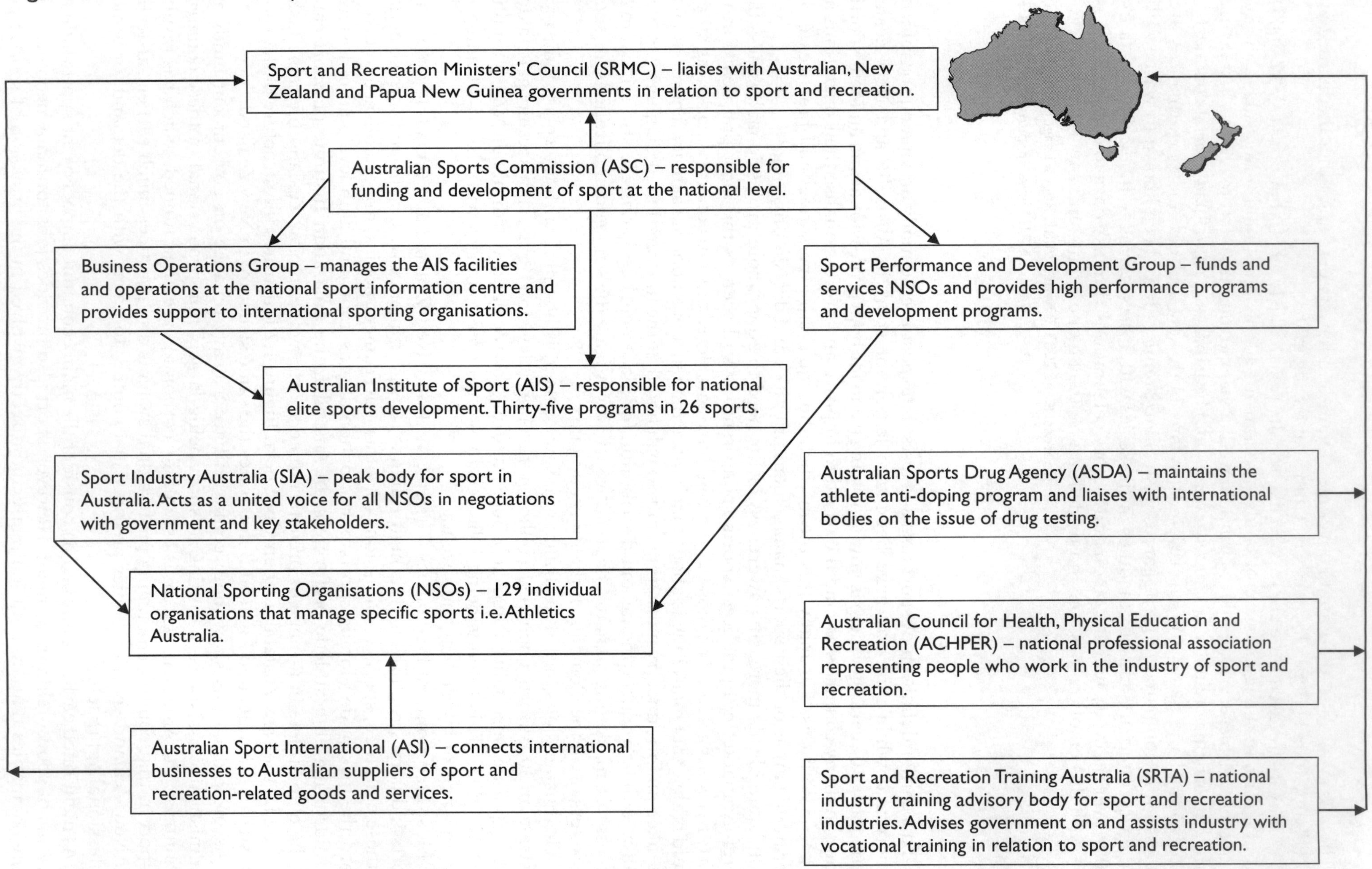


Adapted from www.abs.gov.au

**Figure 1.3:** Structure of the New Zealand sport and recreation industry

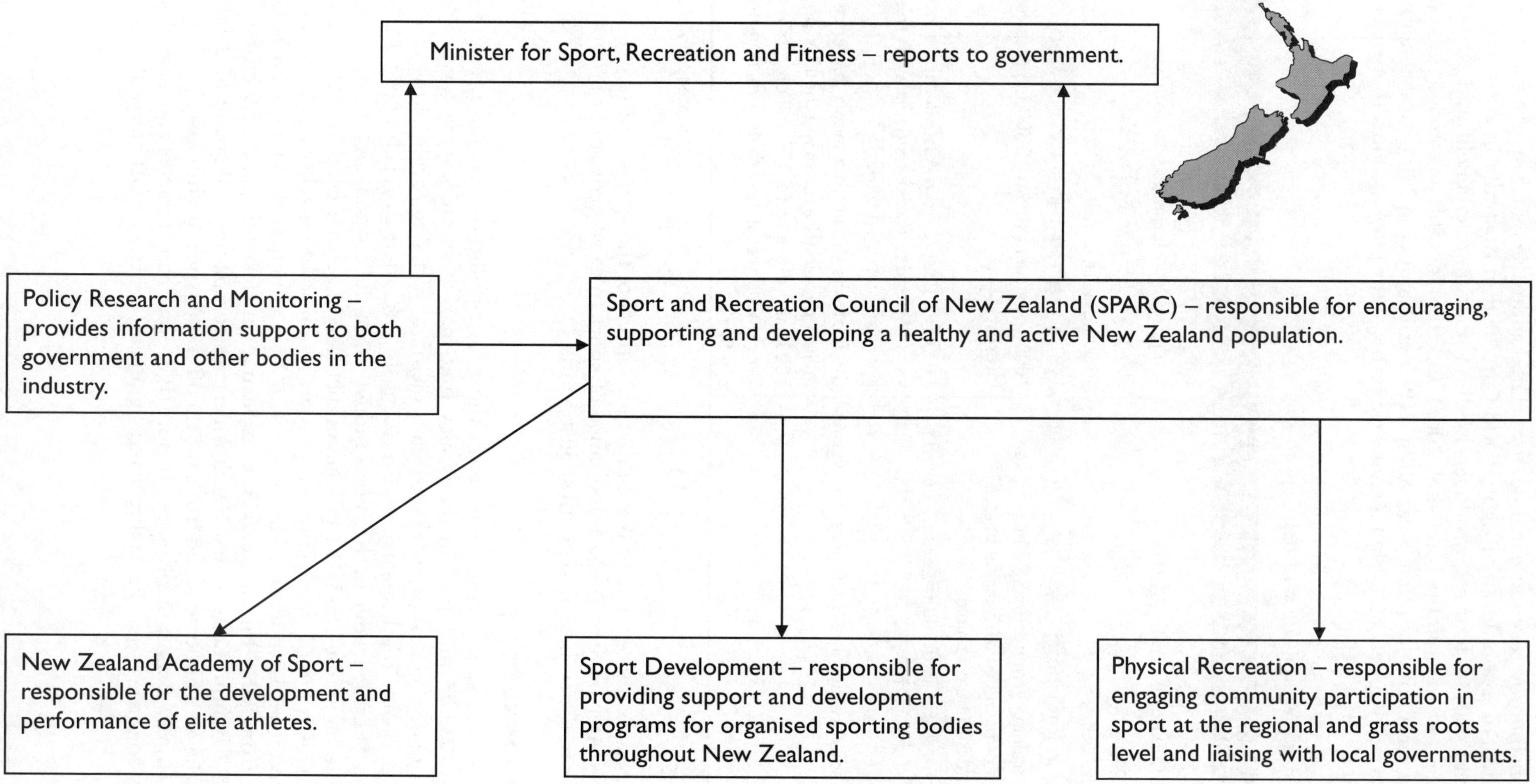
Minister for Sport, Recreation and Fitness – reports to government.
Policy Research and Monitoring – provides information support to both government and other bodies in the industry.
Sport and Recreation Council of New Zealand (SPARC) – responsible for encouraging, supporting and developing a healthy and active New Zealand population.
New Zealand Academy of Sport – responsible for the development and performance of elite athletes.
Sport Development – responsible for providing support and development programs for organised sporting bodies throughout New Zealand.
Physical Recreation – responsible for engaging community participation in sport at the regional and grass roots level and liaising with local governments.

Adapted from http://www.sparc.org.nz/pdfs/sparc_vision_web.pdf

is also responsible for revenue earnings for related industries such as travel, hospitality, and entertainment. For example, the Rugby World Cup, held in Australia in 2003, was expected to lure more than 400 000 tourists, produce $1 billion in economic benefit and attract about $60 million in corporate hospitality (Stensholt 2003). In actual fact it far exceeded these predictions, realising a net profit of more than $192 million (Planet-Rugby.com 2004), and generating greater revenue and tourist appeal as Table 1.1 shows. In terms of the players alone, there was substantial economic gain!

**Table 1.1:** Rugby World Cup statistics

| Player-related statistics | Visitors |
|---|---|
| 600 players | 2 million spectators |
| 64 Hotels (36 000 hotel room nights) | 400 jumbos of international tourists |
| 980 coach trips | 500 000 Australian bed nights |
| used 900 rugby balls | 40 000 overseas visitors |
| 700 tonnes of freight in total | 1181 accredited journalists from around the world |
| 150 different training grounds using 2040 marker cones, 28 scrum machines, 200 tackle bags, 570 tackle suits and 300 bump shields | 1000 volunteers (from 10 500 expressions of interest) |
| 100 000 litres of water and 100 tonnes of ice with an additional 40 ice baths | 1 837 547 people from Australia and around the world attended the 48 matches, with the final attracting a crowd of 82 957 |
| 900 team laundry washes and 8000 personal washes | the final was shown to a media audience of 4.34 million people (the most watched TV program of 2003) and there were 495 million hits on the Rugby World Cup website, with 44.5 million on the day of the final. |

Adapted from Kaless 2003

We will now examine some of these different aspects of the sports industry on a global scale to provide a better picture of the importance of sport to most economies and of the size and impact of the industry, beginning with sponsorship.

## Sports sponsorship

In Australia sports sponsorship now ranks third ($1.6 billion) – behind press ($3.36 billion) and television ($2.75 billion) – in the money that marketers are paying for exposure and its growth has outstripped all other mainstream media advertising (even taking out the Olympic effect) (Lloyd 2001). Total television advertising is estimated to reach about $2.7 billion this year with the AFL the leader in the sports industry. For 2005, sponsorship spending in the USA is predicted to be about US$11.14 billion, an increase of 8.7 per cent from 2003 (Sponsorship.com 2005). This trend of increasing use of sport in corporate marketing is also noted in other developed countries with worldwide spending in 2005 anticipated to be US$28 billion, a rise of 8.1 per cent from $45.9 billion in 2003. European countries will spend $7.9 billion, Pacific Rim countries $5.2 billion, Central and South American companies will spend $2.3 billion, and all other countries will allocate an additional $1.5 billion to sponsorship investment (Sponsorship.com 2005). However sport involves much more than employing athletes and gaining sponsorship, and in many countries sport has a direct and significant impact on GDP as well.

AFL is Australia's most popular sport for marketers

## Impact on GDP

The impact of sport on GDP for any country can be assessed through its impact on employment, participation and on ancillary services. We will look at the statistics for the major sporting countries in the world: Australia, Europe, New Zealand and the USA.

## Australia

In Australia, sport provides a significant employment opportunity for more than 98 267 people (ABS 2003); see Table 1.2. The volunteer rate for males (6.9 per cent) was higher than that for females (5 per cent), with the rates for both males and females peaking for those in the 35–44 year age group (ABS 2003). About one-third of Australians 15 years of age and over are involved in sport, either as players or non-players, with participation rates being slightly higher for males (39.8 per cent) than females (25.2 per cent) and declining as age increases. There are also high levels of participation in sport by school children and the promotion and support of sport is also funded by many businesses. In 2001 businesses gave $1.447 million to sporting organisations, $408 million of which was for sponsorship, $109 million for donations and $39 million for business community projects related to sport.

More than 7 million people aged 15 years and over had been to a sporting event in the 12 months ending March 2002. Australian Rules was the most popular spectator sport, attended at least once during the reference period by almost 2.5 million people. Horse racing (1.9 million) followed and rugby league and motor sports were the third most popular with equal numbers attending (http://www.abs.gov.au/ausstats/abs@.nsf/94713ad445ff1425ca25682000192af2/daaada81176e2f89ca256f7200833023!OpenDocument).

During the year, total attendances at Australian Rules and rugby league were estimated to be 14.4 million and 8.5 million respectively, while for horse, harness and dog racing combined, there were about 10.6 million admissions (ABS 2003).

**Table 1.2:** Sport-related statistics for Australia

| | |
|---|---|
| **Employment** | 98 267<br>178 837 volunteers |
| **Participation** | Males – 39.8 per cent<br>Females – 25.2 per cent<br>15–24 yrs – 50.5 per cent<br>65 yrs> – 17.8 per cent |
| **Most popular organised sports** | Swimming, aerobics and golf |
| **Most popular spectator sports** | AFL, horse racing and rugby league |
| **Total outlays on sport, recreation and gambling by households** | $5.9 million |
| **Government outlays** | $550 million (over four years) with $400m aimed at elite development and $82 million at participation programs |
| **Investment in the AIS facilities** | $65.4 million |

Adapted from ABS 2003

Total outlays on sport, recreation and gambling by government and households amounted to about $10 million and households spent $4146 million on sport and recreation goods and services, while their net outlays on gambling amounted to $1779 million (ABS 2003). Only 51 per cent of organisations in this sector are 'for profit' organisations.

Australian exports of sport and recreation goods during 1995–96 amounted to $358 million while, for the same time, the corresponding value of imports was $970 million. In 2001 the sport and recreation industry added $1942 million of value to the Australian economy (ABS 2003). Some of the major commodities traded included boats, yachts and pleasure craft, bicycles and live horses. The main destinations of Australian sport and recreation goods are New Zealand, Japan and the USA. Asian countries are the source of about one-half of the imports of these commodities, and the USA is the largest individual supplying country.

## Europe

In Europe, it is estimated that 1.5–2 million people work in the sports industry, with sport accounting for 1.61 per cent of all employment in Britain alone. In relation to ancillary revenue, sports clothing and equipment account for a further 60 000 jobs in the EU (EU Report of Sports and Employment 1999). In Germany, sport accounts for 1.4 per cent of GDP, while in the UK, it accounts for 1.6 per cent with consumer expenditure on sport accounting for £6983 million in 1995. It is estimated that the sports industry accounts for 3 per cent of world trade and that Europe accounts for 36 per cent of this activity, while the USA accounts for 42 per cent (Commission of European Communities 1999).

In terms of participation, about 125 million people participate in sport (more than a quarter of all EU citizens). It is estimated that 2 per cent of all private spending relates to sport. On average, European men participate in 10 minutes of sport each day on average, and women five minutes per day on average. While figures on participation vary from country to country, in most countries people participate in *some* sport. Countries with the lowest participation rates are Italy – 77 per cent do no sport and 40 per cent no physical activity; Spain – 43 per cent no sport and 26 per cent no physical activity; and Finland – 19 per cent no sport and 3 per cent no physical activity (European Commission 1999).

In terms of funds generation, TV rights provide a significant boost to most countries, with Olympic years seeing the highest expenditures – US$1504 million was recorded for the Athens Games in 2004.

## New Zealand

In New Zealand, approximately 70 per cent of all young people (5–17 year olds) and 68 per cent of adults participate in sport with men taking part in slightly more activity on average than women. Golf is the most popular sport in New Zealand for men, followed by tennis, touch rugby, cricket and rugby union. Netball is the number one sport for women (SPARC 2001).

In 1999 the gross output from the sport sector in New Zealand was NZ$1.973 million with the largest contributor being sports clothing. New Zealanders spend about $1 billion on sport and physical leisure activities and services (2.5 per cent of all household spending) and an estimated 41 000 people are employed in sport. New Zealand also has a large volunteer population associated with sport with more than 500 000 people giving their time to sports clubs and associations (worth another NZ$1.9 billion per year). Finally about 1 million tourists per year travel to New Zealand to take part in one or more sports or physical activities during their stay (worth another NZ$120 million) (SPARC 1999).

## The USA

In the USA, the top sport sponsors are the Anheuser-Busch Cos, spending an estimated US$190 million to $195 million in 2002 on sports sponsorship. This is then followed by Philip Morris Cos ($175 million to $180 million), General Motors Corp. ($150 million to $155 million), the Coca-Cola Co. ($115 million to $120 million) and PepsiCo, Inc. ($110 million to $115 million).

Participation in sport in the USA is still at a reasonably high level with 20.5 per cent of the population engaging in regular exercise. Extreme or Millennial sports such as snowboarding, wakeboarding, wall-climbing, surfing and mountain biking are the fastest growing sports in the USA, often at the expense of the more traditional team sports such as baseball and basketball.

Latest estimates suggest that in excess of 4.5 million people are employed in sports-related jobs in the USA at all levels and this figure is still increasing. The volunteer network involved in sport in the USA is not as important nor as large as is found in Australia and Europe.

One of the major revenue earners for sport in the USA is the heavy involvement of media. More Americans watch sport on television than attend live games (even though game attendances are large). Network broadcasters continually vie with each other to secure broadcast and cable rights for sporting events and they pay large amounts of money to succeed. As an example, NBC and Turner sports recently paid US$2.64 billion to televise national basketball.

As illustrated in these statistics, much of people's everyday behaviour and working life involves the consumption of sporting (or leisure) goods and services. Sport can be classified as a type of consumption because, in the simplest form, it involves the purchase (or rental), use and disposition of a good or service. People's choices of what sporting events to attend or what brand of sporting goods to purchase can be, and have been, explored in some detail by both academics and practitioners over the years (Bettman 1979). Let's look more closely at the issues involved in sports consumption.

# Sports consumption

The previous section gave a fairly comprehensive overview of the level of economic impact and community involvement in sport worldwide. It is therefore important to understand more about how people choose to watch or become involved with sport in order to better understand this market. When people watch, listen to or play sport this activity is termed *sports consumption*. Sport can be consumed directly – through watching a game played live or by participating in a sport – or indirectly – through watching a game on television, listening to it on the radio or reading about it in a newspaper or magazine.

An interesting trend in most industrialised countries is the growth in indirect consumption of sport (via television or other media) so that in many cases it exceeds direct sporting event attendance. Large sporting events are classic examples of this – such as the Sydney Olympics where approximately 10.5 million Australians (95 per cent of the Australian population), as well as millions of people internationally watched the opening ceremony, while only a few hundred thousand people actually attended the event (Kaye 2000).

It has also been shown that the process of consuming sport fulfils a number of social functions for many people. Sports consumption allows individuals to share something with others in the community on an equal basis, regardless of social standing, age or gender (Beisser 1967). Sport allows consumers to build bridges with others who might be termed 'socially distant acquaintances' (such as people you work with or people you meet at a function). This is possible because sport provides a common interest that can be free of social restrictions or stigmas (Voight 1971; Beisser 1967). This issue will be further explored in Chapter 3.

Some have even likened the current phenomena of the reality TV boom to sports consumption, calling this form of television 'unscripted drama'. Like sport, they say, this form of entertainment has specified rules, structure and players, but the resulting action and outcomes are unknown, making the attraction of the consumption event even more addictive and popular (Malanowski 2003). People use this form of entertainment as a pseudo-social key, allowing them to have conversations with many others with whom they otherwise would have little in common.

Finally, sports consumption can provide an outlet for the exercise of a person's aggressive combative instincts and can allow the channelling and releasing of otherwise socially unacceptable behaviours (yelling, shouting at authority (the referee) and jeering). Interestingly this outlet for aggression is equally enjoyed by both men and women and sport provides a socially acceptable mechanism for this behaviour.

This aggressive and combative nature of sport is also attractive for participants. One of the latest fitness crazes to reach our shores is 'bootcamp' training. This is where seemingly well-adjusted and well-paid executives pay money for ex-military types to yell at them and force them to complete an hour and a half of extreme physical activity each day in order to get fit (ABC News 2004; *Toronto Star* 2004). Apparently this is an increasingly popular activity for both men and women, who insist that it is a great way to get into shape.

Because sport is generally a highly emotional and involving activity for many people, there is also a certain satisfaction in the virtual involvement in sporting events. People comment on feeling exhausted at the end of a game, because they were almost able to 'feel' the action and adrenaline rush of players and athletes. It is this channel for vicarious involvement appreciated by both men and women, as well as the often roller-coaster ride of emotions experienced with sport, which makes it so attractive to modern audiences. You never know what the outcome will be beforehand, and even during a sporting event this can change.

It is this participation in the experience of sport that also brings some unique challenges for sports marketers. When people engage in experiential consumption they do so for a number of different reasons: for hedonic and symbolic motives, self-efficacy, emotional experience motives and interpersonal interaction motives (Arnould & Price 1993). Essentially, experiential consumption is when the consumer takes on an active role in the production and delivery of the consumption experience. For example, a restaurant experience is one where customers take only a very limited role in the production and delivery of the consumption event. Restaurant customers are fairly passive in their involvement. In the main however, sports consumers are very active in their consumption experience, with many commenting on how interaction and involvement with others and with players during the experience heightened their satisfaction. Let's now look at the hedonic or emotional aspects of sports consumption.

## Emotion in sport

The presence of emotion in sport is well documented in the popular press and sports-specific tabloids. It seems that most weekends one hears stories about sports fans either being excessively jubilant, in some cases even rioting, over the performance of their team, a referee's decision or some particular in-game infringement. The press can extend an incident for days with commentary, replays and debates over what should or should not have been. Fans and athletes alike will celebrate for days over successful conquests, and public dignitaries also extend the hype by offering parades and civic receptions for the conquering heroes. Sport has the ability to evoke extremes of emotion in seemingly otherwise generally well-adjusted people. It also leaves some individuals cold, wondering what all the fuss is about (Richins 1983).

Sport evokes strong passions among supporters

Sports entrepreneur Veeck (1962) claims that sport is laden with emotion and it is the anticipation of what will happen and the memories of what occurred that people remember and look forward to. This anticipation and the inability of spectators to influence and predict the outcome is one of the reasons that emotions can be so intense in relation to a sporting event.

The hedonic consumption literature provides some insights into the passions and feelings that sport evokes. Attending a major sporting event, where the outcome is a matter of local, state, national or even international pride is akin to other adrenaline-pumping sporting pursuits. The thrill and excitement that people experience when bungy jumping, sky diving or on a roller coaster are the same as when fans attend a major sporting event. There is a loss of control, the thrill of anticipation and excitement at the possibilities of what might happen. The main difference though, is that at a sporting event, the other spectators who are also present generate much of the excitement. This frenzy and self-abandonment feeds on itself, a phenomenon well known to ancient Romans in gladiator times (McPherson 1979).

Interestingly, there is a major difference in other acts of extreme hedonic consumption to that of attending a sporting event. In the case of a sporting event the skill and toil of others generate much of the emotion. In the case of personally experienced emotion in extreme sports participation, bungy jumping for example, it is the effort and actions of the self that generate the excitement (Shoham, Rose & Kahle 2000). Thus, sporting events are a 'safer' medium in which to vicariously experience the thrill of competition, in that spectators do not have to actually DO anything to gain this experience. They can be unfit, unhealthy, uncoordinated and generally un-athletic and still enjoy the emotions associated with winning, that moment when all else stops as their team scores that extra point that will take them to victory.

## Counterpoint

So why can't traditional marketing principles just be applied to sport? Surely if the customer is the key focus of the organisation, then it is simply a matter of applying the four Ps and the principles of strategic marketing as shown in Figure 1.4.

**Figure 1.4:** Strategic planning process

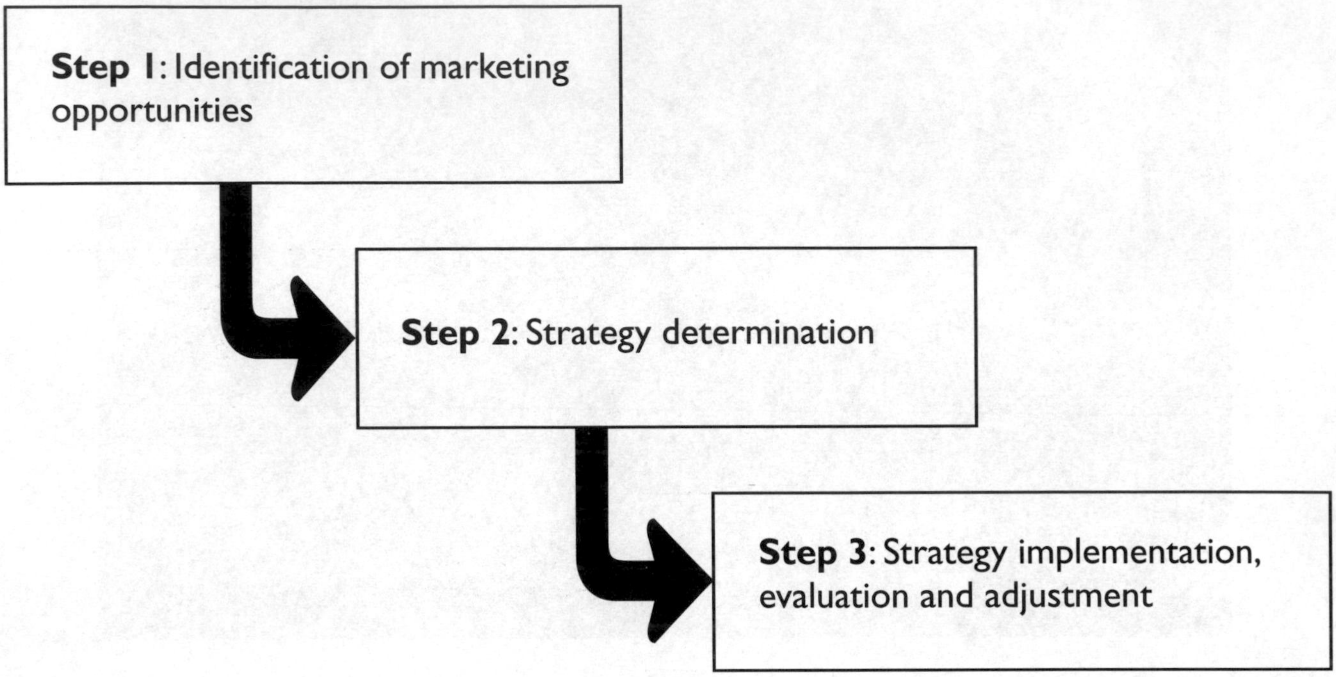


Adapted from Shilbury, Quick and Westerbeek 1998

Well, the short answer to this question is that they can in principle, but it is in the actual application of these basic principles that sport differs. The main problems for marketers attempting to simply apply traditional marketing principles are that firstly the sports product is largely uncontrollable and secondly many of the customers of the sports product have a great impact on the process – more so than in traditional product or service marketing. This influence of others is particularly strong when the role of media is considered. Sport and media make a potent combination of forces and much of the result of this power and influence is outside the control of sports marketers. People love their favourite teams and feel personally affronted if television coverage of their teams and their favourite game is changed; this heightened level of emotional attachment is both a positive and a negative element of sport. The decisions a coach or CEO of a sport makes are carefully scrutinised by both the media and the fans and this pressure can result in considerable influence on management decision-making. The often highly political nature of professional sport is also another factor that makes marketing and management practices in sport difficult and sometimes treacherous.

So in summary, while the consumer should still be the central focus of sporting organisations in relation to their marketing, there are many other factors that impact the strategic decisions of sports marketers and that make this a unique and challenging field.

## Summary

- **discuss the pervasive nature of sport**
  Sports consumption is one of the most pervasive leisure roles in modern society and it pervades all aspects of human life and has worldwide appeal. Sport is seen by many as an integral part of their daily life, their heritage and their history. Sport is also blind to issues of race, religion and culture, which makes it universally appealing.
- **define sports marketing and outline how it differs from mainstream marketing**
  There are two perspectives of sports marketing. One is marketing of sport, which is where sporting organisations apply standard principles of marketing to their business operations. The second is marketing using sport and this is where organisations associate themselves with sporting teams, players or sports in general in order to attract customers, engage in community activity or to provide incentives to their staff and/or clients. In both cases the unique elements of sport – that it has both a services and a physical goods dimension – mean that the application of marketing principles will be different than for pure services or pure goods.
- **describe the evolution of the modern sports industry**
  The modern sports industry has evolved from large international sports events such as the Olympics to one that encompasses all sports at all levels down to the community and school-based levels. The governments of many countries are investing many millions of dollars into the development of sport for economic (improved health), social (improved national identity) and nationalistic reasons.
- **discuss the global size and economic importance of sport**
  For many countries sport provides a significant impact on their GDP, export earnings, tourism revenues and employment. In addition, in most countries a high proportion of people participate in some form of sport. Finally the global audiences of international sporting events are testament to the importance of sport in the lives of many people, regardless of nationality, race or gender.
- **define experiential consumption and its role in understanding sports consumption**
  Experiential consumption is when the customer is actively involved in the delivery and production of the consumption experience. This perspective allows sports marketers to fully consider the important role that emotion and the presence of others has in consumption of sport. Sport is laden with emotion and it is the anticipation of what will happen and the memories of what occurred that people remember and look forward to. This anticipation and the inability of spectators to influence and predict the outcome is one of the reasons that emotions can be so intense in relation to a sporting event.

## Review questions

1. Define sports marketing and the difference between marketing of sport and marketing using sport.
2. Discuss why sport as an industry is so important to many countries.
3. Explain briefly how sport differs from other goods and services in relation to the application of marketing principles.
4. Explain how sports consumption has a social function for many people.
5. What is the significance of the high levels of emotion found in sport to sports marketers?

## Applied activities

1. Provide five recent examples of sports marketing that have been in the news and describe how each relates to our definition of sports marketing.
2. Discuss the advantages and disadvantages of attending a live sporting event as opposed to consuming it via the media (i.e. TV, radio etc).
3. Identify an example of a sports sponsorship and comment on what you think might have been the objectives of the company involved and how successful you feel they may be.

## References


ABC News, 'The Obesity Wars', http://abcnews.go.com/sections/WNT/Living/obesity_wars_040601-1.html, viewed 11 June 2004.

ABS 2003, www.abs.gov.au.

Arnaudon, S. 1993, 'Marketing Australian Sport – the Future', Australian Council for Health and Physical Education and Recreation Proceedings, Darwin, pp.1–9.

Arnould, E.J. & Price, L.L. 1993, 'River Magic: Extraordinary Experience and the Extended Service Encounter.' *Journal of Consumer Research*, 20 June, pp.24–45.

Bawden, H. 2001, 'League Slams Opponents in Sydney and Brisbane Ratings', *B and T Marketing and Media*, 9 July.

Beisser, A. 1967, 'Membership In The Tribe', in A. Beisser, *The Madness in Sports*, Meredith Publishing Company, New York, pp.124–41.

Berich, J. 1995, 'Winning is Everything: Sponsorship in the '90s', *Australian Professional Marketing*, May, pp.12–13.

Bettman, J.R. 1979, *An Information Processing Theory of Consumer Choice*, Addison-Wesley, Reading.

Commission of European Communities 1999, 'Report from the Commission to the European Council: A view to safeguarding current sports structures and maintaining the social function of sport within the Community Framework', Brussels, December.

Cornwell, T.B. 1997, 'The Use of Sponsorship-linked Marketing by Tobacco Firms: International Public Policy Issues', *The Journal of Consumer Affairs*, Vol. 31, pp.238–54.

Daily Research News Online 2002a, 'Superbrands Sports' Sponsorship Research', 21 June, www.mrons.com/drno/news1694.htm, viewed 7 May 2003.

Daily Research News Online 2002b, 'Sponsorship or Not?', www.mrons.com/drno/news1837.htm, viewed 7 May 2003.

European Commission 1999, 'Doping in Sport: Sports Economics and Statistics', Report commissioned by the secretariat of the European Group on Ethics in Science and New Technologies, Brussels, November.

http://tvnz.co.nz/view/sport_index_skin/sport_index_group, viewed 8 May 2004.

Kaless, S. 2003, 'Looking at the Numbers Game', <www.rugbyworldcup.com/EN/Tournament/News/sk+24+11+stats.htm>.

Kaye, L. 2000, 'Seven a Gold Ratings Winner', *B and T Marketing and Media*, 22 September.

Kent, P. 2003a, 'Series Bonds Gould, Johns', June 26, www.foxsports.news.com.au, viewed 14 July 2003.

Kent, P. 2003b, 'History against Blues Dynasty', *The Advertiser*, 11 July.

Lazarus, L. 1984, 'Sports Sponsorship Requires Marketing Expertise, Realistic Expectations and Social Responsibility', *Marketing News*, April, No. 13.

Lloyd, S. 2001, 'Sponsorship: Taking a Sporting Chance', *Business Review Weekly*, Vol. 23, No. 26, Friday 6 July.

Malanowski, J. 2003, 'Reality TV: Why We Can't Stop Watching', *Australian Reader's Digest*, June, pp.106–12.

McCabe, K. 2003, 'Cricket Tops TV Ratings', *The Sunday Telegraph*, 13 July.

McPherson, B. 1979, 'Sport Consumption and the Economics of Consumerism', in *Sport and Social Order*, D. Ball & J. Loy (eds), Addison Wesley Publishing Company, Massachusetts, pp.243–75.

NRL News, www.nrl.com.au/news.cfm?ArticleID=5245&TeamID=22, viewed 14 July 2003.

Pitts, B.G. & Stotlar, D.K. 1996, *Fundamentals of Sport Marketing*, Sport Management Library, Fitness Information Technology, West Virginia.

Planet-Rugby.com, <www.planetrugby.com/Print_page/index.shtml/REDIR?35361>, viewed 8 May 2004.

Richins, M.L. 1983, 'An Analysis of Consumer Interaction Styles in the Marketplace', *Journal of Consumer Research*, Vol. 10 (June), pp.73–82.

Rugby League History, <www.rl1908.com/Origin/States>, viewed 14 July 2003.

RugbyWorldCup.com, viewed 14 July 2003.

Schlosberg, J. 1987, 'Who Watches Television Sports?', *American Demographics*, February, pp.44–9, 59.

Sentara.com 2002, 'Baby Boomers and Sports Injuries', www.sentara.com/explorehealth/2002/BabyBoomers.pdf, viewed 13 May 2004.

Shank, M. 2002, *Sport Marketing: A Strategic Perspective*, Prentice Hall, New Jersey.

Shannon, J.R. 1999, 'Sports Marketing: An Examination of Academic Marketing Publications', *Journal of Services Marketing*, Vol. 13, No. 6, pp.571–34.

Shilbury, D., Quick, S. & Westerbeek, H. 1998, *Strategic Sport Marketing*, Allen & Unwin, Sydney.

Shoham, A. & Kahle, L. 1994, 'Spectators, Viewers, Readers: Communication and Consumption Communities in Sport Marketing', *Sport Marketing Quarterly*, Vol. V, No. 1, pp.11–19.

Shoham, A., Rose, G.M. & Kahle, L.R. 2000, 'Practitioners of Risky Sports: A Quantitative Examination', *Journal of Business Research*, Vol. 47, No. 3, pp.237–51.

SPARC 1999, 'Sparc facts/push play facts II', <www.sparc.org.nz >, viewed 8 May 2004.

SPARC 2001, 'Sparc Facts: the growing business of sport & leisure', www.sparc.org.nz, viewed 8 May 2004.

SPARC 2003, 'Finding the target social market for physical activity (and healthy eating)', www.sparc.org.nz, viewed 8 May 2004.

Sponsorship.com 2003a, Sponsorship spending in North America, extract from IEG Sponsorship Report, IEG, Chicago, <www.sponsorship.com/learn/northamericasponding.asp>, viewed 8 May 2003.

'Sponsorship.com 2003b, 'Sponsorship spending worldwide', <www.sponsorship.com/learn/worldwidespending.asp>, viewed 8 May 2004.

Sport.vic.gov.au 2004, 'The Business of Sport', <www.sport.vic.gov.au/Web/SRV/srvsite.nsf/pages/research_bussport1?OpenDocument>, viewed 11 June 2004.

Stensholt, J. 2003, 'Advantage Sport', BRW, www.brw.com.au/stories/20010129/21460.asp, viewed 8 May 2004.

Summers, J. 2003, 'Sport Marketing', in Janet McColl-Kennedy (ed.), *Services Marketing: A Managerial Approach*, Wiley, Brisbane.

Summers, J., Gardiner, M., Lamb, C., Hair, J., McDaniel, C. 2003, *Essentials of Marketing*, Thomson Nelson, Melbourne, Vic.

*Toronto Star*, 'Bikers Know the Joy of Sweat', <www.thestar.com/NASApp/cs/ContentServer?pagename=thestar/Layout/Article_Type1&c=Article&cid=1084530426635&call_pageid=968350130169&col=969483202845>, viewed 8 May 2004.

TVNZ, tvnz.co.nz, viewed 14 July 2003.

Ukman, J. 1984, *The Official 1984–1985 International Directory of Special Events & Festivals*, Chicago.

Veeck, B. 1962, *Veeck – As in Wreck*, University of Chicago Press, Chicago.

Voight, D.Q. 1971, 'America's Leisure Revolution', in D.Q. Voight (ed.), *America's Leisure Revolution*, Allbright College Book Store, Reading, pp.20–40.

# Chapter 2

# A framework for strategic sports marketing

## Learning objectives

After reading the chapter you should be able to:

- describe why the unique elements of sport impact the strategic planning process
- discuss in general terms the principles of strategic marketing
- discuss the various components of the strategic model for sports marketing
- describe the exchange process and indicate how it is important to the marketing planning process
- discuss the environmental factors that are critical to strategic sports marketing decision-making
- identify the relevant sports publics who have the ability to impact the strategic sports marketing process.

## Scene setter

### Corporate sponsors spend more on fewer sports

Australia is currently experiencing a boom in the number of corporate investors looking to use sport as an element in their marketing mix. The strong performance of Australian teams and individual sports people combined with the increasing number of large, high profile sporting events being staged in Australia are fuelling this growth (see Table 2.1).

**Table 2.1:** Top five sports sponsors for 2003

| | |
|---|---|
| **Foster's Group** | $22 million on AFL, Formula One and horse racing |
| **Telstra** | $20 million on Rugby League, AFL and stadia |
| **Kia Motors** | $10 million on tennis, golf, Rugby Union |
| **Orange** | $6.5 million on cricket |

In spite of this increased interest and preparedness to spend, corporations are becoming more discerning about how and where they spend their money.

Sporting organisations need to be professional and to be able to demonstrate to potential investors how money spent on sport can improve the bottom line. The challenge then for sporting organisations is to recognise the opportunities for corporate investment and to be able to market themselves professionally to be able to attract this interest.

One of the latest strategic moves by corporations in relation to sport is in the areas of technology development. One example of this is Telstra's internet services brand, BigPond, who have recently announced a major sponsorship deal with the V8 Supercar Championship Series.

The 3½-year deal, with two four-year options, will also see BigPond become the technology partner for the Series, with plans underway to develop a new-look broadband channel. Telstra plan to be able to directly measure their sponsorship return through monitoring of traffic and through new subscriptions to BigPond and in addition it is anticipated that the move will also add significantly to company revenues.

BigPond is also sponsoring the development and operation of a new high-tech mobile media centre that will provide the media with satellite broadband communication for the series. The mobile media centre will travel to each round and enable 21 working media to file stories and transmit images as well as to provide up-to-the-minute live timing, point scores and steward's information. This move will not only impact the V8 motor racing sponsorship, but may also have an effect on Telstra's other sporting sponsorship deals by providing a new broadcast platform not yet well developed in Australia, placing Telstra in the forefront of the new wave of sports broadcasting for international sport businesses.

Adapted from Stensholt 2003; http://www.onsport.com.au/

## Introduction

Effective strategic planning and marketing of sport can bring many benefits to a sporting organisation including: raising funds; recruiting members; maintaining and building loyalty; creating and ensuring positive attitudes and perceptions; and attracting and maintaining sponsors and investors. One of the first stages in developing a strategic marketing plan is to be clear about what you are trying to achieve and where you intend to go with the organisation.

This chapter overviews the strategic environment for sports marketing decision-making and provides the introductory framework for a strategic sports marketing decision-making model. The chapter will begin with a review and introduction of the basic principles behind strategic marketing in general terms before turning specifically to strategic sports marketing concepts. A discussion of the unique aspects of sport in relation to strategic marketing decision-making is then presented followed by an overview of environmental elements that impact this process. The various stakeholders that need to be considered in the development of sports marketing strategy then follow, before the chapter finally concludes with a strategic model of sports marketing.

## Unique elements of sports marketing

Never before have consumer leisure choices been more varied and more complex and this, combined with an increase in the demand for shrinking consumer leisure time, has resulted in the sports industry becoming increasingly competitive and dynamic. As discussed in Chapter 1, sport differs from other consumer products or services in a number of ways and these factors impact the strategic marketing planning processes for sporting organisations.

Similar to service encounters in other industries, consumers' satisfaction with sporting events is largely determined by the quality of their experiences. Further, these experiences are impacted by other consumers, the physical surroundings (servicescape) and by the consumer's moods or feelings. As sports marketers cannot control or predict either a consumer's emotions (moods and feelings), or the interaction of others in the consumer's consumption experience, they are only able to exert limited control over the physical surroundings.

Thus, sports marketers must make marketing decisions in an environment where the outcomes of those decisions are unpredictable. However, this issue does not seem to discourage companies from utilising sport as part of their marketing strategy. In addition, these conditions mean that sporting organisations need to become more professional and more organised in their marketing activities.

In general, there are five main facets of sport and sporting products that have unique qualities and considerations of which marketers need to be aware (Mullin 1983). These are: (1) the market for sports products and services; (2) the sports product itself; (3) the price of sport; (4) the promotion of sport; and (5) the distribution of sport. These unique qualities are summarised in Table 2.2 and will be discussed in more detail in later chapters. Essentially, though, in spite of these differences, the traditional processes involved in strategic marketing planning can still be effectively applied and thus need an overview and general discussion as they apply to sport.

**Table 2.2:** Differentiating characteristics of sport

| Category | Specific differences |
|---|---|
| The market for sports products and services (people) | • Sporting organisations simultaneously compete and cooperate.<br>• Sports consumers consider themselves experts, due to the salience of sport and the personal identification that the consumers have with it. |
| The sports product | • There is wide fluctuation of consumer demand in relation to sport.<br>• The sporting product is intangible, ephemeral, experiential and subjective.<br>• Sports products are simultaneously produced and consumed.<br>• Sports products are publicly consumed and satisfaction is affected by social affiliation.<br>• Sporting products are inconsistent and unpredictable.<br>• There is no control over the composition of the core product and there is frequently only limited control over product extensions.<br>• Sports products can be classified as both consumer and industrial products.<br>• The sports product has universal appeal and pervades all elements of people's lives. |
| The price of sport | • The price of sports products is usually small in comparison to the total cost paid by the consumer when consuming sports products.<br>• Indirect revenues are frequently greater than direct operating revenues.<br>• Sport has, until recently, been able to operate on a not-for-profit basis. |
| The promotion of sport | • Widespread media exposure has resulted in growing emphasis on sponsorship as the main element of sports marketing.<br>• High visibility of sport has attractions for businesses in terms of association through sponsorship.<br>• Promotion and marketing emphasis can only be placed on the product extensions rather than the core product. |
| The distribution of sport | • Sport does not physically distribute its product.<br>• Sport is produced and consumed simultaneously |

Source: Summers & Johnson 2000

## An overview of strategic marketing principles

Marketing strategy is the process of planning, implementing and controlling marketing efforts to meet organisational goals and to satisfy consumer needs (Shank 2002). Specific strategic marketing efforts include identifying appropriate and profitable market segments, understanding the behaviour and needs and wants of the customers in these segments, developing different products, pricing strategies, distribution systems and promotional plans for each segment and then monitoring the effectiveness of all this effort to ensure that the customers in each segment are experiencing satisfactory exchanges. In sport there is often little difference between the overall organisational strategic planning process and the marketing planning process (Shilbury et al. 1998) so we will consider the two simultaneously.

The strategic planning process can be summarised into a number of key steps or phases. These are: (1) Clarify and decline organisational and marketing goals; (2) Conduct situation analysis; (3) Identify and describe target markets; (4) Develop marketing mix for each segment; (5) Implement and coordinate marketing plans; and (6) Control and evaluate performance. This process is illustrated in Figure 2.1 and each step will be briefly discussed.

**Figure 2.1:** The strategic marketing process

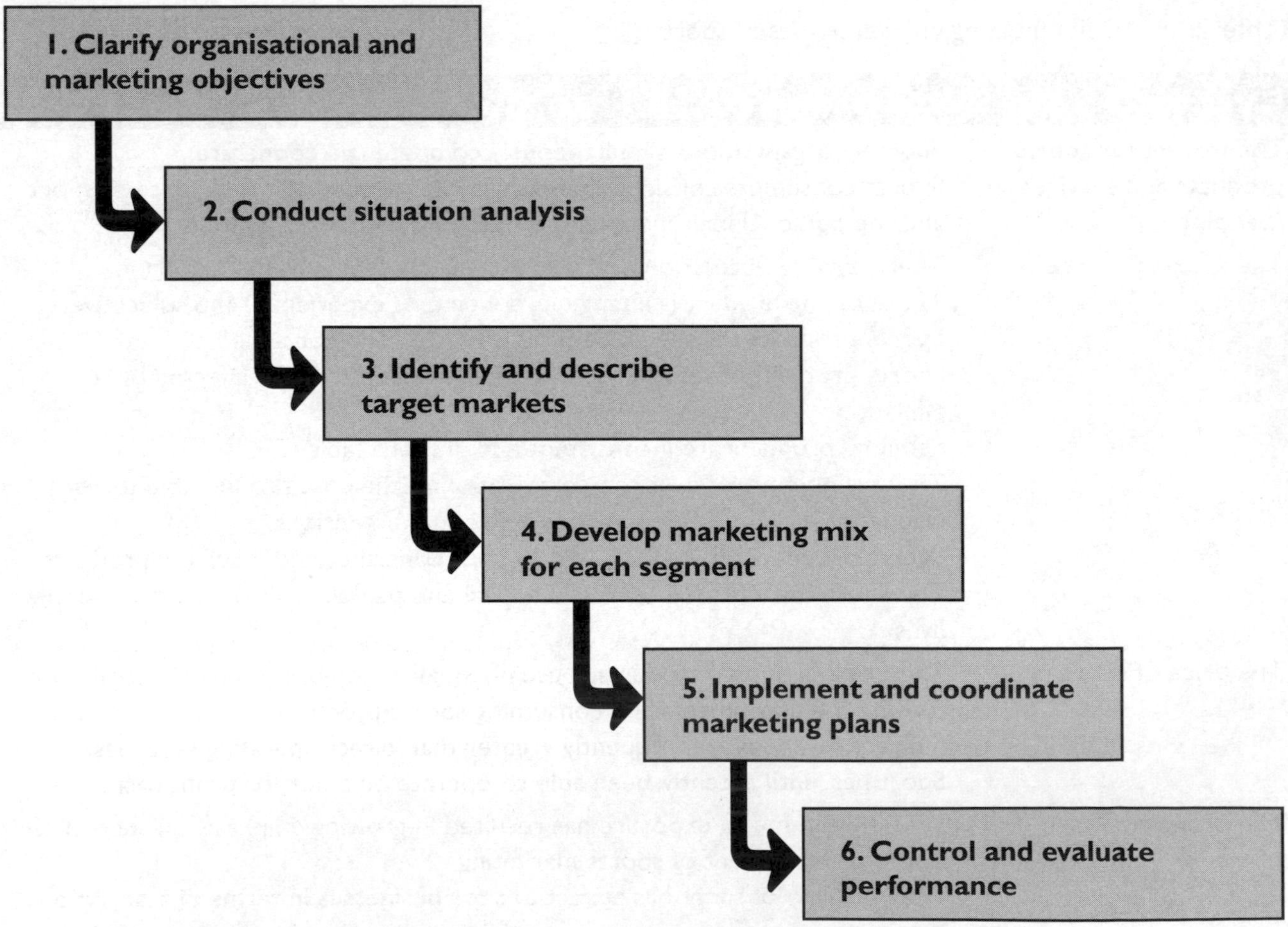
1. Clarify organisational and marketing objectives
2. Conduct situation analysis
3. Identify and describe target markets
4. Develop marketing mix for each segment
5. Implement and coordinate marketing plans
6. Control and evaluate performance

### Step 1: Clarify and define organisational and marketing objectives

Strategic marketing planning involves designing activities relating to the marketing and organisational objectives of the firm in a constantly changing marketing environment. This means that the critical first step in any strategic marketing planning process is to understand and review the overall goals and directions of the organisation. Once an understanding of the organisational direction and mission is achieved, then the marketing objectives can be determined.

Marketing objectives are statements of what is to be accomplished through marketing activities and they need to be SMART. That is, Specific, Measurable, Attainable, Realistic and Time-framed. For example the overall objectives of a local soccer club might be, *'To increase junior membership for the club by 20 players by the start of the competition season'* and from this the specific marketing objective might be, *'To actively promote the benefits of soccer participation to 6–10 year old boys and girls within a 15-minute drive of our club during the months of October to March 2003'*. You can see how the general organisational objective is translated to a more specific and measurable marketing objective that still has the same overall strategic direction.

Setting realistic sports marketing objectives and undertaking strategic marketing planning is not just restricted to local or national sporting bodies. Even governments make strategic plans in relation to sports participation. For example the New Zealand Government's objectives in relation to sport for 2003 were, *'To promote and develop sport, fitness and leisure among New Zealanders and to increase participation in adults by 10 per cent during the 2002/2003 year'* (Mallard 2001).

The New Zealand government has realised that increasing adult participation in sport by 10 per cent would have cost savings of at least $55 million per year and would also prevent hundreds of premature deaths due to obesity and other diseases related to a lack of good health and fitness. These savings in health care expenditure are common incentives for many governments around the world who are now interested in stimulating the activity levels of their populations.

## Step 2: Conduct a situation analysis

A situation analysis consists of an environmental analysis that examines the external forces impacting on the organisation and its markets and an internal analysis that aims to investigate the organisational capacity to take advantage of any opportunities in the external environment or to counter any threats found there.

Tools that can be used in conducting a situation analysis might include a SWOT analysis (Strengths and Weaknesses – internal to the organisation, Opportunities and Threats – external to the organisation) and/or environmental scanning, which is a process used to collect and interpret information about the forces, events and relationships present in the external environment (Summers et al. 2003). There are generally five external forces that can impact any organisation and all are applicable to sporting organisations. These are: governments and politics, technology, demographics, social trends and economic forces. These are illustrated in Figure 2.2.

**Figure 2.2:** External environmental forces

In addition to considering the external forces and their impact on the organisation, it is also essential to consider competition and industry structure on a more detailed level. Sporting organisations are often as competitive with each other for funding opportunities, memberships and for space and facilities as the sports they represent. In Australia and New Zealand the sports market is quite small, due in part to their relatively small populations and also to the regulated structure of the industry. It is important when conducting a competitive analysis that sporting organisations consider not only other sports as potential competitors, but also other recreational pursuits and leisure opportunities.

Porter's competitive forces model (1985) provides a useful framework for sporting organisations to consider the impact of competition on their operation and the attractiveness of a particular industry. Porter suggests that firms consider five forces that include:

1. the intensity of competition between existing firms within an industry
2. the bargaining power of buyers
3. the threat of substitute products
4. the bargaining power of suppliers
5. the threat of new entrants.

Using this model, an industry is deemed attractive if it can be shown to be profitable. Profit per se is often not a good measure for sporting organisations as many are actually non-profit entities. Therefore they might be more inclined to use performance of their teams, membership levels, socio-economic and demographic profiles of their members and the long-term financial viability of the sporting organisation as more useful indicators of attractiveness of a particular sport or market. This approach is shown in Figure 2.3; it allows a sporting organisation to consider the wider implications of competition and the relative power and influence each force might have on the long-term direction of the sporting organisation under review.

**Figure 2.3:** Adaptation of Porter's five forces model for a sporting organisation

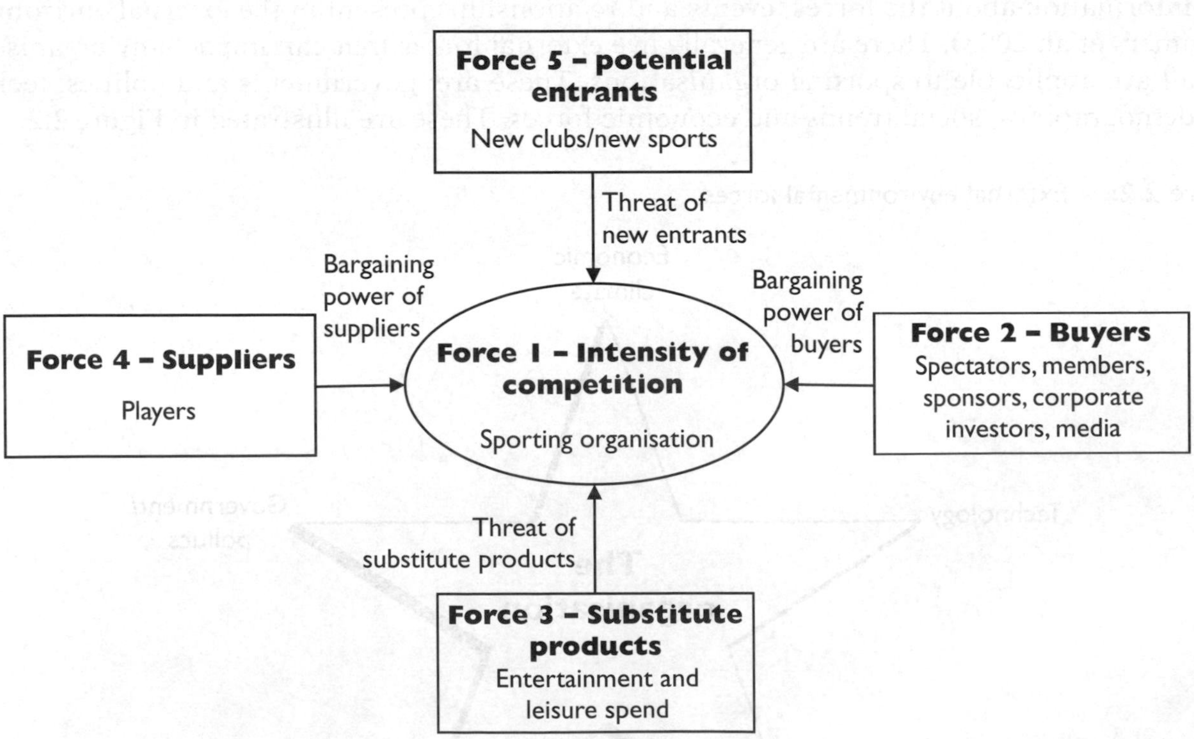


Source: Porter 1985, p.5

This approach forces a sporting organisa-tion to think of competition in its broadest sense and not just in terms of other sports or even other clubs within a particular sport. Each sports customer makes decisions about how to best spend their leisure time and money and sport is only one leisure/entertainment option available. Watching movies, attending music concerts, going to the theatre, eating in restaurants, travel and spending time with friends and family are all possible competitors for a person's leisure time and money.

Understanding the competitors can help a sporting organisation improve the quality of its service, and allow it to stay abreast of trends and changes in customer preferences. In addition it can help to minimise duplication, can assist with the development of more effective and efficient pricing strategies and can help an organisation to focus on its key strengths.

At this stage of the strategic planning process it is critical to have an effective and well-designed marketing information system (MIS) and access to effective databases. An MIS usually consists of a combination of internal and external databases and other secondary data that an organisation can access for timely and reliable information upon which to make strategic decisions. Chapter 5 will investigate the issue of market research and MIS in more detail. In addition to the internal information used by a firm, there are many publicly available databases that can be accessed for information about general behaviours of people in relation to sports participation and also about sports investment on the internet.

## Step 3: Identify and describe target markets

Once the internal and external environments have been examined, the next step involves identifying and describing the company's target markets. Target marketing essentially involves the identification of groups of potential customers who have a number of either personal, physical or buying characteristics in common and who have the desire to purchase your products or services and who can be reached by your communication efforts. Most products and services do not appeal to everyone equally and targeting different groups of customers who have similar motivations to purchase and/or similar characteristics can increase the effectiveness of any planned marketing efforts.

For some sports, identifying the potential target groups is relatively straightforward – this is particularly true for niche sports like extreme sports and also for sports that have specific or specialised equipment or skill sets such as equestrian sports, skiing, mountain climbing or even cycling. These sports have a very specific and narrow group of customers that they appeal to. Other sports like soccer, tennis, or golf tend to appeal to a wide range of different people or to different market segments. The following 'Sport spotlight' discusses the target markets for surf sports, particularly looking at the customers for Quicksilver products.

Extreme sports have a specific group of customers to which they appeal

## Sport spotlight

### Extremely popular sports

Have you ever heard of Torah Bright, Matt Fairbairn, or Corbin Harris? I bet that even if some of you have heard of these extreme sports superstars that your parents certainly haven't! This fact alone makes extreme sports popular with the youth market. For those of you who haven't heard of Torah, she is the first Australian athlete (snowboarding is her game) to pass from the fringe of extreme sports into a mainstream marketable commodity. She has seven major US sponsors, her own video game where she battles Shaquille O'Neil, and all this because she is a highly attractive sports star for the teen market.

Extreme sports are the fastest growing segment of the international leisure market with nearly two-thirds of all American teenagers as regular viewers of extreme sports on TV. In Britain the Extreme sports channel broadcasts in eight languages and into 50 countries. The audiences for these programs see extreme sports as cool, hip and even a bit crazy. The fact that they are removed from the structured masculine team sports preferred by older generations makes them even more popular. In these sports, the individual who goes highest, hardest and heaviest can become an instant hero. There are no rules and participants can create their own boundaries. Some of the extreme sports will fade over time and others will maintain their popularity. Snowboarding is one sport that looks like it might be here to stay with over a quarter of those skiing on Australian slopes in 2003 being snowboarders.

So who are Matt Fairbairn and Corbin Harris? Matt is a vert BMX specialist (that's BMX riding on a vertical ramp) whilst Corbin is a skateboarder. Sports marketers who are attempting to progress the popularity and momentum of these types of sports need to carefully understand their consumers and the external environments that impact them if they are to survive. Followers of extreme sports (mainly teenagers and early 20-somethings) are known to be extremely fickle, suspicious of traditional marketing approaches, sceptical of big business and fiercely protective of their cult-like status. These characteristics present unique challenges for marketers attempting to work in this industry and highlight the reasons why it is so important to really understand the context and behaviours of one's customers and one's business to successfully develop marketing plans.

Source: Safe 2003

Once the various customer groups or segments have been identified, it is important to understand as much as possible about their buying behaviour and how they approach the exchange process. More information about exactly what this entails is covered in Chapter 4. Needless to say, market research is important at this stage to better understand consumers' needs and motives for participation, loyalty and investment. An important point to remember is that sports consumers can have many different motives or reasons for their involvement in sport and the different motives can often represent different target groups.

The classic research in this area by Wann (1995), which examined sports fan motivations, identified eight different motives of sports fans. These are: eustress (a positive form of stress); self-esteem; escapism; entertainment; economical concerns; group affiliation; aesthetic value; and finally family motives (Wann et al. 1999). A sports marketer attempting to increase involvement and participation of fans would be wise to understand that not all fans are motivated by the same things, and further, that these motivations tend to also influence the types of sports preferred and the level of involvement and loyalty to that sport.

In order to assist marketers in their understanding of how consumers behave in relation to sports consumption, it is important that they also understand the characteristics of the exchange process in general. The exchange process is central to any marketing strategy, with an exchange being defined as, 'a marketing transaction where a buyer gives something of value to a seller in return for goods, services or other benefits' (Shank 2002). Exchanges are generally described as value-creating processes as they normally leave both parties to the exchange better off. The simple exchange process for a sports product is shown in Figure 2.4.

**Figure 2.4:** A simplified model of exchange for sports products/services

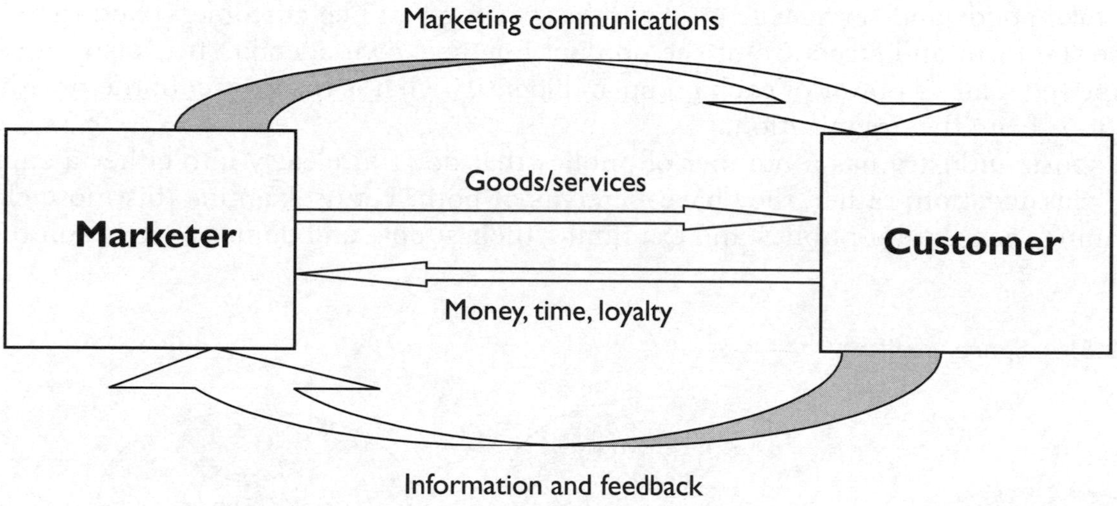


Adapted from Kotler 1980

For exchange to occur there must be:

- at least two parties
- each must have something of value to offer the other
- each must be free to accept or decline the offer
- there must be a means for communication between the parties
- each must believe it is desirable to deal with the other (Shank 2002).

When marketers attempt to understand the buying behaviour of their customers they must first understand how their customers approach the buying situation. For example, is this an important and risky decision for them or is it a decision of little personal or financial consequence? Understanding the importance of the decision, how much time and effort the customer is prepared to spend on the decision and the various alternatives they consider when making decisions is important to the development of more targeted and effective marketing plans.

Whether marketing a particular sport or conducting marketing using sport, end consumers are only one of the various publics (market segments or stakeholders are other words that can mean the same thing as publics) that organisations may target. Generally there are five main groups that marketers need to consider and often the demands of these groups are in conflict with each other. These groups are: sports publics; player or participant publics; business/media publics; support goods and services publics; and government publics. Managing the various publics is a difficult job for sports marketers and we need to understand more about each public in order to better develop effective marketing strategies.

## Sports publics

As with any industry, identification of relevant publics, or those key groups of individuals who impact the organisation – sometimes also referred to as stakeholders – is important. In the sports industry we generally classify seven publics or groups who need to be considered in addition to sports consumers in the marketing planning process. These groups are: (1) Players or participants; (2) business investors and/or media; (3) support goods and services organisations; (4) governments; (5) spectators; (6) other sporting clubs; and (7) sports governing bodies (see Figure 2.5).

In addition their relative impact on the organisation needs to be determined. Is their impact of a supply nature? That is, do they supply goods and services to the organisation with no ability to influence the form and structure of the product? This means that they simply supply goods and services to facilitate the product offering. Or is their impact of a demand nature? That is, do they take goods and services from the industry (in effect like customers) and therefore can influence the form and structure of the product for their own agenda? It is also important to determine the relative power of each group and identify what is the impact of them withholding transactions from the organisation.

The sports industry has a number of publics that don't fit clearly into either a supply or a demand classification; rather, they have elements of both. Let us examine this more closely by first defining the relevant publics and examining their supply and demand effects on the sports product.

**Figure 2.5:** Sports publics

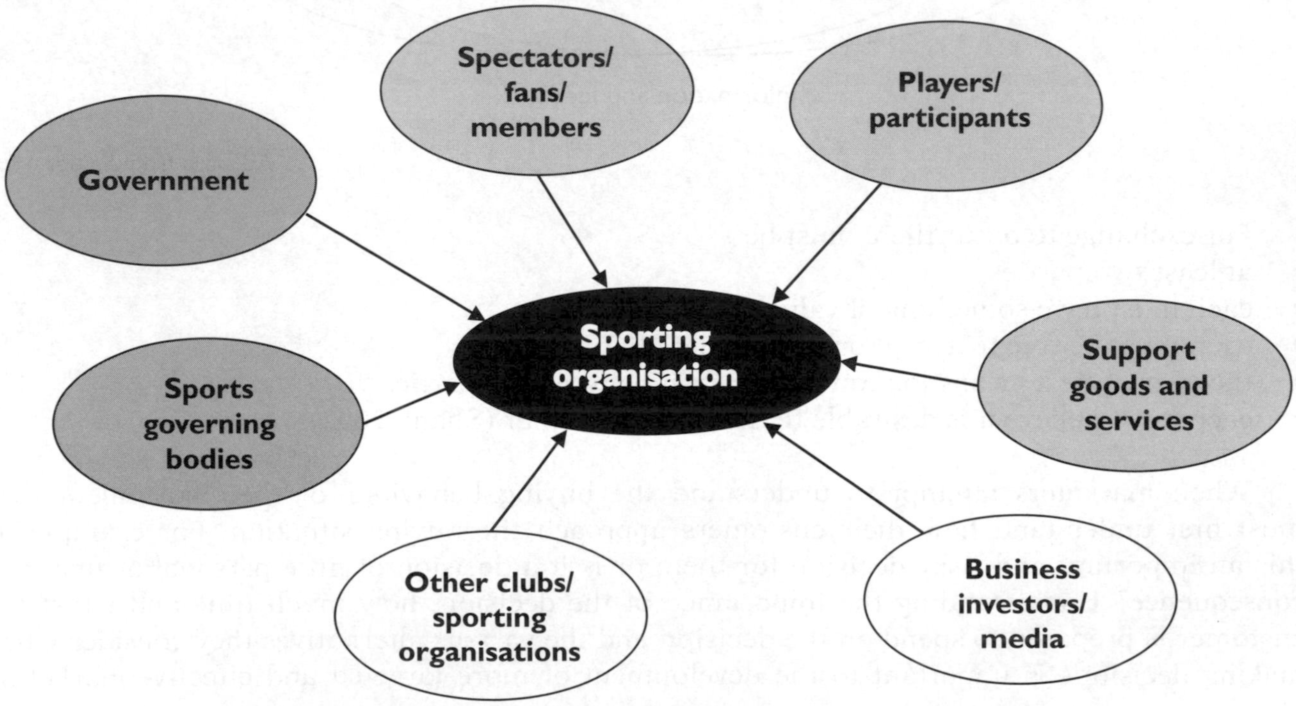


Adapted from Shilbury et al. 2002, p.26

### Player or participant publics

At the centre of any discussion regarding the sports marketing publics is the organisation as discussed earlier; we also need to take into account that sport is essentially about competition. Therefore the sports participants or the players and administrators are very important publics to consider in any strategic marketing decision-making. If their needs are not reasonably well met, then it is likely that there won't be a sports product to market.

These player or participant publics have both a supply and demand effect on the product. That is, they supply services to the sports product and withholding of those services can immediately effect the provision of the product (consider the year that the entire nation's baseball players went on strike in the USA in 2001). They also have a demand effect in that they can and do influence the form and structure of the product and act like customers of the game, particularly when the marketing emphasis is on recruitment of players or members.

Modern marketing has taken a new perspective on participant publics. Where traditional sports marketing took games played by people and found ways to market them to attract more people or to attract business investment and media interest, modern sports marketing has taken the reverse approach. That is, it has identified market opportunities and business and media investment needs and created new 'sport' products, especially to meet these opportunities and also to support and sell other goods or to support particular brands. These marketing decisions have all been made without participants initially being considered in the process. Examples of this are the extreme sports phenomena originally created by the Pepsi Company to sell soft drink. The entire culture, development of participants and design of the sport was engineered to suit the needs of a soft drink company. Now of course, the sport has taken on its own life and persona and exists independently of Pepsi's influence. Other sports such as Championship Bull Riding and Pro Rodeo have also been created using this model.

### Business/media

Business/media publics also tend to have both a supply and a demand impact on the sports product. Business publics are those that look at investing in and/or are involved in the sports product for a business purpose (usually with the long-term aim of making a profit). Media publics are those that use the sports product from a media perspective, once again usually to satisfy a profit objective.

These publics require the sports product to be structured in such a way that they can generate a required return for their investment (demand effect). In the case of business publics, these groups may impact things like competition draws (who plays whom and where) and possibly also the administration of a sport to ensure that significant decisions made in relation to the future and the structure of a sport are made with their requirements in mind. Media publics also have demand effect on the sports product through their influence in things like schedules and venues (schedules designed to suit viewing audiences and venues that are best designed for telecasts).

In terms of their supply effects, both of these publics provide essential services and resources that allow the sports product to function. In the case of business publics, the investment and support they provide often allow a sport to attract a higher profile and thus become more profitable and successful. In the case of media publics, they allow the sports product to be delivered to the various spectator publics at a time and place other than the game venue (through television broadcasts and print coverage of the sports events and issues).

Support goods and services appear on the supply side of the sports industry program

### Support goods and services publics

Support goods and services publics appear on the supply side of the industry diagram and consist of those organisations and individuals who provide essential support goods and services to those at the core of the sports product. These publics could be those that provide catering services, player and worker unions, companies that manufacture and supply specialised sporting equipment and clothing, security personnel and even transport companies that bring the spectators to a sports event or take the participants to a venue to play a sport.

These publics generally do not have any influence over the form or functioning of the sports product and thus, are shown only to have a supply effect in relation to the sports industry. They simply react to the changes and demands of those involved at the core of the sports product.

### Government publics

Many sports in Australia and New Zealand are, to varying degrees, funded by both local and federal governments. Government publics, while maybe not directly funding large high-profile sports, are often involved at the local community development levels of many sports. They provide infrastructure investment in things like facilities, coaching clinics and sporting scholarships, and generally help to encourage sport as a worthwhile and valuable contribution to community life. The total Australian government investment in sport in 2000 was just over $2000 million, while the New Zealand government spent $534 million in the development of sport (Statistics New Zealand 2000). Both countries aim to invest even more in future years as they recognise the contribution of sport to their national economies. In Australia the contribution is about 1.2 per cent of GDP and in New Zealand this figure is about 0.9 per cent (ABS 2000; Statistics New Zealand 2000).

Government publics, similar to business/media publics, are shown to have both a supply and demand impact on the sports product. They have a supply function in terms of their funding and support for the generation and infrastructure of sport. They also have a demand impact where governments require consideration for their involvement in the form of votes or general political mileage.

### Spectator publics

The final group that needs to be considered when looking at the sports industry are the spectator publics. This group is probably the most important public from a marketing perspective, because without them, the sports product would not usually have a very viable future. These publics encompass spectators of sport in all forms – live game spectators and those who participate through the media delivery of the sports product (both in electronic and print form). These publics are shown to have a demand effect on the sports product because ultimately any sport becomes devalued and loses its importance both from a business and participant perspective if it loses its spectator publics. As such, they often can affect the form of a sport, its rules and regulations, its venue and sometimes even who participates in the sport through their influence and opinion.

Many of the demand publics attempt to influence the sports product based on the level of their financial involvement in the sport. In contrast the supply publics provide essential goods and services to the sports industry to allow it to function efficiently. As mentioned previously the conflicting needs of both the demand and the supply publics are difficult for sports marketers to manage. Specifically, demand publics generally attempt to influence the product offering to suit their particular motivations and agendas while the supply publics are more likely to want status quo with the product offering to suit their business requirements and planning schedules. This direct conflict means that sports marketers constantly need to think strategically about how they satisfy these groups within the constraints of the marketing mix, and within their own strategic objectives.

### Other sporting clubs

Understanding the impact of competitor sporting clubs and how their activities can impact your organisation is also important. Other clubs will have similar objectives of recruiting members and players and targeting business investment that, depending on the size of the market in which the sporting organisation is operating, can result in a highly competitive environment.

This is particularly true for sporting organisations operating in regional areas where business investment opportunities and membership growth are limited.

Rural and regional areas of Australia are currently dealing with social and economic factors, including deregulation of the finance sector, privatisation of government business enterprises, microeconomic reform and the introduction of the National Competition Policy. The effect of many of these larger issues impacts local business and its capacity to invest in sport, and in turn impacts the demographic profiles of these regional communities. Thus, other sporting clubs have a supply effect on the sports organisation as they can limit the size of the potential market.

### Sports governing bodies

The governing bodies of various sporting organisations tend to have both a supply and demand effect on the sporting organisation. Governing bodies are responsible for setting rules and regulations for the conduct of sport and can also be of assistance to sporting organisations for things like insurance, coaching and management training.

For example, Surfing Australia aims to service surf clubs throughout Australia from the grassroots club and regional level through to the Association of Surfing Professionals (ASP) standard. The association is involved in sports administration and management, surf coaching, event management, athlete development, educational programs and environmental issues and concerns. It also acts as a central point of contact for any inquiries regarding surfing and the ocean. It provides its members with insurance options, travel assistance, entry into accredited competitions and information about the industry (www.surfingaustralia.com).

## Step 4: Develop marketing mix for each segment

At this stage marketers need to consider each of their target markets separately and to develop an appropriate marketing mix to suit their specific needs. The basic marketing mix elements for all products and services includes: price, product, promotion and distribution (place) and it is possible that each target market will need a different combination of marketing mix strategies to suit their particular needs. This means considering alternative product or service offerings for different segments, perhaps different pricing strategies, different distribution systems and certainly different promotional programs. Once the marketing mix for each segment has been determined, marketers can then consider whether there are any similarities between the groups and whether some efforts can be combined to save resources.

It is important that sports marketers consider how each of the marketing mix elements is integrated and related to each of the other elements. For example sports products that are not strategically priced or even incorrectly or unfairly priced can end up having a major impact on how consumers view the organisation and the product. Distasteful, inappropriate and discriminatory promotional efforts can also have the same impact as would a situation where tickets to a popular sport were not available to people who wanted to attend. Let's have a brief look at what is involved with each of these marketing mix variables at a strategic level; the detail of these strategic decisions is covered in Chapters 6 to 8.

## Product strategies

In the case of sport the product is often the game itself, but there are also some tangible components that need to be considered. The tangible elements of a sports product are things like the participants who play a sport, the type of competition or game it is, merchandising decisions (T-shirts, hats, equipment etc), and venue facilities. The intangible elements are the impressions, experiences, emotions and interpretations that people have about sport whether they are participants or not.

The sports product itself is inconsistent and highly unpredictable and this is what makes it so attractive to many people, but it also makes marketing more difficult. Imagine trying to make strategic marketing decisions about a product that you have no control over! Sports marketers don't know how their teams will perform, whether players will involve themselves in scandals, or whether the schedules for play (often determined by others) will impact their success and/or desirability in the marketplace (Chapter 6 deals in detail with these issues). The intangible elements of sports products take on many of the same characteristics of services in that they are:

- perishable – once a sporting event has passed there are no more 'live' sales possible
- inseparable – sports products are produced and consumed simultaneously when players, coaches, officials and fans create the event that they consume
- heterogeneous – sports products are subjective and based on the experience of the person consuming or producing the sport and therefore each sporting event and each sporting experience will be different
- intangible – many of the elements of the sports product are intangible.

## Pricing strategies

Pricing is both a critical and sensitive issue in many strategic marketing decisions and in sport it is also a complex one. The purchase price of a ticket to a sporting event is based not only on the dollar value of that ticket, but also on the perceived value of the experience and expectations of the performance of the sports players that the person will encounter. In addition, for many sports products a differential pricing strategy is common. This is where different prices are charged for different seats, or different benefits included in the ticket.

For most professional stadium-based sports, the revenue from the ticket prices is less than the revenue expected from media rights and corporate hospitality sales. This is not the case for smaller amateur or regional sporting organisations that often have to rely on ticket sales as their main source of revenue. Therefore different pricing strategies would need to be applied in each case (Chapter 8 considers in more detail the issues involved in pricing in sporting organisations).

## Distribution strategies

Distribution decisions deal with where consumers can buy the product and where the product is consumed. Issues such as inventory management, warehousing, retailing, transpor-tation and channel management are all considered when making strategic distribution decisions for physical goods. Some of these decisions will also apply for the tangible elements of the sports product (merchandise and sports equipment for example).

Decisions about sports facilities such as stadia can also fall under the distribution banner

The intangible elements of sport are also affected by strategic distribution decisions. Where do we sell tickets, where are supporters' clubs located, how do we get people to games and how do we get our players in contact with our supporters are all distribution-related decisions relevant for a sporting organisation. In addition to these elements, decisions about sports facilities can also come under the banner of distribution. Where to place fields or stadia, how should they look, what access issues should we consider and how will people get there are questions that need answers (Chapter 8 deals with these issues in detail).

### Promotional strategies

A strategic promotional strategy deals with the promotions mix, five elements of promotion that need to be combined in the best way to ensure that the targeted consumers of the organisation know about the products and services offered and how to access them. The five elements of the promotions mix are:

- advertising
- personal selling
- sales promotion
- public relations
- direct marketing.

The main objective when making promotional decisions is to ensure that all these elements of the promotions mix are integrated with the marketing objectives and that they consider the decisions and directions chosen in relation to the other elements of the marketing mix. An integrated marketing communications (IMC) program is the ideal outcome of strategic promotional decisions and this is covered in Chapter 7.

## Step 5: Implement and coordinate marketing plans

At this stage of the process the marketing plans are put into action and consideration is given as to who will undertake and be responsible for the various activities, what financial and other resources are needed and what the timelines are for the activities. This stage involves considerable coordination and communication efforts among all areas of the company. There are many cases where great strategic plans have failed at this stage of the process. Generally the reasons are:

- failure to consider the impact on all functional areas within the organisation at the planning stage
- lack of communication about the objectives of the plans
- resistance to change.

Strategic planning is a concept or a way of thinking but developing an 'actual written plan' is an essential part of the planning process. A strategic plan should be written and then delivered to all of the relevant functional areas and players within the organisation. Different strategic plans may be needed for different initiatives. For example a sporting organisation may have one strategic plan on how to raise sponsorship among corporate partners, and another strategic plan on how to increase amateur participation in their sport. For some clubs a sports participation business plan may assist in this area. These plans generally contain information about the strategic focus of the club, a synthesis of the situation analysis, information about the product and market focus and then financial data projections and evaluation and implementation strategies.

## Step 6: Control and evaluation of the strategy

Once the marketing strategy and plans have been implemented, then it is essential that there is an evaluation of their success and an ongoing monitoring of their progress. Marketing control involves measuring and evaluating performance and taking corrective action should it be required. This is why clear and measurable objectives (Step 1) are so important. If this stage is not well done then it is almost impossible to determine how well or how badly a marketing strategy has performed.

This section has provided a brief overview and revision about the strategic marketing process in general and some of the relevant aspects of this for sports marketing organisations.

**Figure 2.6:** A model of sports marketing

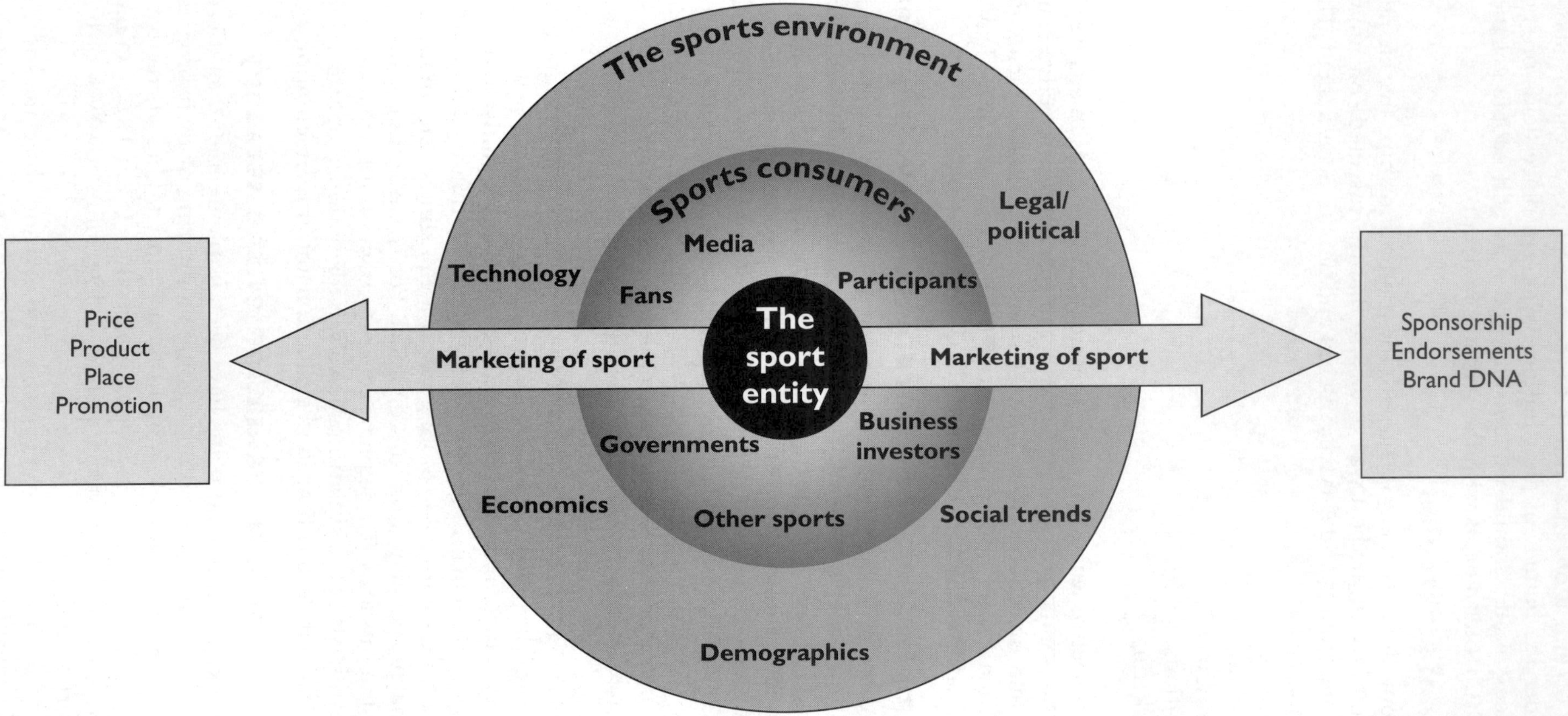

## Strategic sports marketing

Sport is a complex product with multiple publics, which requires careful planning, and strategic manipulation of the marketing mix variables. Figure 2.6 shows a model of the relationship of the marketing mix variables and the sports publics. This model clearly indicates that the marketing mix functions and strategic decisions need to consider the impacts and demands of the various sports consumers and sports publics in the context of the external environment in order to be effective. The demand effect of many of the publics can affect the core product itself, while the supply effect of other publics is in turn impacted by any resultant changes in the core product. Each of the areas highlighted in this model is discussed in more detail in subsequent chapters.

## Counterpoint: Is sport a business?

The money generated from sport around the world has become so excessive that it is now taken for granted that sport is indeed a business. It is listed as national assets, its management and marketing is taught as part of business programs, government and private sector managers are dedicated to its control. However, is this contrary to the social, physical and emotional purpose of sport, i.e. involvement? Surely the inventors of our national games and sports did not design individual and team challenges with the view that they be packaged, televised, sold off, merchandised, commercialised and digitised?

The answer to this question could be debated, and is debated by different members of the community. The bottom line in our contemporary business and social environment though is that sport is a business so that people can enjoy watching and participating in the sport of their choice. In considering some of these arguments you should remember that profit is not the objective of all sporting organisations. Just as some other large public companies are 'not for profit', so too a sporting organisation can exist for the purpose of protecting the sport, making sure that participation opportunities exist, etc. The reason a small social cricket club needs a strategic plan is that they have to protect their playing facility. They need to make sure that they will have members (i.e. players) in the future and that those members will have a ground to play at and perhaps some local sponsors to help them with uniforms and registration fees.

The reason that the Australian Cricket Board (ACB) has to have a strategic plan is that they must be held accountable to all of their stakeholders. They are entrusted with the fair and equitable management of one of Australia's national sports and they need to ensure that cricket is a popular sport in the future both as a social game and an international competitive sport. Strategic planning has led the ACB to the realisation that they must encourage the development of cricket in other countries.

The ACB sponsors player and official development of sport in South-East Asian countries so that Australian cricketers will continue to have competitors in the future. Sport without competition isn't sport. In developing competition, the ACB not only fulfil the needs of Australia's international cricketers but they also protect Australian sport consumers' interests by ensuring they will have cricket to watch in the future. Strategic planning can and does help them identify opportunities for profit, but this profit in turn can help fulfil non-financial goals through programs aimed at causes such as social involvement, physical activity and development of team skills among youth.

Strategic planning should not be considered an exercise for the mega-sports only. In fact strategic plans are vital to the survival and growth of all sports and sports-related organisations from national governing bodies to the local under 8s league. So at the end of the day, perhaps sport has no right to be marketed. Perhaps sport is just sport. Why should everyone from small social cricket clubs to the Australian Cricket Board be pushed to craft elaborate strategic business plans? Isn't their basic purpose just to provide facilities for people to play and/or watch cricket? Why do they need to identify 'strategic' business opportunities? Is strategic planning just a way to dream up money-making schemes? What do you think?

## Summary

- **describe why the unique elements of sport impact upon the strategic planning process**
Satisfaction with sporting events is largely determined by the quality of the sports spectator's experiences and these experiences are impacted by other consumers, the physical surroundings (service-scape) and by the consumer's own moods or feelings. As sports marketers cannot control or predict either a consumer's emotions (moods and feelings), or the interaction of others in the consumer's consumption experience – and indeed they have no control over the outcome of a particular game – they have unique challenges to overcome and traditional marketing principles are not always able to cope with these challenges. Thus, sports marketers must make marketing decisions in an environment where the outcomes of many of their marketing decisions in relation to product, placement and satisfaction are unpredictable.
- **discuss in general terms the principles of strategic marketing**
Marketing strategy is the process of planning, implementing and controlling marketing efforts to meet organisational goals and to satisfy consumer needs.
Marketing efforts include identifying appropriate and profitable market segments, understanding the behaviour and needs and wants of the customers in these segments, developing different products, pricing strategies, distribution systems and promotional plans for each segment and then monitoring the effectiveness of all this effort to ensure that the customers in each segment are experiencing satisfactory exchanges.
- **discuss the various components of the strategic model for sports marketing**
The strategic planning process can be summarised in a number of key steps or phases. These are:
    1. Clarify organisational and marketing goals.
    2. Conduct situation analysis.
    3. Identify and describe target markets.
    4. Develop marketing mix for each segment.
    5. Implement and coordinate marketing plans.
    6. Control and evaluate performance.
- **describe the exchange process and indicate how it is important to the marketing planning process**
The exchange process is central to any marketing strategy. An exchange is a marketing transaction where a buyer gives something of value to a seller in return for goods, services or other benefits. Exchanges are generally described as value-creating processes as they normally leave both parties to the exchange better off.
- **discuss the environmental factors that are critical to strategic sports marketing decision-making**
Environmental factors that are critical to sports marketing are generally external to the organisation and can be grouped into five key forces. These are: governments and politics, technology, demographics, social trends and economic forces.
- **identify the relevant sports publics who have the ability to impact the strategic sports marketing process**
As with any industry, identification of relevant publics, or those key groups of individuals who impact the organisation, is important. In the sports industry we generally classify seven publics or groups who need to be considered in addition to sports consumers in the marketing planning process. These groups are:
    1. players or participants
    2. business investors and/or media
    3. support goods and services organisations
    4. governments
    5. spectators
    6. other sporting clubs
    7. sports governing bodies.

## Review questions

1. What are the unique elements of sport that impact on the strategic sports marketing planning process?
2. What are the external environments that a sporting organisation needs to consider when developing a strategic plan?
3. Why does a sporting organisation need to understand their consumers and how should they go about doing this?
4. List and discuss the various publics that sporting organisations need to consider when developing a strategic plan and outline whether they have a supply or demand function.
5. Why should a sporting organisation plan when the environment is constantly changing?

## Applied activities

1. Go to the Queensland Swimming association web page www.qld.swimming.org.au and see if you can identify any evidence of strategic planning activity. Specifically see if you can identify who the target market is for Queensland swimming, if they have taken account of environmental factors, whether they communicate their mission, and if they provide a service for their consumers (other small swimming clubs and individuals). What conclusions can you draw from this and what recommendations would you make?
2. Choose a local sport and conduct the equivalent of a Porter's five force analysis (see Figure 2.3). What marketing conclusions can you draw for this organisation?
3. Conduct a strategic situation analysis for a local sporting organisation. What are the implications for this organisation in terms of how they present themselves to their consumers and publics and what specific marketing recommendations could you offer?
4. Internet exercise: Go to www.sparc.org.nz and also to http://www.ausport.gov.au/info/statistics.htm and have a look at the general sporting information freely available for sporting organisations in New Zealand and Australia. Comment on which website has the easiest layout for sourcing information. Can you find and compare the data for the proportion of 18–25 year olds who participate in sport for each country? Which has the best figures?

# References

ABS 2003, www.abs.gov.au.

Bloggs, J. 2002, *I Will Survive*, John Wiley and Sons Australia, Brisbane, p.12.

http://www.onsport.com.au/ 'BigPond Makes Big Splash', Issue 74, 23 July 2003.

Kiel, G. 1997, *Marketing: A Strategic Approach*, Nelson ITP.

Kotler, P. 1980, *Marketing Management*, Prentice Hall, New Jersey.

Mallard, T. 2001, Report of the Sport, Fitness & Leisure Ministerial Taskforce, www.executive.govt.nz/minister/mallard/sflreview/taskforce/part3.htm, viewed 20 March 2004.

Mullin, B. 1985, 'Characteristics of Sport Marketing', in G. Lewis & H. Appenzellar (eds), *Successful Sport Management*, Michie Co, Charlottesville, VA.

Porter, M. 1985, *Competitive Strategy*, Free Press, New York.

Safe, M. 2003, 'An Extremely Bright Future', *The Weekend Australian Magazine*, 28–29 June, pp.14–19.

Shank, M. 2002, *Sport Marketing: A Strategic Perspective*, Prentice Hall, New Jersey.

Shilbury, D., Quick, S. & Westerbeek, H. 1998, *Strategic Sport Marketing*, Allen & Unwin, Sydney.

Shilbury, D., Quick, S. & Westerbeek, H. 2002, *Strategic Sport Marketing*, Allen & Unwin, Sydney.

Statistics New Zealand 2000, www.stats.govt.nz.

Stensholt, J. 2003, 'Sport for Sponsors', *Business Review Weekly*, 13–19 March, pp.58–62.

Summers, J., Gardiner, M., Lamb, C., Hair, J. & McDaniel, C. 2003, *Essentials of Marketing*, Thomson Nelson Publishing, Melbourne.

Summers, J. & Johnson, M. 2000, 'Sport Marketing', in J.R. McColl-Kennedy & G.C. Kiel, *Marketing: A Strategic Approach*, Nelson ITP.

Wann, D.L. 1995, 'Preliminary Validation of the Sport Fan Motivation Scale', *Journal of Sport and Social Issues*, Vol. 19, pp.377–96.

Wann, D.L., Schrader, M.P. & Wilson, A.M. 1999, 'Sport Fan Motivation: Questionnaire Validation, Comparisons by Sport and Relationship to Athletic Motivation', *Journal of Sport Behaviour*, Vol. 22, Issue 1, pp.114–40.

# Case studies for Part 1

## Cowboy up!

### Dr Jane Summers

Professional rodeo is gaining in popularity both here in Australia and in the USA. In the USA, rodeo attendance rates as the seventh most attended sport in the country ahead of golf and tennis, with about 23 million fans attending (www.texasstampede.org). This trend appears to be catching in Australia, with the Mt Isa Rotary Rodeo now noted as the largest rodeo in the southern hemisphere with about 30 000 people invading the town for a two-day festival, including a country music festival, ute show, 'best dressed premises' competition, balls and concerts, and for the $200 000 prize money on offer at the rodeo itself.

The Mt Isa Rodeo was the brainchild of the Mt Isa Rotary Club 40 years ago, when it decided to stage an event that could help to raise some funds for the local community and to 'put Mt Isa on the map'. The committee that began the event had no rodeo experience and no knowledge of event management, but they did have sound business experience and good marketing advice.

The committee undertook a strategic review and analysis of their problem. They considered their objectives (to raise money and community profile), they conducted a SWOT analysis and a competitor analysis and from this they identified that there was a market opportunity to create a mega sporting event – a rodeo. So why did they choose a rodeo?

First, Mt Isa is located in the Selwyn Ranges in north-western Queensland. It is considered by the immediate communities as the 'capital' of north-western Queensland. The main industry around the area is mining and agriculture, so when considering a sport that would foster local community support and wider audience appeal, the committee needed to find a sport that was not already over-saturated and over-commercialised by the main city centres, and rodeo fit the bill nicely. Many from the local area owned and rode horses for a living, the cowboy culture was alive and well, and the committee noted a trend for many to get back to their heritage – and what was more indicative of the 'outback' than rodeo?

Having done their analysis, the Rotary Committee of Mt Isa decided that rodeo was to be their sport. They also noted that they had a perfect venue for a rodeo in Kalkadoon Park. This venue gave them the largest rodeo arena in Australia, seating for over 30 000 spectators, 10 food outlets, and merchandise pavilions and areas for three bars and permanent entertainment rides.

So who should be their target audience? In the early days the rodeo attracted men and women from local stations and the local community. Today people travel from Brisbane, Sydney and Melbourne to watch and attend the event, and the town boasts 100% occupancy during the August weekend when the rodeo is in town. It appears that the excitement, the music and the tough cowboy image is attractive to a large proportion of the population, particularly those in the 15–30 age group. The sport attracts men and women equally, though mainly men compete in the more dangerous events like bull and bronc-riding.

Since its inception, the rodeo has generated in excess of $2.5 million to charitable, community, cultural, sporting and service organisations in and around Mt Isa – not bad for a group of people that couldn't even ride a horse! Today, the Mt Isa Rotary Rodeo and its smaller cousin the Warwick Gold Cup are promoted as family sporting events and they generally have a festival atmosphere with country music festivals and other similar and related events happening simultaneously to create maximum entertainment for their audiences. The question for Mt Isa now is what should be their next step? Where should they take the marketing of the rodeo and how should they tackle their strategic marketing plan?

## Questions

1. Do you think that the Mt Isa Rotary Rodeo has followed the strategic marketing planning process outlined in Chapter 2? Justify your answer with the theory from this chapter.
2. Considering the strategic marketing planning process from Chapter 2, what would you recommend the Mt Isa Rotary Rodeo do next in terms of their processes and why?
3. What recommendations would you make to the committee of the Mt Isa Rotary Rodeo about how they could market their event in the future (maybe do a web search to see what other rodeos are doing worldwide to assist you here)?

Sources: http://www.isarodeo.com.au/; Lewis, P. 2000, 'True Rodeo lovers head for Mt Isa', *Landline*, 20 August; www.texasstampede.org/rodeo.

# Telstra Stadium: A sporting partner from the ground up

## Dr Jane Summers

Sportscape is a term commonly used in sports marketing to refer to the physical surroundings of a sporting stadium that affect spectators' desire to both attend and to return to that stadium to watch sport (Shank 2002). Factors that impact on the sportscape and thus on the spectator's perceptions of that venue are things like: stadium access; aesthetics; scoreboard quality; seating comfort; and accessibility of the layout of the stadium generally. Research has shown that spectator feeling of pleasure and displeasure associated with the sportscape can positively and negatively impact on not only the enjoyment of a specific event, but also a person's propensity to return to that venue for future sporting events.

This has meant that modern stadium designers are concentrating their attention on customer satisfaction in their designs, and facility managers are also offering more choices and a larger range of quality in everything from seating to food and beverage choices. Gone are the days when a hard cement seat, a cold pie and a warm beer were all OK if you could watch your favourite team play. Stadia are now installing club seats, exclusive members' areas, choices of gourmet meals, and extensive wine and mixed drinks menus. Modern stadia have to compete with the comfort and convenience of the average living room – complete these days with large flat-screen TVs and surround sound. So the critical ingredient that modern stadia have to sell is the live experience, the crowd interaction and the emotions that can't be replicated in a lounge room.

One such modern stadium is the Telstra Stadium in Sydney. Construction of the stadium commenced in September 1996 and was finally completed in October 2003; it hosted its first sporting event (a national rugby league game) in March 1999 with 104 000 people in attendance. The stadium now boasts a capacity of 80 000 seats and capacity for a further 3500 in corporate boxes, and was host to the 2000 Sydney Olympics. The state-of-the-art seating arrangement allows the lower eastern and western seating areas to move 15 metres closer to the action for rugby union, soccer and rugby league games, or to remain back for the extended fields required for AFL and cricket games.

Telstra Stadium is one of the world's most technically advanced stadia, with digital and fibre optic systems for broadcasting and data communication. There is also extensive mobilenet coverage throughout the stadium. Other statistics are shown in Table 1.

**Table 1: General statistics about Telstra Stadium**

| | |
|---|---|
| Construction cost $690 million | 92 turnstiles cater for 1400 people per turnstile |
| Stadium height is 58 metres | 284 corporate suites and boxes |
| 12 restaurants and members' lounges | 124 food outlets |
| 53 bars | 4 dressing rooms |
| 24 escalators | 350 television sets |
| 4 Boeing 747s would stand side by side under the span of the main arch | Largest crowd – Olympic soccer gold medal match 112 000 (opening ceremony 99 772) |

The stadium is owned by the Stadium Australia Group (SAG), which have a 31-year lease on the ground from the state and federal governments. This means that in order to pay for the considerable costs involved in stadium management, the SAG group have to recruit and keep large contracts for sporting fixtures and events as well as cultural activities that may be scheduled in the Sydney area. The seven-year naming rights with Telstra have helped, however it is the large 'blockbuster' sporting events that have mainly contributed to the stadium's $12.4 million operating profit (Telstra Stadium 2003). These events include the NRL preliminary and grand finals, the ARL state-of-origin games, a number of well-attended AFL games, the ARU Bledisloe and Rugby World Cup games, as well as a number of cricket internationals. During 2004 almost 750 000 spectators attended events at Telstra Stadium, an increase of 150 000 on 2003.

Interestingly, in spite of this impressive attendance record, venue rental from these events does not represent a significant revenue source to the stadium. Instead, the majority of the revenue is generated from the sales of corporate hospitality via suites, boxes and restaurant packages, subscriptions from Telstra Stadium Club members (all gold and platinum memberships were sold for the first time in 2004), naming rights and signage, food and beverage revenue and merchandise revenue. Competing with the stadium's commercial requirement to be profitable is the considerable involvement from the NSW government in the stadium, which also mandates that sporting development and support form a role in the marketing strategies implemented by the stadium.

One example of this is the involvement of Telstra Stadium's involvement in the Australian Rugby Union, which has resulted in the growth and financial viability of that sport in general terms. In relation to the ARU's bid for Australia to host the 2003 Rugby World Cup, not only could the stadium provide a state-of-the-art venue attracting large paying international audiences, but it was also able to provide a facility that was clean of stadium naming rights and venue signage. This, coupled with the extensive corporate hospitality commitments possible at the stadium, was the clincher in the submission. For a $14 million fee, the ARU was able to rent a clean stadium. This, along with tournament costs of about $120 million, represented a considerable cost for the ARU to recoup. However, the large seating and corporate hospitality capacity of Telstra Stadium meant that the ticket sales alone for games played there would recoup in the order of $135 million, while corporate hospitality would recoup more than $1 million.

Currently Telstra Stadium is attempting to assist Australian cricket in a similar way. They have suggested that if the one-day international cricket matches were played at Telstra Stadium instead of the Sydney Cricket Ground, Cricket Australia would have an increase in revenue of about $1 million, and this is just due to the increase in seating. If corporate hospitality rights were included then this figure could easily double.

So why would a company like Telstra want to secure the naming rights of a sporting stadium, particularly when they also hold naming rights to a similar venue in Melbourne (the Telstra Dome). One of the reasons cited is the leveraging opportunities that Telstra get from their involvement. Often these large sporting events will partner with Telstra to give maximum exposure and coverage to products and services offered by the telco. In addition Telstra also use the stadia for staff training, incentives (by offering tickets and access to corporate facilities), customer rewards and product launches. In addition Telstra have sole operating licences for all telecommunications within the stadium including wireless applications, and if you have been to a large sporting event lately you will know that if you are not on your mobile phone talking or texting someone during the game, then you are in a minority. Telstra also leveraged their involvement in the NRL grand finals by having competitions for those in the audience where you were required to SMS your answer to various questions throughout the night – all of which earn considerable revenue for Telstra.

Telstra Stadium has only been in operation for 4½ years and has already changed the landscape in relation to sporting events in Sydney and Australia. However in order to maintain their advantage over the average living room, Telstra need to stay aware of the factors that impact the sportscape and to continue to offer high quality entertainment options to the market. They also need to develop new markets (such as cricket), find and grow new fans and members, and to continue to provide a superior customer experience for those who visit the stadium.

## Questions

1. There are five factors that are suggested to impact upon the sportscape. Discuss how you think each of these individually might impact upon the attendee's satisfaction with a particular stadium.
2. The contract between the ARU and Telstra Stadium comes up for renewal in December 2005. If you were the manager of the ARU what considerations would you give to your decisions to renew or not and what would your decision be?
3. If the naming rights of the stadium were relinquished by Telstra, what other sorts of companies should/could consider taking these up and what would some of the considerations for this decision be?
4. This case has presented mostly factors that can be controlled by stadium management to impact upon spectator satisfaction when attending a sporting event. However, some of the factors that impact upon a spectator's enjoyment of a sporting event attended at a stadium are outside the control of the stadium management. For example, the crowd behaviour, the weather and the performance of the sporting teams being watched. What strategies would you recommend to a stadium management team to assist them when these things go horribly wrong for spectators?

# Part 2

# The sports environment

# Chapter 3

# Sport and society

**Learning objectives**

After reading the chapter you should be able to:

- describe sport as an element of culture
- identify examples of the role of sport in defining national identity
- understand the subcultural power of sport
- outline the benefits to and responsibilities of government in relation to sport
- explain the role of sport in the socialisation of children
- discuss the agents and issues involved in the socialisation into sport.

## Scene setter

**Bush school with a difference**

Statistics can be very depressing, especially when you're looking at something like Aboriginal education.

Why are literacy and numeracy so low and how do you get children to go to school?

These were the questions facing Colin Baker and his wife Sandra when, near retirement, they decided to take on the challenge of running a remote Territory school that was threatened with closure.

The answers – not surprisingly – came from within the community itself.

Colin Baker had learned to ride horses while commanding the Hunter River Lancers from 1983–86 as a member of the Army Reserve.

When an old Aboriginal stockman saw him out riding at Warrego, he suggested the key to getting the community's 12 often uninterested Aboriginal primary school children to school would be to teach them to ride.

Colin took the advice seriously, and to this day, three years later, he has a 100 per cent attendance at the school.

Reading, writing and mathematics are all spinoffs from an hour of riding class every day.

Colin and Sandra also commandeered the pool from the Warrego Mine to teach the kids to learn to swim.

The pool closed with the mine, but the Bakers have seen so many health benefits from swimming that they take the children to the Tennant Creek pool, 55 km away, three times a week.

The children compete every Friday night and have travelled to other Territory swimming centres for tournaments.

> The breakthrough in Aboriginal education is to give children a reason to come to school, says Sandra.
>
> 'It's giving them something to add their literacy and numeracy to.
>
> 'Here we've got the swimming and the horses and their whole education is built around those.
>
> 'Because these children don't speak English – except to me and Colin ... it doesn't have a meaning to them.
>
> 'So you've got to give them a meaning, and that's what we've done here.'
>
> Source: Richards 2002

# Introduction

Sport in all of its manifestations involves millions of people and millions of dollars all around the world. In understanding the magnitude and importance of sport in society we must explore the concepts of culture and society. Sport has an important role to play in defining who we are and what we believe in. It can help to define our own national identity and help us to distinguish that of others.

This chapter will explore the concepts of culture and subculture. Sport has been recognised as a cultural phenomenon in its own right and subcultural sports markets are also becoming a contemporary challenge for sports marketers.

This chapter will also investigate the benefits to and responsibilities of government in relation to sport. The central issues explored will include the benefits of health and fitness to the government and the wider community; the impact of international sporting success; and the community issues associated with the hosting of mega sports events.

Finally the chapter will explain the role of sport in the socialisation of children in society and also look at the separate issue of socialising children as sports consumers. The agents involved in these processes and the related opportunities will be discussed.

# Sport and culture

Sport has been defined as a cultural phenomenon. Like music and the arts, sport has been a part of the history of every culture in the world and continues to be a contemporary vehicle for cultural definition. Individuals and communities can define and express their own identity and communal belongingness through sports and the rituals that are associated with sports. We only have to look at the Olympics to find hundreds of examples of cultural expression *through* sport. The opening ceremony with all its pageantry is really a cultural demonstration, with the waving of national flags and displays of national dress. Chants and war cries allow participants and spectators to reinforce their cultural belongingness and heighten the emotion of the events.

As much as sport is a vehicle for cultural expression, it also helps to define a culture in its own right. Australians are often described as being 'laid back and outdoorsy' by foreign travellers. Much of the outdoor cultural stereotype is related to Australians' participation in recreational land and water sports. Other cultural icons in Australia include cricket and football. The playing and/or watching of sport are actually seen as being 'Australian' things to do.

Not all sports stay confined to their cultural heritage and with the increase of exports and global business generally, sports have migrated to new countries. This is an interesting phenomenon because much of the ritual and spirit of the sport may be grounded in another culture. In this case the sport that has its origins in one culture may be adapted and changed when incorporated into another culture, *or* the incorporation of the sport may bring with it some cultural transference from the original culture. In this section we will consider these issues, define exactly what is meant by culture, and consider how sport contributes to cultural identity.

## Culture defined

There are literally hundreds of definitions of culture in marketing literature, many of them stemming from sociology and anthropology. For marketers, the main focus on cultural studies should be how elements of culture impact upon the thoughts, attitudes, behaviours and experiences of consumers. For the purpose of our investigation into sport, culture may be defined as:

> The totality of socially transmitted cognitive and behavioural patterns defined by communal beliefs, institutions, rituals, the arts, physical activities and all other products of human work and thought.

Essentially this means that people learn acceptable or normal patterns of thought and behaviour from other members of their society as they express them through things like school, government, laws, religion, sports, dance, music, and even theatre.

It is important that we distinguish culture from race or ethnicity here. The term culture makes no references to biological characteristics such as skin colour or other physiological make-up. This is because culture is learned or 'socially transmitted' as the definition suggests. The other essential characteristics of culture are that it is pervasive, functional and dynamic. Further definitions of these characteristics are outlined in Table 3.1.

**Table 3.1:** Characteristics of culture

| Characteristic | Definition | Sporting example |
|---|---|---|
| Culture is **learned** | Individuals are not born knowing the values and norms of their society. They learn what is acceptable from family, teachers and friends. | From an early age, parents and coaches teach children to shake hands after competitive sports matches in both team and individual sports like football and tennis. This sign of respect and fairness we term sportsmanship. |
| Culture is **functional** | Human interaction creates values and prescribes acceptable behaviour for each culture. Culture gives order to society. | It is a cultural expectation that the word of an umpire or official is final in a sporting event. It is not acceptable to disregard the instructions of officials during a game. |
| Culture is **dynamic** | Culture adapts to changing needs and an evolving environment. | The rapid growth of technology has inundated us with media images and given children unprecedented access to sports legends and icons. Where physical violence used to be expected and even keenly anticipated in sports like rugby league, it is now seen as an unacceptable message to children and society in general. |
| Culture is **pervasive** | Culture encompasses all the things consumers do without conscious choice because their culture's values, customs and rituals are ingrained in their daily habits. | Friday night football, which is now so popular in Australia, was actually predicted to fail by some critics who thought it would never replace the cultural norm of going to the footy on Saturday afternoon. In a very different example, have you ever used the terms 'It's just not cricket!' or 'Come on, Aussie'? Why do these terms have meaning in our culture? |

Perhaps the most defining element of culture is values, those enduring beliefs shared by society that certain types of behaviour or modes of conduct are more personally or socially acceptable than others. Individual and collective values are of great importance to sports marketers as they underlie the attitudes that shape the behaviours and experiential interpretations of consumers.

In other words, they define whether or not something is entertaining, appealing, attractive and even important.

Cultural values are often used as segmentation variables as shared values give marketers an insight into how a group might respond to marketing stimuli. Australia and New Zealand have relatively similar value systems and are usually described as being individualistic, competitive, romantic, masculine, youthful and parent-oriented societies. However, in keeping with the recognition that culture is dynamic, several cultural shifts are apparent in both countries. While youth has always been highly valued in the pioneering mentality of the Australian and New Zealand cultures, a demographic ageing of the population and an increase in the political and economic power of older citizens, has seen a reversal of this cultural value. The ever increasing multiculturalism of Australia and New Zealand and an emerging recognition of the importance of the indigenous Aboriginal and Maori cultures have also contributed to the consumer recognition of older consumers. Migrants from Europe and Asia and indigenous cultures have long held the elders of their communities in high esteem. People, especially in Australia, can learn from immigrants who bring their own cultural norms to the country.

With an increase in the value of older consumers in our cultures come products and services to satisfy them. Sport is no different, with age being an important segmentation variable in many sectors of the industry. Many gyms offer special classes for senior members, the Masters Games receives increasing exposure in the media, and the Senior Golf Tournament and the Masters Tennis tournaments are excellent vehicles for targeting older markets and are no longer second fiddle events to the much younger competitions. With Baby Boomers now entering retirement and having increased leisure time, sports marketers should consider adjusting their strategies to suit this significant target market.

Another cultural shift in Australia and also the USA is the recognition of women in society and the rising power of women. In traditionally masculine oriented societies this is quite important as it gives rise to whole new markets and new marketing solutions in sport. Despite the obvious dominance of men's sports around the world we see an increasing acceptance and enjoyment of women's sports and female athletes. Many governments, including Australia, New Zealand, the USA and the UK are investing taxpayers' money into developing women's sports in those countries. There has even been a noticeable increase in the number of women who reach the iconic status normally reserved for sports men like Michael Jordan, Ian Thorpe and Tiger Woods. Both Venus and Serena Williams are internationally recognisable and Australia's Cathy Freeman is perhaps the best known track and field athlete in Australia.

Whether you are marketing a sport or using sport as a marketing tool, you should be very aware that all marketing stimuli is transmitted and received within a cultural context. Cultural traits can give marketers important insights into how best to satisfy consumers' needs.

It is hard to tell whether or not some values were derived from their sporting significance or whether sport is simply a forum for their expression. In the USA and some parts of Europe, successful sports stars are quickly elevated to iconic status with almost hero-like qualities. Michael Jordan has proved to be a marketing lottery for Nike, who have cashed in on not only his basketball success but on his huge fan base who consider him a legend. The hero worship of these American sports superstars seems to make them immune to the normal scrutiny and moral values placed on other members of society. Even those convicted of serious crimes somehow make their way back to the spotlight and even the sporting arena. Mike Tyson, convicted rapist and violent offender, has made more than $25 million per fight since he was released from jail. There has also been much speculation that O.J. Simpson's fame as a football player influenced the not guilty verdict in the trial about his wife's murder.

Australians seem to impose a much different kind of value structure on their sporting heroes. Rather than earn them some moral leniency, Australian sports stars are expected to be beyond reproach by the sporting public. Australians like to support the 'underdog' or the 'battler' in competition and don't like anyone to take advantage of their fame. This perpetuates what is known as 'tall poppy syndrome' in Australia, where sports stars are often criticised or scrutinised if they become too successful and/or too confident. The values of the country include the importance of giving everyone 'a fair go' or equal treatment and so sporting icons are considered very privileged. This privilege is taken seriously by the sporting public and violations by sports stars are not tolerated. The incident where Australian AFL player Wayne Carey committed adultery with his team mate's wife is a good example. This incident had no relevance to his sports performance and while morally questionable was not illegal or life threatening. However, the Australian public and his own fans were outraged by this moral indiscretion and his career and the performance of his AFL club were adversely affected. More recent controversies involving football players from AFL and NRL in Australia, football in the United States and soccer in the UK engaging in questionable sexual activities and being accused of sexual abuse have raised questions about the example being set by these highly influential sporting celebrities. Most professional codes and clubs in Australia now invest a certain percentage of their budget on programs designed to educate high-profile athletes on issues such as public speaking, anger management, socially acceptable behaviour and financial management. Some concern has been expressed that many successful athletes go straight from high school to clubs and codes where they achieve iconic status without ever gaining the degree of social value training and streetwise experience that the general public receives.

## Sport as an element of culture and national identity

Sport exists within cultures but it also is a cultural phenomenon in its own right and has an important role to play in defining national identity and satisfying many individual and social needs. That means that not only does sport operate as part of a culture but it also helps to shape that culture. 'In all its forms and expressions and at all levels sport is determined by both material and spiritual culture' (Leska 2001, p.10).

Sport and culture is seen as an important national and international issue. The two portfolios are often linked in government offices and in 1995 a group of sports leaders from 24 different countries formed the International Sport and Culture Association (ISCA). Today the ISCA has over 100 affiliated member organisations in four continents, totalling more than 20 million individual members. The association defines its purpose as:

- Promoting an understanding between people across borders through sports and cultural activities.
- Underlining the view of sport as a bearer of local, regional or national cultural identity, thereby placing it at the centre of international exchanges of ideas, opinions and cultural expressions.
- Encouraging the broadest possible participation of the affiliated members in sports and cultural activities within and outside their organisation (International Sport and Culture Association 2001).

The ISCA considers sport a very powerful medium and believes that sport is instrumental in strengthening civic behaviour and a feeling of belonging to a society. Sport does indeed bring people together physically and can also bond people emotionally through the mutual support of a team and even a country. When *Australia II* competed in and won the America's Cup, breaking the 132-race winning streak of the New York Yacht Club, the campaign created new icons with boxing kangaroos and Men at Work music blaring, 'We come from a land down under' … Many Australians had not even heard of the America's Cup race before the win but the national celebration was huge and even promoted the very famous words of then Prime Minister Bob Hawke who gave the nation a day off, declaring, 'Any boss who sacks an employee for not turning up to work tomorrow is a bum' (Wilkins 2003).

Think about how sport is linked to the way in which we celebrate or enjoy different holidays. Playing cricket in the backyard at Christmas is an Australian tradition and people in the USA traditionally watch football on Thanksgiving weekend. These are not the only examples of how sport and culture meld. A very interesting cultural phenomenon is the use of the 'haka' by New Zealand sporting teams as a signal of their origin and as an intimidation factor. The original purpose of the haka was to unite tribal men and warriors, to give them courage and create fear in the hearts of their enemies (Thomas & Dyall 1999). The sporting use of the haka started with the All Blacks rugby team and has become a cultural symbol of New Zealand on the world sporting field. It is a unique ceremony that gives contemporary sporting warriors the same sense of unity and courage that was felt by tribe members and is a sporting war cry for New Zealand sporting fans. It is interesting to note, though, that the haka is not supposed to be performed by women and could be seen as an insult if its use were to carry over into women's sports.

New Zealand players perform the haka

There are many sports that we consider part of different nations' identities. Aussie Rules football is as iconic as meat pies and kangaroos in Australia. Soccer is the essence of English sport. Baseball is as American as apple pie and sumo wrestling is undeniably Japanese. Canadians live for ice hockey and Norwegians are born on skis. That doesn't mean that each of these countries has a monopoly on these sports. Soccer is popular in countries throughout the world, especially Europe and South America. Similarly, ice hockey, snow skiing, baseball and even sumo wrestling are popular in more than just their country of origin. For sport to become part of culture or a cultural icon or phenomenon, it doesn't have to have originated in the region or even the country.

Rugby is an immensely popular sport in New Zealand and the All Blacks rugby team are internationally famous. However, rugby was transplanted to New Zealand as a rough and physical game reminiscent of the happenings on English public school fields. Scholars believe that rugby became so immensely popular and part of the social fabric and national identity of New Zealand because of the role it played in unifying the colony. Crawford (1999, pp.7–8) writes:

> In nineteenth century New Zealand cultural forms of expression such as music, art, drama and literature failed to produce an international figure that may have helped in the development of a national feeling of identity. Rugby, as a dramatic form in colonial New Zealand, offered opportunities for people to play a significant part, and to communicate common experiences and shared meanings ... for a transplanted fame, brought out as 'cultural baggage', that very quickly became the national pastime and, arguably, a symbol of nationhood and national identity in a far-off fragment of the Victorian British Empire.

Playing sport in the backyard is part of everyday life in Australia

Some sports have been absorbed into national culture not in their original form but as modified and localised versions of the game. In our consideration of sport as culture it is useful to examine ways in which a sport that has its origins in one culture may be adapted and changed when incorporated into another culture (Thomas & Dyall 1999). For example Samoan cricket or kirikiti as it is known, was adapted from the British game and became integrated within Samoan cultural styles and context (Thomas & Dyall 1999). Kirikiti is played by very large teams of 20 to 25 players of both genders, using a ball and a long bat resembling a baseball bat, but with a triangular cross-section. Only the local people understand the rules and it is a marvellous example of the 'inculturation' of a cultural sports import (Burge 2001).

The cultural power of sport cannot be understated and the Olympic Games are perhaps the only true example of world harmony that we have. Despite the occasional boycott by some countries standing their political or moral ground, the Olympic Games bring together not only people of different nations but people of different ethnicity from within those nations. On the one hand the Olympics and the sports they showcase can define an athlete or spectator's national identity and strengthen their cultural belongingness. On the other hand the sports and that same sense of belongingness can help to overcome national identities that would otherwise exclude some ethnic groups or keep races separated. Despite the universal nature of the games it is also true that this makes them a target of political and religious groups who have used the events as platforms of protest and for the staging of terrorist acts.

*Sports Illustrated* commented on the cultural power of sport in an article about the binding power of basketball in Yugoslavia (Wolff 2001). In 2001, in a collaborative effort between the United Nations, the NBA (the USA's National Basketball Association) and FIBA (the International Basketball Federation), 50 children gathered together for Basketball Without Borders. The significance of the event was that the 50 children were drawn equally from the five successor states of the former Yugoslavia. Even as religion, ethnic backgrounds and alphabets divided the cultures of the old Yugoslavia, basketball had always bound them together.

# Subculture

Sport has stamped its mark on many economies around the world, as employment and revenue generation figures have shown. More than just a factor of contemporary economics, sport itself is very much part of most country's culture and lifestyle. In this section we will discuss the concept of subculture and how some sports foster subcultures of their own.

Broadly speaking, a *subculture* can be defined as:

> a homogeneous group of people who share elements of the overall culture as well as unique elements of their own group.
>
> Summers, Gardiner, Lamb, Hair & McDaniel 2003, p.41

In sports marketing the concept of subculture is very important. Almost every aspect of sports participation and spectating reflects subcultural affiliation. Fans and participants gather for a mutual purpose, wear uniforms or sometimes team merchandise to identify their affiliation. They often use similar terminology when discussing their chosen sport and have rituals such as the team song, warm-up routines, chants and mascots. Considering these factors, it is very useful to consider the definition of a *consumption subculture* in sports marketing:

> A consumption subculture or community is a distinctive subgroup of society that self-selects on the basis of a shared commitment to a particular product class, brand or consumption activity. These groups have an identifiable, hierarchical social structure, a set of shared beliefs and values, and unique jargon, rituals and modes of symbolic expression. As such, these communities act as reference groups for the members as well as for those who aspire to join (or avoid) them.
>
> Neal, Quester & Hawkins 2002, pp.372–3

The self-selection in the case of sport is on the basis of participation in or spectating of a particular sport and/or a particular individual, group or team within that sport. Understanding the subcultural attraction of a sport is very important to a marketer. This could lend insight into new product opportunities, help with promotion design and delivery and is definitely a key segmentation variable. By understanding the attraction and/or repulsion of certain subcultures, marketers can use reference group appeals to market sport and also market other products and services using sport.

The idea of aspirational reference groups is easily applied to sport. Many people aspire to be their favourite sports person. Who wouldn't want to be the next Tiger Woods, Lleyton Hewitt, Lisa Curry, Dawn Fraser, Alisa Camplin, Steve Waugh or Serena Williams? But reference group influence doesn't always have to be positive. Dissociative reference group influence refers to those groups we do not want to be associated with. For example if you have a negative opinion of surfers and don't want to be like them, then you won't dress the way they do or use the same jargon they do.

There are also complicated subcultural situations that involve both associative and dissociative influences. For example, James is a huge basketball fan and in particular he supports the Chicago Bulls. He considers himself a loyal member of the Bulls extended family and likes to get together with other fans to watch games. His favourite player of all time is Michael Jordan and he owns several Bulls T-shirts and caps. He likes to read about the team and has followed Jordan's career closely. James has a lot of respect for Jordan and if he could emulate any one sports person it would be him. James did have one big problem with the Bulls and that was when they signed Dennis Rodman. Despite his basketball achievements, James had real problems with Rodman's attitude and his cross-dressing antics. At the height of Rodman's media attention, in full flight and sporting a wedding dress, James actually felt embarrassed to be a Bulls fan. He even stopped wearing his Bulls jersey to the sports bar on Sunday when he watched the games. Rodman was just too over the top for James and he didn't want to be associated with him in any way.

In this case a marketer really needs to understand his target market. If you were a sponsor of the Chicago Bulls trying to leverage your investment you might think very carefully about including and especially featuring Rodman in any of the conservative or traditional markets you had. On the other hand, if your target market was alternative or in this case perhaps a transsexual or cross-dressing market then you might actually choose to spotlight Rodman in your marketing campaign. Subculture is a powerful cognitive and behavioural influencer but marketers should be sure that they understand all of the factors at work, especially in a group or team situation.

## Sport as subculture

Whether you are marketing a sport or using sport to market your product or service, understanding how to leverage the subculture of the sport is essential. Sport is a complex phenomenon that involves products, services and many intangibles such as emotion, pride, loyalty, competitiveness and determination. Because of this it is not enough to just consider a consumer's satisfaction with a sport or the importance of that sport to them. We should be taking a more holistic and experiential view of customers' relationships to the subculture of the sport.

Research in sports marketing suggests that consumers' enjoyment of sports events derives, at least in part, from their identification with the sport's subculture (Green 2001). This is very important to marketers as it means that the consumption of sport and sports-related products not only fulfils some need for leisure and recreation but may also represent a kind of symbolic consumption for the consumer. In wanting to identify with a sports subculture the consumer is borrowing from the sport to demonstrate their personal identity. So why is sport so important and why does it hold such important subcultural meaning? There are several reasons. Sport provides a highly visible, easily accessible and particularly salient setting for the formation of subculture and the expression of subcultural values by either participants or spectators. We make a distinction between participants and spectators here because they are two different interactions and the attraction of each type of consumer involves different marketing strategies. What is important is that the notion of subculture can be equally applied to either group.

It is important to realise that sport itself is not one subculture. Each different type of sport offers its own unique set of behaviours, values, beliefs and symbolic expression. Even variations of sports can present two different subcultures. The subcultures of cricket and indoor cricket are quite different and the cultural adaptation of kirikiti involves a much different subculture again.

Board sports such as surfing, skateboarding and snowboarding have developed a unique set of meanings that impact heavily upon participants' lifestyles. While closely influenced by surfing and skateboarding, snowboarding has developed its own unique subculture. Born as a rebel snow sport in the 1960s, and banned by many ski resorts, snowboarding popularity saw the sport reach Olympic status in 1998 (Thomas 1998). Snowboarding subculture has an underlying anti-establishment sentiment and participants are seen as the rebels of the winter sports world. When snowboarding hit the Olympic big time in 1998 many commentators regarded it as an anarchic sport. The US snowboarding team mascot was 'Animal' from the Muppets and competitors were conspicuous in their baggy clothes, backward caps and abundance of body piercing. Some snowboarders even refused to wear their country's team uniform while competing in Nagano as it contradicted their snowboard image. Michele Taggart from the US snowboarding team competed in regulation uniform but fought US officials over the right to wear her own style of clothes in the Olympic village. Taggart said:

> 'It's hard for snowboarders in general to accept the authority deal … I want to be unique and individual, and wear clothes that represent me,' she said. 'I'll fight it as long as I don't get kicked out.'
>
> Thomas 1998, p. 1

Snowboarding and snowboarders are anything but mainstream and their rebellious clothes, language and actions help them to identify themselves and each other. In direct comparison, skateboarding devotees use the sport's meaning and value system as a way of expressing and understanding their relationship with the world around them. Skaters display almost tribal behaviour as they gather in absurdly baggy clothes worn in unconventional ways ranging from back the front to inside out, and speak to each other in unique jargon. They are most often young males who are attracted to the sport because of its unpopularity with adults and authority figures. As a subculture, skating is for participants only and often attracts troubled teens and those rebelling against a troubled youth.

Hard-core bodybuilding represents an elusive and fanatical subculture that also has its own unique set of values and morals. Bodybuilders are easily identifiable with pumped up physiques and often deep tans. At first glance this subculture would appear to be a very healthy group with strict and dedicated routines. When someone is fully immersed in the bodybuilding culture, however, there can be very dark implications in pursuit of their ideal selves. Hard-core bodybuilders often take great pride in learning about and using drugs to enhance their physiques. Although considered a *necessary* part of the subculture, the overuse of steroids can lead to physical and psychological problems (Berardi et al. 2002). The rituals of bodybuilding are very apparent and they even have their own sporting jargon. Did you know that a bodybuilder's ultimate goal is to be a 'freak'?!

Rodeo riding is a subculture with very distinct visual representation and a strong value system. Table 3.2 gives an overview of some of the tangible and intangible aspects of the rodeo subculture.

**Table 3.2:** The rodeo rider subculture

| Tangibles | Intangibles |
| --- | --- |
| **Appearance:**<br>• Cowboy style clothes – boots, hats, western shirts, large belt buckles<br>• Drive utes/trucks<br>• Tanned and weathered | **Values, behaviours and lifestyle:**<br>• Family<br>• Masculinity<br>• Tradition<br>• Sensitivity<br>• Nostalgia<br>• Toughness<br>• Romance<br>• Adventure<br>• Adrenaline<br>• Disregard for physical safety<br>• Nomadic lifestyle |

One of the interesting paradoxes of sport as subculture is that a subculture in itself is different from the mainstream culture in some way and is either not appealing to the wider population or the subculture does not welcome 'outsiders' from the wider population. Surfing is a good example of a subculture that doesn't readily welcome the part-time enthusiast or non-surfer crowd. In fact most board sports like their subcultural make-up to include participants only. Whereas a more mainstream sport like tennis attracts large crowds of spectators, who may or may not have ever actually participated in the sport.

The transferability of a sport's values and experiential emotion are quite important to marketers. A sport that tries to protect itself heavily from the commercialisation of its subculture will prove to be a very difficult market to get into. Snowboarding and skateboarding are both in the top five growth sports in the world but marketing big shots like Nike have had very limited success breaking into the skate shoe market using traditional sports sponsorship and promotion tactics. Australian surf company Billabong has had more success by adopting an inner circle strategy where they are seen to be ploughing money back into the sports they are trying to break into. Rodeo sports are one subculture that is actively trying to find commercial exposure for their stars and sports in general. Rodeo in Australia is an old-fashioned provincial subculture pushing hard to embrace the age of commercialism. It is a country sport seeking recognition and credibility in the predominantly urban, professional sporting arena (Hicks 2001).

# Sport, politics and government

The political environment is an important variable in any marketing analysis. In sport, government and politics can impact upon the environment in which the sport is marketed but can in turn have an impact on government and politics. In addition, sport as a product and as a social mechanism can be changed and/or regulated by government policy. Some sports events are so large and so important that they impact upon the very infrastructure of the country and therefore must seek involvement from the government. The three major responsibilities of government in relation to sport are shown in Figure 3.1. It should be noted that these benefits and responsibilities are largely true for developed, western nations but that the role and/or philosophy of the government in relation to sport might be quite different in other countries. This section will examine some of the larger government issues with regards to sport including the role of government in physical fitness, government intervention and provision in sport, hosting mega sporting events and the importance of international sporting success to government.

**Figure 3.1:** The responsibilities of government in sport

## The role of government in physical fitness

There is a range of possible outcomes from sport that are potentially beneficial to individuals, to society and to the governments of those societies. These outcomes include:

- personal satisfaction and better social life
- enhancing the environment
- improved educational outcomes
- improved health through physical fitness
- crime reduction.

The first of these potential outcomes, personal satisfaction and a better social life, are beneficial to a government in so much as they improve the quality of life of their constituents and make for a more balanced society. The environment can be enhanced by sport as sporting facilities often require large capital investment and can be built on sites that need redevelopment. We will look at the rest of these outcomes in a little more detail.

### Sport and educational performance

Improving education is a central goal for many governments in both developed and developing countries and it has been argued that sport can contribute to improving educational performance.

There are three theories that can be used to argue the link between sports participation and educational performance:

1. **Pre-existing conditions**. Athletic participation has no effect on academic performance and grades and any correlation between them is the result of pre-existing conditions such as individual personality traits like motivation or drive.
2. **Zero-sum theory**. Students allocate time and energy from a finite reserve to different activities. Therefore, the more time that is allocated to sports, the less is available for academic pursuits.
3. **Developmental theory**. Through participation in sports and other extracurricular activities, a student is exposed to social relations such as school personnel and other achievement-oriented peers who may generate and/or reinforce the individual's academic goals. Participation can also enhance the visibility and popularity of the student and thus have a positive influence on his/her educational motivations. Activities like sports help the students to acquire skills and qualities like organisation, time management, discipline, self-esteem, motivation and inter-personal skills. These skills can lead to future educational success.

Cabinet Office (UK) 2002, p.53

The continued investment of time and money into sport by both public and private educational facilities, and a substantial body of sociological research, support the arguments of developmental theory. The scene setter from the start of this chapter shows how the introduction of sport brought relevance to the learning of indigenous students in a remote school in Australia's Northern Territory. However, it is difficult to say whether it is the participation in sport or the positive impact derived from increased attention from adults (such as coaches, parents etc.) that bring about the changes in children and their educational performance.

## Sport and physical fitness

Few people would argue that physical activity and physical fitness are not personally beneficial and important in maintaining good health. However, health and fitness are not just personal concerns. Governments are concerned about their constituents' health and fitness because of the implications this can have on the economy of the country. The costs of inactivity or lack of physical fitness can put a strain on a country's healthcare budget and facilities. Table 3.3 shows the estimated cost of physical inactivity in Australia, New Zealand, the United Kingdom and the United States of America.

The high cost of inactivity and the potential savings from getting people to engage in more physical activity are both motivators for government-sponsored fitness campaigns. The physical health benefits of physical activity for adults include reducing the risks of obesity, cardiovascular disease, some forms of cancer, strokes, osteoarthritis, osteoporosis and non-insulin-dependent diabetes (Cabinet Office [UK] 2002).

In promoting physical fitness, governments around the world promote a combination of physical activity and sports involvement for their constituents. Most recommend a minimum of 30 minutes of moderately intensive exercise four or more days a week (Cabinet Office [UK] 2002).

There are many things that governments do to encourage people to participate in sport and get their daily minimum recommendation for physical activity. They develop educational promotion campaigns to tell people what they can do to improve their health. They provide public facilities such as parks, basketball and tennis courts, football fields, bike paths and walking tracks. They also offer grants to sporting bodies to increase the rate of participation in their sports and in some cases for the development of new sports or existing sports to new target markets.

**Table 3.3:** Cost of physical inactivity by country

| Country | Estimated yearly cost of physical inactivity | Yearly potential savings from a 10 per cent increase in adult |
|---|---|---|
| Australia | A$377m | A$90m |
| New Zealand | NZ$135m* | NZ$48m |
| United Kingdom | £2b | £500m |
| Canada | C$2.1b | C$150m |
| United States of America | US$24b | US$7.6b |

*Indirect costs from obesity alone

## Sport and crime reduction

There are two mechanisms via which sport might have a positive impact on crime reduction: displacement and therapeutic prevention. In a report on their role in sport, the UK Government explain the displacement and therapeutic prevention theories as:

1. Displacement – where individuals involved in sport are not available to commit crime;
2. Therapeutic prevention – where sports participation may lead to crime reduction through being:
   - i An antidote to boredom. The extent that crime is encouraged by boredom, sports participation might provide a socially acceptable source of excitement;
   - ii A way of enhancing self-esteem through physical fitness and achievement. Low self-esteem may increase the likelihood of an individual committing a crime. If sporting achievement enhances self-esteem it may reduce crime;
   - iii A way of improving cognitive skills. Sports participation may improve cognitive skills (e.g. self-discipline and empathy) which can lead to a reduction in the propensity towards criminal behaviour;
   - iv An alternative to participating in delinquent peer groups. The theory of differential association proposes that adolescents conform to the values and norms of particular social milieu, which may be dysfunctional. Sport offers an alternative social milieu; and
   - v A creator of positive relationships with 'significant others'. Sport links participants with a range of individuals (e.g. coaches and teachers) who may act as appropriate role models and espouse conventional values and conformist behaviour.

Cabinet Office (UK) 2002, p.58

Other governments have investigated crime prevention through sport and physical activity. The founding premise of the Police Citizens Youth Clubs in Australia was to foster relations between young people and law enforcement through the neutral field of sport and to keep young people active and involved as a potential diversion from criminal or mischievous acts.

A New Zealand government taskforce lists crime prevention as one of the 'social goods' achieved through sport. The Australian Institute of Criminology cautions against the solitary power of sport to prevent crime, but highlights cases where sport and sporting organisations have positively impacted on local crime statistics. The 'Sport spotlight' in this section highlights some of their findings.

## Sport spotlight

### Community crime prevention through sport

Professional sporting clubs involve themselves in communities, with the intention of producing an explicit or an implicit crime prevention outcome. Perhaps one of the best known clubs internationally is the Liverpool Football Club. The Liverpool Football Club is one of the biggest, richest, and most successful teams in world soccer. The club has confronted violence and other problems. Particularly in Europe, soccer has been associated with hooliganism and organised violence, often with racist motives and outcomes.

As part of its response, the Liverpool Football Club established a community development and public relations program. In the late 1980s, the Professional Footballers Association started a pilot scheme at six football clubs, with the aim of improving the connections between football clubs and local communities. In 1993 the program expanded and, with government funding, staff were placed in football clubs as part of a Football and the Community Program.

Examples of community-based activities with relevance to crime prevention are numerous. They included football camps involving high-profile players who promoted quit-smoking and anti-drug themes. A program addressed truancy, whereby children with a history of truancy who attended school for increasing periods of time received a Liverpool Football Club sticker and certificate. Those with improved attendance were invited to the club for a presentation. Another program with the Merseyside Fire Brigade aimed to reduce the 7000 hoax calls received by the brigade each year. To send the message to schoolchildren, the club produced a video starring senior players (Hall 1995 in Cameron & McDougall 2000).

In Australia, professional football, cricket, and rugby clubs participate in community development. For example, the Australian Football League (AFL) is investing $3 million over three years into junior development in Queensland. A Cape York development officer hopes that the AFL Kick-Start program will address many social problems, including petrol sniffing. Part of the program involves AFL footballers who grew up in the general area, visiting, coaching, and talking to young boys and girls about healthy lifestyles and participation in sport (Burke 2000 in Cameron & McDougall 2000).

Individual clubs have also participated in crime prevention programs. For example, as positive role models, members of Carlton and Kangaroos (formerly North Melbourne) Football Clubs visit the Parkville Youth Residential Centre (Inform 1999). Hawthorn players also work with young Aboriginal students, in the hope that they will not drop out of school (Dubecki 2000, p.A4 in Cameron & McDougall 2000).

Programs based on mentoring or role modelling often operate without policy development (Drummond 1999). However, the Raiders, a rugby league team in Canberra, seems to have developed an effective program (Gearin 1999, pp.16–17 in Cameron & McDougall 2000).

A program being delivered in the United States and New Zealand, known as 'Going for Goal', is a promising approach to teach young people life skills that can be transferred from one context to another, for example from sport to the classroom (Tatz 1999, p.138 in Cameron & McDougall 2000).

Source: Cameron & MacDougall 2000

While measuring the actual effectiveness of crime prevention through sport programs is very difficult, most people would agree that these programs have some positive effect and that any reduction in crime whether short- or long-term is beneficial to the general community. It is obvious why this phenomenon is of interest to law enforcement and governments but what relevance does it have for sports marketers and managers?

It is important that any marketer understand the characteristics of their product and the feelings, emotions and behaviours elicited by that product. Marketers of sport or marketers using sport need to understand the social value attributed to sport and the powerful and positive feelings and behaviours that can be associated with sport. Marketers of the clubs mentioned in the 'Sport spotlight' are motivated for their clubs to participate in those community crime prevention programs as it is a great public relations exercise that can help them attract publicity and perhaps even additional community and government funding. The sponsors of those clubs also receive some of this good publicity in a rub-off effect where they are seen as good corporate citizens sponsoring those who are helping to better the community. Finally the children and even adults recruited in such programs actually become part of the sporting target market, probably loyal to the clubs that help them and converts to the sport in general.

## The role of government in organising and funding international sporting events and hosting mega events

The benefits of sport at the grassroots level have been outlined but what about benefits of competitive sport at the national and even international levels? The benefits of hosting a mega event and those associated with international sporting success are inherently linked as most mega events involve international exposure.

International sporting success may have little association with a nation's participation in sport at the grassroots level. Similarly, success at the international level may not be a contributing factor in building higher levels of sports participation. Figure 3.2 compares level of mass participation in sport and the ranking of each nation in terms of elite sporting success. For example, the USA ranks first in an aggregate score of international sporting success but has one of the lowest levels of sports participation in the general population. Finland on the other hand has one of the highest levels of sports participation generally but ranks 20th in terms of international success at the elite level.

**Figure 3.2:** Comparing levels of mass participation and elite success

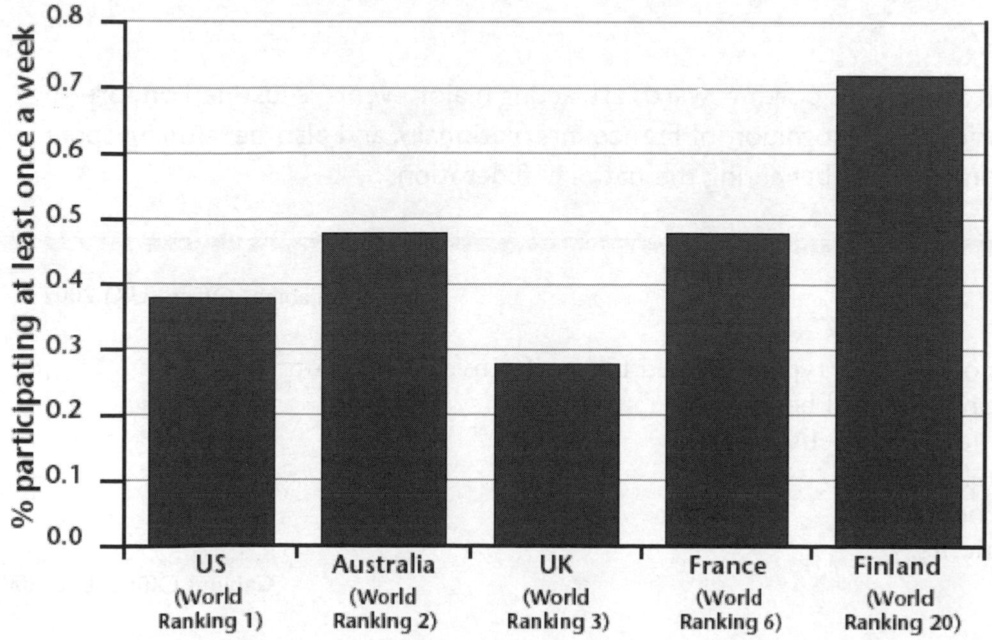


Source: Cabinet Office (UK) 2002

Then why do governments, sporting bodies and corporate entities organise and fund international sporting events? What are the benefits? The benefits fall into two distinctly different categories; one is tangible and the other is intangible. The intangible benefits can be loosely grouped together and termed the 'feelgood factor', which refers to the sense of national identity and pride and the positive impact that international sporting success can have on the image of the country (Cabinet Office [UK] 2002). The tangible benefits include the possibility that international sporting success can lead to economic benefits.

Hosting a 'mega event' has similar benefits, some tangible and others intangible. A mega event usually refers to a large elite sporting competition and the best examples include the Summer and Winter Olympics, the Rugby World Cup and Soccer's World Cup. Countries usually make bids to host these events and it is worth therefore exploring the motivation behind these bids. There are many other sporting 'events' that a country might host including the World Masters Games, Formula One Grand Prix, and any other 'world' championship or elite level competitions at any age group. Figure 3.3 shows some international attitudes towards hosting mega/major sporting events.

**Figure 3.3:** International attitudes towards mega/major events

**Australia**

The Australian Sports Commission in their review 'Beyond 2000' stated that one of their objectives should be to 'assist in securing further international sporting events'. As part of the Commission's international focus this would help to 'generate benefits for Australian sports and Australian athletes, provide commercial returns for the Commission and meet government policy and foreign relations imperatives'.

**Canada**

Sport Canada identifies a wide range of benefits they perceive from sporting events. These include benefits for the athletes, coaches, officials and volunteers involved, benefits for sporting federations (exposure, experience and influence), and benefits through increased sports participation. Other perceived benefits include the economic (job creation, regional development, tourism, exports, infrastructure and tax revenue), social (including youth training and participation) and cultural (the expression of Canadian identity).

**France**

The Ministry of Youth and Sports policy towards attracting major events is justified on foreign policy grounds, ensuring the recognition of France internationally, and also developing sport in France, especially in terms of benefiting the national federations.

Source: Cabinet Office (UK) 2002

There are five types of benefits typically used to justify investing in a mega event:

- celebration, social and cultural benefits
- urban regeneration legacy benefits
- sporting legacy benefits
- tourism and image benefits
- wider economic benefits.

Cabinet Office (UK) 2002

## Celebration, social and cultural benefits

The first factor, 'celebration, social and cultural benefits', is much like the 'feelgood factor' mentioned previously. This refers to the sense of national pride, and a host of psychological factors that are hard to measure. The social and cultural benefits of a mega event or any international sporting competition are difficult to quantify and cannot always be predicted. The Sydney 2000 Olympics are a classic example of a mega event that had a powerful psychological impact on the nation and provided an international arena for celebration and expression of national pride. From a business perspective we should always be concerned with the return on investment of such a large and capital-driven event, however the generation of such powerful positive feelings is also vitally important to marketers. Being associated with an event that can generate that level of pride, celebration and positive emotions is something that a marketer cannot buy on a regular basis and therefore represents a fantastic sponsorship opportunity if leveraged correctly.

From a government perspective there is some belief that hosting a mega event is also a public reward to the constituents of a nation. Szymanski (2002) believes that:

> Rather than thinking of an event as an investment in generating an economic return, it should be considered a form of public consumption – a reward for past efforts.

The remaining economic benefits – urban regeneration, sporting legacy and tourism may or may not be realised depending on the event and the planning and management of that event.

Staging mega events generates a 'feelgood factor' among the public

## Urban regeneration

Hosting a mega event typically requires an overhaul of the host city's facilities including accommodation and transportation services, and public spaces and facilities. This often includes scrutiny of the city and country's administration and public policy and even their human rights performance and policy. However, while it is true that hosting a mega event such as the Olympic Games can involve urban regeneration and the development of sporting infrastructure such as stadia and arenas, this often comes at enormous cost to the host country. In addition to the obvious disadvantages of large public debt, the infrastructure created can also go underutilised once the mega event is over.

## Sporting legacy benefits

Development of sporting facilities is an obvious requirement of hosting a mega event such as the Olympics. In addition, many existing facilities are often updated and renovated, particularly during events like the Rugby World Cup, which requires multiple facilities and training grounds. The 2003 Rugby World Cup in Australia provided a US$150 million surplus for the International Rugby Board and a AUD$43 million profit for Australian Rugby Union. Australian Rugby Union devised a five-year strategic plan for this money, including a AUD$22.6 million investment in strategic programs aimed at maximising participation numbers, commercial opportunities and elite player development. A further AUD$20 million was earmarked as capital reserves (Harmon 2004). Legacies of this size allow for the future development of the sport at all levels.

## Tourism development

The tourism dollars sought through a mega event can occur directly at the time of the event and indirectly through enhancement of the international image of the host country or city. The Sydney 2000 Olympics put Australia under the worldwide travel spotlight. The Olympic sponsorship undertaken by Visa provided international exposure by featuring Australia in over 500 Visa Member programs in over 50 countries around the world, which is believed to have resulted in a 7 per cent increase in tourism and a 23 per cent increase in Visa volume during the games (Li 2003). However, the investment in the mega event isn't always recouped through increased tourist dollars and very careful independent analysis should be carried out when estimating the impact of the event in both the short and long term.

## Wider economic benefits

Hosting a mega event allows a country to showcase more than just their sporting facilities. Many countries take advantage of the international spotlight by showcasing trade and business opportunities. The Australian Government hosted many large trade functions during the Sydney 2000 Olympics and the 2003 Rugby World Cup, which resulted in several lucrative export and trade agreements. In addition, wider economic benefits are enjoyed via the many products and support services that are consumed as a direct result of the mega event, injecting cash into the host country's economy at large. Mega events are also invariably responsible for both short- and long-term job creation. Industries such as sports marketing, media and event management also benefit from the experience gained at mega events, and the resultant injection of skills into the domestic labour market.

Governments must carefully consider the benefits of investing in international sporting programs and the hosting of mega events as the investments they make come from taxpayer dollars. Australian research into taxpayer subsidies for major sporting events (Mules 1998), found that despite the generation of tourist dollars and the development of community infrastructure, the taxpayer is generally the loser in the hosting of major sporting events. This can be a particularly sensitive issue when causes such as public safety, housing and community welfare groups are competing with the sporting event for government dollars. Perhaps the most interesting finding from the research in Australia was the classification of those events that are more likely to achieve high national economic gain. First we should clarify the distinction between spectator events and participatory events. A spectator event is one that relies on masses of people to watch a few competitors in elite competition, such as a Formula One Grand Prix or a Rugby World Cup. A participatory event not only attracts spectators but also relies on mass participation from athletes, such as the World Masters Games, the Australian Surf Lifesaving titles (5000+ competitors) or any number of carnivals and games like bowls carnivals and the Police and Firemen's Games. Participatory events such as these can involve literally thousands of competitors who in turn bring their spouses, children, friends and relatives with them. It is these participatory events, rather than spectator events, which are believed to have superior economic advantages for the host nation.

Research shows that the general characteristics of participatory events with potential to achieve a high national economic gain are that they should:

1. appeal to and involve middle aged, middle class people as participants
2. be popular in affluent countries, such as the United States and Scandinavia
3. be popular in countries where the population has a propensity to travel
4. not lend themselves to mass television exposure, and
5. not require expensive new infrastructure (Mules 1998).

This profile points to events that attract a target market of active, time-rich individuals with increased disposable income. The preferred events are those that don't require expensive capital infrastructure or dependency on inflated media rights.

Sport may have positive benefits for the community in general, but we shouldn't ignore the negative consequences of sport in society. Like the positive benefits, the negative aspects of sport can be classified as tangible and intangible. The tangible negatives include the direction of public funds to sport and leisure facilities and activities that could be otherwise spent on community priorities such as education and health. Often the high-profile status of sporting celebrities holds an irresistible attraction for politicians looking for voter support and the favour that comes from being seen with sporting heroes and legends. The short-term advantages of supporting sporting events and proposals may overshadow the objective assessment of whether or not the event is really in the best economic interest of the community or the nation at large.

The highly emotional arena of sport can also foster intangible negatives like defeat, disappointment and even anger. While a positive sporting experience can result in the 'feelgood' factor, a negative outcome can lead to widespread disappointment or more seriously to sporting violence and hooliganism. This is particularly evident in soccer where fanatic spectators have provided some of the most violent incidents in sporting history.

# Sport and socialisation

We have considered sport as an element of culture and the role of government in sport, which are two larger environmental forces. Now we will consider sport and its role in social development generally and then more specifically the issues involved with socialisation into sport. Consumer socialisation is the process by which individuals develop, through interaction with others, specific patterns of socially relevant behaviour and experience (Hanna & Wozniak 2001). Sport can be an important vehicle through which parents, teachers, coaches and players can teach children life skills such as respect, team work, fitness, dedication, commitment and loyalty. The concepts of sport and socialisation are also important as children are not only taught about life through sport but also taught about sport in life. This section will look at socialisation through sport and also socialisation into sport.

## Socialisation through sport

Sport is an important forum that offers structured and supervised opportunities for growth, interaction and development much like other socialising institutions such as school and church. In fact a Canadian study shows that sport at the community level is among the most positive forces in the lives of Canada's youth, more so than such influences as school, friends and peers, the music/entertainment industry and even religion (Decima Research 2002). Only the family is considered to be as influential in shaping the development of the younger generation.

Socialisation is a process and an end in itself and is a lifelong journey rather than an age-specific event. A variety of socialisation outcomes are believed to be developed through sport, play and games. These outcomes can be classified into three types:

- the development of individual traits and skills
- learning about the environment
- learning to interact with the environment.

In addition to tangible and physical skills, sport can teach and/or reinforce a number of values and attitudes. It would not be fair to list only those positive factors here, so Table 3.4 shows both the positive and negative values and attitudes associated with sport. The key in designing, funding or supporting any sports program is to emphasise the positive attributes and minimise the negative attributes. Sports marketers must be keenly aware of the sporting culture that is fostered by their sport or individual club. Any potential sponsor or strategic partner is going to want to harness the powerful positive attributes that sport can deliver to an individual, family or larger target market.

**Table 3.4:** Positive and negative values and attitudes associated with sport

| Positive values and attitudes | Negative values and attitudes |
|---|---|
| Teamwork | Winning is everything |
| Commitment to a goal or purpose | Dishonesty and cheating are OK sometimes |
| Hard work | The end always justifies the means |
| Striving for excellence | Violence and aggression are acceptable in some cases |
| Fair play | Strength and power dominate |
| Courage to try | Harassment |
| Acceptance of new things | Intolerance and racism |
| Respect for others | Performance-enhancing drugs aren't 'real drugs' |
| Respect for tradition | |
| Respect for rules and boundaries | |

## Socialisation into sport

Sport is a very important part of some people's lives and they can develop deep psychological connections to sport regardless of whether they are participants or spectators. The Psychological Continuum Model (PCM) is a conceptual framework for understanding an individual's psychological connection to sport. Figure 3.4 shows each of the four levels of the PCM. Stage 1 is awareness, which is triggered by external factors and essentially refers to how children are socialised as sporting beings. How did you learn the rules of cricket? Tennis? Soccer? When did you first become aware that different sports and teams exist? This process is sports socialisation and marks the beginning of the level of psychological connection you have to sport.

Socialisation into sports roles, whether they are primary participant roles or secondary spectator roles, involves many of the same agents as consumer socialisation. Parents, teachers and peers progressively input their sporting influence and preferences as a child develops. Parents shape a child's interest in games and activities, and fathers play a primary role in introducing children, particularly boys, to sport (Funk & James 2001). After age 5 when children are exposed to the wider influences of school and peers, parents continue to play a role in sports socialisation. Of particular note is a parent's role in introducing children to televised sport. Through primary or secondary experiences, children become aware of individual teams or athletes, and develop preferences and loyalty for one sport or team or individual over another. Again, parents and peers are very influential in establishing these patterns of preferred sports and teams. Of course, not exposing children to primary or secondary sports involvement can have just as big an impact in not developing a child's sporting interest or involvement.

Socialisation into sport is a very interesting and important concept for sports marketers as it represents an opportunity to shape the beliefs, attitudes and behaviours of future sports target markets. The AFL in Australia invest millions of dollars every year in its Auskick Program, to encourage young children to play Aussie Rules Football. While the stated purpose of this program is to give children the opportunity to develop skills and be physically fit, the AFL also benefits by helping thousands of children become socialised into the role of AFL participant. They not only get to develop a database of future players and supporters, they also provide a forum for children, parents and coaches to interact, all of whom are potential target markets of the AFL.

**Figure 3.4:** The Psychological Continuum Model (PCM)

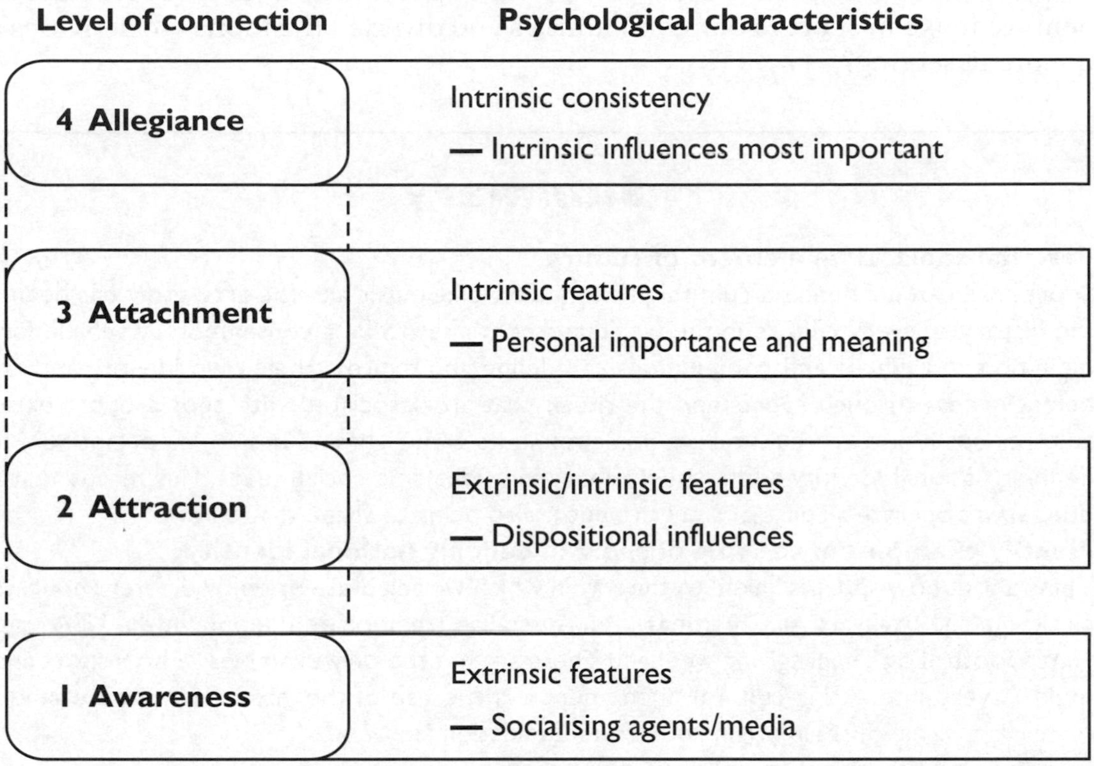


Source: Funk & James 2001

Simpson Australia, manufacturer of white goods, sponsors the Auskick Program and is harnessing the positive power of socialisation through sport to market its home products. In an environment that promotes honesty, integrity, togetherness and commitment, Simpson is seen to be helping parents teach their children life skills. Parents with young children are also a key target market for Simpson and therefore a very good strategic match for their promotion campaign.

# Counterpoint: The 'not-so-feelgood' factor

As much as sport contributes to the positive development and socialisation of children it can also supply negative role models, reinforce the validity of violence and aggression, and lead to unhealthy stereotyping. A study of sports media in the United States (Messner, Hunt & Dunbar 1999) concluded that in sports media:

- Aggression and violence among men is depicted as exciting and rewarding behaviour.
- Sports coverage emphasises the notion that violence is to be expected.
- Athletes who are 'playing with pain' or 'giving up their body for the team' are often portrayed as heroes.
- Commentators consistently use martial metaphors and language of war and weaponry to describe sports action.
- Sports commentators continually depict and replay incidents of athletes taking big hits and engaging in reckless acts of speed and violent crashes.
- Games are often promoted by creating or inflating conflict between two star athletes.
- Sports programs occasionally reinforce racial stereotypes or call attention to race/ethnicity in commentary.
- Women athletes receive very little coverage on sports programs that supposedly feature both men and women athletes.

- Women are largely absent from the sports programs that boys watch and when they do appear they are portrayed in stereotypical ways.

Considering the violence, negative role models and unhealthy stereotyping apparent in sport, should we try to minimise the role of sport in our society? Is it time we reconsidered the huge investment we make in sport in our communities and diverted the money to activities and issues that are more deserving?

## Summary

- **describe sport as an element of culture**
  Sport has been defined as a cultural phenomenon. Like music and the arts, sport has been a part of the history of every culture in the world and continues to be a contemporary vehicle for cultural definition. Individuals and communities can define and express their own identity and communal belongingness through sports and the rituals that are associated with sports. Sport exists within cultures but it also is a cultural phenomenon in its own right and has an important role to play in defining national identity and satisfying many individual and social needs. This means that not only does sport operate as part of a culture but it also helps to shape that culture.
- **identify examples of the role of sport in defining national identity**
  Think about how sport is linked to the way in which we celebrate or enjoy different holidays. Playing cricket in the backyard at Christmas is an Australian tradition and people in the USA traditionally watch football on Thanksgiving weekend. These are not the only examples of how sport and culture meld. A very interesting cultural phenomenon is the use of the 'haka' by New Zealand sporting teams as a signal of their origin and as an intimidation factor.
- **understand the subcultural power of sport**
  In sports marketing the concept of subculture is very important. Almost every aspect of sports participation and spectating reflects subcultural affiliation. Fans and participants gather for a mutual purpose, wear uniforms or sometimes team merchandise to identify their affiliation. They often use similar terminology when discussing their chosen sport and have rituals such as the team song, warm-up routines, chants and mascots.
- **outline the benefits to and responsibilities of government in relation to sport**
  The political environment is an important variable in any marketing analysis. In sport, government and politics can impact upon the environment in which the sport is marketed but can in turn have an impact on government and politics. In addition, sport as a product and as a social mechanism can be changed and/or regulated by government policy. Some sports events are so large and so important that they impact upon the very infrastructure of the country and therefore must seek involvement from the government. The three major benefits to and responsibilities of government in relation to sport are physical fitness of constituents, hosting mega events and international sporting success.
- **explain the role of sport in the socialisation of children**
  Consumer socialisation is the process by which individuals develop, through interaction with others, specific patterns of socially relevant behaviour and experience (Hanna & Wozniak 2001). Sport can be an important vehicle through which parents, teachers, coaches and players can teach children life skills such as respect, team work, fitness, dedication, commitment and loyalty. The concepts of sport and socialisation are also important as children are not only taught about life through sport but also taught about sport in life.
- **discuss the agents and issues involved in the socialisation into sport**
  Socialisation into sports roles, whether they are primary participant roles or secondary spectator roles, involves many of the same agents as consumer socialisation. Parents, teachers and peers progressively input their sporting influence and preferences as a child develops. To understand an individual's psychological connection to sport we can use the Psychological Continuum Model (PCM), which describes the psychological characteristics associated with four different levels of connection.

## Review questions

1. What is culture and what role can sport play in cultural expression?
2. How can sport help to define a nation's identity?
3. Why is the concept of sporting subcultures important to marketers?
4. What are the five possible benefits of physical fitness through sport to the individual, society and the governments of that society?
5. What is socialisation and how can sports facilitate this lifelong process?

## Applied activities

1. Collect three sport-related advertisements that you think use national pride or cultural identity as their main themes. Identify the values being expressed and comment on how successful you think the ad might be.
2. Identify three sporting subcultures (such as skateboarding, motor bike racing and soccer) and make a list of the tangible and intangible attributes that define each one. How could a marketer use this information to relate to each subcultural target market?
3. The Sydney 2000 Olympics were considered to be a huge success for the host country, Australia. How do you think success was measured? How should it be measured and why? Find statistics and commentary that help you explain the major advantages and disadvantages of the 2000 Olympic Games for Australia.

## References

Berardi, J., Lowery, L. & Fortney, R. 2002, 'The Bodybuilding Subculture', http://www.johnberardi.com/articles/philosophy/subculture_pr.htm, viewed 9 May 2003.

Burge, E. 2001, *Our Visit to Samoa*, Bootsnall.com, http://www.bootsnall.com/cgi-bin/gt/travelstories/pac/mar02samoa.shtml, viewed 14 May 2003.

Cabinet Office (UK) 2002, *Game Plan: A Strategy for Delivering Government's Sport and Physical Activity Objectives*, DCMS/Strategy Unit, Cabinet Office, London.

Cameron, M. & MacDougall, C. 2000, 'Crime Prevention Through Sport and Physical Activity', Australian Institute of Criminology, trends and issues in crime and criminal justice, AIC, Canberra, p.4.

Crawford, S. 1999, 'Rugby and the Forging of National Identity', in *Sport, Power and Society in New Zealand: Historical and Contemporary Perspectives*, John Nauright (ed.), ASSH Studies in Sports History, No. 11, pp.5–19.

Decima Research Inc. 2002, *2002 Canadian Public Opinion Survey on Youth and Sport*, Canadian Centre for Ethics in Sport, Ontario, July.

Funk, D.C. & James, J. 2001, 'The Psychological Continuum Model: A Conceptual Framework for Understanding an Individual's Psychological Connection to Sport', *Sport Management Review*, 4, pp.119-50.

Green, C. 2001, 'Leveraging Subculture and Identity to Promote Sport Events', *Sport Management Review*, 4, pp.1–19.

Hanna, N. & Wozniak, R. 2001, *Consumer Behavior: An Applied Approach*, Prentice Hall, New Jersey.

Harmon, S. 2004, *Case Study: The 2003 Rugby World Cup – Lesson to be Learnt by the Sports Industry*, presented at the 2nd Annual Sports Business Summit, Australian Financial Review Conferences, Melbourne, 16 September.

Hicks, J. 2001, *Australian Cowboys, Roughriders & Rodeos*, Central Queensland University Press, Rockhampton.

International Sport and Culture Association 2001, 'About ISCA', www.isca-web.org/presEng.asp, viewed 19 September 2003.

Leska, D. 2001, *Culture – Sport – Politics During A Period Of A Society Transformation in the Slovak Rebuplic*, Gymnica, Vol. 21, No. 2, p.10.

Li, S. 2003, *Sports Sponsorship – A Global Business Affair*, presentation on behalf of Visa at the AFR Sports Business Summit, 16 October 2003, Sydney, Australia.

Messner, M., Hunt, D. & Dunbar, M.A. 1999, *Boys to Men. Sports Media*, Children Now, Oakland, CA.

Ministry of Health 2003, *DHB Toolkit: Physical Activity*, Ministry of Health, New Zealand, www.newhealth.govt.nz/toolkits/physical.

Mules, T. 1998, 'Taxpayer Subsidies for Major Sporting Events', *Sport Management Review*, 1, pp.25–43.

Neal, C., Quester, P. & Hawkins, D. 2002, *Consumer Behaviour Implications for Marketing Strategy*, 3rd edn, McGraw Hill, Australia.

Richards, D. 2002, 'Bush school with a difference', ABC Central Australia, 27 June, www.abc.net.au/central/stories/s591619.htm, viewed 19 September 2003.

Summers, J., Gardiner, M., Lamb, C., Hair, J. & McDaniel, C. 2003, *Essentials of Marketing*, Thomson, Australia.

Szymanski, S. 2002, 'The Economic Impact of the World Cup', *World Economics* 3-1, January, pp.169–77.

Thomas, D.R. & Dyall, L. 1999, 'Culture, Ethnicity, and Sport Management: A New Zealand Perspective', *Sport Management Review*, 2, pp.115–32.

Thomas, P. 1998, 'Snowboarding – A Subculture Hits the Olympics', BBC News http://news.bbc.co.uk/1/hi/sport/winter_olympics_98/snowboard/53826.stm, viewed 9 May 2003.

Wilkins, I. 2003, 'Nationality Issues At Stake in America's Cup Outcome', Official America's Cup website, http://americascup.yahoo.com/story1806.html, viewed 14 May 2003; http://www7.boot.de/cipp/md_boot/custom/pub/content,lang,2/oid,5702/ticket,g_u_e_s_t, viewed 18 February 2005.

Wolff, A. 2001, 'Basketball Binds Former Yugoslavia', *Sports Illustrated*, http://sportsillustrated.cnn.com/inside_game/alexander_wolff/news/2001/07/03/hoop_life, viewed 9 May 2003.

# Chapter 4

# The sports consumer

## Learning objectives

After reading the chapter you should be able to:

- explain the basic principles of consumer behaviour and why it is an important concept for sports marketers
- explain the different types of consumer decision-making
- discuss the various types of perceived risk and how they impact upon the decision-making process
- outline the stages in the consumer decision-making process
- identify and discuss the psychological and social factors that impact upon the consumer decision-making process
- discuss the importance of involvement and motivation to understanding sports consumption behaviour
- explain the process of market segmentation and the relevance of positioning in developing a sports marketing strategy.

## Scene setter

### Anyone for sport?

For many Australians and New Zealanders, sport is almost a way of life and both countries are generally regarded as sporting nations. Certainly it is the trend with many western countries that sporting success can help to define their place in the world and illustrate who their people are. Thus, sport acts in many countries as the central agency in developing a sense of community and identity. Interestingly though, in many countries the development of various types of sport and their popularity has been related to social status and social class. In Australia in the 1900s croquet, golf, lacrosse, yachting and polo were all pastimes of the elite and genteel Australian society. The middle class enjoyed organised team sports like cricket, football and horse racing, while the working class were more likely to be found in taverns than on sporting fields, and this group enjoyed drinking, gambling, horse racing and boxing.

Even today there is evidence to suggest that preferences for sport involvement (be that attendance or participation) are still influenced by social class and education (Wilson 2002) and, further, that the media also has a large part to play in a person's commitment to and involvement with sport (Viseu 2001).

Modern sports consumption provides potential sports customers with many different options and choices for participation in sport. Sports consumers can consume sport by: attending live games; watching sport on TV or listening to the radio; participating in the game; playing in a fantasy league or participating in on-line chat rooms; and/or by purchasing sporting merchandise or memorabilia. Therefore sports marketers have to consider all these forms of sports consumption and to understand the reasons for their target consumers' choices.

Sports marketers also need to know what motivates people to consume sport, why they might choose to become involved or not involved with a particular sport, and how their personal make-up (demographics, social characteristics, personality, education and culture) all impact upon their decisions and preferences. Recent research on sporting preferences in the USA has shown that traditional sports like golf and tennis are rapidly losing their live audience to new sports like Pro Rodeo. In 2004, over 23 million people attended rodeos across the country making it the seventh most attended professional sport in the country (Texas Stampede 2004). What are the reasons for this change of attitudes and shifting of consumer preferences?

To answer this question, sports marketers need to have a very clear and detailed understanding of their target audience, their consumers' characteristics and their psychological make-up. In other words, they need to have a detailed understanding of consumer behaviour.

## Introduction

On current figures, the most popular participation sport in Australia for adults (16–65 years of age) is swimming (59 per cent of the population listed it as number 1) with about 3¼ million Australians swimming at least once during 2002. This is followed by outdoor cricket (57 per cent) and then tennis (55 per cent) (Sweeney 2003). In New Zealand the most popular participant sport is walking (70 per cent) followed by gardening (65 per cent) and then swimming (40 per cent) with nearly half

Swimming is Australia's most popular participation sport for adults

of the population admitting to swimming at least once (Sweeney 2003). Bushwalking/hiking, going to the gym and fishing are also popular participation sports in both Australia and New Zealand with about 2–2½ million people partaking. In terms of television consumption of sport, 96 per cent of Australians admit to watching sport on television with cricket, Australian Rules and tennis being the most popular, with at least one in two people watching them (Sweeney 2003).

During 2003, three quarters of those living in urban areas attended a sporting event at least once. AFL attracts the highest proportion of the population with 27 per cent of 16 to 65-year-olds attending at least one game, and cricket is a close second with 25 per cent attending a live game. The other football codes then attract the most attendance with around 15 per cent attending at least one game of rugby league, rugby union or soccer. Tennis (13 per cent), horse racing (13 per cent), motor racing (11 per cent) and basketball (11 per cent) round off the attendance figures (Sweeney 2003).

As you can see from these figures a large proportion of both the Australian and New Zealand populations attend and/or participate in sport. For those involved in the marketing of various sports, it would therefore be important to know why these people have the preferences they do, whether there are any connections between participation and watching or attending, whether they support their teams or clubs fanatically or only socially and what would get them to participate or attend more often.

The processes that a sports consumer or sports participant goes through in determining whether to attend or play sport and then what sports to support can be examined through an understanding of the consumer decision-making process. Understanding the consumer decision-making process is a fundamental building block in the development of any successful marketing strategy and this is no different in a sports context. This process consists of five stages that are influenced by a number of situational factors, as well as by the personal characteristics of the consumer themselves. In addition, external factors such as the influence of other people, culture and social class also impact the decisions that consumers make in relation to sports consumption. We will now examine the consumer decision-making process in detail.

## The consumer decision-making process

Consumers' preferences are constantly changing and it is therefore important that marketers understand how their customers make their purchase decisions, what is likely to impact their choices and what the important criteria are in their decision-making. Consumer behaviour is the study of actions directly involved in obtaining, consuming and disposing of products and services, including the decision processes that precede and follow these actions (Neal et al. 2002).

Generally, the consumer decision-making process can be summarised into five phases or steps as shown in Figure 4.1. These steps are shown as occurring one after the other, but of course in many consumer decisions, this is not the case. Often consumers move backwards and forwards through this process until they feel confident enough with the information they have to make a final decision. After a decision is made, consumers then tend to reflect on the outcome – are they happy/satisfied or not? This information is then used in future decisions to assist in making better choices (see the feedback loop).

We also need to understand that there are differences in the types of decisions that consumers make. For example, the decision to attend a sporting event at a local sports ground may be a fairly quick and straightforward decision for most consumers. This type of decision is termed low-involvement decision-making. In contrast, the decision to buy tickets to the final of the Rugby World Cup in Sydney, complete with airfares and accommodation, is more likely to be a more involved and difficult decision where alternatives and different options are likely to be considered. This type of decision is known as a complex or high-involvement decision.

Complex or high-involvement decisions tend to result in the decision process being a lengthy one. With these decisions, consumers also tend to spend considerable time searching for information from both marketing- and non-marketing-related sources to assist with their choice and they often consider a range of options (Assael 2004). In complex decision-making the entire decision process is followed – all the steps are included – and consumers generally take their time with their decisions. In addition, consumers often experience considerable doubt (or post-purchase dissonance) about the purchase after the decision is made.

**Figure 4.1:** The consumer decision-making process

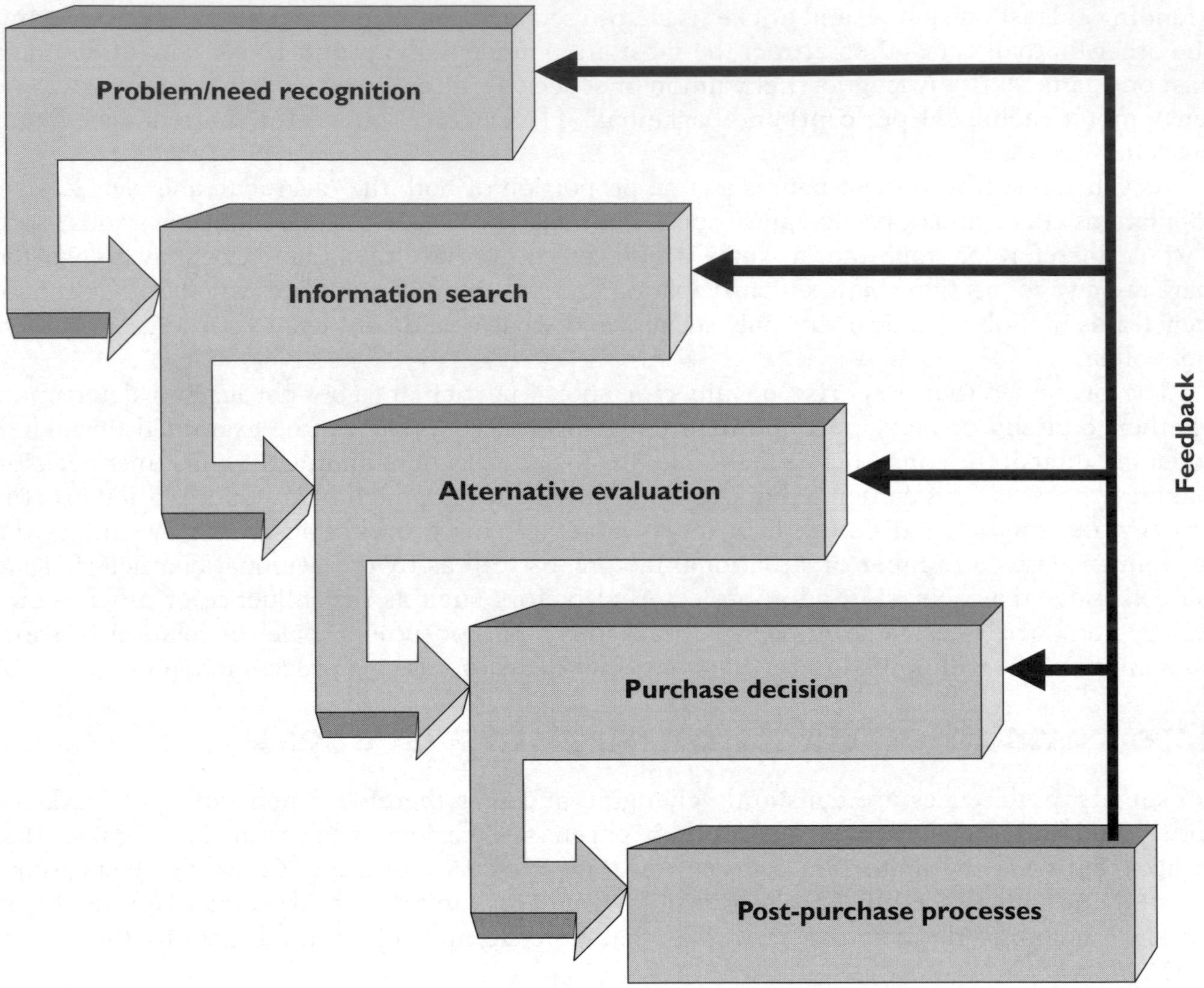


Complex decision-making generally occurs when the following conditions are present:

- high levels of perceived financial, social, physical, functional or psychological risk
- complex products and also products where the differences between alternatives is hard for consumers to perceive
- durable or long-lasting decisions
- lack of experience with this purchase or lack of knowledge about the product category.

In contrast, low-involvement decisions are generally characterised by the following conditions:

- low levels of perceived risk
- simple convenience products
- products purchased regularly and often habitually
- products that have a short life span.

In low-involvement or simple decisions, consumers often skip the information search and alternative evaluation stages of the decision-making process, relying instead on their experience with prior purchases to guide their choice. They also rarely experience post-purchase dissonance or doubt about these types of purchases. Figure 4.2 illustrates these decision types as a continuum with some of the characteristics of each noted.

**Figure 4.2:** The continuum of consumer buying decisions

| | Routine | Limited | Complex |
|---|---|---|---|
| Involvement | Low | Low to moderate | High |
| Time | Short | Short to moderate | Long |
| Cost | Low | Low to moderate | High |
| Information search | Internal only | Most internal | Internal & external |
| Number of alternatives | One | Few | Many |

Source: Summers, Gardiner, Lamb, Hair & McDaniel 2003, p.31

In a sports marketing context, many decisions will be simple or low-involvement ones, however for some consumers the decision to participate in a sport and/or to attend a sporting event can be complex and highly involving. Which type of decision it is will depend on the individual characteristics of the consumer, how much risk they perceive, and the situation in which they are making the decision. Because the levels of perceived risk are important in determining the types of decisions made, this concept needs further exploration.

## Types of perceived risk

Perceived risk is an important factor determining how much time and effort people put into decision-making. The term 'perceived' risk is used, because the level and type of risk only exists in the minds of individual consumers and thus it can be different for different consumers of the same products and services.

It is almost like a continuum where at one end we have those consumers who have high levels of risk tolerance and rarely 'perceive' risk in purchase situations. Sometimes these individuals even seek risk in their purchases – like buying heavily discounted sporting goods from street vendors or at markets with no product guarantees, or buying over the internet or using other non-traditional media. These people don't feel concerned about making a wrong decision; they are often the first to buy and try new products and actually like the *thrill* of uncertainty in decision-making.

At the other end of the continuum we have consumers who are risk-averse and feel very concerned about making the wrong choice. They tend to take a long time with decisions and carefully consider all options and alternatives before making a choice. These consumers avoid risky purchase situations (like markets or the internet) and even decisions like whether to play 'risky' sports would be treated with caution and consideration. You would probably not find these individuals hiking up Mt Everest, playing contact football or downhill skiing. You probably wouldn't even see them riding a horse or scuba diving. Then, of course, there are consumers who are in the middle of this continuum. Where a consumer sits on this continuum in relation to risk will direct the amount of risk felt and by association how they make decisions.

When we discuss perceived risk, we generally group the types of risk felt by consumers into five main categories. These are: financial risk; social risk; physical risk; functional risk; and psychological risk. Each of these will now be briefly discussed.

## Financial risk

In relation to the levels of risk associated with a purchase, financial risk relates to the cost of the item being considered. Products and services that have high prices are generally considered more carefully by consumers. The levels of financial risk felt by consumers will be directly related to their socio-economic background and also to their perceptions of *value*. Culture and family influence are also factors that will impact on how a particular consumer is likely to approach financial risk in relation to various products and services.

For example, a consumer is likely to carefully consider the purchase of a $3000 set of golf clubs unless of course they are very wealthy or perhaps they are a professional player, in which the clubs represent the tools of their trade and may be needed for that person to achieve a high standing in the game. In addition some cultures would not even consider playing golf as an acceptable or desirable sport, so the thought of spending $3000 on a set of clubs might be inconceivable.

## Social risk

Social risk relates to the consideration consumers give to the thoughts and views of others about their purchases. That is, will others think it was a good purchase and will they judge me because of this purchase? Social risk is usually felt where purchases can be easily seen by others (clothing, cars, attending sporting events or playing a particular sport). There are many highly visible products and services that consumers are likely to feel more social risk about. By highly visible we mean that others can clearly see them and make judgements about them. Your brand of refrigerator, for example, would not be a highly visible product, while your car would be.

Questions like, 'Do I have the "right" gym or work-out outfit?', 'Will others judge me if I don't?' 'Is he using the "right brand" of cricket bat?' 'Are her shoes Nike?' are all the sorts of questions that consumers experiencing social risk might pose. Interestingly, personality also plays a role in this type of risk with some consumers allowing themselves to be more influenced by the opinions of others than other consumers.

## Physical risk

Concerns about physical risk relate to concerns for personal safety. People may be concerned about attending large sporting events because of a fear of terrorist attacks or maybe a fear of becoming inadvertently caught up in violence, e.g. at an international soccer match. Additionally they may be concerned about playing a particular sport because it has a high injury rate or perhaps is a high-contact sport.

## Functional risk

Functional risk, on the other hand, relates to a person's concern that the purchased item will perform as expected. In the case of sporting events, this might translate into a concern about the quality of seating. 'Will I be able to see the action from where I am sitting?' or perhaps, 'If I purchase tickets now for a Rugby World Cup final, will I get to see my favourite team play or not?'

When applied to decisions about participating in sport, functional risk might cause a consumer to ask questions like, 'Will I lose weight if I take up this sport?', 'Will this club be the best one for giving me the opportunity to improve my skills?' and 'How much will I need to train in order to be selected into a national or international team?'

## Psychological risk

The last type of risk that consumers are likely to feel, and that in turn impacts the decision-making process, is psychological risk. This relates to a concern about the amount of time and effort that a person puts into making a decision and whether this psychological investment was warranted. Sometimes this sort of risk manifests itself when we take so long to make a decision that the item we are considering is no longer available or has been bought by someone else, and then we will be very frustrated that we have wasted our energy for no return.

For example, a person that is weighing up the value of purchasing accommodation and airfares now for the AFL grand final in order to save money would also be considering the likelihood of their team getting to the finals and the possibility that tickets may not even be available for them should their team make it. How to make the best decision in this case is one fraught with psychological risk.

Now that we understand how the decision process works and some of the differences in the types of decisions, we need to better understand the various stages of the process and how this understanding can assist sports marketers in the development of better marketing strategies.

## Problem recognition

The first stage of the consumer decision process is problem or need recognition. This stage is defined as occurring when a consumer recognises a discrepancy between their actual state (how they are now) and their desired state (where they would like to be). In addition, the discrepancy has to be sufficiently large that it motivates the consumer into taking some action to resolve it.

Take, for example, a person looking at themselves in the mirror in spring after a long and cold winter all wrapped up in loose and woolly clothes. They may feel some degree of dismay and discomfort with their appearance, particularly with the warmer months and skimpier clothes about to appear. This person may have experienced a discrepancy between their actual state (slightly overweight) and their ideal state (thinner) such that they are motivated to do something about it – join the gym or start running.

Marketers can influence consumers' desired and actual states through marketing communications. On a simple level, a marketer can appeal to basic human drives and physiological needs that they know will arise in certain situations. For example, the marketer of a range of high protein supplement food bars may advertise the nutritious and performance-enhancing properties of their products in gyms and other places where people exercise and are likely to want to consume food and drinks afterwards.

In contrast, marketers also attempt to understand more complex subconscious or psychological motives of consumers called *wants*, which occur when there is an unfulfilled need. Wants are not based on necessity; rather they are based on desires or on perceptions of how someone perceives themselves. For example, marketers might highlight the benefits of participation in a particular sport as social, physical and cultural, all of which are desirable but none of which is essential. Macquarie Bank uses its association with the ACT Brumbies as a means of creating interest in their products for consumers and they also use the attraction of meetings with famous players and the opportunity to participate in rugby development clinics as a way of stimulating the desired states in their various customer bases. See the example of the involvement of Macquarie Bank in sport as a means of influencing their customers' decision processes in selection of financial services in Appendix 1 of this chapter.

Consumers recognise unfulfilled needs and wants in a number of different ways. One of the most common is when a current product or service is not performing as required and therefore a change is needed. You need new running shoes as your old ones have holes in the sole, or the players in your team are not committed and you need to change clubs to find serious players.

Consumers can also recognise wants when they are exposed to information about products and services that are superior to the existing ones in some way. This is usually done through marketing communications: 'If you want to play like Michael Jordan you need to wear Nike products.' Marketers spend a lot of time and money on attempting to create desires and wants for their products and services in the minds of consumers. This process is sometimes easier for physical products (sports clothes and so forth) than it is for services and experiences. For example, marketers attempting to create a desire for tickets to attend a sporting event have to focus on communicating the likely atmosphere of the event, the excitement of being there and the fact that once the event is over it can never be recreated – as was done for the 2003 Rugby World Cup advertising.

## Information search

The second stage of the consumer decision-making process is the information search stage. It is here that consumers consider what additional information they might need to assist with their decision. Information search can occur internally and/or externally depending on the level of consumer involvement with the decision and the level of confidence the consumer has in making the correct choice.

When consumers are not particularly concerned about the decision outcome (low involvement) and the decision is one that is made regularly, they will usually simply rely on information they have stored in their memories and not seek extra information from external sources – this is called internal information search. On the other hand, when consumers are more concerned about the decision outcome (more highly involved) and not confident that they have all the necessary information to make an informed decision, they will seek external sources of information to help them. This is called external information search. This external information can take the form of marketing controlled material such as ads, sales people or packaging information, and non-marketing controlled information such as information from friends, relatives, news items and other non-biased sources.

For most consumers, the most persuasive information is that from non-marketer controlled sources, and more importantly from trusted friends or relatives. This is referred to as word-of-mouth communication. For purchases like sport, which have a high degree of intangibility and are largely based on individual experiences, non-marketer controlled sources of information become even more important to potential customers. In addition, marketing controlled information has to rely on attempting to communicate the emotions and feelings associated with a sports purchase as this is the main benefit consumers are seeking.

When making decisions then about how to present information to potential customers, sports marketers generally rely heavily on visual images to communicate the emotions and excitement of sport. Television, which provides both audio and visual images, is generally the most successful

**Figure 4.3:** The evoked set

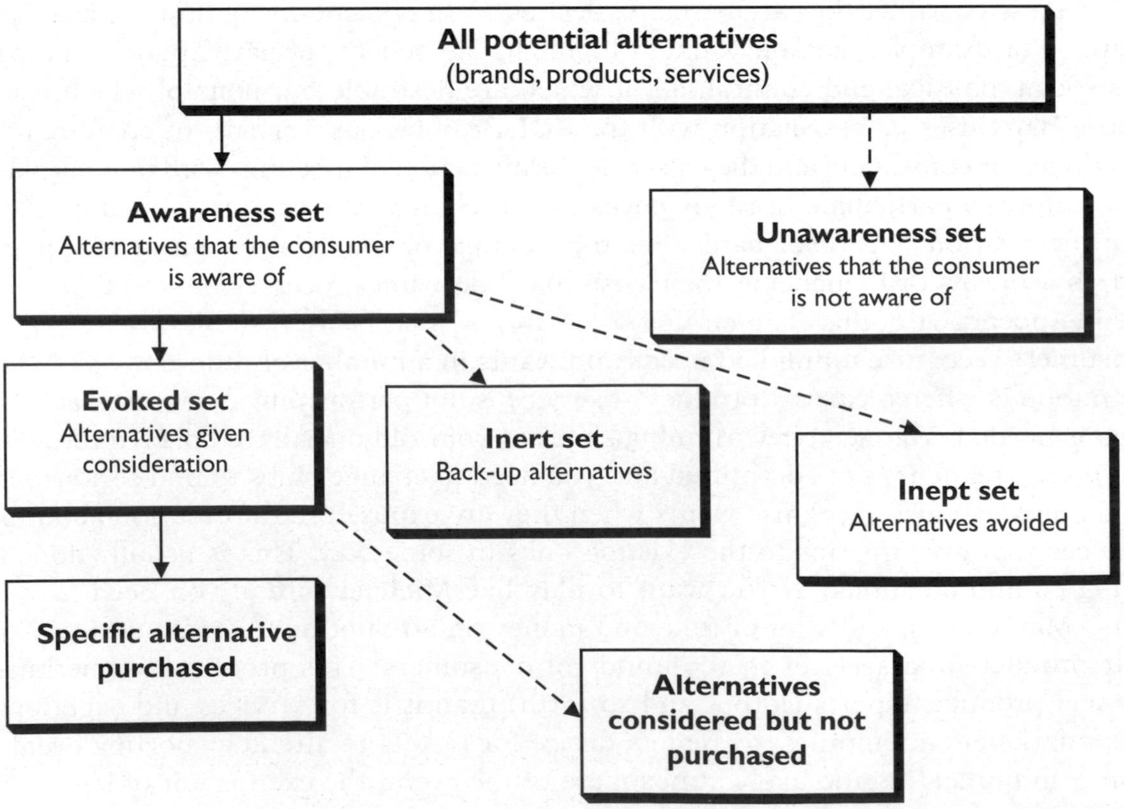


Source: Neal, Quester & Hawkins 2002, p.78

medium for communication of sports benefits. In addition, many sports marketers have also made use of the internet to provide information about their products and services, capitalising on the interactivity of this medium and the ability to use both visual and auditory information.

## Alternative evaluation

Once a consumer has all the information they need to make a decision, they then consider their final list of alternatives. During the information search phase the consumer usually ends up with a list of options from which they will make their final choice. This final list of options is called the 'evoked set' (see Figure 4.3).

Consumers employ a range of different decision rules to help them make their final choice and the complexity of the decision rules used depends largely on the individual consumer and the type of purchase. For most consumer decisions, some sort of evaluation of the major features or attributes of the various alternatives is conducted to determine the best alternative. In the case of sports consumption decisions, the lack of tangibility and lack of easily identifiable and comparable alternatives makes this a little harder. Therefore, when evaluating sports options, consumers might use criteria such as value for money, social acceptance and relevance and the quality of relationships with sales staff or other service providers to help with their decisions.

## Choice

Once the alternatives have been considered, the consumer makes a choice and in doing so they undergo a further decision-making process to decide on how they are going to pay, when they are going to pay and where they might make the purchase. At this choice stage, consumers become interested in delivery options – 'How will I get my tickets?', 'When does my first gym class start?' or 'What nights do we train and what days are the competition?' Once the choice is made, consumers immediately begin an evaluation stage where they consider their satisfaction or otherwise with the choice they have made.

## Post-purchase processes

When consumers purchase complex products they will often undergo a considerable degree of reflection about the decision and consideration about whether or not they have made the right choice. This process of reflection and doubt is called post-purchase dissonance. The more perceived risk involved in the purchase and the less confident the consumer with the decision-making process, the more dissonance is felt. For purchases that are routine or habitual there is rarely any post-purchase evaluation and dissonance.

A person who joins a gym might judge membership satisfaction by their increased level of fitness

In the case of sports consumption, the decision to participate in a sport often has considerable post-purchase evaluation. The consumer will question the value of their effort and the worth of the initial expense. Sports marketers therefore need to have a detailed understanding of the motivations for participation in their various sports as this will provide a guide to the strategies needed to help reassure consumers and to help reduce dissonance.

A consumer's motivation for making a purchase is directly related to the criteria they would use to evaluate their satisfaction. For example, a person who joins a gym in order to get fit will use their resultant level of fitness to gauge their level of satisfaction with the purchase. Another person who joins a gym to meet people will use their resultant social interactions to gauge their satisfaction with the decision.

A consumer's decision-making process is something that is unique to each individual and it will also change with different purchase situations and when purchases are made in different contexts. In order to better understand how the decision process is likely to differ from consumer to consumer, we need to gain a clearer understanding of the factors that impact the process. Essentially these can be divided into two groups, internal or psychological factors and external or social factors. We will explore each group next.

# Psychological or internal factors

A consumer's internal make-up has a significant impact on how they view the world and interpret information presented to them and these psychological factors are unique to each individual consumer. Factors such as personality, perception, learning and attitudes are all important internal factors that need to be understood. We will examine each of these in brief next.

## Personality

Personality is the blend of characteristics that make a person unique and these characteristics are reasonably consistent and enduring. This means that a person's fundamental personality characteristics rarely change. A person's personality determines how they are likely to respond to the environment around them and how they are likely to act in social situations.

There are four main theories used to describe personality. These are: (1) psychoanalytic theories, (2) social-cultural theories, (3) self-concept theories, and (4) trait theories (Assael 2004). These four theories vary widely in their approach. Generally however, the psychoanalytic and social-cultural theories are qualitative in their approach, the trait theories are quantitative or empirical and the self-concept theories sit somewhat in the middle.

Psychoanalytic theories have long been used in marketing and are useful for providing insights into why people make purchase decisions. Self-concept theories, by contrast, look at how self-image impacts purchasing behaviour and is often more difficult to use effectively in marketing strategies as they rely on people understanding and being honest about their self-image. Social-cultural theories of personality are derived from an understanding of people's social and cultural backgrounds and context in relation to decision-making and, once again, the qualitative nature of these theories makes them less applicable to marketing strategy. Probably the most widely used theoretical approach to personality in sports marketing is the trait theory approach.

Trait theories suggest that personality is comprised of a set of traits that describe general response predispositions (Assael 2004). A consumer's personality is quantified by asking them to respond to a range of questions about particular traits or personality factors from a large bank of personality inventories. Once a group of personality traits are identified, combinations of these traits can then be used for segmentation, purchase prediction and marketing communications.

In relation to sport, researchers have often attempted to predict a relationship between personality and sports performance and even choice of sport, however their results have been far from consistent. There has been no specific personality profile that consistently discriminates athletes from non-athletes for example and between male and female athletes. In spite of this there have been some interesting findings in the area of athlete personality traits as shown in Table 4.1. This table shows the personality traits that have been noted in various studies and how they relate to choices of various types of sport – team versus individual and male versus female. For example those who choose team sports are likely to be: less abstract; have strong egos; are more likely to be extroverts and have dependent types of personalities. Those who prefer individual sports, however, are more likely to be: objective; have low anxiety; be abstract thinkers and introverts.

**Table 4.1:** Athlete personality traits

| | Team sports | Individual sports | Female athletes |
|---|---|---|---|
| **Personality traits noted** | Less abstract reasoning | More objectivity | Achievement oriented |
| | Strong ego | Low anxiety | Independent |
| | Extroversion | Abstract thinkers | Aggressive |
| | Dependent | Introversion | Emotionally stable |
| | | | Assertive |

Adapted from www.Academic.uofs.edu/faculty/OAKESM2/spperson.html

Researchers have also attempted to answer the question, 'Does sport change personality or are certain personalities drawn to different sports?' and although personality tests can provide indicators about personality trends, strengths and weaknesses, they can merely provide an *indication* of potential performance not predict *actual* performance. Figure 4.4 shows a profile of various personality traits and how these relate to a number of different sports. You might find some of these findings to be a little controversial.

Finally, researchers have also suggested that genetics has much to do with personality and with sports performance and sports choice. The most famous of these theorists is William Sheldon (Arraj & Arraj 1988) who theorised that there were three basic body types, endomorphs (fat, round, soft bodies), ectomorphs (thin, frail bodies) and mesomorphs (hard, strong, muscular bodies); see Figure 4.5. He suggested that each body type was predisposed to particular personality traits and an understanding of this would help to predict sports preferences and participation rates.

**Figure 4.4:** Your personality/your sport

**VERY HIGH** — **SOCIABILITY** — **VERY LOW**

Golf→Tennis→Martial arts→Downhill skiing→Aerobics→Dance→Bodybuilding→Cross country skiing→Walking→Running→Cycling→Swimming

**VERY HIGH** — **SPONTANEITY** — **VERY LOW**

Tennis→Downhill skiing→Martial arts→Dance→Aerobics→Walking→Cross country skiing→Cycling→Bodybuilding→Swimming→Running→Golf

**VERY HIGH** — **DISCIPLINE** — **VERY LOW**

Running→Bodybuilding→Cycling→Swimming→Cross country skiing→Martial arts→Dance→Walking→Aerobics→Tennis→Golf→Downhill skiing

**VERY HIGH** — **AGRESSIVENESS** — **VERY LOW**

Martial arts→Bodybuilding→Tennis→Downhill skiing→Golf→Cycling→Running→Cross country skiing→Aerobics→Dance→Swimming→Walking

**VERY HIGH** — **COMPETITIVENESS** — **VERY LOW**

Tennis→Golf→Downhill skiing→Martial arts→Dance→Running→Bodybuilding→Cycling→Cross country skiing→Swimming→Aerobics→Walking

**VERY HIGH** — **MENTAL FOCUS** — **VERY LOW**

Tennis→Golf→Dance→Martial arts→Downhill skiing→Bodybuilding→Cycling→Aerobics→Cross country skiing→Swimming→Running→Walking

**VERY HIGH** — **RISK TAKING** — **VERY LOW**

Downhill skiing→Martial arts→Tennis→Golf→Cycling→Bodybuilding→Dance→Cross country skiing→Aerobics→Swimming→Running→Walking

Source: www.sasked.gov.sk.ca/docs/physed/ physed2030/ypysport.pdf

However these theories have not been found to be applicable with modern testing and research. It does however provide an interesting point for conversation and some food for thought for sports marketers (www.age-of-the-sage 2003).

**Figure 4.5:** Sheldon's body types, personality and sport

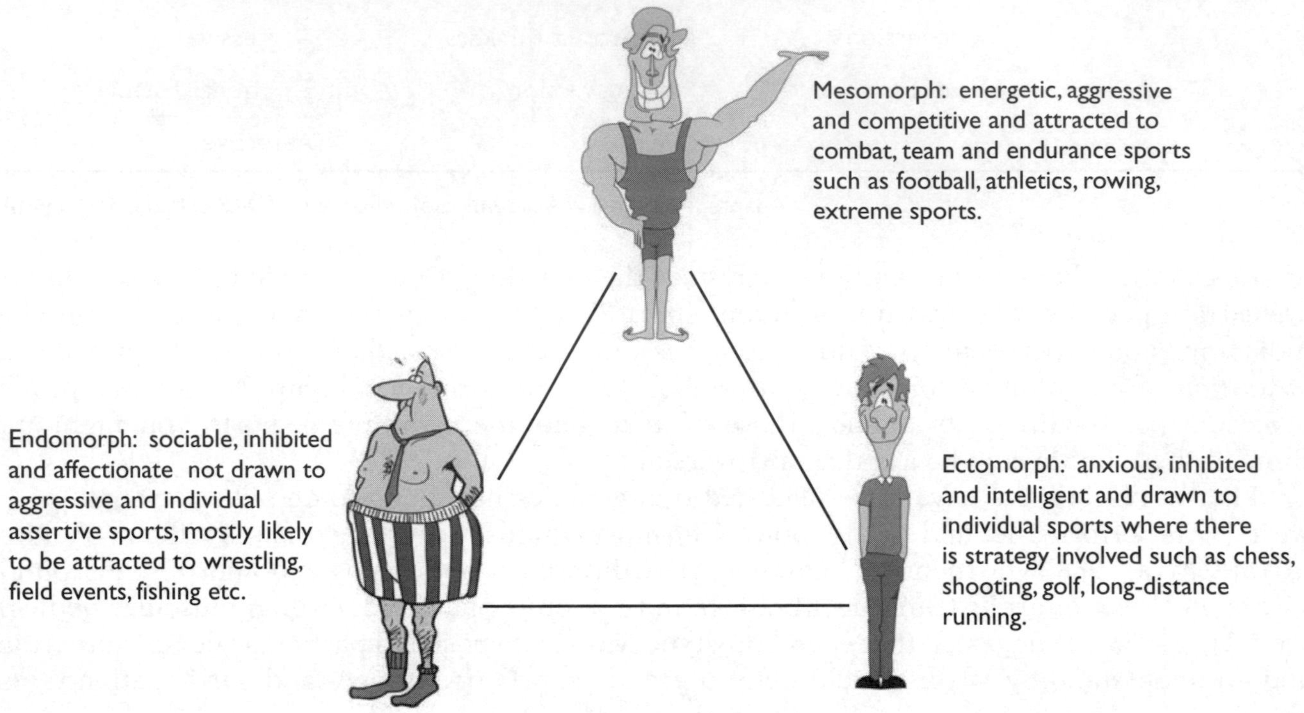
Mesomorph: energetic, aggressive and competitive and attracted to combat, team and endurance sports such as football, athletics, rowing, extreme sports.
Endomorph: sociable, inhibited and affectionate not drawn to aggressive and individual assertive sports, mostly likely to be attracted to wrestling, field events, fishing etc.
Ectomorph: anxious, inhibited and intelligent and drawn to individual sports where there is strategy involved such as chess, shooting, golf, long-distance running.

Adapted from http://www.innerexplorations.com/psytext/3.htm

Although there is evidence linking personality and body type to sports participation and choice of sports, one has to be careful to remember that such links are only suggestive in nature and not causal. That means we can't predict with any degree of certainty the links between sport and personality, or between body type, personality and sports choice. We can only provide indications of the likely groupings and relationships between these factors.

In addition to personality, we also have to understand a consumer's perceptual processes, or how they interpret information from the outside world. For example some people may perceive that rugby union is a high-contact, dangerous and aggressive sport. Others think it is about teamwork and inner strength and endurance and yet both groups of people are reflecting on the same sport. Marketers attempt to influence perception by creating images of brands, products and services in the minds of their target audiences. We therefore need to understand perception more fully to appreciate its impact on consumer decision-making.

## Perception

Perception is the process by which consumers select, organise and interpret information from the external environment through one or more of their sensory receptors (sight, taste, touch, smell, sound). In this case we are interested in understanding how sports consumers are likely to select, organise and interpret marketing-related information about sport and how their perceptual processes are likely to influence this process. Our image or perceptions about various sports are shaped by our interactions with friends, family, marketing information and other media exposure. Personal experiences also help to shape views. This process is shown in Figure 4.6.

The first stage of the perceptual process is exposure. If consumers are not exposed to marketing communications then they cannot begin to process the information. In addition this exposure can be both random and/or deliberate. Random exposure occurs when a customer sees or hears a marketing communication that gets their attention almost by accident or without any searching or planning on their behalf. For example, a person driving their car might hear an ad for tickets to a cricket game in the location they are travelling to and decide that they will attend. The exposure to this information was random.

In contrast deliberate exposure occurs when a customer seeks out marketing information to assist in their decision-making. Examples of this might be if a person reads the local paper for information on sporting events or times. Their exposure to the information is quite deliberate.

This means that sports marketers have to try to ensure that the intended audience will be exposed to their communications and the more times they are exposed to it, the higher the likelihood that they will pay attention to it. This is why sports marketers attempt to make use of all available media in their marketing efforts in an attempt to increase the likelihood of exposure. For example, for a particular sporting event there could be ads on television, billboards, newspapers, radio and an internet site all used in an attempt to gain maximum exposure.

**Figure 4.6:** Perception and information processing

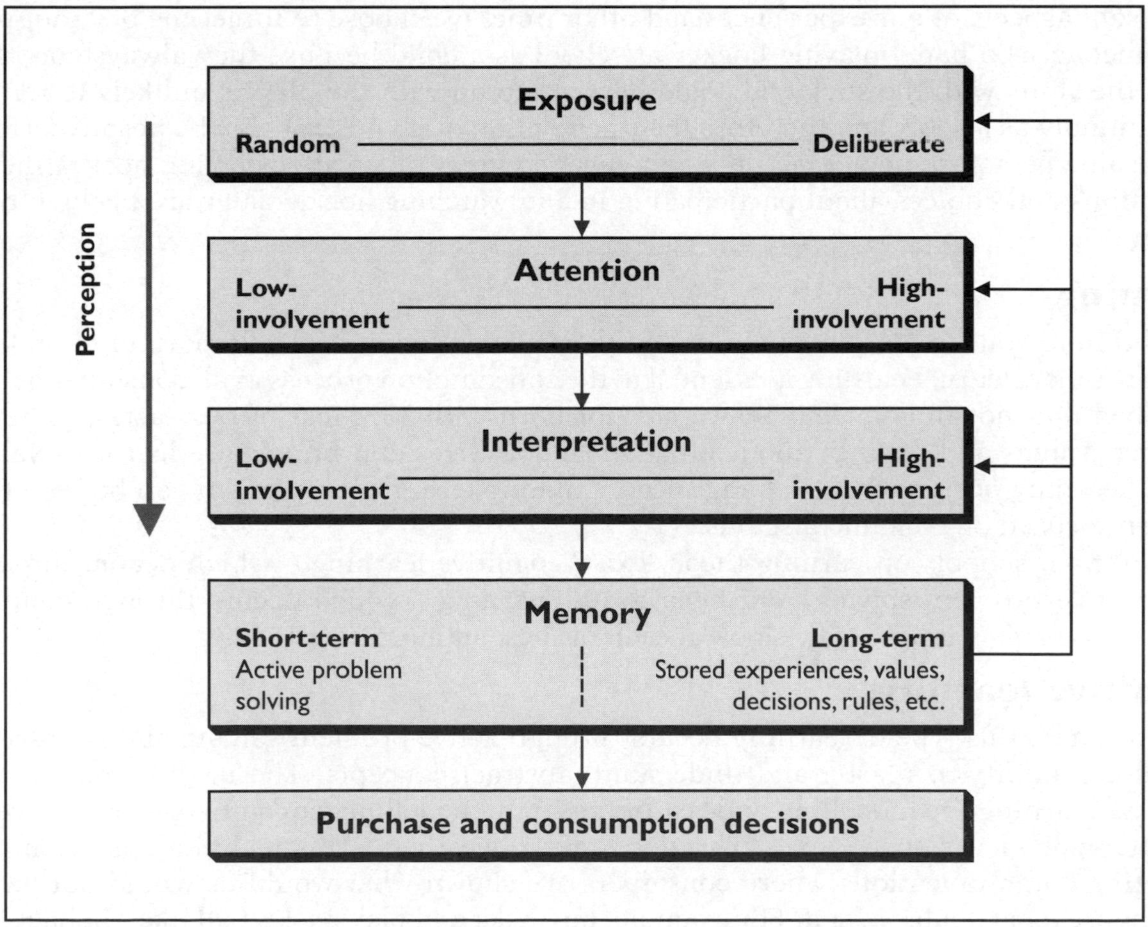


Source: Neal, Quester & Hawkins 2002, p.181

Once a consumer is exposed to the marketing stimuli they then have to determine whether to pay attention to it or not. Because consumers are exposed to many millions of advertising messages a day, they often choose not to pay attention to much of it. This screening out of stimulus is called selective attention. Consumers who are already in the need or problem recognition stage of the decision-making process are most likely to pay attention to information that will assist with their decision. For those consumers not actively seeking information, marketers attempt to get their attention by creating contrast in their communications.

This means they try to make their communications stand out in some way from all the rest so we are forced to pay attention even if not really interested. Have you noticed that ads on TV are generally louder than the program? This is to get our attention. Or sometimes ads use no sound at all – once again to get our attention. Other techniques used are the use of humour, intrigue and colour. Often ads for extreme sports like snowboarding make good use of the principle, showing beautiful scenery and spectacular sporting skill.

Once consumers have paid attention, marketers then attempt to get them to interpret the information correctly. That is, to take the same meaning from the information that the marketer intended. A recent series of ads from Nike specifically targeted women and attempted to depict the fact that Nike is about more than just running shoes and sweat. They were aiming to communicate to women that Nike can provide all the apparel (both sport and recreational) for all aspects of their life, and further that they understood that fitness is both a state of body and of mind. Visit the Nike site and see if your interpretation of their ads matches the intent of the marketing department of Nike (Nike 2003). Notice the difference in imagery and concepts between the men's and women's sites. What does this tell you about how Nike wants you to perceive them?

Finally, once a consumer has paid attention and interpreted marketing information, marketers then hope that they will retain this information for future reference and purchases. Retention, just like attention and interpretation, is also selective. Sometimes we choose not to remember unpleasant aspects of our experiences and other times we choose to forget the pleasant parts.

Someone who hated playing hockey at school as a child because they always got whacked across the shins with the stick and could never keep up with the play, is unlikely to remember hockey fondly as a sport and therefore their perception of it will probably be negative. However, if that same person remembered only the wins and great times after playing hockey then their perceptions and choices about participating in and watching hockey later are likely to be quite different.

## Learning

In addition to consumers' personalities and their perception, it is also important to understand how consumers learn. Learning is essential to the consumption process as all consumer behaviour is learned and not innate (that is: we are not born with it). Most of our tastes, preferences, attitudes, values and feelings about products and services and brands are learned (Neal et al. 2002). Learning occurs when a change occurs in long-term memory and it can be both focused and non-focused or even unconscious.

Two main schools of learning theory exist: cognitive learning – which occurs through the act of active problem solving; and behavioural learning – which occurs through conditioned response to some stimulus. Let's look at each of these in more detail.

### Cognitive learning

As mentioned, this type of learning occurs through active problem solving and is based on an individual's ability to reason and understand abstract concepts. The most common types of cognitive learning are modelling and reasoning. With modelling, consumers learn by observing the outcomes of various courses of actions taken by others. This technique is often used in marketing communications where consumers are shown what would or would not happen if they choose a particular brand. For example, buy Nike and play basketball like Michael Jordan, wear Speedo and swim like Ian Thorpe. In addition, in sport particularly we see this type of learning occurring when people have role models or heroes whom they try to emulate through dress, behaviour and even preferences for brands and products.

In the case of learning through reasoning, consumers engage in complex thinking and often abstract thought. Marketers using this technique generally make their case, giving consumers a range of scenarios or possible consequences of behaviour, and then allow consumers to draw their own conclusions about what behaviours to adopt.

For example, a consumer who has decided to lose weight may read an ad for a gym that offers a range of activities and facilities for all levels of fitness and health. They may conclude that this gym is a good option for them as it will provide long-term benefits through extension classes and activities as they lose weight and become fitter. The important thing for marketers using reasoning in the development of their strategies is that they have to be convinced that consumers will be motivated enough to use complex problem solving. In addition they also need to have a clear understanding of consumers' motivations and goals.

## Behavioural learning

Behavioural learning theories are based on conditioning and repetition. In the case of classical conditioning, consumers learn to associate a particular emotional or behavioural response to an unconditioned stimulus through constant repetition. For example, a person who has a strong desire for a close-knit family, may see ads designed to increase participation in soccer as positive images where happy, healthy families are shown playing soccer together. The positive responses felt by the consumer to images of families sharing and playing together may then be transferred to the concept of playing soccer, thus developing a desire to take up this sport for the family. This concept is often used by marketers where positive emotions or feelings for images, people, scenery or those evoked by music are paired with a product or idea in the attempt to get consumers to transfer those emotions to the product or service being advertised.

In contrast, operant conditioning uses repetition and reinforcement to encourage learning. This technique is often used by coaches to encourage better performances from their players. Reinforcement can be either positive (winning) or negative (losing) and sometimes even punishment is used to shape a desired behaviour (being dropped from the team). In a marketing sense consumers can be rewarded for a positive behaviour (purchasing the product or service) through things like incentives – when you buy this product you are eligible to enter the draw to win a car. Negative reinforcement can occur through the threat of missing out on a reward by not making a purchase – only those who send in three bar codes of XYZ product can purchase this special edition football jersey signed by all the players.

Learning techniques are also used by marketers to moderate and influence consumer attitudes. We therefore need to look at attitudes next.

## Attitudes

Attitudes are enduring and consistent combinations of emotional, behavioural and cognitive responses to a given object in the environment (Neal et al. 2002). Attitudes are learned and they are consistent, which means that while marketers have the ability to influence them, once formed they are hard to change. Attitudes ultimately guide all decision-making and like all evaluations they can range from positive to negative and can be either fiercely held or be very weak.

Generally, attitudes are comprised of three elements – emotions, behaviours and thoughts – and Figure 4.7 shows this. These three components interact to form our overall attitudes and all components have to be consistent. This means if we believe that playing netball is good for our fitness and teaches valuable teamwork skills, then we will feel positive about netball as a sport and we will support the idea of playing it or at least we will be interested enough to watch it when the opportunity allows.

The really interesting part about attitudes is that beliefs and emotions do not have to be factual. For example, you might believe that the most dangerous sport is mountain climbing or extreme skiing and therefore you do not like these sports and would not participate in them. However statistically, the most dangerous sport in the world is rock fishing with 11 to 24 people drowning each year (Royal Life Saving 2003). So reality and beliefs are often different. This then is the challenge for marketers who attempt to create positive attitudes about products or services where there has been misperception in the past.

Sports marketers need to understand consumer attitudes in order to either encourage or foster already positive attitudes, or to attempt to alter negative ones. Often marketers focus on attempting to change or impact the emotional aspect of attitudes as this is generally easiest to target, although for low-involvement decisions, getting trial behaviour can also be an effective way to create positive attitudes.

Figure 4.7: Model of attitudes

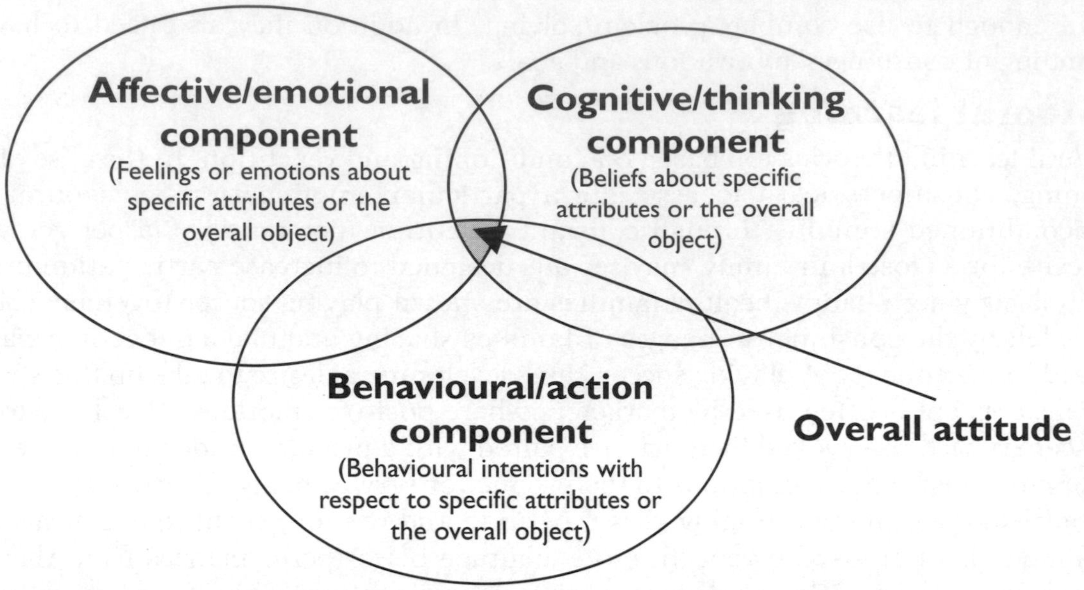


# Social or external factors

Now that we have provided an overview of the main internal factors that impact a consumer's decision-making process, we need to briefly examine the external or social factors that can affect the choice outcome. The factors we will consider are culture, reference groups, family and situational influences.

## Culture

Culture is a complex combination of language, demographics, values and traditions that are shared by groups of people and that are passed down through generations. Culture is dynamic, learned and enduring, which means that while it does change, it does so slowly and is not something we are born with. Cultural values impact our decision-making by contributing to norms, customs, rituals and values that we use to make consumption decisions. What we buy, where we buy it, how we use it and what we don't buy are all culturally embedded decisions.

Chapter 3 illustrated some of the ways that sport can play a role in socialisation and development of culture. In contrast in this chapter we will examine how a person's culture can impact their decision-making processes and why it is a concept that sports marketers need to consider. In relation to sport, participation in sport has been something that has been valued by nearly all cultures for many centuries (see Chapter 1). Sport also pervades all cultures and societies, and transcends religious and language barriers.

As Chapter 3 suggests, we learn our cultural values through a process known as socialisation, which occurs naturally through the influence of family members, experiences and friends. Sports marketers interested in targeting children and families particularly need to understand the impact of culture and socialisation on the choices made. Many of our core values as a society are also closely linked to sports participation. Values like success, independence, self-confidence, empathy and teamwork are all said to be developed through sports participation and these values are also reinforced in the school system where sports participation is encouraged and sometimes enforced.

It would seem obvious to state that cultural values will differ with different groups within society, independent of national boundaries. However many consider nationality to be synonymous with culture. In Australia, as with many countries, this is not the case. For example, we have large populations of Europeans, Asians and New Zealanders as well as our own Indigenous people living here, all bringing aspects of their various cultures to our everyday lives.

Thus it is very important to understand that culture is not homogeneous with nationality and that different cultural groups can easily be offended by insensitive remarks and behaviours. The 'Sport spotlight' highlights this problem. Here, the Real Madrid football team, intending to woo the Chinese fans, ended up with some serious issues when they insulted dignitaries all through a misunderstanding of differences in culture. It might be interesting to debate in class how, as a potential sports marketer, you might salvage any positive attitudes by the Chinese people towards this team!

## Sport spotlight

### How cultural differences can impact sport

Real Madrid, in an attempt to win fans in China, played a number of high-profile promotional games there in 2003. However it would appear that cultural differences were not something that they considered in their preparation with the result that their visit came dangerously close to a public relations disaster.

In the first three days of their visit the Spanish League champions managed to offend just about everyone involved in their sweep through Asia. They got off on the wrong foot when the players astounded Chinese officials by snubbing the ancient Chinese rite of passage for first-time guests, leaving a meticulously prepared banquet in their honour a mere 15 minutes after its start. 'It was chaos. They had a quick drink and left without eating,' said a Kunming official present at the dinner. 'Everyone was shocked. I was shocked,' he said. The team management later explained that the team was under a strict dietary regime and didn't realise that they were expected to attend the banquet as a matter of statesmanship and politeness.

Later in the visit, hundreds of fans anxiously awaiting the arrival of David Beckham, Luis Figo, Ronaldo, Zinedine Zidane and the rest of the superstar squad for their first official practice session on Saturday were left stranded when the team failed to show. Real blamed that debacle on a misunderstanding on the part of local organisers, saying they had never intended to practise that morning.

Then on Sunday, the nine-time champions of Europe decided to practise on a neighbouring field that offered no view to ticket-holding Chinese fans sitting in the stands of the original pitch. Real said the field was rain-soaked and chewed up through use, which proved little consolation for those who had braved pouring rain for an hour to see their heroes.

Confusion about scheduling and strict regulations including no access to Real's newest superstar David Beckham, meanwhile, had angered the Chinese media. 'All the Chinese media are dissatisfied because there is so little to write about,' said Henry Yu, a reporter from Beijing.

One Real Madrid official defended the club, saying: 'We haven't received any complaints so far.' He may not be aware that it is also part of Chinese custom to save face by not criticising guests' cultural gaffes or rude behaviour.

This visit was supposed to be a three-week promotional stint for Real Madrid and included visits to Beijing, Tokyo, Hong Kong and Bangkok. Marketing officials have said the club will pocket £8 million from the jaunt. However the local Asian press are so far less than impressed, with some describing the team as 'bloodsuckers' and 'mercenaries', accusing them of demanding three times more than other clubs in appearance fees.

Real said they were disappointed in the comments and defended their actions. 'We know what we are, we know what we are doing, we have nothing to hide,' said Stephan Attia, chief executive of Asia Sports Development, Real's Asia marketing group.

Source: iafrica.com 2003

## Reference groups

Reference groups are individuals who have the ability to impact a consumer's attitudes and buying behaviours and who, in some cases, can set norms of behaviour or codes of conduct. Some reference groups are aspirational, which means that consumers aspire to be a member of them even if they don't have any direct contact with them. Elite tennis players such as Alicia Molik and Lleyton Hewitt would provide an aspirational reference group for young tennis players and elite swimmers like Ian Thorpe and Jodie Henry may be the same for young swimmers.

Other reference groups can provide more of an informative role and thus are used to provide information that helps consumers make decisions. People in these groups are those from whom we would seek word-of-mouth information and they are seen as experts in some way. Still other reference groups can have a value-expressive influence on behaviour. This means people express who they are by being a member of this group. Some of the gangs and groups you might have belonged to in high school might be like this – your identity is partly formed due to your membership of these groups. Finally, some reference groups have a normative influence over behaviour. This means that they have the ability to set rules and regulations that need to be followed in order to maintain membership. Many sporting clubs have this type of influence on their members.

## Family

The most important reference group for any consumer is their family. Families also make buying decisions together, which differ from the sorts of decisions that individuals might make. In sports marketing, families are a very important group particularly for those sports targeting children. If the parents are not prepared to spend the time, money and effort in getting children to and from training and games then the children won't participate in that sport. Similarly, parents are often targeted for sporting apparel and sports spectating marketing as they will be the ones with money to spend and hopefully an interest in watching their child. For example, parents of Pony Club members would be a good potential market for tickets to equestrian events as their children will be interested in learning more about their sport and seeing their heroes perform.

The changes in family structures from the traditional mum, dad and two children model to one with single parents, multiple parents and step-parents and even multiple step-siblings is also impacting the sports marketing arena. In some cases, split families mean more money spent on children and more money spent on sport/leisure activities such as attending sporting events, while in other cases this change in family structure can result in less money and time for extra-curricular activities as a family. Sports marketers can take advantage of the opportunities (and note any potential threats) presented by these changes. They also need to consider them in their advertising and promotional material by not ignoring these different family groupings in photos and other imagery used to promote their sport.

## Situational influences

All consumption decisions occur in the framework of various situational influences that impact how we behave. When faced with crowded stadia and noisy shops we may feel anxious and stressed and be less likely to spend money or take time with our purchases. If we are happy and enjoying the company of others, we are much more likely to spend more money than if we are alone, and finally we make decisions differently if we are buying things for our own use as opposed to gifts for others. In marketing terms we consider five different types of situational influence: these are physical surroundings, social surroundings, temporal perspectives, task definition, and antecedent states. We will now briefly discuss each.

### Physical surroundings

Physical surroundings refer to the geographical location, décor, sounds, aromas, lighting, weather and visible configurations of the purchase setting. In sports spectating this would refer to the stadium location and layout, in the case of sports participation it would refer to the location of the club or playing fields and in relation to sports products it would refer to the layout and atmospherics of the store. Sports marketers have the ability to significantly influence the physical surroundings and they need to ensure that they consider things like consumer comfort, safety and general wellbeing in their decisions relating to this factor.

## Social surroundings

Social surroundings relate to the presence of others and their ability to influence the consumption experience. Because sport is usually consumed in a social setting, this influence is an important one for sports marketers. Unfortunately sports marketers can do little to impact this particular factor as the behaviour and interactions of others is largely outside their control.

## Temporal perspectives

The temporal perspective relates to time issues such as time of the day, or year, seasonality and even the time constraints perceived by the consumer themselves. Temporal perspectives have the ability to impact how sports consumers make decisions in a number of different ways. Seasonality is an obvious influence in sport, with a number of sports only being played at certain times of the year. Many sports marketers have attempted to address this by extending playing seasons, incorporating northern hemisphere competitions and by modifying the game being played to allow for seasonal variation.

This is something that the Australian Cricket Board have done very successfully. Cricket is generally a summer game and this limits the playing season in the southern hemisphere to September to March. By playing test matches with teams in the northern hemisphere, they can extend the playing season through their summer (our winter) and increase the potential revenues for the game. During 2003, Australian cricket has also hosted test matches in Australia's northern states (NT and north Queensland) during our winter months in an attempt to further generate interest and loyalty for the game and to also increase revenue opportunities. The only negative aspect to all this is from the player's perspective, where they now only have two to four weeks a year not travelling and playing cricket.

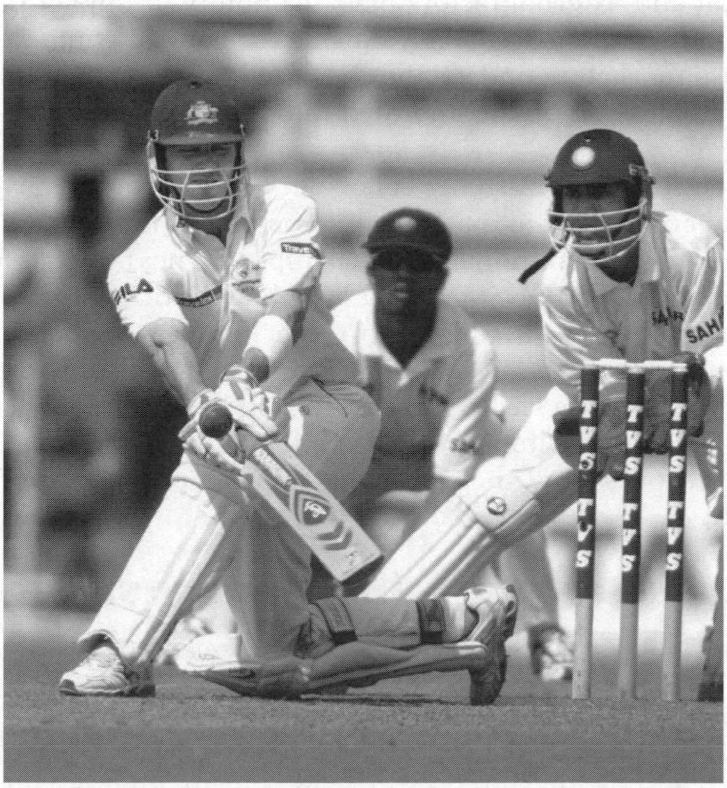

Test cricket is played year-round, increasing potential revenue

### Task definition

Task definition relates to the intended use or reason for purchase. Purchases made for others, such as gifts, often have very different meaning and intent than those made for one's self. Similarly the reasons why a person might choose to play a particular sport will be influenced by their intended outcomes or results of the involvement.

For example a person who joins a touch football team to meet others of their own age and to get fit, will base their selection of team and club on these motivations. That is, they will choose the club that is most likely to offer these outcomes. Another person who wishes to play touch competitively and win and possibly be selected for a state or national team, may make quite different team and club selections as the reasons for their involvement (or product use) differ.

### Antecedent states

The final situational influence is antecedent states. This refers to temporary mood states or temporary conditions as opposed to long-term factors. For example, a person who wins $300 on a Scratch-it might suddenly feel that they are able to afford tickets to the Rugby World Cup, whilst in contrast someone who suddenly receives a number of large bills in a month might curtail any spending on sport for that month. A person who is very busy at work may not play sport during this period and so on.

Similarly, research has shown that when people are happy and in a positive mood, they tend to spend more money than when they are anxious or sad. Marketers often attempt to influence a consumer's mood in their marketing communications by using humour or other positive feelings so that consumers have a higher likelihood of transferring these positive mood states to the product (using classical conditioning principles as discussed in the section on behaviour learning). In the same light, sports marketers can influence the potential mood states of consumers at live sporting events, through management of the physical surroundings – including things like cheer squads, music and other atmospherics – in an attempt to create a comfortable, pleasant environment.

All of these internal and external factors have the ability to impact the consumer decision-making process and many of them are largely outside the control of marketers. In spite of this it is important that sports marketers understand the potential effects and understand their target consumers so that strategies can be incorporated into marketing activities to account for likely impacts.

It is important when studying consumer behaviour to understand that all consumer decision-making is an individual process. Even though many consumers may make the same final decision (to buy tickets to the opening ceremony of the Olympic Games), their motivations for making that decision can differ significantly. Some may have bought tickets to impress others, some to be patriotic, some for the benefit of children or other family members, some because they've always wanted to do so and so on. So even though large groups of consumers can make the same purchase decision (to buy tickets) we need to take a step back and look at their motivations for purchase as these motivations will impact on how they have made their decision, the information they used to assist the process and their ultimate satisfaction with the decision outcome. We look at motivation next.

## The role of motivation in the consumer decision-making process

Motivation is the driving force that compels us to take action to satisfy particular needs. Individuals are driven by different motives and to satisfy different needs at different times. Motivation is essentially an internal state that arouses, directs and maintains behaviour. Marketers are particularly interested in three questions in relation to motivation. What causes a person to initiate a behaviour or action? What is the level of involvement in the chosen activity? What causes a person to abandon or give up a chosen behaviour? As a sports marketer, an understanding of motivation can not only help us interpret why our customers make the decisions that they do, but it can also help us to predict why people participate in particular sports and activities and why they choose not to participate.

Motivation can be internally triggered, with the rewards of a particular action also being internal to the person, such as happiness, self-satisfaction or success. This is known as intrinsic motivation. Or motivation can be externally triggered, with the rewards being external to the person, such as money, fame or career development. This is known as extrinsic motivation. Whichever is the primary driver, motivation is always goal-directed, which means there is always something (a need) that consumers are striving to accomplish or to satisfy.

In the 1960s Abraham Maslow proposed a hierarchy of needs as a method of classifying human needs and motivations into an order of importance as a way of assisting researchers to understand motivation. He proposed that humans are driven or motivated to satisfy these various needs in an hierarchal fashion with the lower order needs taking preference and higher order needs only being sought when the lower order needs were satisfied. He generally represented this approach in the form of a pyramid (see Figure 4.8).

**Figure 4.8:** Maslow's hierarchy needs

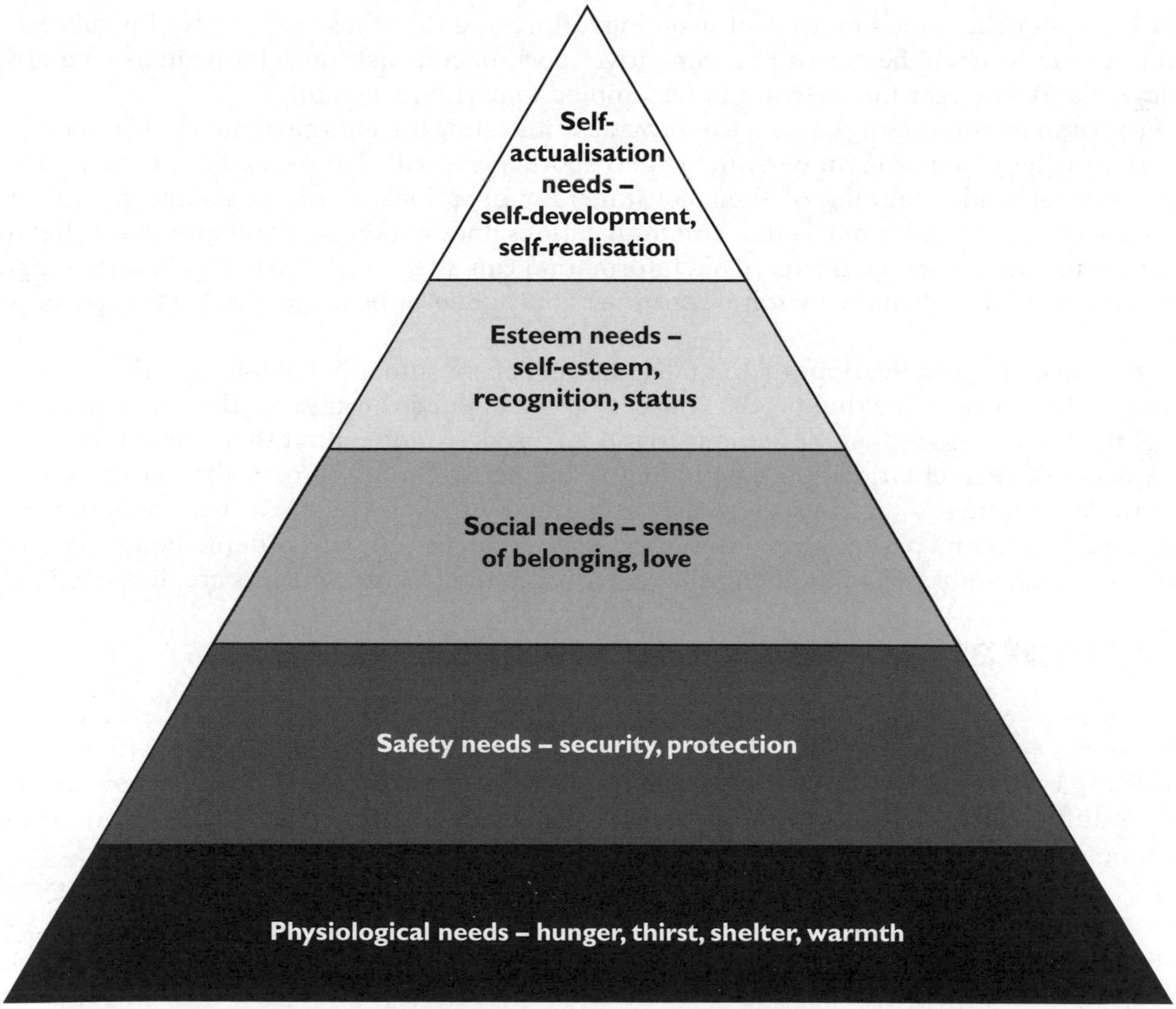


Adapted from Maslow 1968

In the case of sports marketing, this concept can be used to consider why someone might participate in sport – need for belonging (social needs), need for recognition (esteem needs) or maybe need for self-development (self-actualisation needs). All of these needs of course are higher order needs – that is they are above the basic needs that are physiological and safety needs.

This implies that participation in sport is not a basic motivation, rather it is something we might learn to enjoy and learn to develop both intrinsic and extrinsic motivations for once our basic or lower order survival needs have been taken care of. Societies where people are starving and without safety and shelter are generally not interested in playing sport, staying fit or striving to better themselves. In addition, when we consider professional athletes, some may be motivated by the desire for money or fame, which are often in turn being driven by a desire to never have to worry about the lower order basic needs of safety, belonging and physiological needs that may have been major drivers in their lives as children. A recent study into the success of baseball in Latin American countries has found that the main reason the sport is so popular is that it provides many underprivileged people with a chance to change their lives. They are driven by a special hunger because they don't want to go back to a standard of living they tried so hard to leave (*Hispanic Magazine* 1999).

Why people participate in sport and exercise and the rewards that are derived from this have long been the interest of sport and exercise psychologists and now sports marketers. Most conclude that motivation for participation in sport is a complex area and is really part of a dynamic cognitive-behavioural process (Scully & Lowry 2002). The classic works by McClelland (1961) and Atkinson (1957) suggest that to be motivated to achieve, one's motive for success must be higher than one's motive for avoiding failure and that those who strive for success and do not fear failure will be drawn to competitive sport. In contrast those individuals who are low achievers and who fear failure will not be tempted to participate at all.

From a sports marketing context this provides interesting insights particularly when combined with the earlier discussion on personality and sports personality in particular. If marketers can gain a deeper understanding of their consumers' motivations, fears, goals and personalities, they may be able to tailor marketing communications and marketing strategies more effectively to appeal to various target groups. This information can also assist marketers in analysing why some efforts might fail and why some consumers may not ever be in the market for sports goods and services.

The marketing implications of an understanding of consumer behaviour and the factors that influence the decision-making process have been highlighted throughout this chapter. However one of the main reasons that marketers attempt to discover more about their consumers is to aid the process of segmentation and positioning. It is impossible to segment the market without a clear understanding of the characteristics of that market, characteristics that are both physical (age, gender etc.) and psychological (motivations, personality etc.). In order to better clarify how consumer behaviour aids in segmentation and positioning, these concepts are discussed next.

# Segmentation and positioning

Strategic marketing processes all begin with an examination of the potential markets for products and services and decisions about whether and how to segment them (see Chapter 2 for a refresher on this topic). In addition, it is important to position the brand or product so that consumers are able to differentiate its features from those of its competitors. Positioning, therefore, is about creating an image that marketers can use in communicating with potential consumers.

For some goods and services, market aggregation is a feasible option. This means to consider the entire marketplace as a homogeneous unit. Generally, however, this option usually only applies to simple goods that are commodities or where there are few variations or options, and not to more complex goods or to service-type products where there can be many variations. In the case of sports marketing, therefore, market aggregation is unlikely to be a feasible option. Most sports marketers adopt a market segmentation approach, which means that they consider that their potential markets have groups of consumers with different needs, motives and possibly even different physical characteristics that require some modification of the marketing offering (including the product) to encourage them to buy.

Market segmentation is the dividing up of a potential market into smaller homogeneous subgroups that are viable in terms of their size, potential revenue generation and accessibility.

Market segmentation is a process that works very closely with an understanding of consumer behaviour, as both consider differences in consumers. The first step in segmentation is to consider how many different consumers exist in the potential market, and whether these consumers have anything in common that would allow them to be grouped to facilitate marketing strategies. Once grouped, marketers then need to consider whether these groups are:

- able to be described through one or more common factors
- large enough to be viable
- able to be accessed through marketing efforts.

Segmentation possibilities are almost endless, however a number of traditional variables or bases are generally used for segmentation and these can be grouped into three classifications. These are: demographic or physical characteristics, psychological characteristics and behavioural characteristics. Table 4.2 illustrates these segmentation bases with some examples. Let's review each.

**Table 4.2:** Market segmentation variables

| Demographic variables | Psychographic variables | Behavioural variables |
|---|---|---|
| Age | Personality | Benefits sought |
| Gender | Lifestyle | Usage situation |
| Occupation | Values | Usage rate (light versus heavy users) |
| Income | Motivations | Loyalty |
| Education level | Attitudes | Place of purchase (Internet versus store) |
| Marital status | | |
| Ethnicity | | |
| Religion | | |
| Geographic location | | |

## Demographic or physical characteristics

Physical characteristics of markets refer to the physical things that describe or differentiate consumers. Demographic characteristics are the main basis used in this form of segmentation; the other is geographic or physical location. Demographics relate to a consumer's age, gender, marital status, occupation, level of education, stage in the family lifecycle, religion, ethnicity and income. All of these segmentation bases are tangible and easily measurable. The main problem with relying on this type of segmentation alone is that it doesn't provide any more detailed information about *why* people buy, it only tells us *who* they are. For some products – like sport – many different types of people buy the same product so demographics alone is often not a good way to group potential consumers. Most sports marketers would use physical characteristics in conjunction with either psychographic factors and/or behavioural factors to describe and group their potential consumers.

## Psychographic characteristics

Most of the possible psychographic characteristics that marketers can use to segment markets have been discussed in an earlier section of this chapter. These would include things like personality, lifestyle, attitudes, motivations and values. All of these are internal to the consumer and are therefore quite difficult to measure and to identify. These variables often provide a better understanding of a consumer's buying behaviour and are therefore more powerful segmentation variables than just physical characteristics. They help us to understand *why* a group of consumers behaves the way they do.

## Behavioural characteristics

Behavioural characteristics include all the elements that would allow us to group consumers based on *how* they buy our products. Bases used in this form of segmentation would include reason for use, usage rate, place of purchase and usage situation. Situational influences were discussed in an earlier section and these can make for very helpful segmentation bases. Behavioural variables alone, like physical variables, are generally not sufficient to give us a clear picture of the groups of consumers we are targeting, therefore these types of segmentation bases are generally used in conjunction with others.

When the sports industry generally is considered, some researchers have suggested models that help us to identify the main types of groups in the market that sports marketers might serve (see Figure 4.9). This model is one example of the way a sports marketer might consider the industry in terms of segmentation potential and how various aspects of the industry might relate to each other.

**Figure 4.9:** The sports industry segment model

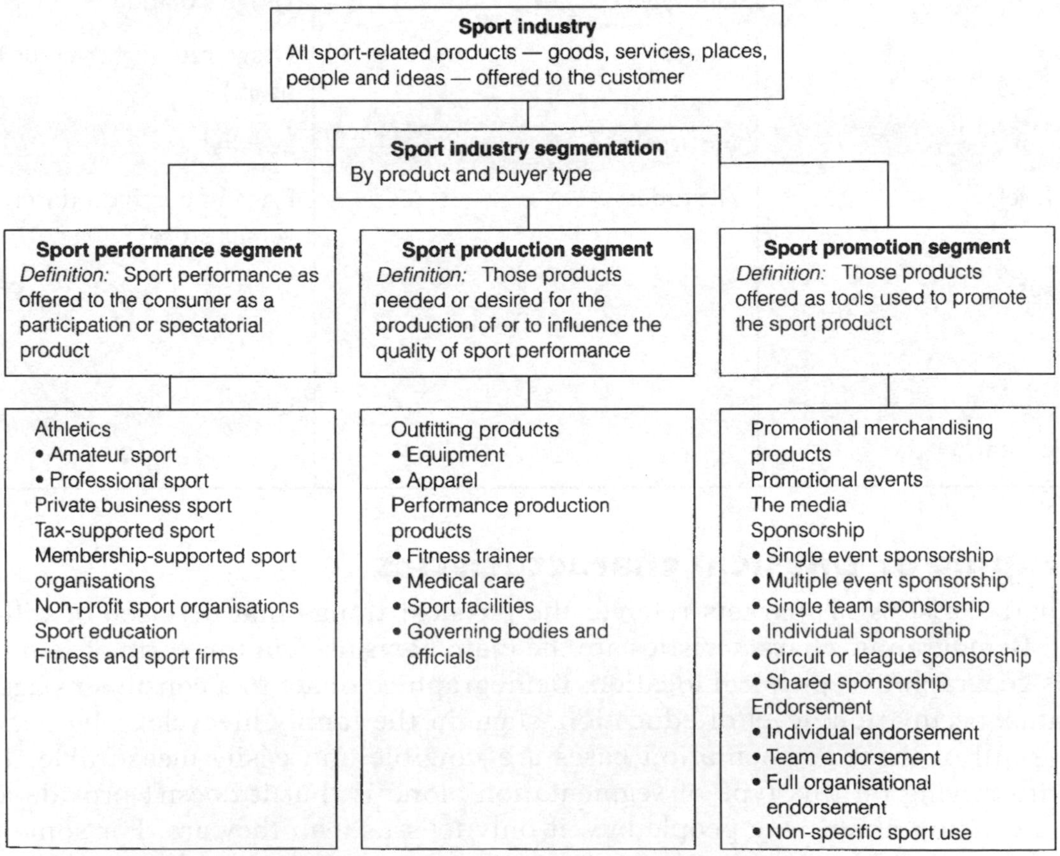


Source: Pitts et al. 1994, pp.15–24

However, new markets are always emerging and sports marketers need to be aware of the potentials offered by these new segments and to be creative in how they approach and consider them. The emergence of the extreme sports market is one such example of a new segment that has distinctly different values, buying habits and preferences from many other youth markets in the sports industry. Additionally, the use of the internet to communicate with customers and to sell sports products has developed an additional behavioural segment with different information style needs and different lifestyles and values to those consumers not using this medium.

Once a sports marketer has segmented their potential market they then need to consider the various positioning strategies that will logically flow from this process. Positioning refers to creating an image of the product in the mind of the consumer relative to the major competitors. For example, snowboarding is positioned as a sport for young people, while skiing is seen as a sport for older, wealthier people.

The Hillary Commission in New Zealand have developed a program called Kiwi Sport (SPARC 2003), which is modified sport designed to appeal specifically to children and to get them to participate and become more active. The New Zealand Government recognised that children's perceptions of many sports were that sport was too hard and not fun. The government has now created this new product positioned as fun, exciting and relevant to children in order to increase the level of participation. The Australian Government has done a similar thing with the Aussie Sports program introduced in the 1980s.

Marketers often use the technique of mapping to assist them in determining how consumers perceive their products relative to others. This technique involves identifying the main criteria on which consumers evaluate or compare products in a particular category and then mapping these in a three-dimensional form so that it is easy to see relative strengths and weaknesses as well as comparative positions. A possible product positioning map for sports shoes is shown in Figure 4.10. The main criteria used in this map for discriminating between brands was price and design (how well they are made for the task). Four main brands have been placed on the map following questions about how people purchase and view sports shoes.

**Figure 4.10:** Product positioning map for sports shoes

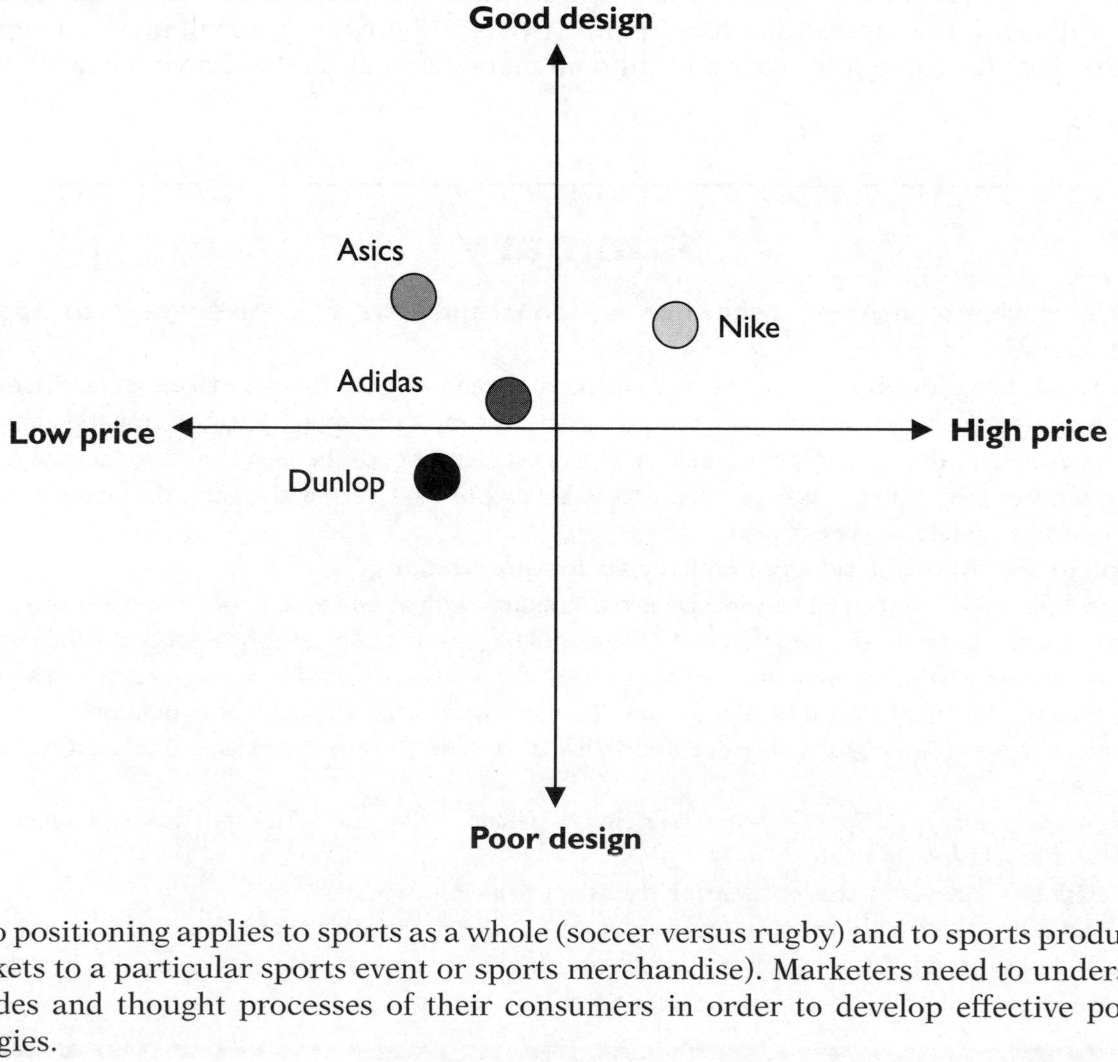


So positioning applies to sports as a whole (soccer versus rugby) and to sports products (such as tickets to a particular sports event or sports merchandise). Marketers need to understand the attitudes and thought processes of their consumers in order to develop effective positioning strategies.

## Counterpoint

The purpose of analysing consumers and their behaviours in most marketing disciplines is to predict consumers' responses, anticipate their needs and satisfy their every desire. A great deal of consumer market research is dedicated to giving consumers precisely what they ask for and taking the 'guess work' out of marketing. Marketing information systems by their very nature are to aid prediction, predictability and proactivity.

However, sports consumers and sports marketing might very well be the exception to this marketing rule. Sports consumers can certainly be researched; segmented, targeted and profiled but the essence of what they want just might be a mystery! This is because what they want is UNPREDICTABILITY. They want competition! It might be true that we can profile a tennis fan and determine that he or she is a dedicated Lleyton Hewitt fan. At the Wimbledon Finals, our consumer, predictably, wants Lleyton to win. However when Lleyton wins in straight sets and the game is over quickly and quietly ... our fan is disappointed. The Hewitt fan should have been satisfied but the means to the end were a letdown.

A recent article in an Indian newspaper lamenting the boring predictability of test cricket is one such example. The writer noted that 'Watching Carl Hooper treat the Indian bowling with the sort of contempt that a Roman Emperor might have reserved for his inefficient valet on a bad day at the office' was not unpredictable at all and that the ultimate result was also well known by all even before the team entered the pitch. The author of this particular article went on to lament the loss of unpredictability in sport with professional sports people and the subsequent loss of the soul of sport. Tiger Woods is generally expected to win any golfing event he enters, Michael Schumacher is expected to win racing events, the Australian cricket team is expected to win when they play and so on around the world (Shekar 2002, p.1).

So how do sports marketers juggle the desire by their audiences to provide predictable and popular results with the same desire for stunning twists and turns that result in an unsung hero winning the day? It's enough to scare a traditional marketer back to the drawing board!

## Summary

- **explain what consumer behaviour is about and why it is important to sports marketers**
  Consumer behaviour is the study of how, when, where and why consumers make the purchase and consumption decisions that they do. It is important to sports marketers because an understanding of the processes that a sports consumer or sports participant goes through in determining whether to attend or play sport and then what sports to support are essential to the development of a successful strategic marketing plan.
- **explain the different types of consumer decision-making**
  Consumer behaviour can be considered as a continuum, with at one end low-involvement or simple decisions, for example, the decision to attend a sporting event at a local sports ground. While at the other end are high-involvement or more complex decisions, such as the decision to buy tickets to the final of the Rugby World Cup in Sydney complete with airfares and accommodation.
- **discuss the various types of perceived risk and how they impact the decision-making process**
  There are five types of perceived risk. These are: financial risk, social risk, physical risk, functional risk and psychological risk.
- **discuss the stages in the consumer decision-making process**
  Generally the consumer decision-making process can be summarised into five phases or steps as shown in Figure 4.1. These stages are: problem or need recognition, information search, evaluation of alternatives, purchase decision and post-purchase processes.

- **identify and discuss the psychological and social factors that impact upon the consumer decision-making process**
  A consumer's internal make-up has a significant impact on how they view the world and interpret information presented to them, and these psychological factors are unique to each individual consumer. Psychological factors or internal factors are things like motivation, personality, perception, learning and attitudes.
  Social factors by contrast, are factors that are external to the individual and include culture, the impact of reference groups, family and situational influences.
- **discuss the importance of motivation to understanding sports consumers**
  Motivation is the driving force that compels us to take action to satisfy particular needs; it is an internal state that arouses, directs and maintains behaviour. Individuals are driven by different motives and to satisfy different needs at different times. Sports marketers need to have an understanding of the motivations of their customers as these motivations are used to direct decision-making, information search patterns and preferences and choice criteria of consumers.
- **discuss how marketers segment markets and the relevance of positioning**
  Strategic marketing processes all begin with an examination of the potential markets for products and services and decisions about whether to and how to segment them. In addition, it is important to position the brand or product so that consumers are able to differentiate its features from those of its competitors. Positioning therefore is about creating an image that marketers can use in communicating with potential consumers.

## Review questions

1. What are the stages of the consumer decision-making process?
2. What are the characteristics of a high-involvement or complex decision?
3. Discuss the difference between risk averse and risk tolerant consumers.
4. How do situational influences impact the consumer decision-making process?
5. What are the three components of attitudes?
6. What are the three main bases used for segmentation?
7. What is meant by positioning?

## Applied activities

1. In small groups consider the decision-making process a person considering taking up a sport in order to keep fit might adopt. Comment on what would happen at each stage of the process and on any factors that are likely to affect the final decision. Each group should agree on a different sport and then compare responses.
2. How has the internet impacted on the decision-making process for someone considering purchasing tickets for a live sporting event? Choose a particular event in order to comment.
3. Review Figure 4.4 – sports personalities. Choose three different sports representing different traits from this figure and interview 10 people about

their perceptions of the personality traits of these sports. Comment on any discrepancies in your findings, using other consumer behaviour theory to assist your response.

4. In small groups, visit the Australian Football League website (www.afl.com.au) and comment on the different markets you believe they are targeting and what segmentation bases they are using. In addition, comment on what criteria the AFL have been positioning themselves and whether or not you believe this to be appropriate.
5. Internet exercise: Have a look at the Rugby World Cup site (www.rwc2003.com.au) and comment on how it has provided information that will assist potential ticket buyers in their purchase decision. Is there information that they could have provided that is missing? Do you think the site encourages and inspires you to want to purchase tickets? What changes would you recommend? Compare this now with the polocrosse World Cup site (www.polocrosse.com.au) and comment on the differences. Why do you think this might be the case?

# References

Arraj, T. & Arraj, J. 1988, *Tracking the Elusive Human, Vol 1: A Practical Guide to C.G. Jung's Psychological Types, W.H. Sheldon's Body and Temperament Types and their Integration*, Inner Growth Books, Chiloquin, Oregon.

Assael, H. 2004, *Consumer Behaviour: A Strategic Approach*, Houghton Mifflin, Boston.

Atkinson, J.W. 1957, 'Motivational Determinants of Risk Taking Behaviour', *Psychological Review*, Vol. 64, pp.359–72.

Hispanic Magazine 1999, www.hispanicmagazine.com/1999/apr/Cultura/

Maslow, A.H. 1968, *Toward a Psychology of Being*, D. Van Nostrand Company,

McClelland, D.C. 1961, *The Achieving Society*, Free Press, New York.

Neal, C., Quester, P. & Hawkins, D. 2002, *Consumer Behaviour*, 3rd edn, McGraw-Hill Irwin, Sydney.

Nike 2003, www.nike.com.au, viewed 30 March 2004.

Pitts, B., Fielding, L. & Miller, L. 1994, 'Industry Segmentation and the Sport Industry: Developing a Sport Industry Segment Model', *Sport Marketing Quarterly*, 3, (1), pp.15–24.

Royal Life Saving 2003, www.royallifesaving.com.au/_uploads/media/2_116.pdf.

Scully, D. & Lowry, R. 2002, 'Why We Do – And Why We Don't', *The Psychologist*, www.bps.org.uk/publications/thepsychologistdet.cfm?ID=444.

Shekar, N. 2002, 'Oh How Boring (?) and Predictable', *The Hindu*, Wednesday 17 April 2002, http://www.hinduonnet.com/2002/04/17/stories/2002041701332200.htm, viewed 28 August 2003.

SPARC 2003, www.sparc.org.nz, viewed 30 March 2004.

Summers, J., Gardiner, M., Lamb, C., Hair, J. & McDaniel, C. 2003, *Essentials of Marketing*, Thomson Learning, Melbourne.

Sweeney Sports Report 2002/2003, Sweeney Sports Pty Ltd, Victoria.

Texas Stampede 2004, www.texasstampede.org/rodeo/, viewed 14 March 2004.

Viseu, J. 2001, 'Sport Consumption Through Media', Minho University Working Paper Series, Issue no. 5.

Wilson, T. 2002, 'The Paradox of Social Class and Sports Involvement: The Roles of Cultural and Economic Capital', *International Review for the Sociology of Sport*, Vol. 37, Issue 1, pp.5–16.

www.Academic.uofs.edu/faculty/OAKESM2/spperson.html, viewed 28 March 2004.

www.age-of-the-sage.org/psychology/sheldon.html#William_Sheldon 2003, viewed 28 March 2004.

www.iafrica.com/pls/cms/iac.page?p_t1=4&p_t2=6&p_t3=0&p_t4=0&p_dynamic=YP&p_content_id=257549&p_site_id=2, viewed 28 March 2004.

www.innerexplorations.com/psytext/3.htm.

www.sasked.gov.sk.ca/docs/physed/ physed2030/ypysport.pdf, viewed 20 August 2003.

# Appendix to Chapter 4

## How does Macquarie Bank use its involvement with sport to influence the consumer decision-making process?

Giulia Santamaria, Marketing Executive – Foreign Exchange for Macquarie Bank, works with the sports marketing arm at Macquarie Bank and specifically manages their Sports Camp Program and support of charitable organisations, including management of major fundraising initiatives for the Australian Schoolboys Rugby Union and the Layne Beachley Aim for the Stars Foundation.

Macquarie Bank use sport as a way of linking with the community, entertaining clients and building a positive brand image. They believe that sport is a powerful vehicle to build relationships with key clients and stakeholder groups. Sport is the preferred method for building and strengthening relationships in business because the appeal of sports crosses socio-economic and cultural barriers, providing a backdrop for developing personal connections.

Their specific involvement in sports marketing includes the following:

- Association with individual athletes, e.g. Matthew Hayden (cricket), who are then used exclusively for advertising and promotional activity, as guest speakers at client functions and for sporting clinics with the children of staff and clients.
- Sponsorship of professional sporting teams, e.g. ACT Brumbies, who are used in a manner similar to the individual athlete association to extend both the external and internal marketing activity of the firm.
- Sponsorship and support of community events and sporting organisations, e.g. Balmoral Burn (community fun-run) and Gosford Netball Association, as community involvement initiatives and for social responsibility.
- Purchase of corporate hospitality at elite sports events, e.g. corporate suite at the Super 12 matches, for use as staff incentives (internal marketing) and for sales and client incentives and product and promotional rewards.

Macquarie Bank evaluate their sports involvement through the use of an audit that examines the cost-effectiveness of the activity compared to the amount it would cost to receive the same level of brand exposure through other marketing activities such as advertising, or editorial publicity. They also consider sales increases or value to the business of any new relationships and cost this in addition to brand exposure. Finally, Macquarie also look at the impact of their association with sport on staff morale and on customer relationships by evaluating formal feedback (letters, emails, faxes) and informal feedback through discussions and comments.

The decision to support a sporting organisation (professional or community-based) or elite athletes is based on the appeal the sport or individual will have to the company's target markets – either internal or external. It is important to the bank that internal stakeholders, including the staff, be able to take ownership of the sponsorship property or sports involvement and feel some connection and degree of emotional attachment to the activity. For example, Macquarie Bank have a high level of involvement with rugby union at a community and professional level and there is a high level of acceptance among staff of this association. Non-mainstream sports with a low level of appeal to staff would not be as readily embraced by the company.

Clients are another important target audience, and any sports supported must have a high level of appeal to this group. Individuals and sports supported must also reinforce Macquarie's brand values, and therefore the values of the sporting organisation and those of any individual and of the bank must be consistent.

Macquarie Bank use their involvement with sport to influence key clients; through support of community sporting organisations a key client may be involved with, their relationship with the bank can be significantly strengthened. They specifically target the problem recognition and information search phases and they attempt to develop loyalty and preference for Macquarie brands so that at the evaluation stage key benefits of its products are uppermost in the minds of these customers.

The target audience can vary from one key individual to a group of clients or to a broader audience – for example, funds managers. Determining the appeal of a sport to each target audience so that a relationship can be forged through sport is really the key marketing task. The emotive nature of sport provides a perfect vehicle to build links beyond the business context and to create an emotional tie or link with the bank.

Macquarie Bank will determine the success of the sports investment by measuring against key performance indicators. For example, they may be aiming to increase by 20% the awareness of the brand in regional communities in NSW. By research into brand recognition before and after the activity the success of the sponsorship can be measured.

It is important to recognise that many of the intangible benefits of sports investment are difficult to quantify. Hence the value of introducing elite sports people to key clients is hard to measure, however informal feedback and improved relations may follow these activities.

Source: Giulia Santamaria, Foreign Exchange Marketing, Macquarie Bank, 2003 personal communication

# Chapter 5

# Sports marketing research

**Learning objectives**

After reading the chapter you should be able to:

- explain the importance of marketing research in sports marketing
- define and explain secondary versus primary data
- outline the steps in the basic marketing research process
- understand the different types of sports marketing research designs
- describe the process for questionnaire development.

## Scene setter

### Sport problems = sport questions = sport data

The National Rugby League (NRL) in Australia has had more than its fair share of problems in the last decade. From the divisive Super League fiasco to sex scandals and player violence, NRL clubs and officials have had their marketing skills strongly tested. In addition to these image problems, NRL has also suffered because of a commercial perception that rugby union is more popular, and therefore a better sponsorship vehicle, than rugby league. While many companies see rugby union as the number one sport in Australia it is actually not true in terms of either participation or spectating. However, the statistical reality of this popularity contest is irrelevant if the perception exists in the commercial world.

Despite these perceptual problems, rugby league has enjoyed increased TV ratings, match attendance figures and merchandise sales since 1998. About 3 million people attended the NRL's 191 premiership and final matches in 2003, compared with the 2.9 million who attended 250 matches in 1998. The Nine Network's weekly TV audience for rugby league in 2003 was 2 million, up from 1.85 million in 1998. The pay TV operator Fox Sports' NRL coverage has 900 000 viewers a week. Merchandise sales climbed from $33 million to $50 million over the same period (Shoebridge 2003).

The sex scandals that rocked the NRL in 2004 have no doubt taken their toll on the image of the game in the eyes of both the viewing public and the corporate sponsorship community. The exact impact however has not yet been assessed. Speculation that the NRL has lost the female market, or that viewers and sponsors alike will switch codes or sports, is not enough reliable information on which marketers can base decisions.

Both the NRL and current or potential sponsors need reliable research to answer questions such as whether or not rugby union is more popular than rugby league, and what the current perception of the NRL and its players is among various target markets. Marketing of sport and marketing using sport is heavily dependent upon good information.

## Introduction

The scene setting article on the NRL quotes a lot of data and asks a lot of questions. Sponsorship spending, television ratings and game attendance statistics were just some of the figures used to explain the NRL's predicament. Where did this information come from? How does the NRL know that companies think rugby union is more popular than rugby league? How can the NRL change sponsors' perceptions of the popularity of the sport? The answer to all these questions begins with RESEARCH. Research is a key business tool in any marketing arena and sports marketing is no exception. This chapter will explore the role of sports marketing research, the different types of sports marketing research and the steps in a sports marketing research project.

## The role of sports marketing research

Marketing research can be defined as the function that links the consumer, customer and public to the marketer through information – information used to identify and define marketing opportunities and problems; generate, refine and evaluate marketing actions; monitor marketing performance; and improve understanding of marketing as a process.

This definition applies equally well to the specific area of sports marketing research. Whether you are marketing sport or using sport in your marketing strategy, information is necessary for making sound strategic decisions. Research can provide information in all key areas including: consumer attitudes and behaviour, financial performance, product development, pricing and distribution strategies and promotional development and effectiveness. Without research the company runs the risk of making uninformed decisions. Uninformed decisions are little more than guess work and you will not survive in the highly competitive sports industry without taking advantage of sound marketing research.

Research can provide valuable information about why people watch sporting events

Sports marketing research ranges from very simple information gathering to highly complex research projects. The type of research conducted depends on the information required and often the budget available. Deciding what information is required usually starts with a thorough examination of the problem or decision faced. Table 5.1 shows some examples of problems that might be faced by different stakeholders in the sports marketing industry and the types of marketing research information that could help address those problems.

Research plays a vital role at every stage in the strategic sports marketing process. Traditionally, marketing research was considered to be most valuable at the strategy planning and development stage, in helping marketers to understand consumers. However, contemporary sports marketers now understand that marketing research can contribute to every stage in the marketing strategy process, including the implementation, control and evaluation stages of all sports marketing programs.

**Table 5.1:** Information provided by marketing research

| Stakeholder/ Decision-maker | Problem or decision faced | Information provided by marketing research |
|---|---|---|
| **Sports marketers** | Game attendance is down | • How do our game attendance figures compare with our competitors?<br>• What are the national averages for live game attendance in various sports?<br>• Who attends our games and why?<br>• Who used to attend our games and why don't they now?<br>• How satisfied are game attendees with their experience at our games? |
| | We need to raise revenue through team merchandise | • What types of merchandise sell well in our sport?<br>• What types of merchandise would our fans be interested in?<br>• How much would our fans be prepared to spend on merchandise?<br>• Where would fans expect to purchase merchandise?<br>• How should we make fans aware of our merchandise? |
| | Our amateur league players are unhappy and numbers are dropping | • Who are our players?<br>• Why are they unhappy?<br>• Do they play other sports?<br>• Are they satisfied with the league, including game times etc.?<br>• Who else could we target to join the league?<br>• Could we change the game or competition structure to better suit players? |
| | Our sponsors pay considerably less to sponsor our sport in relation to other sports at our level | • What is the current sponsorship value of our sport and how does this compare with competing sports?<br>• How many people currently play our sport nationally?<br>• How many people currently attend games in our sport nationally?<br>• What is the perception of our sport and its popularity among our sponsors? And potential sponsors? |

| Stakeholder/ Decision-maker | Problem or decision faced | Information provided by marketing research |
|---|---|---|
| **Sport sponsors** | Is our sponsorship effective? | • What were the goals of our sponsorship and have we reached those goals?<br>• How popular is the sport that we sponsor?<br>• Are our values and goals compatible with the goals and values of the sport we sponsor?<br>• How does the cost of our sponsorship compare with similar sponsorship deals in the same and competing sports? |
| | How should we leverage our sponsorship? | • Which forms of promotion are most effective among our shared target markets?<br>• How do sports fans perceive our product?<br>• What types of special offers or promotions would appeal to the target market(s)?<br>• What types of leveraging activities have our competitors engaged in? Were they effective? Why/why not? |
| **Government** | Which sports should we direct public funding to? | • Who participates in sports, and what sports are they participating in?<br>• How often do people participate in different sports and where do they participate?<br>• Which sports would benefit most from public funding? |
| **Television network** | What sports should we buy the broadcasting rights to? | • How much are the rights to various sports and how do they compare?<br>• What have the past audience figures been for each sport season or sporting event?<br>• What are the demographic profiles of the audiences for each sport?<br>• How do they profile compared with our target audience? |

There are two general ways that sports marketing research might be conducted. The first way in which research might be instigated is in response to a specific problem or situation, such as those outlined in Table 5.1. The second way that research might be conducted is as part of a continual environmental monitoring program, or as part of the marketing information system.

## Situation specific research

Situation specific research is conducted by sports marketers when they are faced with a specific problem or decision. The research question is designed to specifically answer that question and provide the sports marketer with the information they need to make informed decisions. We are referring to the purpose of the research here, rather than the type of research or how it is conducted. The research can be as simple or complex as it needs to be.

An example of situation specific research was the Indigenous Participation project that was carried out by the Albury Netball Association as part of a grant from the Commonwealth Government's Living in Harmony initiative. The project aimed to increase participation in netball among local Indigenous women. As part of the project, the association conducted a survey to see if the project had achieved its aims. Their research gathered feedback from the Indigenous participants, and also from the other association members.

## Environmental monitoring research

Environmental monitoring is a strategic management task that involves continually analysing business and social environments. The purpose of this monitoring is to identify opportunities and threats, identify marketplace trends and gauge relative competitive position in the industry.

In the marketing research process, environmental monitoring is now largely formalised under two different kinds of systems. The first is the *marketing information system (MIS)*, an internal monitoring system that utilises internal records, marketing intelligence and the results of situation specific research. The second is the *decision support system (DSS)*, a database driven system that allows decision-makers to obtain and manipulate information at the same time. The characteristics of a good DSS system include:

- **Interactivity** – the system should be user friendly and allow managers to give simple instructions and retrieve useful information.
- **Flexibility** – the system should provide the level of information required by each user – e.g. sophisticated data manipulation for market analysts and simplified summary reports for managers.
- **Discovery orientation** – good systems will allow users to model different market situations and ask 'what if' questions to aid in decision-making.
- **Accessibility** – the technology driving the DSS needs to be as seamless as possible, with simplicity and user friendliness adding to the overall value of the system (Summers, Gardiner, Lamb, Hair & McDaniel 2003).

Decision support systems are becoming more and more important in the contemporary sports marketing environment and many sporting organisations are realising the marketing power that comes from developing large consumer databases. The Australian Football League for example use their junior development program, AFL Auskick, as a way of gathering participant and fan data from children and their families and following these consumers through their lives as fans and participants. The database forms the backbone of a very powerful and valuable direct marketing program that the AFL believe will ensure the long-term financial and social success of their sport.

# Types of sports marketing data

There are two basic types of sports marketing data: secondary data and primary data. Secondary data is any information that has already been gathered for some purpose, other than the research project at hand. For example, any report available on the Internet, statistics you read in the paper, even this textbook, are all secondary data. Primary data, on the other hand, is information that is developed or gathered by the researcher for the specific purpose of addressing the research question(s) at hand. That means that if you were to ask the season ticket holders of your football club if they intended to buy season tickets next year, you would be collecting primary data.

The decision on which type of data to use depends largely on the importance of the research project, and the temporal and financial budgets available. Both primary and secondary data have advantages and disadvantages. Generally, secondary data is cheaper to collect than primary data and can be collected relatively quickly; however it doesn't always address the specific research problem at hand. Primary data is usually more expensive and more time-consuming to collect, but it can yield more precise data if it is collected and analysed using the appropriate processes and techniques. A summary of the basic advantages and disadvantages of each type of data can be seen in Table 5.2.

**Table 5.2:** Advantages and disadvantages of primary and secondary data

| | Advantages | Disadvantages |
|---|---|---|
| **Primary data** | • Specifically addresses the research question<br>• Reliability, credibility and accuracy are known<br>• Can address almost any research question | • Collecting and analysing data can be expensive<br>• Researcher must have the necessary skills to conduct primary research<br>• Primary research is time-consuming |
| **Secondary data** | • Can be very cost-effective<br>• Can usually be gathered quickly<br>• Doesn't require the same expert skills as primary data collection | • Reliability, credibility and accuracy may not be known<br>• Units of measurement may not be appropriate<br>• Data may not be presented in a usable format<br>• Interpretation and analysis skills are still required<br>• Data may be untimely or out of date<br>• Source or sponsor of the research may not be known |

Primary and secondary sports marketing data will be discussed in more detail in the following sections. It is important to consider the advantages and disadvantages of each type of data, but it is not always a choice between primary and secondary data. Most primary data collection research projects utilise secondary data in the preparation and analysis phases.

For example, if the Australian Cricket Board wanted to determine which sports are most popular in schools in Australia among both boys and girls in various age groups, they would begin by seeing what information already exists. The ACB could consult state and federal education authorities to see if they have this type of information already. They could purchase secondary data reports on sports participation from a specialist research company or consult the Australian Bureau of Statistics census data. A search of the Internet might also return some sports magazine or newspaper articles related to children and sports participation. If after consulting some or all of these secondary data sources they find that they have enough adequate information, they may not proceed any further. However, if the secondary data is not detailed enough, is too old or just isn't adequate in answering their questions, they may design a primary data research project. The secondary data they did collect will almost certainly have helped them refine their information needs and may also help them decide how to collect the information they need.

We will consider secondary data in more detail now and cover a whole range of issues associated with primary data collection later in the steps of the sports marketing research project.

## Secondary sports marketing data

Secondary sports marketing data is organised into two main locations, internal sources and external sources. *Internal secondary data* is that found within the organisation. For a sports marketing organisation this might include game attendance figures, merchandise sales records, sponsorship revenue etc. Organisations in sport-related fields or using sport to market their products and services may also have relevant internal secondary data such as regional sales figures and/or customer demographics. Much of this internal data can be part of the organisation's marketing information system or decision support systems that we discussed previously.

*External secondary data* is all the information that exists outside the organisation. A considerable amount of local and international information available about sport, sports consumption and sport-related issues exists and is available. Sport is a pervasive social issue that attracts research attention in areas such as health, psychology, business, sociology, community studies, government accountability, economic impact and education. As such there are numerous sources of external secondary data coming from private industry, government studies, popular press articles, industry and association reports, national and international sporting bodies and academic institutions.

Many of the external secondary reports, statistics and commentaries have long been collected and developed by government and industry bodies. However, the Internet has seen a revolution in the dissemination and use of this information. The Internet makes it cheaper and quicker to collect secondary data, and the power of search engines means that locating relevant data is more possible than ever before. Secondary data has always been cheaper than collecting primary data but the Internet vastly magnifies this advantage and puts a global information network at the fingertips of sports marketers and managers.

The Internet has made collecting data easier than ever before

Table 5.3 lists some major sources of external secondary sports marketing data in Australia, New Zealand, the United States and Great Britain.

**Table 5.3:** External secondary sports marketing data sources

| Source | Description |
|---|---|
| Australian Bureau of Statistics<br>http://www.abs.gov.au/ | Government reports stemming largely from the comprehensive national census project. In addition, the ABS conduct special sport related studies like sport participation surveys. |

| Source | Description |
|---|---|
| Australian Sports Commission<br>http://www.ausport.gov.au | The Australian Sports Commission administer and fund sport in Australia on behalf of the federal government, developing elite sporting excellence and increasing community participation. They have an excellent website with links to the Australian Institute of Sport and Active Australia. The most exciting feature of their website is their Sports Information link, which will take you to the National Sports Information Centre and a searchable database of reports, articles and web links. Check out their Starter Kit for Sports Web Research. |
| Sweeney Sports Report<br>http://www.sweeneyresearch.com.au | A private marketing research company that conduct an annual national survey of Australians' sporting interests, sports sponsorship in Australia and other issues including sports and the media, brand image and the Olympics. The resulting reports can be purchased in whole or part. |
| Roy Morgan Research<br>http://www.roymorgan.com | Roy Morgan Research is a very well-known Australian marketing research and public opinion polling company. Originally specialising in public opinion, corporate image and media measurement, the company have expanded to cover all aspects of marketing research information gathering whether by personal interviews, the telephone, self-administered or the Internet. Try using 'sport' as a search term on their site and look through their comprehensive list of findings and articles. A great deal of secondary data, including statistics, graphs and interpretation are available free of charge. |
| Amateur Athletic Foundation of Los Angeles<br>http://www.aafla.org | This American foundation provides their own research reports online and also allows you to search a number of different important sport-related journals. Their own research includes such topics as:<br>AAF/ESPN Children and Sports Media Study<br>Gender in Televised Sports, 1989, 1994 and 1999<br>Gender Stereotyping in Televised Sports: A Follow up to the 1989 Study<br>Gender Stereotyping in Televised Sports<br>Boys to Men: Sports Media Messages about Masculinity<br>Children and Sports Media<br>Coverage of Women's Sport in Four Daily Newspapers<br>Portrayal of Race, Ethnicity and Nationality in Televised International Athletic Events<br>Crossing the Color Barrier: Jackie Robinson and the men who integrated major league baseball. |

| Source | Description |
|---|---|
| Statistics New Zealand<br>http://www.stats.govt.nz | Statistics New Zealand is New Zealand's official statistical agency. This is an excellent site for locating sport-related information about New Zealand and its citizens. Try typing 'sport' as a search term on their site. You will find great data about sport participation among New Zealanders of all age groups and also industry figures like sport retail trade sales etc. |
| Sport England<br>http://www.sportengland.org | Sport England are responsible for providing the strategic lead for sport in England to deliver the government's sporting objectives. Their website is an excellent source of English sport data including the latest news, policy and recommendations from the government in relation to sport, information according to both sport and region, and a student resource link for sport-related information. |
| ESPN TNS Intersearch Sports Poll<br>http://www.sportspoll.com | The ESPN Sports Poll provides in-depth American information, an extensive range of fan bases, comprehensive sports interest and behaviour data, a broad spectrum of sporting events and daily interviewing. This type of data is useful to evaluate overall sponsorship and sports marketing programs and to price and negotiate sponsorship proposals. This is largely a subscription-based service but some information is available free of charge on their site. |
| The Gallup Organization<br>http://www.gallup.com | The Gallup Organization have 40 offices around the world and are well known for their polling and research abilities. The organisation have sport-related polls and reports on various countries around the world. Their site is based on subscription revenues, where members can download results, findings and reports. |
| The American Sporting Goods Manufacturer's Association<br>http://www.sgma.com/index.html | This association of the sports industry states that they are dedicated to growing the business of sports and fitness worldwide. They have an extensive secondary database on sport and related topics in the USA and all over the world. Members enjoy access to many detailed reports but there are some very interesting reports also available free of charge on their site. Look at their Market Reports and Studies link. |

## Evaluating secondary data

Finding existing sports marketing data is not the end of a secondary research project. In fact in today's information age, finding the secondary data is the easy part. The most difficult and indeed the most important task is evaluating the data. Burns and Bush (2000) suggest that evaluating secondary data can be done by answering five questions:

- What was the purpose of the study?
- Who collected the information?
- What information was collected?
- How was the information obtained?
- How consistent is the information with other information?

It is important as a researcher, a decision-maker and as a marketer that we understand the information that we are using. Some research is carried out in order to 'prove' something or to advance a particular position. If this is the case, it is unlikely to be objective and making decisions using the data could be unwise. In the same sense we need to understand who collected the information, so that we can evaluate the competency of the researcher and speculate on the validity of the information. It may not always be obvious 'what' information was actually collected. Beware of project titles and the labels on tables and graphs. The title may not accurately describe what information was actually collected, what the precise measures were and how they were measured. Finally, it is important to determine whether the information is consistent with other measures of the same variable. Determining consistency will go a long way to establishing the reliability of the information and will also serve as an alert to any large variances that could adversely affect the usefulness of the data. While two different sources may report different measures of the same variable that is not to say that they are not both reputable. However, you will need to find out more about how the measures were taken before you decide on which information or combination of information sources you intend to consider. The 'Sport spotlight' in this chapter describes how two of Australia's leading secondary sources of sports marketing information, the Australian Bureau of Statistics and Sweeney Sports, conducted national surveys of participation in sport but reported quite different results. This is not to say that either survey is not equally useful, however sports marketers should make sure they understand the methodologies used by each organisation and determine the suitability of the data on that basis.

## Sport spotlight

### Lies and statistics

The Australian Bureau of Statistics and Sweeney and Associates, a private marketing research organisation, each conduct national surveys of participation in sport. But the surveys reveal vastly different levels of sports participation, leaving us unsure as to who to believe.

In July 2001, the ABS produced a comparative study of its own sport participation surveys and those done by Sweeney and Associates. At a conference in Rockhampton, Bob Stewart (Victoria University of Technology) discussed the findings of the ABS study and examined the different survey results for 1998–99, the most recent period for which there is comparable data.

Sweeney reports an overall participation rate of 88 per cent, while the ABS indicates a rate of 59 per cent. The Sweeney participation rates for its top 10 sports are typically much higher than the ABS rates. For instance, Sweeney's participation rate for swimming is 39 per cent whereas the ABS is 15 per cent. For other sports the Sweeney/ABS rates are fishing (25, 7); tennis (24, 8); snooker/pool (23, 3); golf (21, 10); cycling (20, 6); and 10-pin bowling (19, 3). The use of different categories makes some comparisons difficult. Sweeney used 'bushwalking and hiking' (27), whereas the ABS used 'walking' (23). Sweeney's 'gym workout' (25) and 'aerobics' (11) compares with ABS's 'aerobics and fitness' (11). For 'jogging, running, marathons and fun-runs', Sweeney reports 20 per cent participation while the ABS reports 5 per cent for 'running'.

Stewart said the main difference between the ABS and Sweeney surveys centred on methodologies used. The ABS sampled one informant from each of 13 000 households. The sample covered all major cities, every state and many rural regions representing 99 per cent of the Australian population. The data was collected from four quarters of one year, and covered adults over 18. Interviews were done face-to-face. By contrast, Sweeney sampled 1500 informants from only Adelaide, Canberra, Brisbane, Perth, Melbourne and Sydney. There were no informants from Hobart, Darwin or regional Australia. The data was collected during December and January, and covered people aged 16 to 65. Interviews were conducted over the phone.

The framing of questions also helped explain the different results, Stewart noted. While the ABS specified a 12-month time scale for participation, Sweeney left the time period open-ended. In addition, Sweeney provided informants with a list of 56 sport activities to assist their recollection of 'interest' and 'participation'. The ABS showed informants prompt cards with examples of 'sports categories' to invite responses on their 'involvement as player or participant'. But, as Stewart asked, what was meant by 'sport participation'?

In summary, potential users of these sport participation surveys should be aware of the different methodologies and definitions used and treat the results with caution.

Source: Booth 2002

## Steps in a sports marketing research project

Conducting marketing research is a sequential process involving seven steps. These steps can be seen in Figure 5.1. In the following sections we will consider each of these stages in more detail. It is important to understand that sports marketing research and, for that matter, any marketing research, must follow a rigorous and sequential process. Researchers and managers alike should take comfort that the marketing research process is basically the same no matter what the project is. For example, if the Brisbane Broncos want to determine how satisfied their season ticket holders are with the stadium seating and facilities, they will use the same research process as Nike would use to determine what the clothing needs of amateur female soccer players may be. Even the Wagga Wagga under-8s rugby league team will follow the marketing research process when their volunteer administration tries to determine how to increase their membership for next year. Regardless of the problem faced or the size of the organisation, the marketing research process guides the project through sequential and interdependent steps, and in doing so ensures that any time and money expended on the project are well spent.

### Define the research problem

We mentioned previously that the marketing research process is sequential and interdependent, which means that any research project can only be as good as the definition of its purpose. If the initial problem or decision is not correctly identified and defined, then all subsequent research efforts will be misdirected. It is advisable to have some preliminary discussions with members of the organisation to discuss issues and ideas surrounding the potential problem. It is important that key decision-makers and those responsible for carrying out possible future directions related to the issues are involved in the preliminary planning of any research.

At this stage, one of the fundamental errors that an organisation can make is to concentrate on symptoms rather than the problems that are faced. One way to avoid this is to have an experienced researcher, either from inside the organisation or from a professional research

**Figure 5.1:** The sports marketing research project

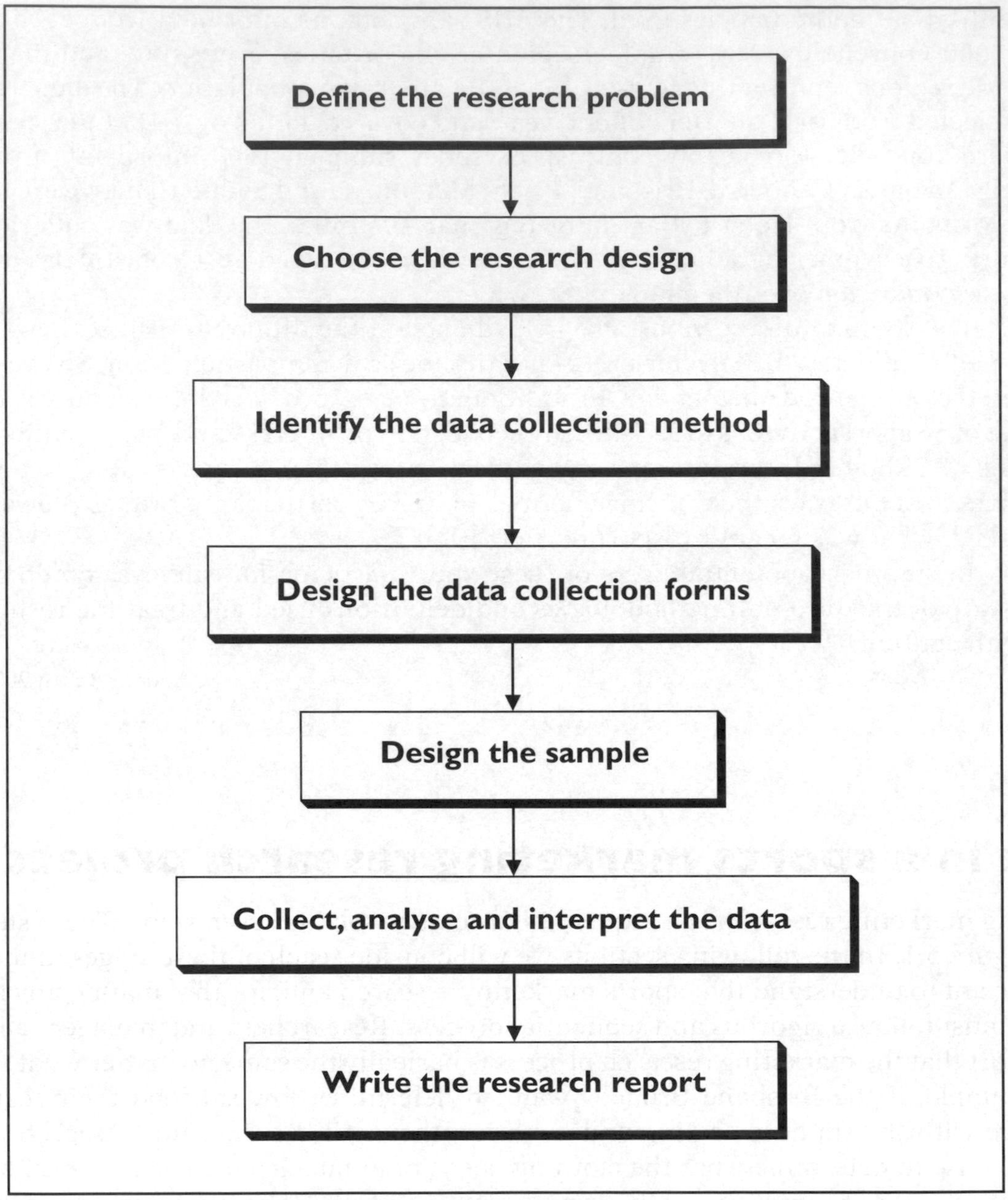
Define the research problem
Choose the research design
Identify the data collection method
Design the data collection forms
Design the sample
Collect, analyse and interpret the data
Write the research report

group, involved in defining the research problem. The research problem should be information-oriented, in that it describes what information is needed to solve the problem or take advantage of an opportunity. The next step is to translate the research problem into more specific research objectives and perhaps a set of related research issues. Look at the example in Table 5.4. These objectives were part 1 of a multi-stage research project. The research problem in this first stage was to get a general profile of sports consumers and determine which sport was the most popular among those consumers.

Don't be overwhelmed by how specific these objectives and issues might appear. Remember that there could have been an extensive amount of secondary data collected by this stage, and that the researcher's experience and intuition also help in clarifying issues.

## Choose the research design

Research of all types can be classified into three categories: exploratory, descriptive or causal. Table 5.5 outlines the research objectives commonly associated with each research design approach.

**Table 5.4:** Example of a research problem and related research objectives and issues

| Research problem | Research objectives | Research issues |
|---|---|---|
| **Develop a general profile of sports consumers and determine the most popular sport among those consumers.** | To identify the most popular sport in a sample of the same population from which samples for later studies will be taken. | What is the respondent's favourite sport?<br>Which sport is the most popular overall? |
| | To develop a measure of sports enthusiasm. | How is sports enthusiasm displayed or enacted?<br>Do respondents show different levels of sports enthusiasm? |
| | To determine if there is any variability in statements measuring aggression and arousal-seeking among spectators of the most popular sport. | How can the respondent's aggressive tendencies be measured?<br>How can a respondent's arousal-seeking tendencies be measured? |
| | To develop a general demographic profile of spectators of the most popular sport. | What is the average age, income, occupation, etc. of spectators whose favourite sport is the most popular among respondents? |
| | To examine attitudes towards sports spectating among spectators of the most popular sport. | What factors impact upon sports spectating?<br>How important are each of these factors to respondents? |

**Table 5.5:** Research design and objectives

| Research design | Research objectives |
|---|---|
| **Exploratory research** | To gain background information, to define terms, to clarify problems and hypotheses, to establish research priorities and gain insight into variables to be considered. |
| **Descriptive research** | To describe and measure marketing phenomena at a point in time, answer the questions of who, what, where, when and how. |
| **Causal research** | To determine whether one variable causes or determines the values of other variables. |

There are those who believe that the three basic designs are stages in a continuous process where exploratory research is the initial step that then serves as a guide for descriptive and causal studies. However, this is not necessarily true and research does not have to follow any type of sequential design order at all. Due to the iterative nature of research, we could begin with a descriptive study and later use a smaller exploratory study for further definition of the findings. In sports marketing research it is likely that the research budget and time frame, along with the overall managerial importance of the study, will largely dictate the design choice. In general terms it is fair to say that research becomes more costly, time-consuming and complex as we move from exploratory, to descriptive, to causal research. This relationship is shown in Figure 5.2.

**Figure 5.2:** The research design time, cost and complexity continuum

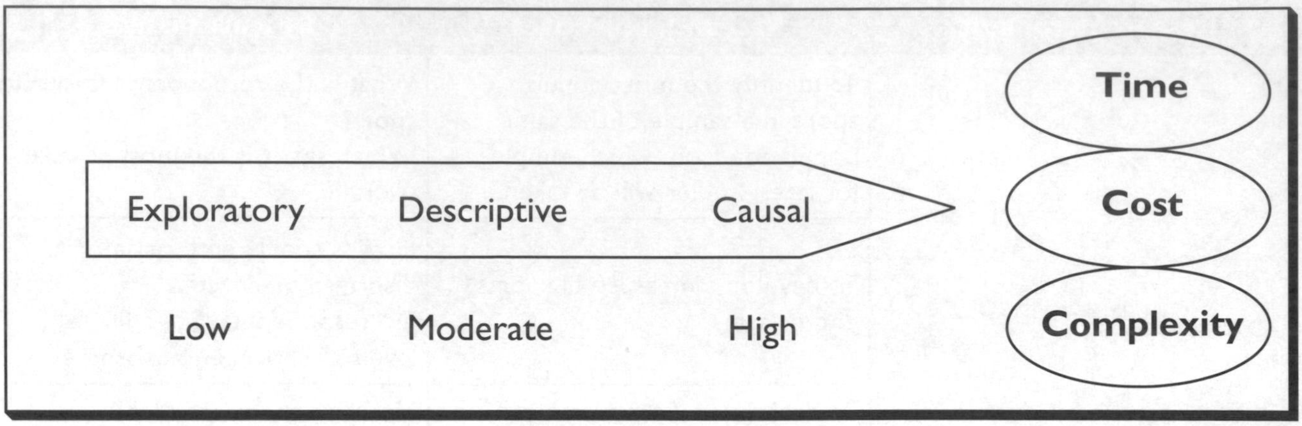


## Exploratory research

Exploratory research is useful in more clearly defining the research problem or objectives and is usually characterised by its unstructured and informal nature. This type of research can be very constructive in the early stages of a project or when the problems and opportunities are new or not well understood. When an organisation is considering entering a new market or is exploring new product opportunities, using exploratory techniques can be a flexible and insightful research design. Burns and Bush (2000) advocate the use of exploratory research in the following situations:

- gaining background information
- defining research terms
- clarifying research problems and defining objectives and hypotheses
- establishing research priorities.

Regardless of the eventual commitment to the research project or the research design used, most researchers will include an exploratory research phase in their design. Common techniques used in conducting exploratory research are outlined in Table 5.6.

**Table 5.6:** Common techniques in exploratory research

| Technique | Description |
|---|---|
| **Secondary data analysis** | Relies on previously collected information. Researcher must ensure that the secondary data sources are evaluated and deemed appropriate for the research problem. |
| **Experience surveys and in-depth interviews** | This involves gathering information from those who are known to be knowledgeable in areas relevant to the research problem. |
| **Focus groups** | This popular technique involves bringing together small groups of people (6–10) and having a qualified moderator guide them through a discussion on the research issues. |
| **Projective techniques** | There are a number of projective techniques including sentence completion, word association and balloon tests. The techniques encourage participants to share their interpretations or understanding of the issues presented. |
| **Observation** | There is some information (particularly behaviours) that is better collected through observation rather than direct questioning. |

Because exploratory research is largely a process of discovery, it is not uncommon to use several techniques that give the researcher differing angles and views about the issues under investigation.

## Descriptive research

Descriptive research is usually associated with survey research but in fact it can involve a number of techniques. The key definitive criteria for descriptive research is that it attempts to answer the questions of who, what, where, when and how. Descriptive research focuses on taking a snapshot of some phenomenon or issue and accounts for the majority of both academic and commercial research.

Like exploratory research, descriptive research will involve well-defined research objectives. Unlike exploratory studies, descriptive research may also involve tentative and speculative hypotheses that the researcher is trying to prove or disprove. Table 5.7 shows some possible sports marketing research problems that could be investigated using descriptive research and some possible corresponding research questions and hypotheses.

Descriptive research involves a variety of techniques and collection methods

**Table 5.7:** Descriptive research, questions and hypotheses

| Research purpose | Research question | Hypothesis |
|---|---|---|
| How should our new team merchandise be distributed? | Where do people buy similar types of merchandise now? | Season ticket holders buy through club catalogues and other fans buy from specialty stores. |
| Who should we target with our new mini ticket packs? | What kinds of people currently buy this kind of ticket package from other clubs? | Families buy mini ticket packs in other sports and clubs. |
| | Who currently attends the games included in the packs? | Singles and young marrieds with no children currently attend these games. |
| How can we change our club catering? | What is the current level of satisfaction with club catering and what are people's perceptions of the services provided? | Satisfaction with current club catering is below average. |

Descriptive research can be very thorough and involve a variety of techniques and collection methods. What descriptive studies do not do is show that one variable causes or determines the values of other variables. This cause and effect type of relationship can only be established using causal research.

## Causal research

Of the three research designs available to researchers, causal research is perhaps the most stringent as it attempts to measure cause and effect. For example, a causal research design might be one that tries to measure cause and effect between ticket prices and game attendance. That is, a decrease in ticket prices will cause an increase in ticket purchases and therefore game attendance.

Causal research is not as common as descriptive designs in social sciences research, which is largely what sports marketing research consists of. However, causal studies can be used equally well to aid in managerial decision-making and can involve some of the same tools and expertise as descriptive studies, such as surveys.

Experimental research is synonymous with causal designs. A variety of experimental research techniques can be used with a combination of measurements (pre- and post-testing), groups (single groups or additional control groups) and allocation of respondents to specific groups. Experiments can be conducted either in laboratories or in the field, with the most common field experiments being test markets. Experiments do raise a number of issues with relation to validity and reliability and controlling and accounting for these require expertise and usually additional time and money. A variety of factors need to be taken into account when selecting an appropriate research design including budget, time, idea and data security, and the level of validity required.

## Identify the data collection method

We have already discussed the difference between primary and secondary data, and explored the issues involved with secondary data collection. As was also previously discussed, the research process is interdependent, and so the decision on what type of data collection method to use is largely a function of the research problem and the research design chosen.

Survey research is a key technique in sports marketing and Table 5.8 compares the characteristics of various types of survey research. This information is key in determining the cost/benefit of different methods of information collection.

In addition to the data collection techniques already mentioned, sports marketing also offers some interesting challenges which can be overcome using innovative collection techniques. Whereas the majority of sports research still relies on the traditional techniques such as focus groups, interviews and surveys, there are a growing number of agencies and individuals exploring the benefits of observation research and ethnographic studies.

Because sport is such an emotional and hedonic phenomenon, some traditional marketing measures don't accurately capture what happens during a sports experience. Ethnographic collection techniques might involve the researcher actually attending games and describing what the atmosphere was like, how people behaved, what they were wearing, the sights, sounds, smells etc. Similarly, an experiential study on sports merchandise might involve giving a representative sample of a target market an amount of money and then accompanying them on a shopping trip to see what they buy, where they buy it from, what language they use to describe products and services and how they make decisions.

## Design the data collection forms

Regardless of the technique used to collect the data, the researcher must decide on how to record the data. This is particularly crucial for survey research that relies on questionnaires and/or response sheets to record data collected in a consistent manner.

**Table 5.8:** Characteristics of various types of survey research

| Characteristic | In-home personal interviews | Mall intercept interviews | Telephone interviews from interviewer's home | Central-location telephone interviews | Self-administered and one-time mail surveys | Mail panel surveys | Computer disk by mail | Internet interviews | Focus groups |
|---|---|---|---|---|---|---|---|---|---|
| Cost | High | Moderate | Moderate to low | Moderate | Low | Moderate | Moderate | Moderate to low | Low |
| Time span | Moderate | Moderate | Fast | Fast | Slow | Relatively slow | Relatively slow | Moderate | Fast |
| Use of interviewer probes | Yes | Yes | Yes | Yes | No | Yes | No | Yes, if interactive | Yes |
| Ability to show concepts to respondent | Yes (also taste tests) | Yes (also taste tests) | No | No | Yes | Yes | Yes | Yes | Yes |
| Management control over interviewer | Low | Moderate | Low | High | n/a | n/a | n/a | High, if interviewer used | High |
| General data quality | High | Moderate | Moderate to low | High to moderate | Moderate to low | Moderate | High to moderate | High to moderate | Moderate |
| Ability to collect large amounts of data | High | Moderate | Moderate to low | Moderate to low | Low to moderate | Moderate | High | High | Moderate |
| Ability to handle complex questionnaires | High | Moderate | Moderate | High if computer-assisted | Low | Low | High | High | Low |

Source: Summers, Gardiner, Lamb, Hair & McDaniel 2003, p.146

**Figure 5.3:** The questionnaire development process

**Plan what to measure**

The research objectives are used to formulate research issues. Exploratory work can be carried out to gain more information on what to measure.

↓

**Format the questionnaire**

Actual questions are developed for each research issue. Recognised scales should be chosen where possible. The response formats should also be selected, i.e. Likert scales, dichotomies etc.

↓

**Refine question wording**

The format of each question should be carefully evaluated for: comprehensibility, and respondent's knowledge, ability, willingness and inclination to answer the questions.

↓

**Decide on sequence and layout of questions**

The questionnaire should start with simple lead-in questions, followed by attitudinal statements about key issues or the key data collection questions and end with any sensitive demographic questions such as age, income, etc.

↓

**Pretest and correct problems**

The questionnaire should be checked for errors by the researcher. It should then be pretested and the time taken to complete the questionnaire should also be determined. Any minor corrections should be made, ready for the final administration of the questionnaire.

The questionnaire design process is a sequential and rigorous process and the steps are outlined in Figure 5.3. There are two basic types of questions that can be used when developing a questionnaire:

1. Open-ended questions – where a blank space is used to encourage respondents to describe their answer in their own words in as much or as little depth as they feel is necessary. This is a good technique in exploratory research to allow for the discovery of issues or even language that the researcher had not considered.
2. Close-ended questions – when the researcher understands more about the issues under investigation, close-ended questions may be used to anticipate that responses will all fall into certain categories. Even a yes/no choice is a close-ended question. Another example might be asking a respondent to choose their favourite sport from a given list that only includes tennis, rugby league, soccer, rugby union, cricket and Aussie Rules. A common and effective form of close-ended questions are scaled response questions that rely on recognised and tested scales to record the magnitude of a respondent's feelings, beliefs or attitudes towards something. For example, you could ask respondents to record how strongly they agree or disagree with the statement 'Professional golfers are paid too much money' and record their answers using a scale from 1 to 5, where 1 = strongly disagree, 2 = disagree, 3 = neither agree nor disagree, 4 = agree and 5 = strongly agree.

## Design the sample

The following steps outline the process that should be followed when designing a sampling strategy. In the interests of time, resources and often accuracy, researchers collect information or 'data' from a sample of the population rather than asking everyone. For example if we wanted to know how satisfied season ticket holders are with their seats and stadium services we might ask a sample of the season ticket holders (drawn at random from a list) rather than asking them all. This would save us time and money and would give us data that was representative of the opinions and attitudes of all season ticket holders. The size of the sample taken is often a compromise between cost and generalisability and is dependent on the potential value of the information collected and the decision being made.

### Step 1: Define population from which sample should be drawn

A population is the entire group under study as defined by research objectives. A thorough understanding of the population is needed in order to define it properly. For example if a stadium is the subject of your research, then in order to define the population you need to understand how wide the catchment area of the stadium is and the demographics of the patrons. The population should be defined in terms of its crucial characteristics including elements, units and time. A unit is a person, or other thing that is actually studied by the researcher; the basic objects upon which the study is carried out. If a sampling unit is actually comprised of several individuals, it will be referred to as a sampling element. For example we might be interested in season ticket holders and their families in the northern suburbs of Sydney in 2004.

### Step 2: Establish a frame of that population

Once the population has been defined, an appropriate sampling frame must be identified or developed. The frame will determine the boundaries. The sampling frame is a list of sampling units from which a sample will be drawn. The list could consist of geographic areas, institutions, individuals or some other definitive unit characteristic. The important consideration here is that the list is as close as possible to the characteristics of the population. Typical sampling frame lists may include telephone directories, electoral roles and client bases including internal fan or member databases, season ticket holders, etc.

Most frames are not perfect and this is the first stage of potential error in the sampling process, that is, *sampling frame error*. For example, if a telephone directory is selected as the sampling frame you should remember that this excludes those people who have silent numbers or who have no telephone at all. The difference between the population and the frame should be reported in the limitations section of a report and should be acknowledged when using the information to make decisions.

### Step 3: Choose the method of selecting the sample units

A decision has to be made between a non-probability versus a probability sampling technique. Probability sampling means that each element of the population has a known and equal chance of being selected. While probability sampling is often more difficult and expensive to achieve it also allows us to determine the reliability of the sample. An example of probability sampling would be to select respondents from a qualified population using a random number generator. Non-probability sampling is often more convenient and less costly but can lead to some biases or error in our sampling. An example of non-probability sampling would be to simply call for volunteers to take part in a study or to approach anyone that walks past to participate in a survey.

### Step 4: Determine the size of sample needed

If a non-probability sampling method is used this may involve a judgemental determination based on cost, time and analysis requirements. However if a probability sampling technique is chosen then a statistical determination of sample size, using the appropriate formula, will be necessary.

### Step 5: Write instructions for identifying and selecting actual members of sample

This involves the methods used to actually draw the sample units from the frame. This step must be considered throughout the entire process so that the 'workability' of the sampling method is assured. For example, if a systematic sampling method is chosen, instructions must be determined for the intervals at which units will be selected.

## Collect, analyse and interpret the data

The fieldwork involved in collecting data is a critical stage in the research process. Errors in data collection can occur both intentionally and unintentionally due to the largely human nature of marketing research. Many new technological innovations in data collection, storage and analysis aim to minimise human error. However, key strategies such as the proper selection, training and supervision of fieldworkers are still essential.

Once the data has been collected, the next phase of the project involves editing the collected data to ensure that it is legible, complete, and that the respondents and their responses are eligible for inclusion in the final analysis and reporting of results.

Data analysis turns the raw data or individual responses to questions into usable managerial information. After data has been entered for analysis, usually into a spreadsheet or dedicated statistical analysis software, the first step is to 'clean' the data. This process ensures that the data has been accurately entered and that it is in the correct format for analysis. Cleaning is also an important phase for the researcher as it often provides them with their first look at the assembled data and gives them a 'feel' for the nature of the data. Decisions on the type of analysis to be used are dependent on the research problem, the research design and the limitations of the type of data collected. Typically, descriptive analysis considers frequencies, measures of central tendency and measures of variability. Descriptive statistics are common in sports marketing research but be cautioned against using any one descriptive statistic as the sole basis of decision-making. These measures should be considered collectively.

If the research project involved hypotheses, the data analysis might require statistical tests such as bivariate analysis (the analysis of two variables). Bivariate analysis typically tests whether or not there is a relationship between two variables and the difference between the two variables.

### Write the research report

Writing the research report is a critical task as it is the communication vehicle for what could have been weeks, months or even years of hard work in collecting the information for the project. Without a well-written and considered report the research is merely data and of little value to the decision-makers who must try to interpret the meaning of it. In writing a research report, the methods used to obtain data must be accurately portrayed and described. It is important that the reader can determine the reliability and validity of the information from the information given.

Researchers have a responsibility to comprehensively and fully report on the methods used to select samples, collect and analyse data, as well as the results of that analysis. This also applies to the presentation of results where scales on figures and graphs should not be manipulated to give a false impression of results.

## Counterpoint: Questioning the dominance of quantitative sports marketing research

Is marketing research and the information it provides really worth it? If you are a good manager and/or marketer shouldn't you be able to make decisions for yourself without collecting all this expensive information?

Successful sports marketing decisions are based on good information. This information, or marketing research data, provides the sports marketer with reliable data concerning the 'market' and the consumers it contains. Marketing research is the process of learning what customers want, listening to their desires and expectations, and determining how to satisfy those wants. In addition, it is used to assess how customers react to a marketing plan. Thus, marketing research cannot only be used to answer specific questions; it is also concerned with the following broad issues about the market:

- Who are the customers and what do they want?
- In what manner and how often should communication be made with customers?
- Which marketing strategies elicit the 'best' responses in customers?
- What responses will each type of marketing strategy elicit?
- What mistakes have been made?

The answers to these questions may be sufficient to generate a marketing strategy, but they can also be broken down into dozens of others in order to produce greater detail. In general, the more detailed and expansive the information collected, the more effective the marketing program is likely to be. However, the catch is the greater the detail, the greater the cost of the marketing research. Thus, the problem facing small and resource-challenged sports organisations is that marketing research is expensive, time-consuming and expertise-intensive. For these organisations, the solution is to find a cost-efficient approach while avoiding the pitfalls of poor research. Qualitative techniques provide a tenable alternative to traditional models based on lengthy questionnaires directed to large sample groups, and the subsequent need for costly analysis.

Source: Smith & Stewart 2001

## Summary

- **explain the importance of marketing research in sports marketing**
  Marketing research is a critical managerial activity in sports marketing and all other areas of business. When faced with problems or opportunities, sports marketing managers can use marketing research to obtain information that they require to make better, more informed decisions. This is essential in the highly competitive field of sports marketing.

- **define and explain secondary versus primary data**
  Secondary data is data that already exists, having previously been collected by someone else. Primary data, on the other hand, is data that is collected for the specific purpose of answering the research problem at hand. Secondary data is widely available, is cost-effective and, with the information explosion of the Internet, more accessible than ever before. It does however have limitations and its use should always be evaluated. Primary data collection involves specific research expertise and can be costly and time-consuming, however the magnitude of the decision faced will often warrant the time and money involved in the primary research process.
- **outline the steps in the basic marketing research process**
  The marketing research process guides the project through sequential interdependent steps, and in doing so ensures that any time and money expended on the project is well spent. There are seven steps in the process including:
  1 Define the research problem
  2 Choose the research design
  3 Identify the data collection method
  4 Design the data collection forms
  5 Design the sample
  6 Collect, analyse and interpret the data
  7 Write the research report
- **understand the different types of research design approach**
  - There are three basic types of research design: exploratory research, descriptive research and causal research.
  - Exploratory research is most commonly used when the research problem is not well understood and has its strength in its flexibility and discovery potential.
  - Descriptive research is the most common research design and frequently involves survey research. It answers the questions of who, what, where, when and how.
  - Causal research tries to prove the cause and effect relationship between two or more variables.
- **describe the process for questionnaire development**
  A questionnaire is a method of consistently collecting and recording data. The questionnaire design process is a sequential and rigorous process involving the following steps:
  - plan what to measure
  - format the questionnaire
  - refine question wording
  - decide on sequence and layout of questions
  - pretest and correct problems.

## Review questions

1. What is marketing research? Explain the role of marketing research in the process of sports marketing management.
2. What is secondary data and what criteria would you use to evaluate a secondary data report?
3. What are the steps in the marketing research process?
4. Define each of the three research design types and give an example of when each design might be used.
5. Compare the advantages and disadvantages of telephone interviews and mall intercept interviews.

## Applied activities

1. Racing Victoria (http://www.racingvictoria.net.au) is trying to decide whether they should make any changes to their website. They are not sure it satisfies the needs of the current users and/or what they could do to improve it. Using your knowledge of the sports marketing research process, define the research problem that Racing Victoria faces and develop corresponding research objectives for them. Also recommend the type of research design that you think would achieve those research objectives.
2. Using the information in Table 5.3 (External Secondary Sports Marketing Data Sources), find out about sports participation rates in Australia, England, the USA and New Zealand. How do they compare and what are the major differences?
3. Using the Internet, find at least four articles that relate to the marketing of basketball in Australia and New Zealand. What issues do you see for this industry and how reliable are the articles that you found?

## References

Booth, R. 2002, 'Lies and Statistics', *Australian Financial Review*, 14 December, p.51.

Burns, A.C. & Bush, R.F. 2000, *Marketing Research*, 3rd edn, Prentice Hall, New Jersey.

Kumar, Aaker & Day 1999, *Essentials of Marketing Research*, John Wiley & Sons, New York.

Shoebridge, N. 2003, 'League Tackles Unpopular Perception', *Australian Financial Review*, 22 September.

Smith, A. & Stewart, B. 2001, 'Beyond Number Crunching: Applying Qualitative Techniques in Sport Marketing Research', *The Qualitative Report*, Vol. 6, No. 2, June, www.nova.edu/ssss/QR/QR6-2/smith.html, viewed November 2003.

Summers, J., Gardiner, M., Lamb, C., Hair, J. & McDaniel, C. 2003, *Essentials of Marketing*, Thomson, Australia.

# Case studies for Part 2

## A league in crisis

### Dr Jane Summers

Many public and private organisations prefer to ignore the reality that 'bad things' can happen, either through denial of their vulnerabilities or through myopia about their successes and strengths. A crisis can be defined as any problem or disruption that triggers negative stakeholder reaction and extensive public scrutiny (Newman 2003). Effective crisis management lies in continuous learning processes designed to equip managers with the capabilities, flexibility and confidence to deal with sudden and unexpected problems or events. Good crisis leaders are those who can make fast decisions under pressure and who can keep the big-picture consequences of actions and words in mind when making these decisions. Managers who do not do these things run the risk of the crisis escalating, coming under the scrutiny of the media, having the crisis seriously interfering with the normal operations of the organisation and jeopardising the reputation of the organisation (Fink 1986).

In 2004 rugby league in Australia was both ill-prepared and ill-advised to effectively deal with what should have been a routine problem with one of their teams.

The key role in any crisis management and crisis communication plan is to be prepared and to have the plan well rehearsed and well known to all key management staff. Essentially the plan should have four main features. These are: (1) to have clearly defined response strategies; (2) to have appropriate resources available and responsibilities assigned; (3) to maintain ongoing corrective action and reactions during the course of the crisis; and (4) to have an evaluation and follow-up stage (Sharon 1999). We will examine each of these areas in brief.

On 22 February 2004 one of the Australian Rugby League teams held a preseason game in a regional town in coastal New South Wales. After the game, which the team won, the players celebrated with some continuing far into the night. The next day a young woman complained to police that she was sexually assaulted by a number of players at the player hotel and from there a crisis emerged. Instead of acting swiftly, transparently and with compassion for the women and players, the club scorned the media, took a superficial approach and generally responded with barely veiled aggression to the efforts of anyone trying to find out the truth. Misinformation and rumour abounded, players spoke to the press, locals speculated and even the hotel manager had something to say. In terms of classic crisis management theory as discussed above, the management of this crisis was badly done.

As a result, a number of key sponsors left the club with over $200 000 in sponsorship also following. Spectators, customers of sponsors and players themselves reacted angrily to the attitudes of players and club management and, worse still, players admitted that this form of behaviour was not only condoned by club officials, it was seen as normal and like a 'rite of passage'. At no time was there any concern shown about the woman in question with all press releases from the club suggesting that their players were the victims here and that women were known to be predators in these situations.

This arrogant approach fuelled anger from other sporting organisations and women began to speak out about similar treatment from other clubs in the league and from other football codes. In classic crisis escalation, what should have been a serious, but easily dealt with problem, became a major reputational and institutional crisis for the individual club, the league in general and its sponsors, players and fans.

Five months after the event, a survey by *Rugby League Week* magazine in May 2004 of players found that 87% of players said that the damaging revelations of these scandals had not forced them to reconsider their attitudes to women (Honeysett 2004). Most suggested that their behaviour was already good around women and therefore there was no need to change it, although 53% also noted that they were embarrassed to be a rugby league player in light of these incidents. Finally, 97% of players suggested that alcohol was an integral part of the lead-up to major games and interstate clashes and that they should not be held accountable when this was the case. There's nothing wrong with a few beers and people having a good time or is there? Well this of course is the main question. At the end of the investigation, the police were not able gather enough evidence to prosecute and so the charges were dropped, however the question still remains: is this the sort of behaviour we want to encourage in our young sports stars?

These actions have caused the NRL to make significant changes to their player code with a signed written code of conduct now being required of all players and a responsible alcohol policy being adopted. In addition players are having counselling and special coaching on how to deal appropriately with women. All of this will certainly help but many are left wondering if maybe it is all too little too late. Interestingly this sort of crisis is becoming more and more common in many sporting codes, and yet sport managers appear to be ill-prepared and unwilling to have appropriate crisis management plans and training in place.

Source: adapted from Honeysett, J. 2004, 'Players approve booze up', *Fox Sports*, June 9.

Boin, A. & Lagadec, P. 2000, 'Preparing for the future: Critical Challenges in Crisis Management', *Journal of Contingencies and Crisis Management*, Vol. 8, No. 4, pp. 185–91

Fink, S. 1986, *Crisis Management: Planning for the Inevitable*, AMACOM, New York.

Robert, B. & Lajtha, C. 2002, 'A new approach to crisis management', *Journal of Contingencies and Crisis Management*, Vol. 10, No. 4, December, pp. 181–91

## Questions

1. How do these players rate in terms of the role models they play in our society and what are the socialisation impacts that need to be considered by rugby league officials?
2. Is this culture of mistreatment of women, binge drinking and outlandish male bonding appropriate for professional sport in this day and age?
3. What would your marketing recommendations be for the NRL to attempt to repair the damage of this type of crisis? Defend your recommendations with theory from Chapters 2 and 3.

# Bowling them over: Building the reputation of women's cricket

**Bridget Marcou**

### *Background*

The Australian women's cricket team dominated the international scene throughout the 1980s and 1990s. Before the team left for the 1997/98 World Cup in India, they were ranked No. 1 in the world in test cricket and second in one-day games.

In spite of this impressive standing, the Australian women's cricket team found they were:

- suffering from little media coverage
- receiving limited sponsorship
- seen as 'unattractive'.

As a result, the team approached a professional PR company to develop a public relations campaign to generate awareness of the unsponsored Australian women's cricket team and promote their imminent matches to key publics, without using advertising support. The campaign was conducted between September 1997 and July 1998, with the goal of 'creating a positive team profile by enhancing the media's interest in the sport of women's cricket and encouraging sponsorship'.

### *Research*

To gain a deeper understanding of why the team received hardly any prematch publicity and why team members were rarely interviewed by the electronic media, the organisation surveyed 50 cricket and sports writers across Australia, gaining a 75% response rate.

Key findings showed that fewer than 18% of sports writers had ever watched the Australian women's cricket team play a match and only 8% had seen the media guide distributed by Women's Cricket Australia. On the other hand, 90% were interested in finding out more about the team. Further, a key concern uncovered in the survey was the perception among sports writers that the team was 'unfeminine' and team members were individually unknown.

### *Campaign goal and objectives*

The overall campaign goal was to create a positive team profile by enhancing the media's interest in the sport and encouraging sponsorship. Specific objectives were to:

- Develop Belinda Clark as a personality. This would be measured by raising the sports media's awareness of her as team captain from just under 65% to 90%.
- Create a positive and attractive image for the team. This would be measured by the quantity, content and tone of coverage in sports and general media during the campaign.
- Generate a significant increase in sponsorship enquiries to the Executive Director, Women's Cricket, within a year.

Targets for the campaign included potential sponsors, sports enthusiasts, women cricketers, potential women cricketers and the media.

### *Key messages*

- The Australian women's cricket team are world-ranked athletes.
- Members of the Australian women's cricket team are attractive sports people.
- Women's cricket is an attractive and legitimate sport.
- The Australian Women's Cricket team needs sponsors.

### *Campaign: The Rose Bowl (Women's Cricket World Series)*

The initial campaign began with a focus on the drawing power of then Australian Democrats leader Cheryl Kernot as patron of Women's Cricket Australia and in this role she was invited to be the guest speaker at the team's farewell lunch before departing for the Rose Bowl Series against New Zealand.

Key elements of the launch included:

- creating an innovative and enticing invitation for the media
- aggressive media follow-up
- a comprehensive media kit
- background on Cheryl Kernot's involvement with cricket, and team member profiles
- Cheryl Kernot's call for sponsorship
- coordinating creative photo opportunities with Cheryl Kernot.

Results:
The launch achieved national, metropolitan and regional electronic and print coverage. It also generated an enquiry from a potential sponsor and positive awareness of the team was generated. Specific results included:

- four television news stories (including one national news program)
- radio news stories (including two interviews)
- seven newspaper articles (including two general news stories)
- the first time that television and non-sports radio stations had attended a women's cricket event.

### *Campaign: The World Cup*

To generate publicity prior to the World Cup, a media launch was arranged for the competition six weeks prior to the team's departure. The timing capitalised on Australia's victory in the Rose Bowl Series by maintaining the media's growing interest in women's cricket.
Key elements of the campaign included:

- A media release announcing the team's mission to become the world's best women's cricket team and the need for a sponsor.
- Organising key members of the team to appear as guests on variety and sports programs.
- Coordinating interviews with players for radio stations and newspapers.
- Inviting New South Wales media to photograph/film the team departing for India.

Results
Women's Cricket Australia received two enquiries from potential sponsors during this campaign, and after the World Cup an anonymous Bendigo businessman reimbursed the team's travel expenses. Specific results included:

- seven-page fashion feature on player Zoe Goss in *TotalSport*, including a tasteful centrefold
- radio news stories (including 13 interviews)
- nine newspaper articles, including a half page in *The Australian*
- team members as guest models on *Sale of the Century*
- captain Belinda Clark featured in *Good Weekend* magazine.

### *Campaign: The Ashes Series*

Based on the success of the media launch for the World Cup, the same strategy was re-employed in June 1998 in advance of the Ashes Series in England.
Key elements of the campaign included:

- A media release announcing the creation of an Ashes competition for women cricketers.
- Inviting Adelaide sports and news media to a media conference at a training camp held in Adelaide.
- Guest appearances by team members on variety and sports programs.
- Team members photographed wearing the latest fitness and evening wear in a leading women's publication.
- Coordinating interviews with players for metropolitan radio stations and newspapers.
- Inviting media to a farewell event with Cheryl Kernot.

Results

The pre-Ashes publicity campaign resulted in a continued increase in calls from potential sponsors. A sponsor for the Rose Bowl Series was confirmed and WIN TV also confirmed non-financial sponsorship. In the first month of the team's three-month Ashes tour, coverage was achieved in 29 newspapers (three regionals) and there were 344 radio reports on the team. Specific results included:

- news of the series announced 42 times on metropolitan radio stations, five television stations and 13 newspapers
- Belinda Clark interviewed on John Laws' national radio program
- a segment on women's cricket on *A Current Affair*
- Minister for the Status of Women independently issued a media release stating the team's need for a sponsor
- four-page fashion spread of team members in *Women's Day*
- player Melanie Jones as celebrity chef on *Who's Cooking?*
- two team members featured on *The Footy Show*
- four-page story on the team and Ashes Tour in the *Herald Sun* Saturday magazine.

### *Evaluation*

In evaluating the overall success of the campaign, it was important to return to the original goals and objectives established at the outset.

**Develop Belinda Clark as a personality**

Awareness of Belinda Clark's captaincy rose to over 90% when the sports media questionnaire was repeated with 50 leading Australian sports writers at the conclusion of the campaign.

**Create a positive and attractive image for the team**

All media coverage was positive. ABC Radio National was even recorded as saying 'Why can't we see more of these attractive women cricketers on TV?' Coverage increased as the campaign developed indicating a growing interest from the media in women's cricket.

**Generate a significant increase in sponsorship enquiries**

The Australian Women's Cricket team had nine enquiries about sponsorship during the campaign and two more after the campaign ended. Subsequently, the Commonwealth Bank of Australia was secured as the major sponsor of women's cricket.

## Questions

1. What role did research play in the development and running of this campaign and why was it an important first step?
2. What other forms of research do you think could be used in the next stage of the media campaign for women's cricket, particularly now that sponsors are involved?
3. What did women's cricket do particularly well in this campaign, that other sports can copy in a drive to attract sponsorship?

# Part 3

# Marketing of sport

# Chapter 6

# The sports product

## Learning objectives

After reading the chapter you should be able to:

- explain what is meant by the term product
- discuss the difference between a good and a service
- explain the service components of sports products
- discuss the various levels of products
- explain how sports products differ from other types of products
- outline the unique influence of media on sports products
- discuss issues relating to sports product management
- explain the relevance of the product lifecycle for sports marketers
- discuss the main considerations involved in branding strategies for sports marketers.

## Scene setter

### Fitness trends and the constant battle of the bulge

The contemporary fitness movement around the world is rooted in the 1960s counterculture, which among many other 'radical' values gave rise to a new focus on psychological and physical self-improvement. Physical self-enhancement branched off on its own, evolving into one of the most dramatic cultural changes of the 20th century: the fitness revolution. This revolution began with the running boom of the 1970s, and in the racquet-dominated 'health clubs' of the same decade; it then proceeded to the aerobics boom of the early 1980s, and a few years later a third generation of low-impact activities, such as fitness walking, soft aerobics and treadmill exercise was noted. Low-impact is the real revolution, because it has now made fitness available to everyone.

In the 1990s, physical fitness around the world once again began to redefine itself with the focus on potentially less strenuous, or otherwise user-friendly equipment including steppers, recumbent bikes, light hand-weights, and elliptical trainers. In the 1990s more than 20 per cent of all health club members were over 55 years of age.

By the turn of the millennium, the most important contemporary subtrend of the fitness industry was the new genre of kinder and gentler fitness: stretching, flexibility, balance and relaxation techniques. By integrating the mental and physical, some of these new mind-body incarnations have defied traditional categorisation as 'fitness' activities.

This new growth industry has seen the emergence of Pilates training, elliptical motion trainers, recumbent cycling and yoga; all activities with a typical older, female focus, though current data and the adoption of these forms of fitness by many high-profile movie stars and other celebrities have resulted in a decreasing median age for these forms of exercise and an increasing interest from men. One reason for their popularity is the claim by western civilisations to have increased levels of stress in their lives and that these kinder and gentler forms of exercise that combine both mind and body relaxation techniques (like yoga and Tai Chi) have a therapeutic as well as fitness benefit for participants.

The fitness industry then is a classic example of a sporting industry that has to be constantly vigilant for changes in consumer preferences that result in opportunities for new product development. No doubt the next five to 10 years will see a new craze or trend emerge with additional sports products to take over from this trend; what do you think it might be?

Adapted from http://www.americansportsdata.com/pr_04-15-03.asp

# Introduction

Sport is found in one form or another in every geographic location on earth. It involves people of all ages, sexes, income levels, occupations and religions and it is generally associated with leisure and motivation, which are considered to be basic needs by nearly all groups in society. The worldwide appeal of sport means that the potential market for it is very large and most people have some interest in sport in one form or another. This level of interest leads to the personal identification with sport discussed earlier and also makes sport as a product very attractive to investors such as sponsors and the media.

Sport is found in one form or another all over the planet

This chapter will examine the sports product in more detail, commencing with a review of the basic elements and multi-dimensionality of the sports product introduced in Chapter 1 by discussing the levels of the sports product in detail. It will then conclude with an examination of the issue of strategic sports product decisions and review the use of product extensions.

As introduced in Chapter 1, the sports product itself is quite complex and multi-faceted and, as previously mentioned, a number of factors differentiate sports products from other goods and services when it comes to strategic marketing decisions. These form a framework that sports marketers need to consider when making strategic decisions about sports products. Before we deal with these issues specifically, we need to look at how marketers generally handle strategic decisions in relation to their products.

# Product defined

Products are generally defined as, 'anything that can be offered to a market for attention, acquisition, use or consumption that might satisfy a need or want' (Kotler et al. 2003, p.344). Based on this definition, products can be tangible goods such as toothpaste or clothing and they can be intangible services such as a haircut or attending a sporting event. Products can also be ideas, such as accepting the 'Don't drink and drive' message, and they can also be destinations, 'Queensland – beautiful one day, perfect the next', or even people – Tiger Woods and Lleyton Hewitt market themselves as products. So the term product refers to the complexity of all items used in the marketing exchange process whether they are tangible goods or intangible services or ideas.

When discussing products we tend to use the term *good* to describe tangible physical products such as tennis racquets, sports shoes and swimming costumes. In contrast, we use the term *pure services* to describe activities or benefits offered for sale that are intangible, inseparable from the consumer, perishable, heterogeneous in that they are not consistent and where there is no transfer of ownership (Shank 2002; Kotler et al. 2003). Examples of pure services in sport would be a sporting event or an actual game.

Very few things are purely service-like or are purely physical products. Sport is no exception with most sports products having both physical characteristics and pure service-like characteristics. For example, when a consumer buys a piece of sporting equipment the equipment itself is a tangible good, while the service at the store and the expectations of performance are all intangible. Even when consumers attend sporting events there are both tangible and intangible elements to that product. Things like the food and beverages available, the merchandise for sale and even the ticket bought are all tangible goods, while the experience of the game and the game itself are intangible.

Marketers generally make strategic decisions in relation to their product offering, about things like the positioning of the product, the product benefits being offered, the product attributes and features and the range of products offered for sale. All of these decisions need to consider both the tangible and the intangible elements of the product in order to achieve the most effective marketing outcome.

Because a sports product has a large service component and because the service component is also generally central to the product itself (particularly in the case of sporting events), we need to briefly explore the service qualities of sport further. As any of you who have completed an introductory marketing course would know, services have many different qualities to goods, requiring different marketing approaches and strategies.

# The service components of sport

The unique elements of services – intangibility, inseparability, heterogeneity and perishability – can all relate to the sports product. Like service consumers, sports consumers do not obtain actual ownership of a sports event and the involvement of others in the consumption of sport is an important part of the product experience. This experiential component is also an important element differentiating sports consumption from that of other services and goods consumption.

Products are said to be experiential in nature when they must be experienced by the consumer in order for them to be consumed. Other products that are experiential are concerts, theatre productions and festivals. Let's examine these service characteristics in more detail.

## Intangibility

Many sports products have intangible elements, and a sporting event or game is completely intangible. The intangibility of services tends to increase the levels of perceived risk for consumers considering the purchase of services (see Chapter 4 for more information about perceived risk), which in turn makes consumers more thoughtful and considered in their decision-making processes. Further, because there is no ownership of a service after purchase, and nothing to really show for the money spent, consumers are more likely to be concerned with value for money considerations and therefore more critical of their experience of the service.

The challenge for sports marketers is to attempt to increase aspects of tangibility in their sports product offering to help customers overcome some of these concerns. Even something as simple as ensuring that sports consumers have something to show for their expenditure, like a memorable ticket stub, T-shirt or poster can assist with increasing the tangibility of an intangible good such as a sports event.

Other things sports marketers can do is to highlight things like the stadium design and comfortable seating, create commemorative tickets which people will keep and possibly even include merchandise giveaways with tickets like tattoos, hats, flags or blow-up fingers and signs. All these things help consumers to perceive a tangible reminder of the experience and thus can help alleviate post-purchase dissonance and perceived risk.

## Inseparability

This aspect of a service relates to the fact that the consumption of the product cannot be separated from the production of the product. For example, a person attending a sporting event (which is the consumption of the sports product), is consuming the event (watching it) while the event is being played out or performed (production of the good). This inseparability is less of a problem for physical sports goods, however these do have an element of inseparability, particularly when we consider the purchase experience. The service offered by the sales person and the expectations of the consumer all occur at the time of consumption. So even though it is possible to separate the good (piece of equipment) and the use of the piece of equipment from the purchase, the two really go together to form a purchase experience.

As discussed earlier, sports marketers have no control over the outcome of a sporting event and no control over how well or how poorly the respective athletes or teams will perform. Therefore sports marketers have to try to create other aspects of the consumption experience that can be separated for consumers and where they have control over the outcome. Things like half-time and pre- and post-game entertainment, venue management and post-game functions are all aspects of a sporting event where marketers have some degree of separation of the product and the consumption experience and where they can control the delivery of that experience.

## Heterogeneity

Another factor that distinguishes services from goods is the issue of heterogeneity or standardisation of offering. With goods, it is relatively easy to develop a standard product with quality controls to ensure that all goods offered for sale meet a specified standard. With services however, because the production and consumption occur simultaneously and because people are involved in the delivery of services, every service encounter will be different.

In the case of sport this is one of the main attractions for consumers. Can you imagine how quickly people would tire of attending sporting events if every event was identical and the outcome of every game was known? The uncertainty of outcome and the excitement and expectation of the unknown are part of the main attraction of sport.

In all service offerings, we are talking about interactions between people and these interactions will always differ purely because of human nature. We all know there are times when we meet people we instantly like and times when we meet people we instantly dislike. These interpretations and inter-personal interactions affect the service delivery and the experiences of customers.

Like many other entertainment products, the consumption of sport is experiential and the benefits of playing, watching or generally being involved in sport will be different for different people. These experiences are also difficult to describe to others, have different meaning for each consumer and are thus difficult to market.

For example, you may love watching football and you have managed to secure prized seats to the final test match of the Rugby World Cup to watch your favourite team play. You have organised the time off work, you book and pay for accommodation near the ground and you are all set for a great evening. The day of the match is fantastic, the sun shines, there is a parade, and it looks like your favourite team will play well. Then it is time to leave for the match and it has started to rain, you get wet, the taxi queue is miles long, the hotel advises you that the restaurant is not open tonight and you have to go back out in the rain to get an early dinner before the game. When you finally arrive, your seats are great, but there is a group of loud obnoxious fans behind you that have drunk too much. They yell and abuse the referee and generally make your viewing of the game unpleasant. To top it all off, your favourite team is playing badly and it looks like they will lose by a big margin. At this point you are wondering why you spent all this money to attend the game live when you could have stayed home and gone to bed when things got bad!

Now most of these experiential factors were out of the control of the World Cup marketers, but all of them combined to impact the overall feelings of satisfaction (or dissatisfaction) of this sporting experience for this individual. The satisfaction of the person who has experienced this will depend on how much they love rugby, their expectations and many other factors that are unique to the individual. Others who engaged in exactly the same consumption behaviours could have had a fantastic evening and been extremely satisfied. In spite of all this, sport still has a universal appeal to many people, regardless of nationality, sport type, socio-economic background and gender.

## Perishability

When we deal with tangible goods, marketers are able to store any unsold goods for sale at a future time. They can also stockpile goods for an anticipated future demand peak and they can clear unsold stock through sales and other sales promotion incentives. When we talk about services however, because the production and consumption occur simultaneously and because the service event is a once-only occurrence, we cannot store, stockpile or clear unsold services. We therefore say that services are perishable, meaning they can't be stored. In effect they *perish* once the event is over or the game has started.

In the case of a sporting event, seats for that event are finite in number. So a really popular event (the opening ceremony of the Olympics for example) can only sell tickets for the number of seats in the stadium. We can't stockpile seats and have more available for popular games, for example. We also cannot sell those seats once the game is over, so the stock of seats has a very discrete life. The same occurs if you have a horse riding instructor or swimming teacher who has eight hours in a day when they can give lessons. If students don't fill all these available lesson spots, then the instructor loses the potential income for those sessions and they cannot recoup this loss.

Sports marketers therefore attempt to even out these fluctuations in demand by creating incentives for customers to purchase their services (lessons, game seats) in times when the demand is likely to be low, and then charge a premium for services in times when demand is likely to be high. Tickets for grand final events are always more expensive than tickets for low rating season games for example. In addition, the emergence of extensive media coverage of many sporting events has helped to minimise the perishability factor, by allowing games to be broadcast at times that are more convenient to both spectators and the media planners. This has the additional benefit of also extending the life of these events and increasing the potential audience in excess of the capacity of the sporting venue.

While it is important to have an understanding of both the service and goods components of a sports product, we also need to consider how these aspects merge together to form a product offering. This is generally discussed by examining the different levels of a product (in this case a sports product) and considering how this impacts the marketing decisions made by sports marketers. We address this next.

## The sports product

When we discuss products in general terms we need to think about them on three levels. The most basic level is the core. This refers to the central feature or benefit that a consumer is buying. The core product can be thought of as a solution to the consumers' problem. Then there is the actual product or service elements of the product and finally there is the augmented product that includes any ancillary benefits and services.

When we think of sporting events we generally refer to the core of the product as the competition itself as this is the main reason people spend money to attend sporting events. If we were referring to sports merchandise then perhaps the core might be association with the team or maybe even social acceptance depending on the individual consumer. Figure 6.1 illustrates the differences in how a marketer would think about the three levels of product for two types of sports products, one a sporting event and the other a piece of sporting equipment (a team jersey purchased by someone who is passionate about their favourite team). You will note that by thinking about the product in this way, a marketer is able to consider the elements and benefits that would be important to a consumer (both tangible and intangible) and they should also then be able to reflect these in their marketing communications.

You can see by looking at Figure 6.1 that the sorts of issues marketers would need to take into account when developing their target marketing strategy, their product positioning strategy and their marketing communications strategies for each of these products would be quite different. Generally it is the augmented product factors that marketers would highlight in their advertising and selling approaches for these products as these are the things that are emotive and exciting to consumers. Most of the factors listed in the actual product area are items that people would expect to find when purchasing these products, so there is no real advantage in highlighting these in marketing communications.

When the sports product gets a service component or some element of intangibility, this is when the level of control over the core becomes less evident. Let's explore this further.

## When competition is the core product

Competition, by its very nature, means that there must always be a winner and a loser and this win/loss ratio of sporting teams is totally uncontrollable. In fact, the unpredictability of this core element of sport is the key to the passionate and committed following of many sports fans. Spectators at sporting events can be satisfied with their experience, even if their team does not win, as long as the quality and intensity of competition was of a high standard.

The implications of this lack of control of the core product for sports marketers are that they cannot focus on winning as the central theme of their marketing efforts to attract spectators because they cannot guarantee the outcome of the competition. Rather, sports marketers can only use the past performance or history of the team or players in their marketing communications. Even then this can be awkward if the result is contrary to the high billing. The one-day Cricket World Cup in 2003 in South Africa was a classic example of this, where a miscalculation in the scoring system meant that the home team (South Africa) did not make the finals of the competition. These sorts of outcomes have major implications for both customers (fans) and investors as they can lead to a loss of credibility with sponsors.

If a team loses continuously, then the marketing campaign can also lose credibility and can thus create long-term image problems for both the marketer and the team. As in many other service industries, sports marketers are best not to over-excite the expectations of consumers by promising a level of performance that they have no control over and may not be able to deliver. The actual performance of a sporting team is generally the domain of the coach, who is

**Figure 6.1:** Three levels of product

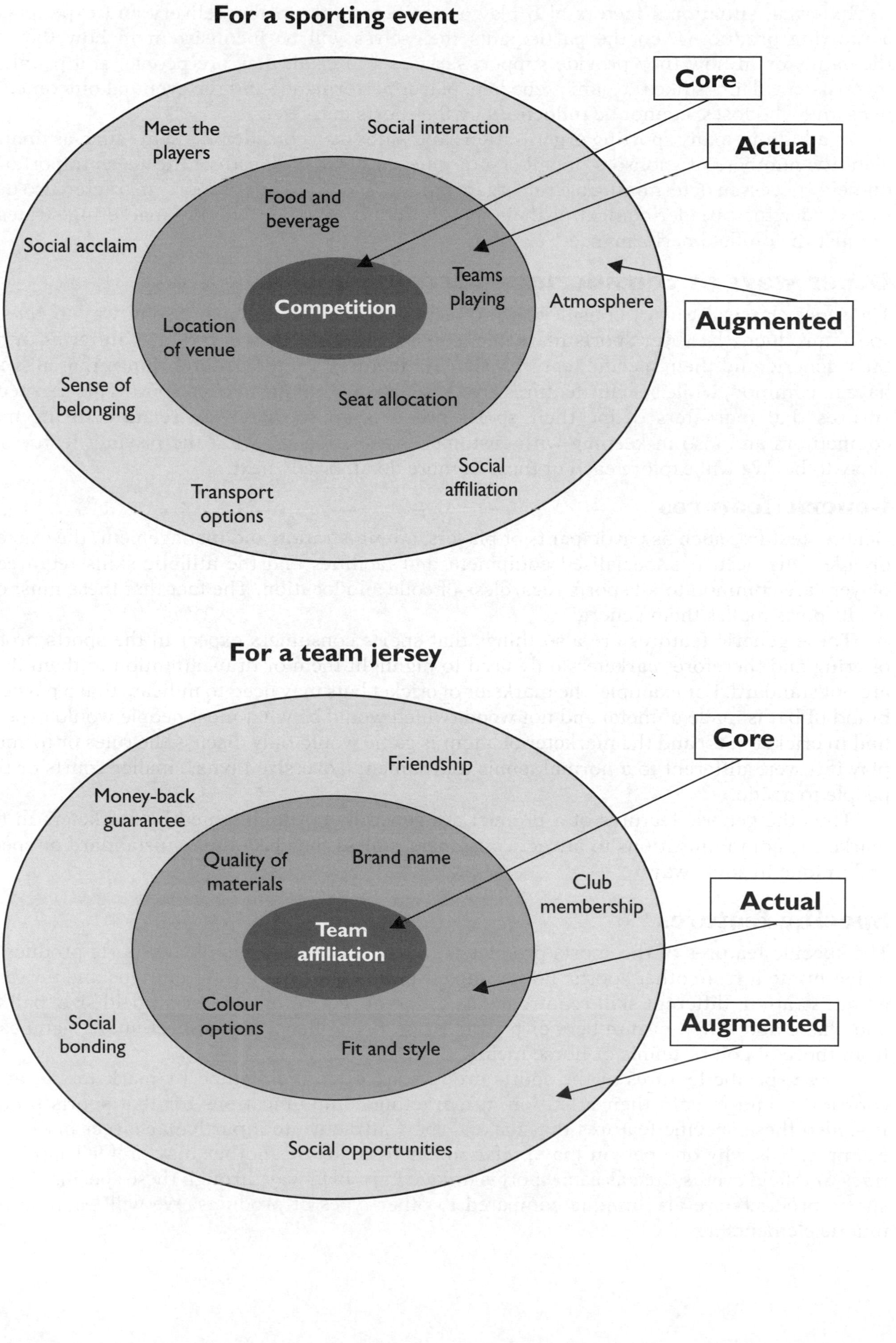
For a sporting event
Core
Actual
Augmented
Meet the players
Social interaction
Food and beverage
Social acclaim
Teams playing
Competition
Atmosphere
Location of venue
Sense of belonging
Seat allocation
Social affiliation
Transport options
For a team jersey
Core
Friendship
Money-back guarantee
Quality of materials
Brand name
Club membership
Actual
Team affiliation
Augmented
Colour options
Social bonding
Fit and style
Social opportunities

more interested in the more tangible elements of the product, such as player fitness levels, skill development and injury issues, than the marketing implications of his team's performance.

External, situational factors also play a significant role in the delivery and experience of a sporting product. Even the participants themselves will be inconsistent in how they play the game, or in how they provide support services – after all they are people, and people are inconsistent. Things like the game schedule, player performance and the eventual outcome, who wins and who loses, cannot be influenced by the sports marketer.

In addition, many sporting organisations and clubs also consider elements such as financial viability, numbers of sponsors, membership rates and media investment to be as important as on-field success in determining overall organisational success. Thus, a sports marketer also needs to consider the broader context of their sports product when developing marketing strategies, not just the on-field performance.

## Other ways of considering sports products

The more classical way of considering products presented already is a useful way to consider sports products, however sports marketers can also consider sports products in terms of both their generic and their specific features. Generic features are the general things that all sports have in common, while specific features are those that are unique to each sport. This perspective ensures that marketers define their sports products appropriately in relation to the major competitors and also in keeping with customer expectations of what the product features are likely to be. We will explore each of these in more detail briefly next.

### Generic features

Generic features such as participants or players, administration and management, the existence of rules, the need for specialised equipment and facilities and the athletic skills required by players are common to all sports regardless of code and location. The fact that these must exist in all sports makes them generic.

These generic features are also things that sports consumers expect in the sports product offering and therefore marketers only need to highlight them or draw attention to them if they are not standard. For example, the marketer of cricket bats may need to indicate that a particular brand of bat is made of metal and not wood (which would be what most people would expect to find in cricket bats) and the marketer of a tennis game would only discuss the rules or format of play if it were different to a normal tennis tournament – oversized bats, smaller courts or three people to a side.

Thus the generic features of a product are generally not highlighted by marketers in their marketing communications to attract consumers, unless they become non-standard or specific and unique in some way.

### Specific features

The specific features of the sports product are those unique aspects of the sports product that differentiate it from other sports. For example, rugby league has a different type and process of administration, different skill requirements, different regulations, different field size, ball type and shape and different numbers of players from those of soccer, and even more significantly from those of golf or tennis or horse racing.

These specific features of the sports product are often highlighted by marketers to attract consumers and to gain their attention in marketing communications for that sports product. It is also these specific features that make a sport attractive to a particular target market. For example, it is why one person may prefer soccer to rugby or another may prefer triathlons to track and field events. Just as each sport is unique in its own way through these specific features, sports products are also unique compared to other types of products. We will examine these unique elements next.

# Factors that make sports products unique

As mentioned earlier, a number of specific characteristics of sports products make them quite unique in terms of marketing planning and implementation. The main reason that sports products differ from other products is the high level of personal identification people have with sport, which results in them being particularly critical of and interested in managerial decisions made by sports marketers and administrators. Other areas where sport is unique includes the influence and role of media on the development and delivery of sports products, the fact that sports products are associated with high levels of emotion, that they are simultaneously industrial and consumer products and that sporting organisations simultaneously compete and cooperate with each other. We will now examine these factors in more detail.

## High levels of personal identification with sport

As with many other service-like experiences, the level and quality of personal interaction between sports consumers and the sporting organisation's employees is an important aspect in the ultimate satisfaction of these consumers. In the case of sport, this interaction occurs at a distance and in a group setting where the involvement of the media and others creates a 'virtual' interface that results in consumers feeling they 'know' the players and the sports managers, and yet rarely does any intimate contact occur. This high degree of personal identification with sport means that consumers often feel that they have expert knowledge of both the game, the players and the strategies that should be employed in order to achieve a winning outcome. Just ask anyone who follows a sport after a competition round! They're all experts and they all have an opinion of who should have played, who shouldn't have, what should have been done by the coach and how they would have played or organised the game differently.

The past experiences of the participants will also affect their current perceptions of the sports product. For example, people who have played a particular sport themselves will have a different view of a game to those who have only ever been spectators. People who have previously attended a major golf tournament at a particular course will know where the best parking is, what to bring and how to maximise their experience, whereas first-timers are more likely to have some levels of dissatisfaction due to their lack of experience and knowledge of how to best enjoy their participation. In services theory this is often called 'scripts' and refers to the fact that experienced customers know how to behave and what questions to ask and are therefore more likely to have a satisfying experience than first-timers.

Even an understanding of the legends and folklore of a particular sport is an important element for spectator satisfaction. Knowing these stories and the importance of particular individuals to a sport allows fans to communicate on a deeper level and create a sense of community and belonging not possible to 'outsiders' or those who are not in the 'know'. Similarly, knowing the rituals, songs, dances or traditions are also part of the sense of community and involvement that are important benefits of sports consumption for many sports consumers.

## The influence and role of media

The universal appeal of sport to people from all walks of life has resulted in an increased interest in sport by the media as a vehicle to generate profits. Sports programming on television now occupies a significant proportion of viewing space in most western countries – just try to watch anything else on a Saturday or Sunday afternoon!

For many sports, television rights are a major source of revenue and sport is also a major source of revenue for many media organisations. This reality is confirmed by the president of the European Television Broadcasting Association in a recent press release, and the sentiment is echoed by most western broadcasters:

> Public service broadcasters cannot fulfil their cultural mission – a mission related directly to the democratic, social and cultural needs of each society, including the need to preserve media pluralism – if they cannot broadcast sports events that are important to their audiences. Nor can they succeed in the contest for audiences without sport.

> It is therefore essential for public service broadcasters to be able to acquire rights to broadcast sports competitions and to produce high-quality programmes from these events. No sport can thrive without broad exposure on television.
>
> Wessberg 2000

Sport offers consumers the chance to forge lifelong relationships with teams and properties and dip in and out of major events when it suits them. It is this passion that broadcasters, properties, advertisers and sponsors will continue to harness and it is their continued financial interest in the order of millions of dollars that have resulted in the high level of involvement by media in sports development and delivery of the sports product. Examples of this investment include the new deal by Ten Sports, who have agreed to pay the Pakistan Cricket Board (PCB) $42 million over the next five years for exclusive television rights to international cricket in Pakistan (Ali 2004), and the billions of dollars invested by companies for the Olympic media rights.

As a result of this enormous dollar investment though, sports media are increasingly influencing aspects of the sports product to suit their interests and stakeholder requirements. Issues such as scheduling (moving the times and even days of games so they don't clash with other popular shows), the rules of games (making the game more open and faster) and even the form of the game have been affected in a number of sports through the pressures by network executives, pushed to show a profitable return on their investment.

The key players in the sports media interaction are shown in Figure 6.2. These are the networks or broadcasters themselves and their affiliates, advertising agencies, corporate clients or sponsors, event management operations, venues and facilities management, the rights holders and the athletes themselves. All interact in a manner designed to achieve the best individual outcomes for themselves, and as all have very different goals and objectives, this interaction can sometimes be the cause of great tension. As Figure 6.2 also shows, the interactions between the players are not always direct and mostly the sporting organisation is required to mediate these interactions – another potential source of tension.

**Figure 6.2:** The key sports media players

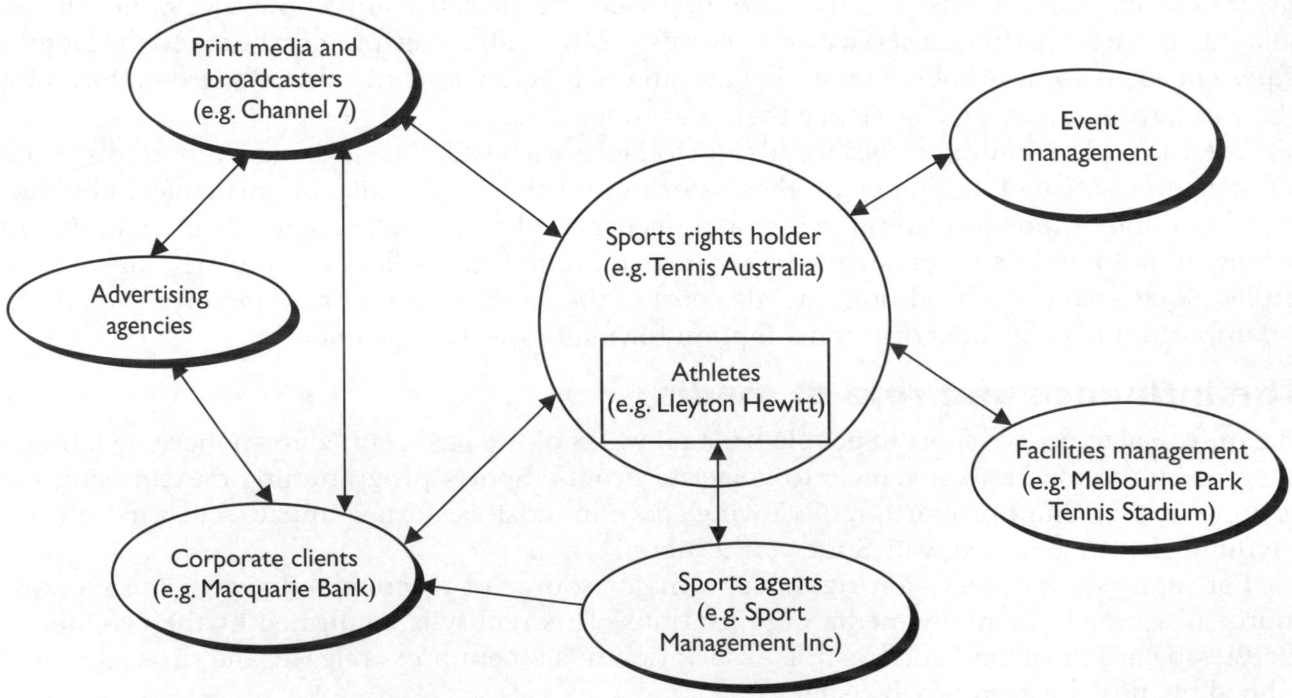


Rights holders include entities such as the International Olympic Committee, NFL, NCAA, Major League Baseball, National Basketball Association, the Rugby World Cup, Tennis Australia, the International Motor Racing Association and others. These organisations own and control events (competitions), which have value to television broadcasters. Television broadcasters, in turn, bid for the right to telecast these events and many times bid against each other for the programming rights, thus driving up the revenues (rights fees) to the rights holders.

Central to the rights holders are the athletes themselves – often they are also managed independently and contracted to the rights holders. They perform their skills in return for large salaries. Of course, these enormous salaries would not be possible if it were not for the tremendous amounts of money paid by the television networks. Virtually all professional athletes are represented by individual agents, many of them attorneys, who negotiate salaries, bonuses, deferred compensation packages, endorsements and other fees in return for a percentage of their total income. Many agents who represent a large number of athletes have considerable leverage and experience in this field and try to negotiate maximum fees while their athletes (clients) are healthy and in their prime.

Broadcasters then package and promote the events to a television audience and they count on advertisers to pay fees for commercial time when the broadcast is aired. Profit on these broadcasts is usually substantial, thus justifying the fees paid by the networks. The price at which commercial television airtime is sold is a function of the number of television viewers and the availability of advertising space (Shilbury et al. 1998).

Facilities/venues are required to stage the events and the host team or facility also needs to make a profit. This model is particularly evident in professional sports where the local team sells in-stadium advertising and tickets and, on occasion, local broadcast rights, thus providing additional revenue to the host team or facility or owner. Management and operations of the sports venues is a large business in itself. The sale of tickets, licensed merchandise, food and beverages and other operational tasks generate revenue and create a sense of excitement around the events. In the case of the Olympics, these local organising committees were created for a short time during which they created their own infrastructure, rented facilities, organised competitions, sold tickets, staged ancillary events and then effectively went out of business, all in the span of approximately six to seven years (Karlis 2003).

Promoters and event managers frequently create their own events. Don King has been the consummate sports promoter by packaging professional boxing events in large venues and negotiating television rights and signing the athletes to fight for a large prize purse. Other sporting events that have been organised outside of an organised competition or playing season would include the recent Polocrosse World Cup, 'friendly games' of sport played between visiting countries, and demonstration events. Quite often golf course managers will organise special events, inviting golfing celebrities and often matching them with high-paying corporate players, actors or other celebrities as both a method of promoting their courses and of raising revenue.

Finally, corporate clients or sponsors pay large sums of money to advertise their messages on the television, in stadia/venues, on radio and in hospitality suites at various sporting events and through the sponsorship of teams and individual players. The Olympics, the 2003 Rugby World Cup and NASCAR have been particularly successful as corporate entertainment opportunities (see Chapter 1 for Olympic and Rugby World Cup sponsorship figures). Of course, other sporting events that are also popular are the American Super Bowl, Wimbledon, the Melbourne Cup, the Grand Prix, Indy and other such events.

Interestingly there are changes taking place within this structure of media involvement in many countries around the world in an attempt to gain greater audience share for sports media. Some television companies that supply sport have started buying sports associations and premises and organising sporting competitions themselves (ESPN – US sports cable station – and the Xgames are an example of this). And some sports organisations have set up television channels. The danger in such vertical integration is that the sporting contest and the events will be arranged solely with television schedules in mind. Many commentators fear that these trends may result in a loss of contact with sport's essential values and cultural foundations and that, as a result, sport will end up becoming no more than just another consumer product of the market economy.

In spite of the need by both broadcasters and sporting organisations for media exposure, most large media organisations are beginning to experience a decline in their audience share for their programming, due mainly to increased fragmentation in the industry. Sports audiences have so many options to choose from that they are becoming far more discerning in their media consumption, a fact that has recently cost the American division of the News Corp group US$387 million in a write-off on its NFL (National Football League) deal, $297 million on its NASCAR contract and $225 million on its NBL (National Basketball League) rights deal. News Corp's net loss in the second quarter of 2001 increased to $606 million from a $23 million loss a year earlier. At the same time, sales rose 7 per cent to $4.12 billion (Battin 2003).

In addition to the increase in options for media consumption, the global sports industry is expected to undergo rapid transition over the next decade as it explores new opportunities in broadcasting. According to a new report released by Screen Digest, 'The Global Business of Sports Television', the industry will aggressively pursue alternative revenue streams via interactive broadcasting. As more and more interactive technologies entice audiences this is expected to result in significant increases in related gambling, advertising, sponsorship and merchandising revenues. Over the next two years these new revenue streams are forecast to increase substantially, reaching $1.39bn by the end of 2005 and $2.79bn by the end of 2008 (The Global Business of Sports Television 2003).

In addition to interactive technologies such as the Internet and digital television, pay TV is also an important player in the shift of media habits. Sports coverage is something which many sections of the public are willing to pay extra to watch and the most popular sports have become drivers that help market new pay-TV services. This forces the cost of these rights to the most popular sports to incredible levels, while at the same time it deprives many people of television access to these events. In Australia and New Zealand the governments have put in place strict anti-siphoning laws in an attempt to minimise this problem.

Anti-siphoning refers to the laws that govern what sport is available to pay TV companies and what sports are offered on free-to-air television. The main rules are highlighted below. It is generally accepted that if thrilling sporting competitions are no longer available to mass audiences through public television, the values connected with sport – values which are essential in the complex relationship between sport and societies – could be undermined. Many sports have a national and cultural heritage attached to them and it is particularly important that these sports are made as freely available to people as possible.

## Anti-siphoning rules

The objective of the anti-siphoning scheme is to ensure that certain events are available to the whole viewing public by preventing pay TV licensees from acquiring exclusive rights to listed events. Under section 115 of the Broadcasting Services Act 1992 (BSA) the Minister for Communications, Information Technology and the Arts (the Minister) may gazette a list of events, or events of a kind, which the Minister believes should be available free to the general public. The current anti-siphoning list comprises domestic and international sporting events in 11 categories including cricket, tennis, golf, motor sports and the football codes.

Pay TV licensees are prevented from acquiring a right to televise a listed event until a right has first been acquired by the ABC, SBS or commercial free-to-air broadcasters reaching more than 50 per cent of the Australian population. The intent of the scheme is to give free-to-air broadcasters priority over pay TV licensees in acquiring rights to listed events.

The Minister may remove an event from the anti-siphoning list in certain circumstances, for example where free-to-air broadcasters have had a real opportunity to acquire the right to televise an event but none of them has done so within a reasonable time.

Source: http://www.dcita.gov.au/Article/0,,0_1-2_10-4_104869,00.html 2003

The move to digital and web-based media is particularly popular among younger audiences who are enthusiastically participating in web pages and feedback channels that are associated with major sports events. Websites are accessed for updated results, player information, information about music featured in broadcasts and online fan chat rooms. Cellular networks are also being extensively used to communicate information and results to fans and SMS messaging at games is becoming more popular as marketers attempt to involve the audiences in competitions and betting opportunities (all in the name of increased revenue).

## Emotions involved in sports consumption

Happiness, the thrill and adrenaline rush of the win, and the depressing emptiness of the loss all contribute to a sports consumer's feelings of satisfaction. Similarly, these emotions are ephemeral and cannot be replicated. Some sports are inherently violent, which is attractive to some participants and some spectators, while other sports are more passive. The nature of the sport and the acceptable levels of aggression and contact, the actual performance of the players and the involvement of the audience all combine to create a highly charged emotional setting for sports consumers, whether they are attending a game or whether they are consuming it indirectly through the media. Rarely are people neutral about the performance of a team or the outcome of a game and often this passion can lead to serious rivalry and unacceptable behaviour.

Hooliganism in sport has been in existence from time immemorial, however it is in soccer where we tend to see the most hooliganism occurring (or at least we hear most about it in this sport). Over 200 countries play this game and with that many people intensely interested in and passionate about the outcome of games, it invariably leads to hooliganism (www.dooyoo.co.uk/speakers_corner/discussion/hooliganism_the_real_sport_behind_football 2003).

Football hooliganism has been regarded as a problem since the 1960s

Wagering in sport has also been in existence from the time man began to bowl, kick or throw a ball. The heavier the wagering, the more potential there is for associated violence. Some even say that hooliganism shows that there is interest in the game and that it signals development, progress and popularity (*Daily News* 2003). Football hooliganism has been regarded as a problem by the authorities only since the 1960s; although it has been a part of the football culture for a lot longer than that, the recognition of the problem was partly due to the media coverage of football matches bringing it to the attention of the general public.

It was around the late 1950s and early 1960s that hooliganism started to take on a somewhat 'organised' state. At first it was just groups of men (usually young) who would get together at the goal end and try to intimidate the opposing fans. Quite often these displays of 'masculinity' would end in fighting inside the ground. Since then things have changed, with the fans becoming more organised and the violence itself getting more and more frightening. Violence is no longer contained to brawls inside the ground, but involves 'gangs' of thugs who front up to one another outside the ground, prepared to use knives and other weapons to kill if necessary (Football Violence 2003).

Most would agree that pointless, senseless violence, cowardly stabbings, vicious assaults, and children terrified out of their wits is not what sport is or should be about. People sometimes get their priorities mixed up, with comments like 'Football is not a game of life and death, it's more important than that' highlighting some of the potential for things to get out of hand. Football is, and always will be, however much money is involved, just a game. Inter-club rivalry and banter between the fans is great; it all adds to the atmosphere and enjoyment of the game but it's certainly not worth dying for. Sport should not be a place for politics of any sort. However, in spite of this, even seemingly 'normal' fans admit that when emotions run high it is sometimes difficult to control themselves, particularly when taunted and faced with equally passionate responses from the opposing fans (*Daily News* 2003).

Football clubs are spending millions of pounds trying to tackle hooliganism, by paying for policing, CCTV systems and by compiling databases of members and known trouble-causers. While all this is helping we are still a long way from really understanding what motivates and drives these types of unacceptable fans (*Daily News* 2003).

## Sports products are both consumer and industrial products

The sports product is delivered to both end users (consumer product) and organisational consumers. It also forms part of new products (industrial product) through such things as endorsements by sporting figures, sponsorship, broadcasting and corporate boxes. This has implications for marketers when they are attempting to understand the decision processes of their markets.

Individual consumers often make more emotive decisions about how they will spend their time and money, whereas corporate customers tend to have more rational and financially solid reasons for their purchase decisions. However, research investigating how corporate management makes decisions about investing in sport (through sponsorship or endorsement) shows that higher levels of emotion are present in decisions relating to sport than in other types of industrial decisions.

As each of these groups has different motives for purchase and as each seeks different benefits, sports marketers need to consider how this impacts their marketing strategies and their product offerings to both groups. For example, the marketing efforts used to target individual consumers may use images of excitement, bonding with others, entertainment and the once-in-a-lifetime aspect of an event to attract these consumers. Marketing efforts aimed at industrial customers may be more focused on rates of return, media coverage, exposure and other more financial or business-like aspects of the involvement.

## Sporting organisations simultaneously compete and cooperate

The very essence of sport is competition and in order to provide organised and structured competition, sports teams need to cooperate with each other in some form of association or league. Things like competition schedules, awards, rules, game structure and even fundraising have more effect if controlled and organised as a result of cooperative effort. Thus sports organisations simultaneously compete and cooperate with each other and it is this mandate of cooperation that is the key factor differentiating sport from other industries.

In most other industries, while there may be advantages to belonging to industry associations or professional bodies, this membership is not a *requirement* of their operation. For sports organisations it is. If an organisation is not a member of the National Basketball League for example, then the team cannot play in this competition. With membership comes rules, game structures and other requirements that mean teams have to cooperate and work together even as they compete passionately.

Thus, the sports product is a complex mix of tangible and intangible elements and emotion also plays a key role in the perceptions of the product by the various stakeholders. This makes managing the product quite a difficult task for sports marketers with many aspects of the sports product being outside their control. So let's now look at how sports marketers make strategic decisions about sports products.

# Strategic product decisions

The strategic use of 'product' in the sports marketing mix refers to product management decisions, product development and design, product lifecycle and branding decisions. Product development and design refers to the introduction and creation of new sports products, whilst product lifecycle decisions relate to the length of time a product has been in the market and its natural cycle. Branding is an important part of any strategic product decision and includes things like image, brand personality and brand value. Each of these areas will now be briefly discussed.

## Product management

Management of a company's product mix involves deciding what products to offer, what lines to carry, when to keep or delete a product and when to add new products. When we consider products that organisations produce or sell, we need to look at the total range of products and services offered by that firm. When we find a group of products that are closely related because they function in a similar manner, are sold to the same customer groups or are marketed through a similar type of outlet this is known as a *product line* (Kotler et al. 2003). For example, Nike produces several different lines of athletic shoes and clothing. Marketers need to decide how long or how short their product lines should be to remain profitable. If adding new products will make the company more profitable then the product line is too short and vice versa.

When we group together all the product lines and all the services offered by an organisation this is known as the *product mix*. For example the product mix for a local gymnasium might offer a variety of fitness classes, learn-to-swim classes, clothing and sporting goods shop, child-care services, restaurant, dry-cleaning service, dietician and physiotherapy services and remedial massage.

The product mix can be expressed in terms of its width, its depth and its consistency. Width refers to the number of product lines offered, depth refers to the number of items in a product line and consistency refers to the similarity between the product lines. Table 6.1 illustrates examples of product mix, lines and items that you might find in a couple of different sectors of the sports industry.

As part of a product management strategy, sports marketers also need to be concerned with product positioning decisions. Product positioning involves attempting to create an image or position of the product in the minds of the customers relative to those products' main competitors. As mentioned in Chapter 4, consumers purchase products to satisfy many different motives and needs, and therefore they attach different interpretations to the value of products relative to the alternatives available to them. Product positioning requires an understanding of perception, branding and personality that will be discussed in more detail later in this chapter.

## New product development

There are a number of different ways to categorise new products. Figure 6.3 illustrates these. As you can see, new products can be anything from a repositioned product to a totally new

**Table 6.1:** Examples of product mix, lines and items in the sports industry

| Sport company | Product assortment (mix) | Product line – items offered in the product line | |
|---|---|---|---|
| Fitness centre | Fitness | Aerobics class | Low impact aerobics<br>High energy classes<br>Kindy Gym<br>Kick boxing<br>Yoga/Tai Chi |
| | Weight loss<br>Restaurant and lounge<br>Aerobics<br>Weight training<br>Tanning<br>Massage<br>Fitness testing<br>Sports leagues<br>Pro shop<br>Medical | Weight training | Body building<br>Free weight training<br>Sport specific strength sessions |
| | | Tennis | Classes<br>Beginners to advanced<br>Club competitions |
| | | Medical | Physiotherapy<br>Remedial massage<br>Chiropractory<br>Dietician |
| Sporting goods manufacturer | Golf equipment and clothing | Golf | Golf clubs<br>Golf shoes<br>Golf balls<br>Golf clothes<br>Golf umbrellas |
| | Tennis equipment and clothing | Tennis | Tennis racquets<br>Tennis shoes<br>Tennis balls<br>Tennis clothes<br>Tennis strings |

Source: Pitts, Fielding & Miller 1994

invention. The further down this list of new product types one moves, the cheaper and easier it becomes to market.

There are many reasons why a company might want to add a new product to its existing product line. Examples include to fill a gap in the market, to stimulate sales, to improve the company's competitive position or possibly even to expand into new markets. In the sports industry new products can include new sports equipment, new types of competitions and even modified versions of games to reach new markets. In the sports industry, additions to product line (often called product extensions) and product modifications or improvements are common. Truly new world sporting events are not common, however new-to-the-world sports merchandise or even sports leagues and competitions are more common.

Examples of additions and modifications that are common in relation to the competition itself are the addition of betting competitions (footyTAB), send-up games (celebrity matches, silly equipment and so on), even board games or computer games based around a sport. The form of the game can also be altered to widen interest and to attract new audiences. For example short course and team triathlons and short course half marathons were all designed to attract

**Figure 6.3:** Categories of new products

| Category | Description |
|---|---|
| New to the world | This category represents inventions. The product is new to the world. For example, the first car, palm pilot, laser printer or antibiotics, XFL football and kite-surfing. |
| New category entries | Products that take the firm into a category that is new to it. Here products are not new to the world. For example, Johnson & Johnson's first insect spray, Hewlett-Packard's first Internet server, Nike's first sport-related computer game. |
| Additions to product lines | This category represents products that are line extensions in the firm's current markets. For example, Cascade light beer, BMW 4WD vehicle, Canon digital camera, junior rugby competitions. |
| Product improvements | This category represents existing products that have been made better. Almost every product in the marketplace has been or will be improved once or several times in the course of its lifecycle. For example, changing rules in a game to allow a faster, more exciting play. |
| Repositioning | This category is reserved for products that are re-targeted for a new application or to a new user. A classic example is the Arm and Hammer baking soda that was repositioned several times from baking to deodorant, fridge deodorant and carpet cleaner, boxing for women or women's rugby. |
| Variations of the above | Variations such as new to the country, new to the channel, packaging improvements and different methods of manufacturing are not commonly accepted as new products, e.g. AFL being marketed in the USA. |

Increasing ease of entry to market

new participants and to provide these sports in a form that could be televised. Horse racing at night is another example of a sport that has been modified to take account of different market needs. The XFL is a classic case of a new sports product where changes to the game form were not successful (see 'Sport spotlight').

Harness racing at night is an example of a sport being modified to take account of market needs

## Sport spotlight

### The XFL story

In 1999, the World Wrestling Federation (WWF) and NBC sports joined forces to present 'outlaw football', XFL (extreme football league). A short three years later the creators of XFL pulled the plug. Why didn't this product take off? The brain-child of Vince McMahon, the WWF chairman, tried to blend sport with spectacle unsuccessfully.

It had a likely audience: football addicts and young men with a demonstrated taste for the fake-mayhem-and-sex circuses put on by the WWF. It had the best publicity, it had sponsors, airtime, and a television audience that was primed and ready for this next generation in football. But it was not to be. It seems that the product offering did not meet the market needs and products that can't deliver on their advertising are nearly always doomed.

The basic premise of the game was to have American football played under the same rules as the national game, but with hundreds of cameras on, around and over the field to allow vision and replays from every angle. Players, coaches and referees had microphones and all conversations were encouraged to be 'bad', 'bold' and controversial. All this was complemented by beautiful, scantily clad women who would hold up score cards, give cheering demonstrations and generally add some aesthetic atmosphere to the game.

What could go wrong, after all this was a tried and tested formula that was successful in the WWF arena? The problem of course was that people were expecting wrestling on the football field and they got second tier NFL players playing football instead. Audiences were presented with an awkward, stumbling and ultimately unengaging show. The curious found too little shock value and scandal, the football fans found too little decent football, with players usually drawn from those who could not make the real football leagues. Their verdict was apparent by the second game, where ratings plunged and received record lows for prime-time television. The league made numerous changes during the year in an effort to stop the ratings from falling. Nothing they tried worked. The XFL discontinued operations in its fourth quarter with an anticipated loss of approximately $35 million.

The trappings of good-looking cheerleaders and the pseudo violence were not enough to keep the audience – they wanted performance. The viewers wanted substance, not just a pretty package. The publicity surrounding the opening was so great that people's expectations were higher than the product could meet. When the fig leaf was pulled away people were disappointed, creating the classic gap between consumer expectations and service delivery capabilities. The game was too violent, and too boring at the same time. There was no fan base, no skills, no well-known names.

In short the game suffered from too much hype and confusion about its purpose. XFL couldn't decide whether it wanted to be more about sport or spectacle. The lesson for marketers is not to get too carried away with the power of promotion and persuasion without solid substantial ability to deliver on promises. In the case of male viewers who were the target audience of XFL, it turns out that they were interested in more than just staged violence and sex – they also want entertainment and skill when it comes to sporting events. In this case the XFL over-promised and under-delivered and for many it will not be missed.

Source: Anon. 2001a; Anon. 2001b; http://www.officialxfl.com/News/endofxfl.asp

## Merchandising

The use of merchandising as a sports product extension can also be very successful. Using this form of promotion, the specific elements of the sport – those attributes unique to the sport – can be extended. The list of potential merchandising options is almost endless, from clothing and equipment, to posters and cards, to books, pictures, music and more. Almost anything that can have a team logo stamped on it is fair game for merchandising. Things like the experiences, emotions and benefits sought can be extended via video footage, action photos and audio footage, so that fans can forever recreate that winning moment.

The Brisbane Lions AFL team have met the merchandise challenge head on, offering their fans baby clothes with Lions colours and logos, pet accessories, pet and baby memberships, children's school accessories and almost anything else you could imagine. Have a look at their website for more: www.lions.com.au. Even the intangible elements of the sport can be extended through merchandising.

Merchandising therefore is a very flexible promotional tool that can be used for sporting organisations at any level to both generate revenue and to foster team spirit, morale and fan loyalty. Licensing arrangements are not only financially attractive to sports marketers, but they can also build a strong and loyal customer base that is also important for the long-term survival of the sport.

## Ticketing

Tickets to games can also be considered to be a sports product extension. While the function of tickets seems quite obvious, the form and structure of the ticket is also important. Not only should the ticket provide the relevant information for the purchaser (such as time and date of event and seat number), but it also can be designed with specific pricing and packaging options in mind. The main objective of tickets should be to build value for the purchaser. That is, tickets should include the game plus entertainment, or a portion of the ticket could be redeemable for a sponsor's product or other items at the venue, thus building in additional value. Some tickets can even be designed as souvenirs and collector's items.

Strategic packaging of tickets can also help to alleviate uneven demand for the product. For example in the case of a basketball team, there are bound to be matches scheduled for the home stadium that are not popular with the potential audience. By offering these games packaged with highly popular games, possibly with preferential seating or some other advantage, the sports marketer increases the chances of maximising revenue for unpopular games and still having satisfied customers.

## Product lifecycle

When introducing new products, marketers need to consider quite different strategies than when they have mature or older products. The product lifecycle allows marketers to consider the course of a product's sales and profits during its lifetime and involves five distinct stages: product development; introduction; growth; maturity; and decline. These stages are often depicted as a curve, as shown in Figure 6.4. This graph also highlights what happens to sales and profits at each stage of the lifecycle and the most appropriate marketing strategies that should be adopted at each stage.

Examples of sports products that are in the introduction stage would be the new 'GoDogGo'™ product recently launched in the US. This is essentially a bucketful of tennis balls that automatically launches balls into the air at a pre-set speed for your dog to chase (www.seegodoggo.com). As a product in the introductory stage, the marketers of this product should expect to see slow growth in sales and low profits due to extensive advertising required to create awareness with customers. The same would also apply to the new *Golf Leisure and Lifestyle* magazine recently launched by Pacific Publications or the sport of kitesurfing (www.kitesurfing.org), both of which would be new products in the sports industry. Not all products at this stage of the product lifecycle are successful, with the failure rate for new consumer products at about 40 per cent (20 per cent for industrial products and 18 per cent for services) (Kotler et al. 2003; Pitts & Stotlar 1996).

**Figure 6.4:** Product lifecycle

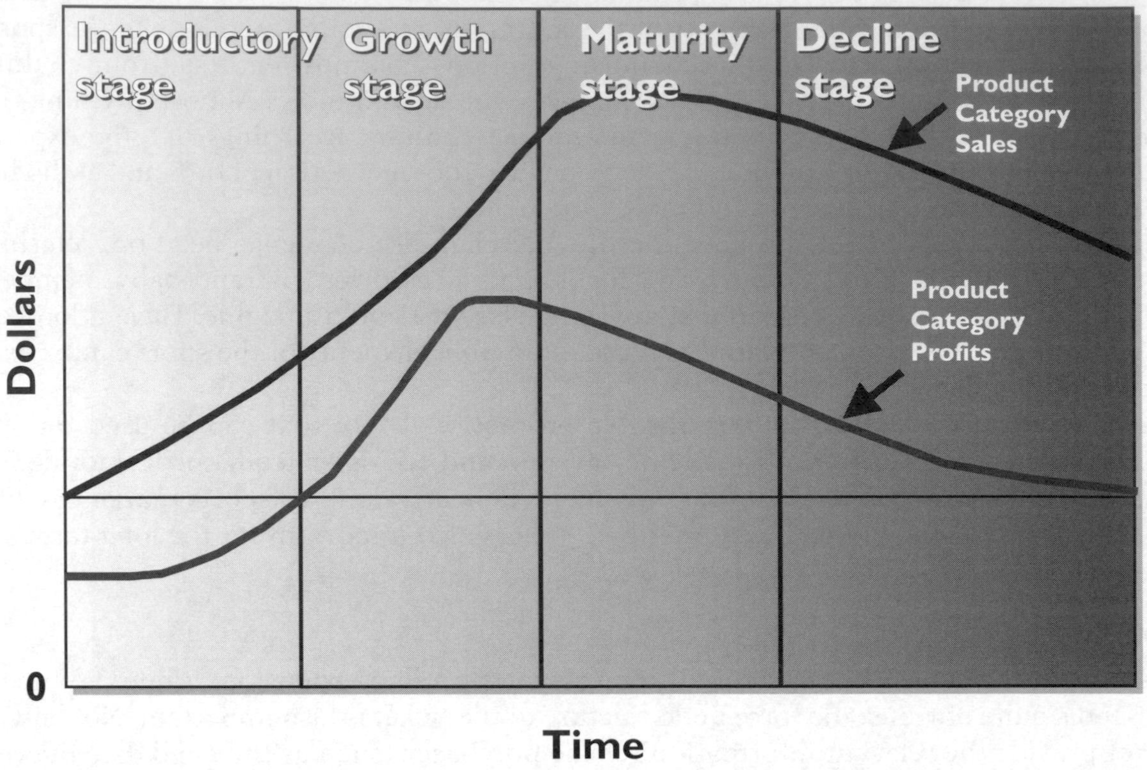


Source: Lamb, Hair & McDaniel 2003, p.302

Products in the growth stage of the product lifecycle experience rapid growth and market acceptance. Examples of sports products in this stage would be SMS text messaging used by many sports to update fans about scores, betting odds and other news. Pilates exercise classes would be another example of a product in the growth phase and most of the categories of extreme sports would also fit into this category. Interestingly, sports products like yoga and aerobics are sports products that have re-entered this growth stage after being in decline or maturity for some time. With modifications and changes to their form, they have once again become popular.

Sports products in the maturity stage would include most professional sports, sports shows like the *Footy Show* and most sports media, magazines and so on. Products in this stage of the product lifecycle experience a slowdown in sales growth or a flattening or levelling off of demand. Quite often profits also stabilise and in some cases even begin to decline. It is at this point that marketers will usually look for ways to revitalise their products to regenerate interest in them. Quite often products at this stage are relaunched, maybe to a new market or given some modifications to make them popular again (like the yoga and aerobics example discussed earlier).

When products enter the decline stage they are usually on their way out with declining profits and sales. Some products can stay in this phase for some time, existing on the lag effect of earlier marketing. Generally products at this point are either phased out completely or reinvented to appeal to new markets, similar to products in the later stages of maturity. Sports products that have been through this stage would be aerobics and jazzercise clothing and accessories of the 1970s, and even the form of exercise itself has fallen by the way. The new forms of aerobics, Body Attack, combat and kickboxing, take many of the same principles and moves of the 1970s style aerobics, but they have been repackaged to appeal to a less image-conscious audience and have a very 1990s feel to them.

The discussion about sports products at different stages of the product lifecycle also highlights the fact that marketers need to consider different marketing strategies at the various stages as each stage has different requirements for each element of the marketing mix. Table 6.2 shows the typical marketing strategies that are best considered at the various stages of the product lifecycle.

**Table 6.2:** Typical marketing strategies during the product lifecycle

| **Marketing mix strategy** | **Product lifecycle stage**<br>**Introduction** | **Growth** | **Maturity** | **Decline** |
|---|---|---|---|---|
| Product strategy | Limited number of models; frequent product modifications | Expanded number of models; frequent product modifications | Large number of models | Elimination of unprofitable models and brands |
| Distribution strategy | Distribution usually limited, depending on product; intensive efforts and high margins often needed to attract wholesalers and retailers | Expanded number of dealers; intensive efforts to establish long-term relationships with wholesalers and retailers | Extensive number of dealers; intensive efforts to retain distributors and shelf space | Unprofitable outlets phased out |
| Promotion strategy | Develop product awareness; stimulate primary demand; use intensive personal selling to distributors; use samples and coupons for consumers | Stimulate selective demand; advertise brand aggressively | Stimulate selective demand; advertise brand aggressively; promote heavily to retain dealers and customers | Phase out promotion |
| Pricing strategy | Prices are usually high to recover development costs | Prices begin to fall towards end of growth stage as result of competitive pressure | Prices continue to fall | Prices stabilise at relatively low level; small price rises are possible if competition is negligible |

Source: Summers et al. 2003, p.216

While it is important for marketers to consider where their products fit in relation to the product lifecycle, the image or positioning of the product is also a critical marketing activity that has to be considered at all stages of the product's cycle. Decisions about branding, identity, image and personality all need to be considered in relation to the strategic product marketing activities.

## Branding

Branding adds value to products and requires a long-term investment of marketing activity. Companies who control their brand names have considerably more market power than those who simply sell products and let the market decide how the brand is to be perceived. A brand then, is a name, term, symbol or combination intended to identify the products of one seller or group of sellers and to differentiate them from their competitors (Shank 2003). Branding allows a consumer to instantly recognise and associate certain benefits with a product. What does the name Nike mean to you? How does your impression of that brand compare to other similar brands like Reebok, Asics or New Balance?

## Brand name

Associated with the concept of branding is the issue of a brand name. This is the element of the brand that can be vocalised and marketers need to ensure that their choice of name symbolises the benefits or images that the company wants for their product. When choosing a brand name for a sporting product, most marketers try to select names that will stimulate positive feelings and associations, be easy to remember and pronounce, and that are distinctive.

None of these rules however seem to apply for marketers of extreme sports products. The more outrageous and uncommercial the brand name it would appear the better for this market. Brand names like Venomous, Black Flys, Alien Workshop, Independent, Shorty's, Darkstar, Spitfire and Blind are all very popular brand names. In contrast if we were to look at popular brand names in the area of golf, we would see names like Cobra, Links, Ping and Wilson. We even see brand names that are based on famous golfers, like Tiger, Tommy Armour and Ben Hogan.

Golf brand names are often named after famous golfers

Even sporting teams have brand names and these are generally chosen to reflect something about the geographic location of the team. The New Zealand All Blacks rugby team manage their brand name with strict rules of conduct and codes of behaviour; all players, once they make the team, are not allowed to have individual identities and personalities that overshadow that of the team and its brand identity. It is quite a different case when you examine sports like basketball, where individuals are encouraged to develop their own brand personality and identity independent to that of the team. Michael Jordan, Denis Rodman and Shaque O'Neil are all examples of this.

Therefore a brand should communicate something about the company's values, the benefits sought by the customer in buying the product and the personality of the product. If this product was a person, what kind of person would it be? Marketers have long known that customers are attracted to brands that have similar personality traits to their own, or that project personality traits that they would like others to think they possess. For example, if following and participating in kitesurfing says to people that you are a fit, daredevil, young in attitude person, with no fear, and that's how you want people to think of you, then this might be a sport for you. Similarly, if wearing Canterbury clothing communicates conservative, tasteful, value- and image-conscious personality traits, and this is how you want to be seen, then you may choose this brand.

## The branding process

When building a brand, most marketers are ultimately attempting to attain customer loyalty and therefore brand loyalty for their products. The branding process begins with creating brand awareness and concludes with creating brand loyalty. Figure 6.5 shows the process.

**Figure 6.5:** The branding process

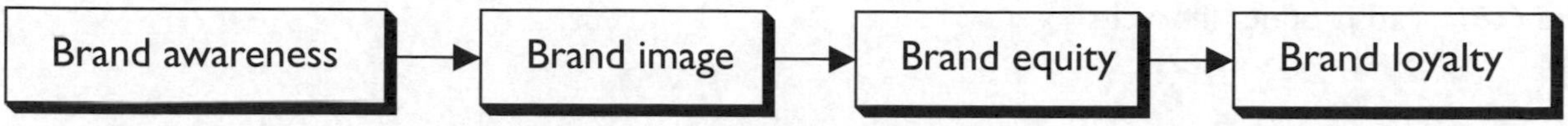


Source: Shank 2003, p.269

Once the marketer has created an awareness of the brand in the market, they can then devote their attention to creating a brand image or brand personality. Sports marketers attempt to create brand images through the management of a number of 'image drivers' (Shank 2003). These drivers include product features, product performance, quality, pricing, service levels, packaging, promotional activity and distribution channels all of which combine to create an image in the mind of the customer.

The final link in the process of developing brand loyalty is to create brand equity. This refers to the value of the brand in the marketplace. Consumers who perceive a brand with high value or equity will be more likely to pay more for the brand, will prefer that brand, and will often be more satisfied with their purchase when they acquire that brand. In relation to sport, this perceived brand equity is often reflected by the perceptions of team success (winning vs losing ratio). When we look at more tangible sports products, brand equity is generally a factor of perceived quality, familiarity with the product and brand loyalty.

Brand loyalty refers to the constant preference or repeat purchase of one brand over all others in a product category. Loyal customers tend to go out of their way to repurchase a particular brand and often will tell others of the superiority of the brand over competitors. Loyal customers act like company salespeople and they are free!

In relation to sports, we often look at loyalty in terms of fan loyalty, or how committed and involved a supporter is with a particular team. Loyal fans are those who stay believing in and supporting a team, even after numerous losses and these customers are obviously very important to sports marketers.

Loyal fans feel a form of bonding or personal association with the team and are often also very involved in the team history or traditions. These consumers also tend to be season ticket holders, or members of some sort, hold team merchandise and can often provide volunteer labour for a team when needed. But it is not just sports themselves that have loyal customers; sports merchandise and sporting apparel brands also have loyal customers who always purchase their brands. Thus sports marketers attempt to create loyal customers no matter what their product offering, as these customers form the foundation for their organisations and act as positive spokespeople for attracting new members and customers.

# Counterpoint

This chapter presented an overview of the traditional marketing considerations that need to be considered when making strategic product decisions. Issues about product mix, product positioning and branding are all relevant regardless of whether the product is a pure good or a pure service. We have also shown in this chapter that the principles hold true for sports products that generally are a combination of both goods and services.

There are however sports products where these traditional models do not appear to apply and this is in the area of extreme sports. These types of sports seem to follow more of a 'fad' lifecycle and, as has been the case for all fad products, traditional methods do not seem to apply. Fads are defined as 'seemingly drastic swings in mass behaviour without obvious external stimuli' (Bikhchandani, Hirshleifer & Welch 1992). The lifecycle of durable goods is generally described as a bell-shaped curve (as is shown in Figure 6.6), which emerges gradually, plateaus and then slowly declines. In contrast the graph of a fad product is generally a very spiky one, showing a sharp increase from the introduction phase with an equally sharp fall after a short maturity phase. It is this very rapid acquisition over a short period of time, with a quick drop off, which is the hallmark of a fad (Bergman 2003).

**Figure 6.6:** Fad product lifecycle

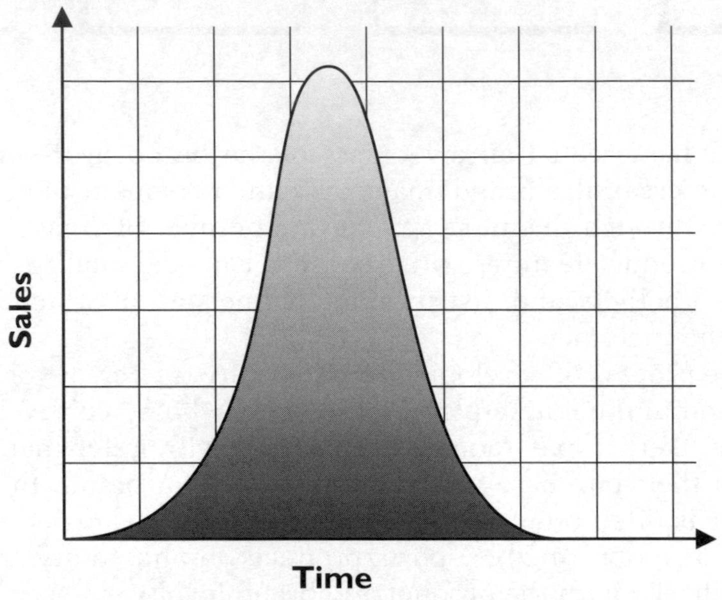


The rapid growth and almost cult-like following of Xgames (extreme games) follows this fad lifecycle quite well. Many different types of extreme sports are very popular at present but few seem to be planning for a long-term run of popularity. In fact it is their very uniqueness and newness that is part of their attraction for their audience. It would seem that the lack of tradition, lack of association with those of an older generation (parents) and lack of history are what makes these sports most attractive to 12 to 22 year olds.

Similarly, traditional branding consider-ations are also not relevant in this market. Extreme sports consumers are known to distrust large corporations and flashy marketing campaigns. They want their brands to be known only to those in the group, to be almost outcast in nature and certainly not commercial. This group particularly does not have the same values as their parents and if their parents don't know about the brands and their associated personalities then this is even better. The trick then for marketers in this area of sport is to use sponsorship, endorsements and other marketing and promotional tools to gain the trust and awareness of the extreme sports consumer without using traditional broadcast media. Websites, chat rooms, retail displays, endorsements and sales promotions are tools that will work well in this market.

So the moral of this story is that even though traditional methods are useful, there are always some products where these methods may not be as appropriate and marketers need to be creative and to understand their customers really well to develop strategies that will work. In addition, marketers educated in traditional marketing methods and principles, and of an age that don't understand this segment, will struggle to make their approaches relevant and legitimate. What tactics would you suggest to a manufacturer of clothing aimed at the skateboard market if they wanted to break into this segment and be accepted?

## Summary

- **explain what is meant by the term product**
  Products are generally defined as, 'anything that can be offered to a market for attention, acquisition, use or consumption that might satisfy a need or want' (Kotler et al. 2003, p.344). Based on this definition, products can be tangible goods such as toothpaste or clothing and they can be intangible services such as a haircut or attending a sporting event. Products can also be ideas and they can also be destinations or even people. So the term product refers to the complexity of all items used in the marketing exchange process whether they are tangible goods or intangible services or ideas.
- **discuss the difference between a good and a service**
  The term *good* is used to describe tangible physical products such as tennis racquets, sports shoes and swimming costumes. In contrast, we use the term *pure services* to describe activities or benefits offered for sales which are intangible, inseparable from the consumer, perishable, heterogeneous in that they are not consistent and inseparable from the consumer and there is no transfer of ownership.
- **explain the service components of sports products**
  Service characteristics of intangibility (sports products cannot be stored), inseparability (production of a sporting game and its consumption occur simultaneously), heterogeneity (each sports consumption experience will be unique) and perishability (once an event is over there is no opportunity to re-consume it) all relate to the sports product. Like services, consumers do not obtain actual ownership of sport and the involvement of others in the consumption of sport is an important part of the product experience.
- **discuss the various levels of products**
  When we discuss products in general terms we need to think about them on three levels. The most basic level is the core product. This refers to the actual thing that a consumer is buying and can be physical or intangible. Then there is the actual product or any secondary service elements of the product, and finally there is the augmented product that includes any ancillary benefits and services.
- **explain how sports products differ from other types of products**
  The main reason that sports products differ from other products is the high level of personal identification people have with sport that results in them being particularly critical and interested in managerial decisions made by sports marketers and administrators. Other areas where sport is unique include the high levels of emotion involved in sports consumption decisions, the fact that sports products are simultaneously industrial and consumer products and the fact that sporting organisations simultaneously compete and cooperate with each other.
- **outline the unique influence of media on sports products**
  Sports media are increasingly influencing aspects of the sports product such as scheduling (moving the times and even days of games so they don't clash with other popular shows), and even the rules and form of the game are seen as fair game by network executives, pushed to show a profitable return on their investment.
- **discuss issues relating to sports product management**
  Management of a company's product mix involves deciding what products to offer, what lines to carry, when to keep or delete a product and when to add new products. When we consider products that organisations produce or sell, we need to look at the total range of products and services offered by that firm. When we find a group of products that are closely related because they function in a similar manner, are sold to the same customer groups or are marketed through a similar type of outlet, this is known as a product line. When we group together all the *product lines* and all the services offered for an organisation this is known as the *product mix*.
- **explain the relevance of the product lifecycle for sports marketers**
  The product lifecycle allows marketers to consider the course of a product's sales and profits during its lifetime and involves five distinct stages: product development; introduction; growth, maturity; and decline.

- **discuss the main considerations involved in branding strategies for sports marketers** Branding adds value to products and requires a long-term investment of marketing activity. Companies who control their brand names have considerably more market power than those who simply sell products and let the market decide how the brand is to be perceived.

## Review questions

1. Explain what is meant by the term *perishability* in relation to sports products.
2. Why is *heterogeneity* a major concern for sports marketers?
3. What is meant by the term *core product*?
4. When a product mix is described in terms of its depth, width and consistency, what is this referring to?
5. What do *anti-siphoning* laws refer to?
6. What are the steps involved in the branding process?

## Applied activities

1. Visit the kitesurfing website (www.kitesurfing.org) and any other links from this site. Comment on whether you think the marketers of kitesurfing products (which are in the introductory phase of the product lifecycle) are following the general marketing mix principles outlined in Table 6.2.
2. Interview five of your peers about their choice of fitness activities. If any of them participate in yoga or Pilates ask them questions about why they like these more passive sports forms and see if you can find out through web research how these sports have been adapted and changed over time to appear new and interesting again. Comment on the marketing tactics used.
3. Choose a well-known sports brand or sports team and ask five people about their perceptions of brand equity and about their loyalty to these brands. What perceived benefits do they see with each brand and what are the brand values that they think the product evokes.
4. Visit the EXPN website (www.expn.go.com) and have a look at the range of extreme games that are presented. Choose one form of extreme game and write a brief explanation of how the game is played and how the direct influence of media has influenced the game form and the competition schedule.

# References


Ali, M. 2004, 'Ten Sports to Cover Pakistan Domestic Cricket', *Daily Times*, 10 October, http://www.dailytimes.com.pk/default.asp?page=story_7-5-2003_pg2, viewed 10 October 2004.

Anon. 2001a, 'No tears shed for the XFL', *Advertising Age*, Vol. 72, Issue 21, p.18.

Anon. 2001b, 'XFL R.I.P', *Advertising Age*, Vol. 72, Issue 20, p.3.

Battin, P.S. 2003, 'Television Sports Rights 2003', *PSB Media*, http://www.gouldmedia.com/nv_rpt_tsr03.php, viewed 30 March 2004.

Bergman, M. 2003, 'When a Fad Ends: An Agent-based Model of Imitative Behaviour', University of Houston, http://www.uh.edu/margo/paper.pdf 2003, viewed March 2004.

Bikhchandani, S., Hirshleifer, D. & Welch, I. 1992, 'A Theory of Fads, Fashion, and Cultural Change as Informational Cascades', *Journal of Political Economy*, 100(5).

Daily News 2003, www.dailynews.lk/2003/09/09/spo05.html.

Football Violence 2003, http://uk.fc.yahoo.com/f/football_violence.html.

Karlis, G. 2003, 'City and Sport Marketing Strategy: The Case of Athens 2004', *The Sport Journal*, United States Sports Academy, www.thesportjournal.org, viewed 30 March 2004.

Kotler, P., Adam, S., Brown, L. & Armstrong, G. 2003, *Principles of Marketing*, 2nd edn, Prentice Hall, Sydney.

Lamb, C., Hair, J. & McDaniel, C. 2003, *Essentials of Marketing*, South Western, Canada.

Pitts, B. & Stotlar, D. 1996, *Fundamentals of Sport Marketing*, Fitness Information Technology Inc., Morgantown.

Pitts, B.G., Fielding, L.W. & Miller, L.K. 1994, 'Industry Segmentation Theory and the Sport Industry: Developing a Sport Industry Segment Model', *Sport Marketing Quarterly*, Vol. 3, Issue 1, pp.15–24.

Shank, M. 2003, *Sports Marketing: A Strategic Approach*, 2nd edn, Prentice-Hall, New Jersey.

Shilbury, D., Quick, S. & Westerbreek, H. 1998, *Strategic Sport Marketing*, Allen & Unwin, Sydney.

Summers, J., Gardiner, M., Lamb, C., Hair J. & McDaniel, C. 2003, *Essentials of Marketing*, Thomson Learning, Melbourne.

'The Global Business of Sports Television' 2003, Report commissioned by Global Media Intelligence Screen Digest, published 1 January.

Wessberg, A. 2000, 'Sport Television and the Internet', Speech by the president of the European Broadcasting Union to the United Nations, New York, 19 November 2000, http://www.ebu.ch/news/press_archive/press_news_1100a.html, viewed 30 March 2004.

www.americansportsdata.com/pr_04-15-03.asp.

www.dcita.gov.au/Article/0,,0_1-2_10-4_104869,00.html.

www.dooyoo.co.uk/speakers_corner/discussion/hooliganism_the_real_sport_behind_football/.

www.officialxfl.com/News/endofxfl.asp.

www.uh.edu/margo/paper.pdf 2003.

www.xfl-football.com/.

# References

# Chapter 7

# Communicating and creating value in sport

## Learning objectives

After reading the chapter you should be able to:

- define promotion and how it relates to communication
- defend the integrated marketing communications perspective for strategic promotional strategy formulation
- discuss the elements of the promotions mix including the emerging forms of promotion and highlight their impact on sports promotional strategy
- debate the advantages and disadvantages of the various promotional elements for incorporation in a sports marketing plan
- discuss the process for developing a strategic promotional plan
- discuss the strategies that can add value to promotional relationships.

## Scene setter

### Fossil gets linked to Davis Cup sponsorship

Fossil is a design, development, marketing and distribution company that specialises in consumer products predicated on fashion and value. The company's principal offerings include an extensive line of fashion watches sold under the company's proprietary FOSSIL®, RELIC® and ZODIAC® brands as well as licensed brands for some of the most prestigious companies in the world, including EMPORIO ARMANI®, DKNY®, DIESEL® and BURBERRY®. The company also offers complementary lines of small leather goods, belts, handbags and sunglasses under the Fossil and Relic brands, jewellery under the Fossil and Emporio Armani brands and Fossil apparel. The company's products are sold in department stores and specialty retail stores in over 90 countries around the world, in addition to the Company's e-commerce website at www.fossil.com. In late 2003, Fossil announced a multi-million dollar sponsorship of Davis Cup tennis that they intend to carry through for a number of years. So what have a watch and fashion company got to do with tennis and how can involvement with international tennis add value to Fossil products and customers?

The International Tennis Federation (ITF) and Fossil signed a multi-year agreement, starting with the final of the 2003 Davis Cup by BNP Paribas between

Australia and Spain in Melbourne in November, to become an international sponsor and the official watch of the Davis Cup (Indiantelevision.com 2003). Fossil will enjoy exclusive on-site and on-court benefits including the provision of the official on-court timer. As part of its watch licensing agreement with the ITF, the company launched the official Davis Cup watch at the 2003 Davis Cup final. The watch is also available at Fossil stores and retailers worldwide. Both parties say publicly that this is a very exciting partnership, but where exactly are the benefits?

Obviously to ITF the main benefit lies in the commercial investment and injection of sponsor capital, but how does Fossil stand to gain from the deal? Fossil intends to use the Davis Cup program as a global communication platform, stating that the Davis Cup and the ITF are driven by the same set of values – passion, authenticity and teamwork, which is evident in the Fossil culture. In a nutshell, Fossil see the international profile of the Davis Cup series and the target audience of young international globetrotters as a neat 'fit' with their target audience. Fossil are always looking for new distribution channels, association with winning celebrities and fashion-conscious high-profile athletes (just consider the Williams sisters). In addition, it is likely that their sponsorship would include some corporate hospitality options at major events, which Fossil can use to woo customers or suppliers, or maybe use as staff incentives, all of which can add considerable value to their product offerings and to their company position. This just might be a game, set and match made in heaven!

Source: http://www.daviscup.com/news/newsarticle.asp?id=12598

## Introduction

Consumers have to know about products and services before they can make decisions about whether to buy them or not. The process of communicating with consumers is known as promotion. As in the 'Scene setter', getting your message to the target audience sometimes involves associating your product or your company with high profile celebrities or events.

Many people think of promotion as simply advertising or perhaps public relations, however promotion is about much more than that and, in fact, includes any act by an organisation that communicates to that organisation's stakeholders. So, even an organisation's packaging and prices communicate information about value and possibly about product contents to consumers. How an organisation's employees relate to customers and to each other also communicates things about that company, and how an organisation looks (physical setting) can also communicate many things to potential and current customers about how much that organisation cares about its staff and its products and corporate image.

This chapter will address the issues of promotion in the sports environment by commencing with a discussion about what promotion is and what it is not and then exploring how a sporting organisation can utilise this marketing mix element to communicate effectively with their intended audiences and how they can create long-lasting customer and investor value through strategically planning their promotional activity. The chapter will begin with an overview of how promotion works and the elements that combine to form a promotional strategy.

## What is promotion?

Promotion is defined as the coordination of all seller-initiated efforts to set up channels of information and persuasion in order to sell goods and services or to promote an idea (Ray 1982). Promotion relates to the strategic targeting of an organisation's communication efforts to a range of targeted audiences both internal and external to the firm. Promotional activities can be used to establish an image for the firm, to reposition images and brands, to create awareness of products and services, to alert customers to special offers and deals, to inform customers about a business's location, changes in staffing and other relevant information and to inform other publics and stakeholders about a business's operation and performance.

In contrast, communication then, involves the passing of ideas or thoughts between a sender and a receiver (Belch & Belch 2004) and is said to occur when an individual attends to a message, decodes or interprets the message and then determines whether to store the information, to act on it or to discard the information (Cravens 1994). Figure 7.1 shows this process.

**Figure 7.1:** The model of the communications process

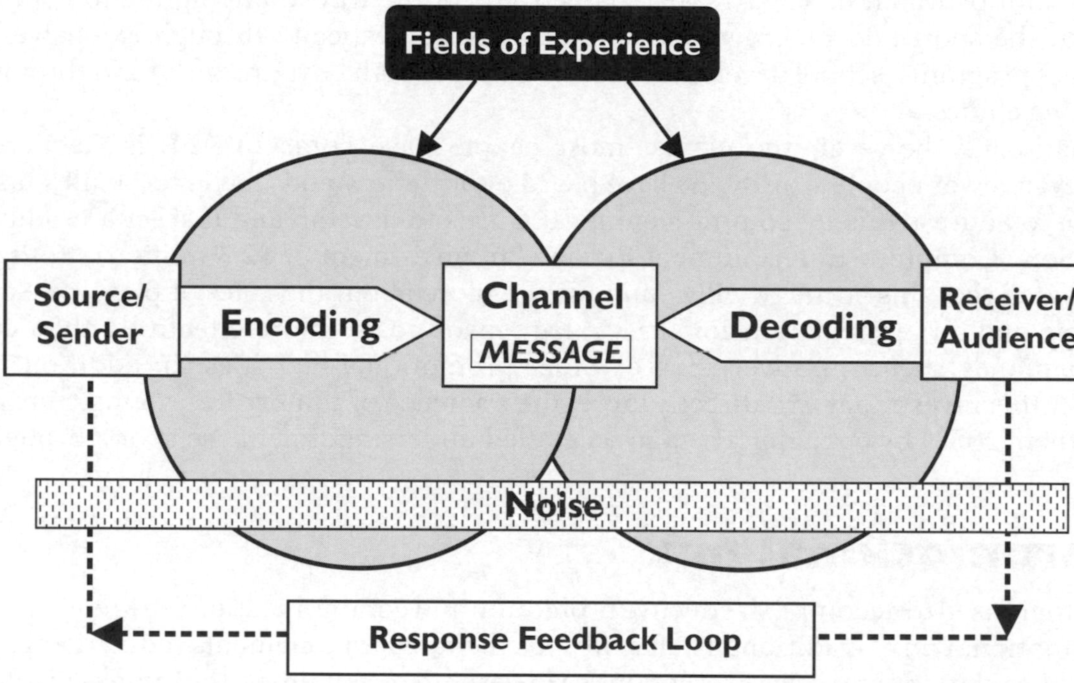


Source: Belch & Belch 2004, p.139

This model of communications highlights how important it is to really understand the receiver of an indented communication and to carefully choose the most appropriate channels of communication to ensure effective transfer of information. If the receiver's fields of experience are not understood, a marketer can fall into the trap of sending communications that make no sense to the intended receiver.

The model of communications therefore begins with the sender or the *source*, who selects words or symbols or pictures in some combination to form a message that will be *encoded* into a form that can be sent to the *receiver*, who *decodes* the message and hopefully understands it the way the sender intended it to be.

The message is sent via a *channel* to the receiver and this channel can be personal (such as a face-to-face presentation) or non-personal (such as in mass media like television or radio). The selection of the appropriate channel is almost as important as getting the message right, because the channel has to be one that the receiver can, and does access.

In addition, the sender also needs to attempt to reduce the potential for distortion and interference (noise) in the process of sending and receiving the message by attempting to reduce clutter and by choosing channels that will be relevant to the receiver. Noise would be a major factor in radio advertising, for example, as most people are doing other tasks (driving, typing, studying, reading etc) when listening to the radio and these activities interfere with the ability of the message to be correctly and clearly understood and received.

Finally, the sender needs to consider the receiver's *fields of experience* when they are composing the message. This refers to the perceptions, attitudes and values that a receiver brings to the process of communication and that they use to help them interpret the various messages they receive or are exposed to. So, it is important to understand your target audience and how they are likely to respond to your communications in order to result in more effective communications activities.

Australian Football League (AFL) is having considerable problems attempting to internationalise and even nationalise their game and to communicate the benefits of attending and supporting the game to a wider audience than Victoria, South Australia and Western Australia. Other states within Australia are less than enthusiastic about AFL in the main, though small pockets of support do exist and these are growing. This enthusiasm becomes even more thinly spread offshore. In fact, most countries have never even heard of the sport let alone understand it or are motivated to participate in it or watch it. The AFL have gone some of the way to attempting to communicate more about the sport and its crowd-pleasing benefits domestically through extensive regional development programs, school development programs (for both boys and girls) and through player and coaching clinics.

Internationally however, the closest most people have come to AFL is Gaelic football. However even fewer people worldwide have heard of or understand Gaelic football! The AFL are attempting to address this by commissioning IR Gurus to develop and market a Gaelic football game for Sony Computer Entertainment Europe (an investment of $2.3 million). Both partners have estimated that this strategy will communicate more about the rules of play, the excitement of the game and an appreciation for the strategy involved far more effectively than could the equivalent money spent on advertising or other promotional activities. In addition, they are hoping that this investment will directly target the audience of tomorrow – young teens and pre-teens (Withers 2003) by engaging them in a detailed understanding of the sport through virtual play.

# The promotional mix

The basic tools used to accomplish effective promotion and communication are known collectively as the promotional mix. Traditionally, this mix has included four elements (advertising, personal selling, public relations and sales promotions). However in recent times, the increased reliance on, and use of, direct marketing and interactive marketing have seen these tools included as separate elements of the promotional mix (Belch & Belch 2004). In the sports context, sponsorship is also sufficiently important to be singled out as a separate promotional element (see Figure 7.2). Thus the sports promotional mix consists of seven elements that need to be considered together in order to be effective in an integrated strategic way. This is known as the process of integrated marketing communications or IMC.

## Integrated marketing communications

For many years the promotional function within organisations was dominated by advertising using mass media and relying on the expertise of advertising agencies to guide most aspects of the marketing plan. During the 1980s, many companies came to see the need for a more strategic integration of their promotion and marketing tools and hence the development of integrated marketing communications.

The IMC approach considers all the aspects of an organisation that communicate with customers and/or stakeholders and therefore goes well beyond mass media advertising. Companies began to see that consumers' perceptions of their brands were a synthesis of a bundle of messages from not only the advertising messages, but also the pricing strategies, distribution strategies, publicity efforts, sales promotional activities, packaging, point-of-purchase displays, corporate uniforms, store or office layout, websites and so on. Adopting an IMC approach allows an organisation to strategically coordinate all of its activities to ensure a consistent and appropriate message is being communicated to its various stakeholders and that more consideration is being given to total brand value (Belch & Belch 2004).

**Figure 7.2:** The sports promotional mix

Therefore, while the activity of promotion is really just another term meaning the communications process, the promotions mix represents the tools and activities of promotion and IMC. Further, IMC is a way of managing the marketing and communications tools, process and activities so that they are coordinated and a synergistic effect is achieved (Semenik 2002).

In order to allow marketers to consider all promotional and marketing activities in a coordinated and strategic manner, we first need to understand a little more about each element and how best to integrate it into a promotional plan. A summary of the strengths and weaknesses of each promotional element shown in Figure 7.2 is provided in Table 7.3 at the end of this section as a summary. Each promotional mix element then serves a different communication and marketing function. The decision on what combination of methods to use needs to be made in light of the overall marketing plan, resource constraints and promotional objectives – more will be discussed about this later. First however we need to briefly overview each element, beginning with advertising.

## Advertising

Advertising is probably the most well-known and first thought-of element of the promotional mix and is defined as any paid form of non-personal communication about an organisation, product, service or idea by an identified sponsor (Belch & Belch 2004). Sporting organisations regularly advertise their products, their events and even their players in mass media outlets (radio, television, newspapers) in an attempt to increase attendances, encourage participation and to stimulate support and loyalty. Some sporting organisations may even use advertising to sell products or to stimulate positive attitudes within the community.

The non-personal aspect of advertising means that it is essentially a transmittal of a message without the opportunity for any interaction or feedback from the audience. It is best used for products and services that are targeted at mass consumer markets and it has the advantages of being able to create brand images and symbolic appeals for companies or brands and of attracting attention easily. Use of mass media in advertising means that it is often a very cost-effective method of reaching a large audience, even though the costs of production per advertisement can be quite high.

Advertising, while the most well known element of the promotions mix, generally does not receive a high level of use in sporting organisations, except when used to inform people about when events are on, what deals are available and to sell merchandise. Sporting organisations tend to make more use of sponsorship and public relations in their promotional programs, though advertising can (and does) play a role. Advertising is more often heavily used by sports investors to communicate their involvement in a sport or to sell sporting-related products and services. Think of signage at sporting events, television ads during sporting events advertising the sponsors' products and so forth.

An important part of successful advertising campaigns is a good creative strategy and execution. However, just because an ad is creative doesn't mean it will be popular or effective. So what is creativity and how can it be managed in relation to advertising?

## Creative strategy defined

Creativity is defined as a quality that enables people to generate novel approaches, generally reflected in new and improved solutions to problems (Belch & Belch 2004). In relation to advertising, creativity is about being able to gain the attention of an audience and to make an impression on them. The challenge for those whose job it is to be creative is to develop advertising messages that incorporate all the information known about the target audience, the communication objectives, the product benefits and features and the organisation's corporate view.

To do this successfully a creative process is generally followed, even though some creative people suggest that creativity cannot be structured through specific processes. One perspective on the creative process is shown in Figure 7.3. This process was developed by the former vice president of J. Walter Thompson Advertising Agency (1975) and it suggests that in order for creativity to have relevance and be effective in advertising strategy development, the objectives of the campaign, the background information about the audience, the product and the problem to be solved all need to be considered. Once the advertising message has been determined, it is important to consider how the message is executed. This is known as advertising appeal or execution style.

An example of creative advertising in sport that attempts to engage consumers and encourage product use was the Coca-Cola campaign based on the Rugby World Cup in 2003. This series of ads was based on the 'thrill seeker' campaign, where satellite and digital technology were used to find 20 owners of bottles of Coke and Diet Coke randomly distributed around Australia. Each winner received VIP World Cup Finals tickets for two, a Peugeot car and $10 000 spending money from Visa. The promotion, reminiscent of the Willy Wonka story where five gold tickets to tour the chocolate factory were hidden in chocolate bars, had thrill seeker teams around the country who found and rewarded the lucky winners live on national radio as they were discovered. In addition to television ads, the promotion also had radio advertisements, point-of-purchase displays in stores and an extensive PR campaign attached to it. David Campese was the main endorser of the campaign, playing the role of 'Secret Agent Thrill Seeker' (Plaskitt 2003a). Activity 7.1 outlines the steps you would need to follow to write a creative brief, which is a planning sheet used by advertising agencies to clearly communicate to all concerned the focus and direction for the creative strategies being used in marketing communications.

**Figure 7.3:** The creative process

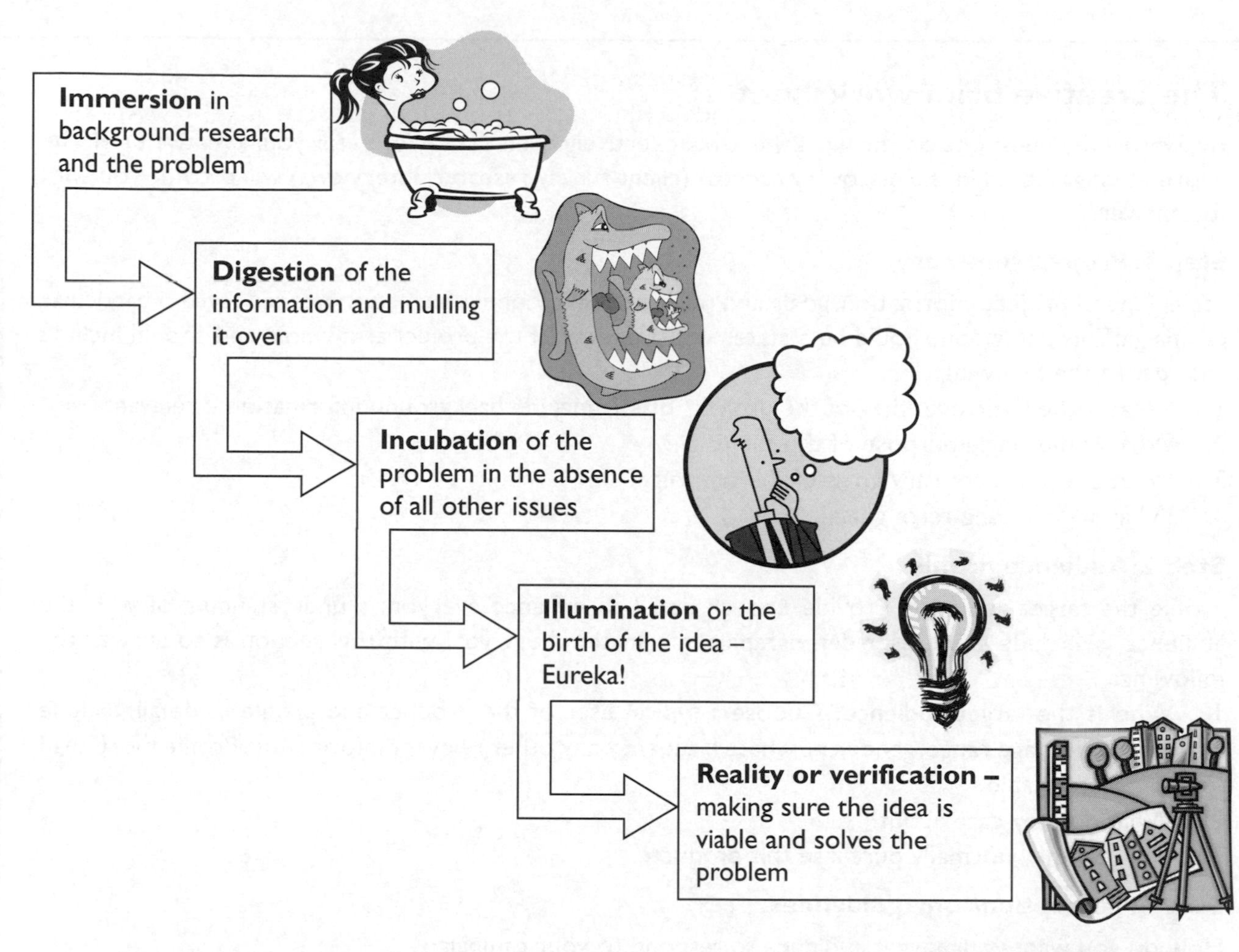
**Immersion** in background research and the problem
**Digestion** of the information and mulling it over
**Incubation** of the problem in the absence of all other issues
**Illumination** or the birth of the idea – Eureka!
**Reality or verification –** making sure the idea is viable and solves the problem

Source: Webb Young 1975, p.42

Coca-Cola
Diet Coke

The 2003 Rugby World Cup attracted creative advertising by marketers

**Activity 7.1:** How to write a creative brief

## The creative brief worksheet

Answering the questions on the worksheet will effectively build the skeleton for your creative brief. The information gathered in the discovery process (client survey, research, interviews) will provide you with the answers.

### Step 1: Project summary

State general project information, goals and relevant background information needed for the particular campaign. This paragraph should be a statement overview of the project as a whole and should include answers to the following:

1. What is the basic overview of the project? Briefly include background information if relevant.
2. What is the single purpose of the campaign?
3. What are the secondary goals of the campaign?
4. What are the long-term goals?

### Step 2: Audience profile

Profile the target audience. Provide enough detail to enhance everyone's understanding of who the audience is. Include some user demographic information. Your goal with this section is to answer the following:

1. Who is the target audience? Choose a typical user of the product and profile in detail. Include occupation, age range, gender, purchase frequency, any other relevant information. Profile more than one if applicable.
2. What do they care about?
3. How do they normally purchase this product?

### Step 3: Perception/tone/guidelines

How do you want your target audience to respond to your campaign?

1. What does the target audience currently think and feel about the company and the current products?
2. What do we want them to think and feel?
3. How will this new campaign site help to achieve this goal?
4. What adjectives can be used to describe the way the product and company should be perceived?
5. What are some specific visual goals the campaign should convey?
6. State a single-minded word or phrase that will appropriately describe the product.

### Step 4: Communication strategy

How will we convince them?

1. What is the overall message you are trying to convey to your target audience? For example: cost-effective, secure, reliable, efficient, etc.
2. How will you convey the overall message? For example: effective messaging through copy, directed path towards goal, specific offer etc.
3. Identify stages of development (if appropriate) used to execute goals.
4. How will you measure the success of the campaign?

### Step 5: Competitive positioning

How you are different from your competition and the factors that will make you a success.

1. How is your company or campaign different to your competition?
2. What specifically sets you apart from your competition?
3. What areas of past campaigns have been successful and why?

Adapted from: http://www.macromedia.com/resources/techniques/resources/define/creative_brief.rtf.

## Advertising appeals and execution styles

The above example of Coca-Cola and the 2003 Rugby World Cup used a highly emotional appeal delivered with drama, humour and personality and was bound to catch the attention of television and radio audiences. The appeal of an advertisement refers to the approach used to attract the attention of the audience. Appeals tend to be grouped into either *rational/informational* appeals or *emotional* appeals depending on the message being sent and the approach needed to gain the attention of the audience. *Rational* appeals tend to focus on the practical, functional or utilitarian aspects of the product or service. *Emotional* appeals on the other hand focus on the social or psychological needs for purchasing a product or service and tend to use feelings or psychological states in their approach.

Many sport-related advertisements use emotional appeals because sport is such an emotional product. Feelings such as joy, nostalgia, excitement, fear, pride, sorrow, grief, arousal, anger, belonging and status can all be relevant in the sporting arena. Rational appeals are also used, but only if there is a serious message to be sent: e.g. 'Don't use performance-enhancing drugs in sport!' Many advertisements use a combination of the two appeals to gain consumer attention, particularly where serious issues need to be communicated.

*Advertising execution* refers to the way an advertising appeal is presented. How you say the message can in some cases become as important as what you are trying to say. Generally there are a number of ways that advertising messages can be presented or executed and some of these are shown in Table 7.1. Organisations can use these as individual styles or in some combination to best achieve their objectives.

One of the execution styles mentioned in Table 7.1 that is often used in sports advertising is testimonial and many sporting celebrities make most of their money from this type of activity. This is where a well-known personality endorses or represents the product in order to encourage others to also support the brand. While this is a great strategy to gain attention and to ensure that the message gets noticed, marketers need to be careful that the power of the celebrity doesn't overshadow the brand and also that the celebrity's values match those of the brand. There are many examples of companies that have had disastrous associations with celebrities. The 'Sport spotlight' highlights some of the things to watch out for when using this form of execution.

**Table 7.1:** Advertising execution styles

| Execution style | Definition |
|---|---|
| Straight sell or factual message | Straightforward presentation of information concerning the product or service. |
| Scientific/technical evidence | Scientific or technical evidence is presented in the ad or there are endorsements from scientific bodies or agencies to support the advertising claims. |
| Demonstration | Illustrates the key advantages of the product or service by showing it in actual use or in some staged situation. |
| Comparison | Directly communicates the brand's particular advantage over competitors. |
| Testimonial | Where a person praises the product or service on the basis of his or her personal experience with it. |
| Slice of life | Based on a problem-solving approach portraying a problem or conflict consumers might face in their daily lives and how the advertiser's product or service can resolve the problem. |
| Animation | Animated scenes such as cartoons, puppets or other types of fictional characters are used. |

| Execution style | Definition |
|---|---|
| Personality symbol | Developing a central character or personality symbol that can deliver the advertising message and with which the product or service can be identified. |
| Fantasy | Popular for emotional appeals, and the product or service is central to the fantasy or escape situation created by the advertiser. |
| Dramatisation | Focus is on a short story where the product or service is the star. Like slice-of-life but more exciting and suspenseful. |
| Humour | Funny situations or statements are used to highlight the benefits of the product or service. |

Adapted from Belch & Belch 2004

## Sport spotlight

### A celebrity ate my brand!

Sports endorsements have been a powerful tool over the years and marketing texts are full of examples of where the values of the celebrity have either deviated from that of the brand or were never aligned in the first place. It is well known that consumer's perceptions of the celebrity will be stronger than those of the brand being endorsed and so a match of the two is essential. When you use a celebrity endorser it means giving part of your brand to someone else and this can be dangerous, but it can also be extremely beneficial.

Take the example of Nike and Michael Jordan. Nike is often said to be the inventor of sports celebrity endorsements and this began with their signing of an unknown young basketballer named Michael Jordan. This relationship ended up very well for all concerned and Nike have gone on to build a successful brand using sports endorsements prolifically, although even Phil Knight (chairman and founder of Nike) admits that the signing of Michael Jordan as a Nike endorser was an example of both genius and luck!

So how can marketers make celebrity endorsements work and what do they need to be careful of? There are 12 key tips that marketers can follow to assist in the planning and selection of celebrity endorsers, and these are shown in Table 7.2. Throughout all of this is the main theme that the brand values of both the celebrity and of the organisation must match and be seen to match by the target consumers. Another important element to remember is that if your marketing strategy hinges on successfully signing a specific sporting celebrity then you probably don't have a very robust or well-constructed strategy. Finally, when considering using a celebrity you need to attempt to achieve brand awareness and not just logo awareness, so all marketing efforts and activities of both the firm and the celebrity need to be focused on this goal.

**Table 7.2:** How to select celebrity endorsers

| | |
|---|---|
| The use of athlete, team or celebrity endorsement should be viewed as a strategic not a tactical decision. | This means that whenever this strategy is considered, it should be part of a larger promotional and marketing plan, rather than just the idea to use a particular athlete at a particular time without consideration of how the other aspects of the promotional plan can be aligned to gain maximum value from the association. |
| Make sure the endorsee DNA and your brand DNA are aligned. | Brand DNA refers to the core values and positioning that make a brand unique and is essentially the building blocks of a brand. A more complete discussion of brand DNA is provided in Chapter 10. |
| Make sure there is a relevant match to your brand promise and that of the celebrity. | Sporting celebrities have their own personal brands and it is essential that any matching with products or services is credible and relevant. |
| Choose a celebrity property where there can be some ownership of any endorsement. | This means that when signing a sporting celebrity, you want to be able to ensure that other products endorsed by them also match your brand values and that you don't end up with a celebrity that loses all credibility by endorsing everything from baby food to telephones. Both parties lose in this scenario. |
| Think 'partnership' rather than just 'endorsement'. | You need to be able to work with your celebrity to achieve both parties' goals. If the celebrity needs funds or equipment to compete perhaps then a mutually beneficial partnership can work. |
| Aim to build both brands – yours and theirs. | The more popular and well known your celebrity's brand the better your brand will fare from the association (assuming the DNA matches, of course!). |
| Understand the risks of putting all your eggs in one basket long-term. | The best relationships in this area have been long-term ones and this means constantly managing both the celebrity brand and your own. If Shane Warne were your celebrity endorser you may have trouble as he is continually struggling to maintain his brand image – this can be a risky option. |
| Be innovative in how endorsements are used. | Many sporting organisations have been very successful by integrating their celebrity relationships into their marketing strategies and not just using sporting celebrities to say good things about their products. Nike, for example, has relationships with elite athletes who are generally at the cutting edge of innovation and therefore provide the highest level of inspiration to Nike's customers (they are also used to test market products and participate in the product development stages). Think 'brand awareness' not just 'logo awareness'. It is important for any organisation to develop good brand awareness – what the logo stands for and what it means – not just recognition. Celebrity endorsers can help achieve this quickly. |
| Performance is more than the last game. | Sporting celebrities are under the spotlight both on and off the field and consumers will continue to associate them with your brand even when they are not appearing in an ad or on the field. Careful management is needed to avoid potential problems in this area. |
| Know who owns the endorsement rights – is it the athlete, the team or the federation or possibly even the media? | This is particularly true when using an athlete who belongs to a well-known team. Is the athlete popular because of the brand image of the team or are they popular in their own right? The case of David Beckham is a good example of this. Will he be just as bankable now that he is no longer with Manchester United? |
| If your brand strategy relies 100 per cent on getting a particular sporting celebrity then you need a new strategy. | Well-known celebrities are expensive and popular and you may not be able to access the people you think you need. It is important to remember where this strategy fits in the larger marketing picture and to have a range of options to achieve your goals. |

Adapted from a presentation made by Mr Carl Grebert, Brand Marketing Director, Nike Australia and New Zealand, 2003, *Australian Marketing Institute*, Premiership Strategies 2003, Sports Marketing and Sponsorship, Melbourne

When implementing advertising strategies, another area that is important for sports marketers to consider is the media planning and strategy development. Because advertising uses mass media it is necessary to briefly overview some important aspects of this part of the process.

## Media planning and strategy

Media planning refers to the decisions involved in delivering the promotional message to a prospective audience using various media as a channel. Essentially the media plan addresses issues of which channel to use (what media or mix of media) and how this media should be scheduled to best achieve the objectives.

The delivery system chosen to send an advertising message is known as the medium and includes broadcast media (radio and TV), print media (newspapers, magazines and so on), direct mail, outdoor advertising and many other forms of support media. The media vehicle is the specific carrier within a medium. For example, *60 Minutes* would be a broadcast media vehicle, the *Financial Review* would be a print media vehicle and so on. The media plan considers all of these options in light of the media objectives that have been decided.

Finally, when media plans are developed, specific decisions about reach (measure of the number of different audience members exposed to the media vehicle) and frequency (the number of times a receiver is exposed to the media vehicle) are important considerations. It is often a challenge for marketers to achieve a balance between these two measures. Each medium has both advantages and disadvantages and Table 7.3 provides a good summary of these.

**Table 7.3:** Media characteristics

| Media | Advantages | Disadvantages |
|---|---|---|
| Television | Mass coverage<br>High reach<br>Combines sight, sound and motion<br>High prestige<br>Low cost per exposure<br>Appealing to senses<br>Attention-getting | Low selectivity<br>Short message life<br>Clutter<br>High absolute cost<br>Fleeting exposure<br>High production costs |
| Radio | Good local acceptance<br>Low cost<br>High frequency<br>Good for hard-to-get audiences<br>Flexible – short lead times<br>Low production costs<br>Well-segmented audiences | Audio only<br>Clutter<br>Low attention-getting<br>Fleeting message<br>Fragmented audience |
| Newspapers | High coverage<br>Good segmentation options<br>Short lead time<br>Timely<br>Reader controls exposure<br>Can incorporate other sales promotional elements<br>High credibility<br>Can use more complicated messages | Short life<br>Clutter<br>Low attention-getting<br>Poor reproduction in some cases<br>Selective reader exposure |
| Magazines | Segmentation potential<br>Quality reproduction<br>High information content<br>Longevity<br>Multiple readers<br>Credibility and prestige | Long lead times needed<br>High production costs<br>Visual only<br>Lack of flexibility<br>May not have guarantee of position |

| Media | Advantages | Disadvantages |
|---|---|---|
| Outdoor | Location specific<br>High repetition<br>Easily noticed<br>Low cost<br>Low message competition | Short exposure time requires short ads<br>Poor images<br>Local restrictions<br>Little audience selectivity<br>Creative limitations |
| Direct mail | High selectivity<br>Reader controls exposure<br>High information content<br>Opportunities for repeat exposure<br>No ad competition<br>Allows personalisation | Relatively high cost per exposure<br>Junk mail image<br>Poor readership<br>Clutter |
| Internet and interactive media | User directed information search<br>Messages can be customised<br>User attention and involvement<br>Can develop interactive relationships<br>Direct selling potential<br>Flexible message platforms<br>Reaches specific market | Clutter<br>Audience characteristics hard to measure<br>Effectiveness hard to measure<br>Limited creative capabilities<br>Technology limitations<br>Limits potential audience<br>Limited reach |

Adapted from Belch & Belch 2004, p.330 and Shank 2003, p.375

While those media mentioned in Table 7.3 are probably the most well-known and popular ones used by marketers in the development of their advertising and media strategies, other support media are also beginning to feature prominently in advertising strategies. The main support media that marketers use for their advertising messages are: out-of-home advertising (things like billboards, transit ads, skywriting, blimps, cab and bus ads and so on), promotional products advertising (such as gifts, T-shirts, prizes, commemorative products, pens etc.), *Yellow Pages*, movie ads, product placements in movies and television shows, in-flight advertising and virtual advertising.

Virtual advertising is very popular in sport right now, offering advertisers the opportunity to seamlessly integrate advertisements into the broadcast of a sporting event and to tailor companies and brands to different geographic and regional audiences all in the one broadcast. Virtual advertising is generally used for ground signage, pitch signage and even scoreboards. First used by the San Francisco Giants baseball team in 1996, virtual advertising is most popular for internationally telecast events allowing local or even regional sponsors to have their product information displayed where relevant. Telecasts of a cricket test between Australia and India for example, can show a billboard or on-field signage with ads for Pepsi to the Indian audience and ads for Coke to the Australian audience while the actual billboard or on-ground signage may not even physically exist at all (Mangla 2003).

This form of advertising is even beginning to branch out into television shows and movies, allowing product placements and messages to be implanted to suit different markets (Burke 1999), and not everyone is happy about it. This type of advertising can be misleading and it is suggested that it may lead to over-saturation and offence, with sporting stars and actors possibly using and/or virtually endorsing products that they did not consent to. So far the Australian Broadcasting Commission is keeping a close eye on the development of this technology and its use in sport in particular.

While advertising is able to access a large number of people simultaneously across a range of geographic and national boundaries, the messages that are sent are impersonal and are easily ignored by the intended audience. A more interactive way of communicating marketing messages to people and of getting their involvement and commitment is to use personal selling. We examine this element next.

# Personal selling

Personal selling involves the selling through person-to-person communication, utilising persuasion and influence. In sports organisations, personal selling is particularly useful for securing corporate sponsorships, season or long-term memberships to clubs, corporate hospitality and even for selling sports products that have largely intangible benefits (such as gym memberships and training programs).

Because personal selling involves interpersonal communications, it has a much lower reach than advertising and tends to also be more expensive per contact. However, in spite of the increased cost, personal selling is the most effective promotional element for products and services that require the development of relationships, demonstration or persuasion. Personal selling opportunities allow the seller to modify and adapt their presentation according to immediate customer feedback, thus allowing a personalised approach and the ability to counter objections and answer questions.

In addition, there is a lack of distraction in a personal selling situation, where the seller and the buyer are engaged in the selling process and committed to listening and processing information from each other. This level of involvement results in a higher level of commitment and increases the chances of a successful outcome for each party. Finally, personal selling can also be a valuable source of research information for an organisation as the discussions about products and services can highlight many product and market opportunities as well as potential problems.

There are however a few disadvantages with personal selling. These tend to be mainly associated with the lack of ability to standardise the messages being delivered and therefore control the interaction between buyer and seller. Conversely this is also a strength of personal selling. Therefore it is also important that comprehensive sales training programs be delivered to ensure a high quality outcome. Because personal selling means dealing with people there is also an increased cost for management of maintaining and developing a sales force, all adding to the costs of this tool.

Like other promotional program elements, personal selling should be used as just one component of an integrated campaign and should rarely, if ever, be used in isolation from the other elements. Advertising, public relations, sales promotions and direct marketing can all help to increase the effectiveness of a personal selling program. Let's examine how sales promotions works next.

# Sales promotion

Sales promotion consists of a variety of short-term promotional activities that offer a direct inducement to make an immediate purchase through the offer of extra value or incentives. Sales promotions can be directed at both end-user consumers and at organisational buyers or sales teams (Belch & Belch 2004; Shank 2003). Therefore sales promotions are distinguished by three key features: (1) they involve an inducement or extra incentive to buy, (2) they are an acceleration tool and therefore have sales targets as an objective, and (3) they can be targeted at different parties in the distribution channel to both end-user consumers and trade members.

Examples of consumer-oriented sales promotions include: samples; coupons; premiums (two-for-the-price-of-one); contests/sweepstakes; refunds/rebates; bonus packs; price-offs; frequency or loyalty programs; and event marketing. In sport, sales promotions are very common with tickets to games often used as prizes for sponsor products (think back to the Coke and 2003 Rugby World Cup example used earlier in this chapter), with premiums such as give-away T-shirts, footballs, hats etc. also being used as well as many other types of consumer-oriented activities.

As the main objective of sales promotion is to increase short-term sales, in end-user consumer marketing this type of promotion is very effective for creating awareness of a new brand or product and generating trials through incentives, for reminding customers of an offer, to move seasonal stock and for winning new customers.

The main objective of sales promotion is to increase short-term sales

When we consider trade-orientated sales promotions, activities such as contests and dealer incentives; trade allowances; point-of-purchase displays; training programs; trade shows and cooperative advertising are common. These sorts of promotions are generally designed to stimulate sales and broaden distribution channels by rewarding the efforts of retailers and other salespeople who are involved in getting the product to the end-user consumer.

There are many examples of companies who have utilised this form of promotion to stimulate their sales team or to encourage new customers. A large insurance company in the United States purchased a corporate box at the athletics stadium for the Atlanta Olympics, which included the opening and closing ceremonies and then proceeded to use these seats to the various events to stimulate sales of their products (by using them as incentives for customers) and to reward insurance agents who recommended their products.

In addition, many retailers are pleased to gain point-of-purchase assistance to help with the movement of product in their stores. Every season there are life-sized figures of sporting personalities or sporting celebrities in bottle-shops around the country, supporting the sales of beverages related to a sporting sponsor. Bundaberg Rum uses the Bundy Bear, as well as various members of the Wallabies rugby team to successfully merchandise its rum based products, while Carlton United Breweries have many different sports sponsorships they use to assist in merchandising various brands in their offering (for example their involvement with Australian cricket).

While sales promotion is a powerful tool to stimulate consumer action, marketers also need to be careful not to overuse it. Continued discounting and inducements can result in the market becoming reluctant to pay full price for products and thus can erode the brand value. Therefore sales promotions are a useful strategic short-term tool, but they should not be used for long-term loyalty development. One promotional tool that is useful for developing long-term brand value is public relations and we will examine it next.

## Public relations

Public relations is defined as a management function that evaluates public attitudes, identifies the policies and procedures of an organisation with the public interest and executes programs of action (and communication) to earn public understanding and acceptance. It is also used to establish and maintain mutually beneficial relationships between organisations and their various publics (Shank 2003; Simon 1980).

Public relations (PR) is often confused with publicity. The difference is that public relations is the management of various activities and processes that communicate with an organisation's publics, and publicity is merely one activity or tool that is used by public relations managers to generate news in the broadcast or print media. The various publics that a sporting organisation needs to consider in the development of a PR campaign have been outlined in Chapter 2 and different approaches need to be considered to meet the information and brand development needs of each group.

In sporting organisations, PR is extensively used as a brand development tool, but it is also increasingly used to defend and counter potentially negative incidents that can damage both the sports brand and that of specific sports celebrities. Australian cricket, and international cricket, have had their fair share of issues with match fixing allegations, drug taking and unethical play (sledging and accusations of racism). These organisations have attempted through their communications and media releases to inform the public about the facts, to outline the courses of action taken (or proposed) and to follow-up with stories about what they are now doing to prevent these incidents from recurring. These types of PR functions are very common in all sports and quick and decisive action is essential for protection of the sports brand image.

In summary, the functions of PR can be to: build marketplace excitement or interest; to create news about products and services; to introduce product or service information; to add value to customer service; to build brand loyalty; and to defend a brand or corporate image. Public relations activities extend to the maintenance of the corporate image in all media and with consumers becoming increasingly technologically focused, the electronic communication media are also important for sporting organisations. The issues involved with the use of Internet and interactive media in the promotional program will be briefly examined next.

## The Internet and interactive media

The Internet began as a US defence department project and has now broadened to be a worldwide means of exchanging information and communication. The most well-known feature of the Internet is the World Wide Web (WWW). Other features include email, Telnet (online databases and library catalogues), search engines and file transfer protocols. While Internet use has grown rapidly around the world, Australia has one of the highest penetration rates of Internet usage (ABS 2003).

Most Internet activities involve the use of a website, which can be as static as an electronic brochure or as interactive as a totally integrated e-commerce destination. The more interactive and exciting a website is, the more chances there are for repeat visitation. One of the main advantages of the Internet as a medium for communication is that it allows considerable creativity and flexibility because it is essentially a combination of different media. That is: it allows communication both to and from customers; it allows for direct response; it allows sales of products and services independent of a physical presence; and it allows organisations to collect certain information about their audience's preferences, information needs and attitudes.

In addition, use of the Internet allows organisations to customise the offering to their audiences and to directly target interested people. The F2 network (www.f2.com.au) allows people to register and then receive news and sport updates and information specifically targeted to their needs and interests. Basketball fans can register their interest and the teams they follow and then information about them, game scores, game results and related information will automatically be sent to them.

This ability to target and tailor the messages also allows communities to be developed. Cyber communities are groups of people with similar interests who share discussions and interaction online. Companies attempt to increase the level of interaction like this where possible as it increases audience involvement and also increases the chances of repeat visitation.

The official website of the Australian Football League is a good example of this interactivity (www.afl.com.au). There are places for children and adults, men and women, and even opportunities to buy products and services online (e-commerce). If you visit this site and look in the Kids Zone you will also note that the AFL have created an interactive game for children with characters based on all the club mascots in an attempt to build loyalty and involvement with both the site and with the brand.

While using the Internet and interactive marketing can greatly enhance a promotional strategy, there are some problems that sports marketers need to be aware of. The first is in the area of measurement. One of the greatest disadvantages is the unreliability and lack of rigour of customer research in this area. As with television viewer ratings (which just measure if the particular show is on or off in a house), many measurements claiming to measure website effectiveness just count whether someone has opened the site, not whether they have processed the messages on it, nor made any positive attitudinal changes based on it. Marketers need to be cautious when interpreting the success of figures such as these.

Another issue that sports marketers need to consider are the technological limitations that can hinder the speed of access of a site or that may limit a potential customer's ability to process the information on that site. Long download times and complicated sites that are hard to navigate will turn audiences off – in some cases for good. Similarly, in Australia, fast and reliable Internet access is still largely confined to metropolitan populations so using this form of promotion without support from other more traditional elements may limit the potential market that can be accessed.

Finally, the amount of information available on the Internet can be enormous and there are many organisations both domestically and internationally advertising and attempting to gain customer attention using this medium. This results in a significant clutter problem and makes getting attention quite a challenge. Use of the Internet in a well-designed promotional campaign is the first step for many sporting organisations when attempting to internationalise their sport. The Internet makes worldwide audiences available, but a clear strategy in this area is also needed. Chapter 11 will address this issue of internationalisation further.

The Internet has also revolutionised how audiences consider sporting information. During the 1996 Atlanta Olympics the national television broadcasts of events in the United States were poorly watched and television networks and their advertising sponsors were very unhappy with the results. It seems that the up-to-the-minute reports, scores and webcasts available from the Internet were far more popular with audiences who wanted to see what they wanted and when it happened rather than having to wait for the homogenised, delayed television broadcast that may only show highlights of their favourite sport. Many international sporting events now offer their audiences live web updates, SMS text messaging of results and scoring opportunities as well as access to game statistics and merchandise sales all from the comfort of their home or work computer or mobile phone and in real-time.

Other interactive media that also need to be considered in the sports context are interactive television and SMS text messaging. Interactive television or iTV allows the viewer of a program to interact with the program and/or the ads. Viewers of football games are able to view aspects of the game from different angles by choosing their preferred camera shots, to see the probability of various plays and game plans, to bet on various aspects of the game (successful kicks, tries made, tackles missed and so on), and even to see what might have happened if substitute players had been included based on a computer store of player statistics.

SMS messaging is already being used extensively in sporting applications as a way of increasing audience involvement in both the game and in sport generally. Audiences can SMS man-of-the-match votes, enter competitions while playing, get game statistics downloaded onto their phones and take pictures and, in the future, will be able to place bets and make purchases all from their mobile phones.

Use of the Internet and other interactive media expand the opportunities for sports marketers to stimulate customers to take advantage of purchase offers and to respond in some way to marketing offers and communications. Let's now look in more detail at how direct marketing actually works.

# Direct marketing

Direct marketing is a system of marketing by which organisations communicate directly with target consumers to generate a response or to stimulate a transaction (Semenik 2002). This contact can take place through telephone, through the mail, through the mass media (television or radio or print ads), through the Internet or through other interactive media. In all cases the direct contact needs to have a 'call to action' which is the incentive to respond to the offer being made, and a contact number or response option for the customer to take.

Many people confuse direct marketing with direct mail, when in fact mail contact is just one form of direct marketing. Direct marketing is essentially interactive marketing, as the aim is to develop an ongoing dialogue with the customer and to generate some form of market-related response. Like sales promotion, direct marketing can be used to stimulate short-term sales but unlike sales promotions, it can also be used to inform customers of offers that are likely to appeal to them directly. It can also be used to develop long-term relationships with customers.

Direct marketing relies on accessing some form of database of customer information generally with more details about the customer than just their contact information. Most direct marketing campaigns are narrowly targeted to specific audiences with specific offers so a reasonable amount of information is needed about purchase preferences, purchase histories and interests.

Many sporting organisations use direct marketing as a means of maintaining contact with their customers and to make offers for future purchases that can be tailored directly to the different types of audience. Most sporting clubs that have memberships will have promotions, special offers and merchandise opportunities that can be tailored and offered to different customers through direct marketing avenues.

Some of the problems with using direct marketing lie with the need to have well-maintained and accurate databases. In addition, in Australia, the National Privacy Principles considerably restrict who can access private databases and how the information in them can be used. Further, unless the direct marketing efforts are well targeted and personalised, the audience can dismiss the offers as advertising or as having no direct relevance to them. So a targeted and personalised approach is essential for high success rates.

The last element of the sports promotional mix that needs to be discussed is sponsorship. This element is a very useful and powerful tool for use in sports marketing programs and although it incorporates aspects of advertising, public relations and sales promotion, it is also sufficiently important to be considered as an element in its own right in the sports context.

# Sponsorship

Sponsorship, after advertising, is probably the promotional method most commonly associated with sport. It can be defined as investing in a sport identity to support an organisation's objectives, marketing goals and promotional strategies (Shank 2003). This investment can take the form of money or trade (Nike supplying shoes for a team) and the sport identity can be an individual athlete, a team, a league or a specific competition or an event.

There has been much discussion about sponsorship over the years with a gradual move by sponsoring organisations to a more strategic and structured investment decision process. In days of old, many organisations sponsored sporting events or teams that individuals within the organisation supported and there was only token effort made to measure the effectiveness or return of that investment. Increased corporate competition, pressure from shareholders and increased accountability have meant that sports sponsorship is becoming more rational and more strategic in its application. This of course also means that it is becoming harder for sports to find key sponsors without a clear understanding of the benefits that can flow and without the ability to measure the return.

Sponsorship is a growth area in sport globally with approximately 1.6 billion dollars being spent in Australia and approximately $9 billion being spent globally in 2003 (IEG 2003). Worldwide the average sports deal is worth about $2 million, with soccer and Formula 1 being the most attractive sports for sponsors (*Sunday Times* 2004).

In Australia, Sponsorship Solutions Group Account Director Craig Dodson commented that, 'the market for top end sports sponsorship opportunities in Australia is going from strength to strength with the total value of the opportunities in the Sponsorship Solutions Top 40 rising by 9.8 per cent in the last 12 months'.

In 2003, the Australian Tennis Open retained its position as Australia's most valuable sports sponsorship opportunity with Sponsorship Solutions valuing it at $9.8 million. Ian Thorpe retained his number one position in the Sponsorship Solutions Top 40 with a value of $480 000, however Dodson stated that, 'the competition was fierce with Lleyton Hewitt and Mark Webber significantly increasing their value in the last 12 months'. Alisa Camplin recorded the biggest increase of any athlete from the previous year's report, rising 14 positions to now be number 13 in the Top 40 which Dodson attributed to, 'an outstanding year of results that helped to raise her profile'. The 12 months has seen Shane Warne's marketing value fall and as a result he no longer holds a position in the Sponsorship Solutions Top 40 (Sponsorship Solutions 2003). A summary of these findings is provided in Tables 7.4 and 7.5.

The Australian Tennis Open is Australia's most valuable sports sponsorship opportunity

**Table 7.4:** The top 10 sport opportunities in the 2003 Sponsorship Solutions Top 40

| Opportunity | 2003 rank | 2002 rank | Change rank | 2003 $value | 2002 $value | Change $value |
|---|---|---|---|---|---|---|
| Australian Tennis Open major sponsor | 1 | 1 | 0 | 9.80 million | 9.25 million | +550 000 |
| Australian Grand Prix naming right sponsor | 2 | 2 | 0 | 9.00 million | 8.50 million | +500 000 |
| AFL premier partner | 3 | 3 | 0 | 8.00 million | 7.75 million | +250 000 |
| NRL major sponsor | 4 | 4 | 0 | 6.80 million | 6.50 million | +300 000 |
| Wallabies naming right sponsor | 5 | 5 | 0 | 6.10 million | 5.75 million | +350 000 |
| Melbourne Cup naming right sponsor | 6 | 6 | 0 | 5.80 million | 5.50 million | +300 000 |
| World Rugby Cup worldwide partner | 7 | n/e | n/e | 5.00 million | n/e | n/e |
| VB Series (one-day cricket) naming right sponsor | 8 | 7 | -1 | 4.75 million | 4.50 million | +250 000 |
| 3 Series (test cricket) naming right sponsor | 9 | 8 | -1 | 4.60 million | 4.25 million | +350 000 |
| Australian Tennis Open associate sponsor | 10 | 9 | -1 | 4.10 million | 3.85 million | +250 000 |

Source: Sponsorship Solutions 2003

**Table 7.5:** The top 10 athlete opportunities in the 2003 Sponsorship Solutions Top 40

| Athlete | 2003 rank | 2002 rank | Change rank | 2003 $value | 2002 $value | Change $value |
|---|---|---|---|---|---|---|
| Ian Thorpe | 1 | 1 | 0 | 480 000 | 450 000 | +30 000 |
| Lleyton Hewitt | 2 | 5 | +3 | 430 000 | 375 000 | +55 000 |
| Pat Rafter | 3 | 2 | -1 | 400 000 | 425 000 | -25 000 |
| Cathy Freeman | 4 | 4 | 0 | 395 000 | 385 000 | +10 000 |
| Mark Webber | 5 | 8 | +3 | 370 000 | 300 000 | +70 000 |
| Greg Norman | 6 | 3 | -3 | 365 000 | 400 000 | -35 000 |
| Adam Gilchrist | 7 | 6 | -1 | 340 000 | 325 000 | +15 000 |
| Steve Waugh | 8 | 7 | -1 | 320 000 | 300 000 | +20 000 |
| Karrie Webb | 9 | 9 | 0 | 290 000 | 275 000 | +15 000 |
| Grant Hackett | 10 | 14 | +4 | 210 000 | 170 000 | +40 000 |

Please note – n/e stands for new entrant

Source: Sponsorship Solutions 2003

With 62 per cent of Australians saying that sponsorship increases their interest in using sponsors' goods and services, it would therefore seem that sports sponsorship would be an important tool for many companies to use in their marketing campaigns. There are however some cautions for sports marketers to consider.

Corporate investors must first understand that sponsorship is not a charity and it is not advertising (Plaskitt 2003c). Sponsorship can do things that advertising can't and often good sponsorship programs use a combination of other media and tools to support them, not just advertising. The discussion about the brand DNA and that of the athlete or team to be sponsored that was presented earlier in this chapter also needs to be considered when looking at the use of sponsorship and both the investor and the sport should have the same value set.

In an example of matching brand DNAs, one might question how Simpson (manufacturer of household appliances) and the AFL could be a good match. The answer, from the chairman of the AFL, was that both companies held similar values. It seems that Simpson didn't see itself solely as a manufacturer of appliances. Rather it viewed itself as a company that made appliances that would allow families to spend more time together. The AFL too, was targeting families and promoting the football as a family outing. So naturally the two companies saw many similarities with their brand image. Both were Australian, both targeted families, both recognised that family time was largely dictated by the ability to get other chores done efficiently, and both had large female audiences. So in this case an association through sponsorship was a good choice for both companies.

Sports sponsorship allows marketers to use emotion and to contact customers like no other element. Sport is also a great way of targeting the youth market and other traditionally hard-to-get groups (such as busy corporate executives who don't traditionally watch television or listen to the radio), but it has to be done in a way that is credible and smart.

In spite of its benefits, measurement of sponsorship has always been an issue and there is no doubt that corporate sponsors are becoming more selective in the properties that they invest in. Boardroom accountability is also beginning to scrutinise the total value of sponsorship investments made and attempting to come to terms with how to value this form of marketing expenditure.

While the way sponsorship is being conducted within Australia is continually evolving, big picture events are still being run, naming rights are still being signed, causes are still being supported, and partnerships across all levels of sponsorship are still being established and renewed. Marketers need to ask a number of questions about their sponsorship such as: How visible was the sponsorship? Did anyone notice it? Did it change the perception of the brand in any way? Is our brand image visible? Did we sell more products as a result of our sponsorship? And should the sponsorship be renewed? (Plaskitt 2003b).

In spite of the call for more professionalism and measurement standards, more than 50 per cent of recent Australian companies interviewed about sports sponsorship did not undertake any formal measurement of this investment. Most sponsorship decisions are made by CEOs and those who have invested in stadium signage as part of their sports investment are not convinced that the investment has been worthwhile (Sponsorship Insights 2003).

While sponsorship can assist in achieving many different communication objectives, the most common objectives linked to it are: awareness; changing or reinforcing brand image; increasing loyalty; employee motivation; and finally sales stimulation. How then can both investors and sporting organisations gain benefits from sponsorship? The key is to ensure that there is sufficient value added to the sponsorship relationship.

## Adding value to sponsorship

The key to successful long-term relationships between sporting organisations or athletes and corporations depends on recognition of mutual benefits, of protecting each other's rights and brand image and restricting the number of investors so that all have meaningful returns. Australian Cricket specifically restricts the number of sponsors to about five in order to ensure they can manage each partnership well and to integrate the activities of both groups to achieve maximum advantage.

Nike suggests that successful partnerships (note the word partnerships is used and not sponsorships) evolve from management of the relationship trinity (see Figure 7.4). This trinity shows that the objectives and values of the sport or athlete, the investor's brand and any other third parties like agents need to be considered and it is in the area of overlap that the greatest gains can be achieved.

**Figure 7.4:** The relationship trinity

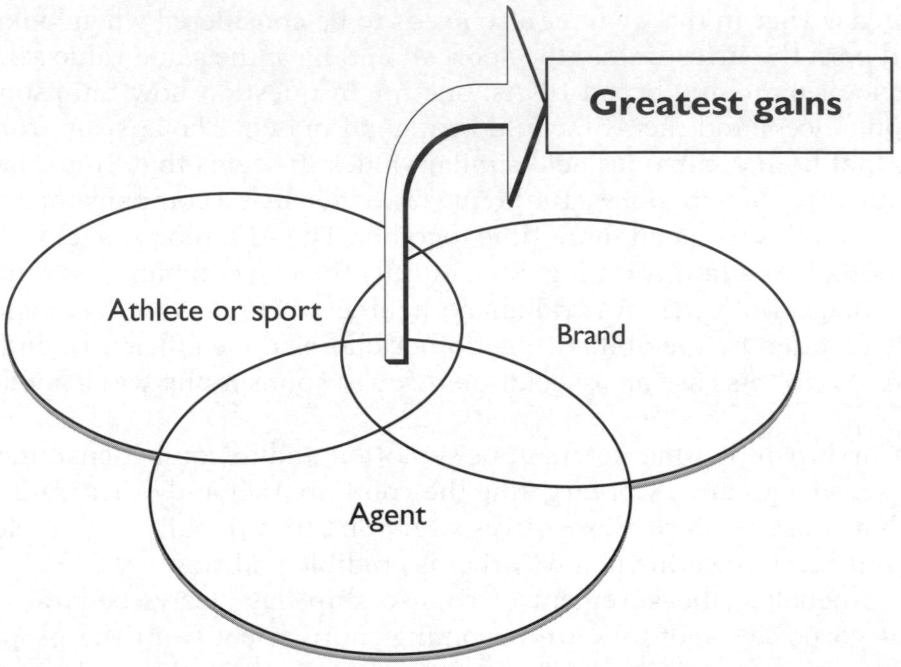


# Ambush marketing

One area where sponsors of major sporting events need to be careful is with ambush marketing. Specifically ambush marketing is where a business markets its goods or services in such a way that it could reasonably be suggested that they have a connection with a particular sporting event or team. Sponsors of large international events like the Olympics and the Rugby and Soccer World Cups invest millions of dollars in their involvement with these events and it is therefore important that their investment is protected. At the 2003 Rugby World Cup in Australia corporate sponsors (there were only 10 official sponsors) each paid close to $5 million for their investment, and unofficial organisations such as travel companies, corporate hospitality events, merchandise and signage were all targeted by the IRB (International Rugby Board) in an attempt to protect the brand equity of both the World Cup and its partners (Sinclair 2003).

Ambush marketers attempt to avoid the high upfront costs involved in sponsorship of these events and yet they see significant advantages of being associated with the emotion and often high levels of spending that occur. Many large event organisers conduct research during these events to measure the effectiveness of their official sponsors and to gauge the impact of any ambush activities. Asking people to recall sponsors and their products is one way to achieve this. Probably one of the most famous ambush cases was at the 1996 Atlanta Olympics when Nike (not an official sponsor) purchased large billboards and sides of buildings around the official Olympic stadium to advertise their products, which were seen to be part of the Olympics just through their physical association with the Games.

Now that we have discussed more about each of the promotional mix elements available to sports marketers, there is a need to consider how they best fit together to develop a promotional plan. Table 7.6 summarises the strengths and weaknesses of the promotional elements just discussed for easy reference.

**Table 7.6:** Strengths and weaknesses of the promotional mix elements

| Element | Strengths | Weaknesses |
|---|---|---|
| Advertising | Creates awareness<br>Informs a large audience<br>Low cost per exposure | Is intrusive<br>Expensive to produce<br>Suffers from clutter<br>Impersonal and therefore not persuasive<br>Not seen as credible |
| Personal selling | Personalised and allows for customisation of the message<br>Most persuasive tool<br>Good for complex products or products that need demonstration and explanation<br>Can develop relationships | Most expensive form of promotion<br>Can be intrusive for customers<br>Has other management problems associated with dealing with people |
| Sales promotion | Stimulates immediate response<br>Can create value<br>Good for creating awareness and product trial<br>Creates excitement and interest<br>Good for trade promotions | Can add to clutter<br>Can erode brand equity if overused<br>Has only a short-term benefit |
| Public relations | Can create goodwill<br>Can place messages in the media in a more credible fashion than advertising<br>Can add value to brand image<br>Communicates with a range of publics | Hard to measure effectiveness<br>Little control over placement in mass media<br>No direct short-term benefits |
| Internet and interactive marketing | Allows interactivity<br>Good for stimulating product trial<br>Can be flexible<br>Allows specific targeting and message tailoring<br>Allows access to additional support information to enhance consumer buying processes<br>Highly creative | Can be hard to create a strong brand image<br>Hard to measure effectiveness<br>Can be hampered by technological limitations<br>Clutter<br>Can restrict potential audience (must have a computer with Internet access – poor mass market reach)<br>Privacy issues |
| Direct marketing | Can be highly targeted<br>Excellent for reaching niche audiences<br>Can customise and create one-on-one communication<br>Offers means for customer feedback | Effectiveness depends on accuracy of database<br>Not always seen as credible and can be discarded<br>Expensive to large audiences |
| Sponsorship | Can be highly targeted<br>Creates a high level of participation and involvement<br>Can contribute to corporate image<br>Creates news opportunities<br>Can be used to motivate sales team, customers and channel members | High wastage as all audience is not relevant<br>Has short message life if a one-off event<br>Can have high cost if not strategically integrated into total IMC<br>Difficult to manage sporting team or celebrity brand image |

Adapted from Burnett & Moriarty 1998, p.114

# The promotional planning process

The promotional planning process commences, as do most processes, with an articulation of objectives. The question 'What is the marketer trying to achieve and by when?' is generally answered at this stage. Promotional objectives are determined based on overall organisational objectives and an understanding of the target market characteristics.

Once the objectives have been set, the budget needs to be considered, as resource constraints can sometimes result in the need to re-evaluate the objectives. Once the objectives and budget have been determined, then the integrated marketing communications program can be designed where all the promotional mix elements are each considered for their strengths and weaknesses in light of the objectives to be achieved. Once the mix elements have been decided, the various media to be used are considered and media plans, creative strategies and implementation plans are then determined. The last stage in the planning process is to design measurement and evaluation tools that can ultimately determine whether the objectives have been achieved or not. This process is shown in Figure 7.5.

**Figure 7.5:** The promotional planning process

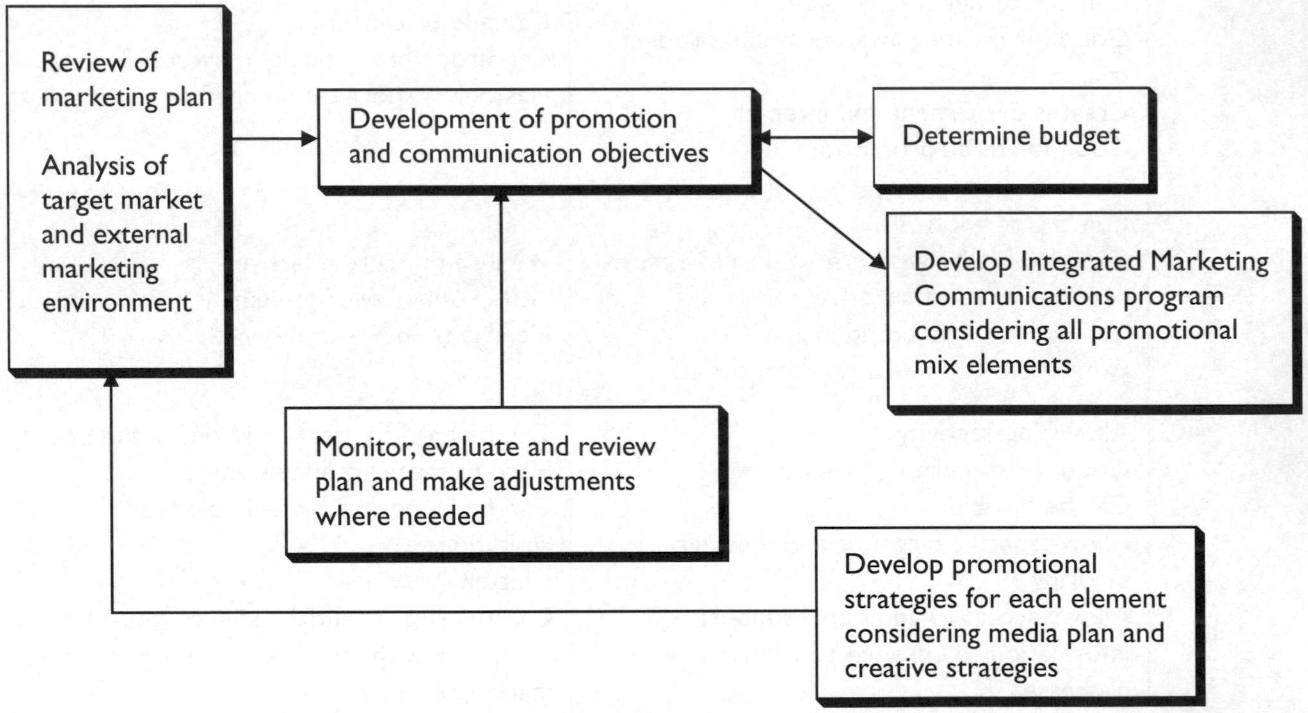


This process is impacted by a range of factors that need to be considered in the planning stages of a promotion campaign. The overall marketing objectives of the organisation determine the specific promotional objectives and these need to be kept in line. In addition, the environment external to the organisation will affect both the development of the promotional objectives as well as the ability to implement them successfully. This includes things like the competitor's activities, technological developments, and changes to rules and scheduling and so forth.

It is also necessary to understand the behaviour of the customers and target audiences to be able to determine which elements will best reach them and how to tailor marketing messages to have maximum impact. In addition the geographic dispersion of the target market will also be an important consideration. A target market that has a large geographic dispersion will need a medium that will have wide reach and be cost-effective. For target markets that are more narrowly defined, marketers can make use of more 'niche' mediums and vehicles to reach their audiences.

One aspect that is generally considered in this developmental stage is whether a push or a pull strategy (or some combination) will impact the promotional methods to be used. When organisations adopt a push strategy they are attempting to move the product into the channels of distribution and to encourage sellers to increase sales. A pull strategy however is focused on end-user consumers and relies on them demanding the product from the re-sellers.

While this promotional planning process seems relatively easy and straightforward it is important that all the available promotional mix elements are well understood and are considered in light of the overall objectives in order for the plan to be successful.

## Counterpoint: When sponsorship goes wrong

So when marketing a sport and considering the promotional aspects, is any publicity good publicity? Probably the management of most rugby league clubs in Australia in 2004 will tell you no, it's not. The reverberations of the sex scandal allegations first from the Canterbury Bulldogs and then from other clubs sent the National Rugby League into crisis-control. A number of team sponsors from the Canterbury team pulled out of their sponsorship contracts for the 2004 season, and there is growing concern from sponsorship experts that the whole league is likely to be hurt by this public furore (Dabkowski 2004). The NRL was hoping to boost its sponsorship revenue by $3 million for the 2005 season. At the time of writing of this book, no further losses of existing sponsors had been experienced, however the expected boost in revenue had been downgraded.

Even more concerning is the fact that many experts feel that this case has highlighted one of the negative aspects of sports sponsorship for corporate investors, the uncontrollable nature of being involved in sport. Sponsors of team sports have always known that it is much more difficult to control the behaviour and attitudes of large numbers of players (upwards of 40 in some codes), but these recent allegations have brought the seedier side of professional sport into the light. Many sponsors also have large female markets and allegations of sexism, poor attitudes towards women, lack of respect for women, binge drinking and boys-only bonding sessions have not helped their future investment considerations.

This of course is not a problem limited to Australian sport. All around the world sponsors of sport are counting the costs of association with characters or teams that have behaved badly. In the USA, allegations of rape against basketball star Kobe Bryant have cost the rising star millions and have forced major sponsors, McDonald's, Nutella, Nike and Coca-Cola to suspend their interest in the player (Dabkowski 2004). In Britain, allegations of gang rape against members of the premier soccer league have alarmed sponsors.

Perhaps the one positive of all this for Australian team sports is that so far the rugby union and soccer codes have remained free of these problems and perhaps they will benefit from sponsors still wanting to be involved in sport, but wanting a safer option. What would be your recommendations about investing in a football team in Australia at present if you were advising your managing director? What cautions would you make and maybe what contract specifications would you suggest to help protect the brand image of your company if things went wrong (Dabkwoski 2003)?

As a postscript to our ominous warning however we should mention that the Canterbury Bulldogs won the 2004 premiership. It appears that the corporate and spectator publics forgave all of the winners ... aahh the power of sport, but oh! the power of winning.

## Summary

- **define promotion and how it relates to communication**
  Promotion is the strategic targeting of an organisation's communication efforts to a range of targeted audiences both internal and external to the firm, and involves the coordination of all seller-initiated efforts to set up channels of information and persuasion in order to sell goods and services or to promote an idea.
- **defend the integrated marketing communications perspective for strategic promotional strategy formulation**
  The IMC approach considers all the aspects of an organisation that communicate with consumers and therefore goes well beyond mass media advertising. Adopting an IMC approach allows an organisation to strategically coordinate all of its activities to ensure a consistent and appropriate message is being communicated to its various stakeholders and that more consideration is being given to total brand value.
- **discuss the elements of the promotions mix including the emerging forms of promotion and highlight their impact on sports promotional strategy**
  The promotions mix traditionally includes four elements: advertising; personal selling; public relations; and sales promotions. However in recent times the increased reliance on and use of direct marketing, interactive marketing and sponsorship have seen these tools included as separate elements of this mix. All elements are used in sports promotional strategies with sponsorship being the one most commonly associated with sport.
- **debate the advantages and disadvantages of the various promotional elements for incorporation in a sports marketing plan**
  See Table 7.2 for a list of the strengths and weaknesses of the various promotional elements. Essentially those elements that have interpersonal contact with the customer are more expensive per customer contact than non-personal methods, but they are more persuasive and are better for more complex or high-involvement products. Those elements (such as advertising) that are non-personal and are inexpensive per customer contact, reach many people but are really best for creative general awareness or gaining customer attention. The best IMC strategies include a balanced mix of these elements.
- **discuss the process for developing a strategic promotional plan**
  The promotional planning process commences, as do most processes, with an articulation of objectives, followed by a review of the budgetary constraints, then integration of an IMC program is designed including the development of media plans, creative strategies and implementation plans. Finally the last stage of the process is to design measurement and evaluation tools that can ultimately determine whether you have achieved your objectives or not.

## Review questions

1. What is meant by the term Integrated Marketing Communications?
2. What is promotion and how is it different to the promotions mix?
3. What are the elements of the sports promotions mix?
4. Which element of the sports promotion mix would you use if you wanted to stimulate interactivity with your target audience?
5. What is meant by the creative process?

6. When would it be best to use personal selling as part of your promotional plan?
7. What are some of the issues that you need to consider when using a celebrity endorser?
8. Why is sports sponsorship so popular?
9. How can you create added value with sports sponsorship?

## Applied activities

1. Visit www.afl.com.au and comment on the mix of promotional elements that have been used in this site. What do you think are the promotional and communication objectives that are being satisfied by this site?
2. If a local sporting club approached you for some guidance in the development of their promotional plan, what would you suggest would be the best place for them to start and what plan of action would you recommend?
3. A family friend who owns a small power-tool retail business has mentioned to you that they are thinking of sponsoring the local cricket team. What would you advise them and what process would you suggest for them to assist with their decision?

## References

ABS 2003, www.abs.gov.au, viewed 1 February 2004, p.35.

Belch, G. & Belch, M. 2004, *Advertising and Promotion: An Integrated Marketing Communications Perspective*, McGraw Hill, Boston.

Bergman, M. 2003, *When a Fad Ends: An Agent-Based Model of Imitative Behavior*, http://www.uh.edu/margo/paper.pdf, viewed September 2003.

Burke, D. 1999, 'Seeing is Believing: Virtual Advertising Hits the Footie Pitch', *SchNews* Issue 237, Friday 19 November, www.Urban75.org/archieve/news092.html.

Burnett, J. & Moriarty, S. 1998, *Introduction to Marketing Communications*, Prentice Hall, New Jersey.

Cravens, D.W. 1994, *Strategic Marketing*, 4th edn, Irwin, p.5.

Dabkowski, S. 2003, 'The Market Says Who's Who in a World of Spin', *The Age*, 16 July.

Dabkowski, S. 2004, 'Off-Field Scandals Threaten Sponsorships', *The Age*, 6 March.

IEG Sponsorship report 2003, www.sponsorship.com.

Kotler, P., Adam, S., Brown, L. & Armstrong, G. 2003, *Principles of Marketing*, 2nd edn, Prentice Hall, Sydney.

Mangla, A. 2003, 'Virtual Advertising', *PC Quest*, Tuesday 15 March, www.pcquest.com/content/cricket/103030402.asp.

Pitts, B. & Stotlar, D. 1996, *Fundamentals of Sport Marketing*, Fitness Information Technology Inc., Morgantown.

Plaskitt, S. 2003a, 'Coke Brand Bubbles Up', *B and T Weekly*, 26 September, p.1.

___ 2003b, 'Centisible sponsorship', *B and T Weekly*, 26 September, p.20.

___ 2003c, 'The Science of Sport Marketing', *B and T Weekly*, 26 September, p.18.

Ray, M.L. 1982, *Advertising and Communication Management*, Prentice Hall, Englewood Cliffs, NJ.

Semenik, R.J. 2002, *Promotion and Integrated Marketing Communications*, Southwestern Canada, p.9.
Shank, M. 2003, *Sports Marketing: A Strategic Approach*, 2nd edn, Prentice-Hall, New Jersey.
Shilbury, D., Quick, S. & Westerbreek, H. 1998, *Strategic Sport Marketing*, Allen & Unwin.
Simon, R. 1980, *Public Relations Concept and Practices*, 2nd edn, Grid Publishing, Columbus OH.
Sinclair, L. 2003, 'RWC Outflanks the Ambushers', *B and T Marketing and Media*, 13 November, p.47.
Sponsorship Insights 2003, www.sponsorshipinsights.com.au, viewed 10 October 2003.
Sponsorship Solutions 2003, www.sponsorshipsolutions.com.au, viewed 3 March 2004.
*Sunday Times* 2004, http://www.suntimes.co.za/2002/03/24/business/news/news04.asp, viewed 7 July 2004.
Webb Young, J. 1975, *A Technique for Producing Ideas*, 3rd edn, Chicago Crain Books, p.42.
www.daviscup.com/news/newsarticle.asp?id=12598.
www.macromedia.com/resources/techniques/resources/define/creative_brief.rtf.
www.zdnet.com.au/newstech/ebusiness/story/0,2000048590,20280239,00.htm.

# Chapter 8

# The pricing and distribution of sport

## Learning objectives

After reading the chapter you should be able to:

- explain the relationship between price, value and other psychological benefits
- explain how a sporting organisation should strategically determine their prices
- discuss the relationship between strategic pricing and the other marketing mix elements
- discuss the impact of supply, demand and price sensitivity on pricing strategies
- identify how external factors affect strategic pricing
- identify the various channels of distribution relevant in a sports marketing context
- discuss the core distribution concepts relevant to strategic marketing decision-making in sport
- identify the major issues inherent in sports facility management and how these impact sports marketing decision-making
- discuss the role of media in distribution of sport to its publics.

## Scene setter

### Are we paying through the nose for sport?

There has been much written lately in the popular press both here in Australia and internationally (particularly in the USA) about the rising cost of attending professional sports and the almost obscene amount of money paid to professional athletes. Fans who do manage to afford ticket prices (sometimes upwards of $26 per ticket) are then faced with $6 beers, $4 cokes, $8 hamburgers and then there's the taxi home or car parking fees on top.

So why is sport becoming so expensive? One suggestion is the increased investment at the professional level in sport by media and the large salaries being paid to sports people. David Beckham is a good case in point – currently he is paid an annual salary of £4.2 million (about $12 million Australian dollars) all before he even kicks a football and then there are his endorsements (about another £18 million per year). Just ask the people who are paying all this money how they feel about it after his disastrous penalty kicks in the recent Euro 2004 Championships that lost England their place in the finals.

Or perhaps consider a 30-second commercial spot at the 2004 American Super Bowl – the annual final game for the pro football season – which cost US$2.25 million (Reid 2004) and the television rights agreement paid by UK television (the BBC) to German giant Kirch to secure coverage of the 2002 and 2006 soccer World Cups – £156 million (£52 million for the 2002 World Cup) and this was considered to be a bargain deal! In addition there are the costs of building and maintaining the stadia themselves that also has to be recouped somehow in ticket prices. With stadia costing hundreds of millions of dollars to build and many thousands of dollars to maintain, someone have to foot the bill.

Is it any wonder that sporting teams and stadium management have to carefully consider their pricing strategies in this complex environment? Delivery of sports product to large audiences can only be done through cooperation of stadia and media, and yet the price of their support eventually has to be passed on to the end consumer. Current trends suggest that consumers may have just about reached saturation point in this area.

Source: Barrnad 2002; Reid 2004

# Introduction

The 'price' of a product is often thought by marketers to be the most important factor influencing customer decisions. However customers actually pay more attention to the 'cost' of an item, which includes not only the actual price, but also less tangible elements. Things like opportunity costs (not being able to do or buy something else if this purchase is made), time costs and frustration and energy costs are also considered by a consumer when they evaluate how much a good or service costs them. In addition, customers also look at the benefits of a purchase to assist them to determine 'value' in their decisions. Thus when sports marketers come to make strategic decisions about pricing, they need to understand that pricing is a complex variable that deals with both tangible factors and intangible psychological factors such as costs and value.

Where a good or service is offered for sale and how difficult it is to obtain are also considered when a customer makes a purchase decision. The distribution strategy used by an organisation can send specific messages to customers about the accessibility and therefore the viability of a particular purchase decision. In sports marketing, distribution decisions include not only service delivery issues, but also stadium and facilities design and management as well as media involvement in delivery of the sports product to the end consumers.

This chapter will begin with a discussion of pricing strategies before moving on to a detailed overview of distribution issues and challenges for sports marketers. We will begin with an explanation of what pricing is followed by a discussion of the factors that affect pricing strategies, before reviewing the pricing process.

# What is price?

As shown in Chapter 2, pricing is both a critical and sensitive issue in many strategic marketing decisions and in sport it is also a complex one. It is part of the exchange process also discussed in this chapter (refer back to Figure 2.4 in Chapter 2 to refresh your memory) and is a way of quantifying the value of objects being exchanged. In sport, the price is generally money that is exchanged for sports products. These sports products can be varied in nature and can include: entertainment experienced by attending a live game; merchandise or sporting equipment purchased at a retail outlet; the opportunity to meet players at a team dinner; or perhaps tuition or coaching in how to play a sport.

No matter what the product, whether it be a tangible good (like a tennis racquet) or an intangible service (like attending a live game), the same basic principles apply. A sound pricing strategy considers the value that the buyer puts on what they buy (Nimmer 1971) and what they are then prepared to pay for that value (Mantanovich 2003). If we accept this approach, then it also makes sense to consider that price does not have to only be restricted to monetary exchange.

### Price versus value

Price can also include exchanges of other things that people value, such as time, effort, attitudes and even items of ownership. For example, volunteers at major sporting events who often assist with ticketing, crowd control and marshalling of athletes exchange their time and effort for free access to that sporting event and the possibility of meeting and mingling with athletes. As Chapter 1 highlighted, the sports industry in most countries has a high proportion of volunteer labour, particularly at the regional and grassroots level of sport. Even children trade sports collector cards with sporting heroes on them, applying the basic principles of exchange by allocating differential value to their cards at the consent of their peers.

Finally, all sporting teams look for, and attempt to foster, loyalty and fan identification with their followers, as these groups of customers are most likely to generate long-term revenue and continued attendance at games. Development of this level of loyalty is a result of an attitude change and motivational drive that impels consumers to prefer a particular team or sport over other sporting and/or leisure pursuits. In this case an exchange of value has occurred (attitudinal loyalty for entertainment and team recognition) without any money changing hands.

Therefore, as mentioned in Chapter 2, the value or perceived benefit of the sports product is generally a combination of both tangible and intangible elements that are interpreted differently by different types of sports consumers. Sports consumers also consider competing demands for their exchange value (money, time, effort, possessions or attitudes) when they are making their consumption decisions. For example, a family considering attending a football game on a weekend might not only consider the total monetary outlay, but also the other costs involved like travel time, anticipated levels of frustration (long queues, traffic congestion, tired and cranky kids), other leisure pursuits forgone to attend (golf games, kids' sporting events, books to be read) and opportunity costs (if we go to this game this weekend, we won't be able to afford to go to anything else for the next three weeks ... is this want we want?).

As such, understanding a consumer's subliminal reaction to the perceived benefits of a sports product, as well as understanding the competing demands on that consumer's time and monetary outlay, need to be well understood by the sports marketer. This becomes even more important when the sports product is a game attendance, because the intangible nature of this form of sports product increases the uncertainty that the outcome (the sports spectating experience) will be of value. When the form of the sports product is tangible (such as the purchase of a sports shoe or an item of sports merchandise) then it is generally easier for customers to determine the value of the exchange. Thus value is generally the result of a mental evaluation of the perceived benefits of the exchange compared to the price (cost) of the exchange (Shank 2003). But how should a sports marketer determine the best way to establish their pricing strategies?

## How to set a price

There are a number of different pricing strategies available to sporting organisations and the strategy chosen will largely depend on the form of the sports product. That is, sporting teams would determine their ticket prices using different criteria than would a sports merchandise retail outlet. Sporting organisations also need to consider the fact that their products are made up of different components (as shown in Chapter 6), the core, the actual and the augmented product, as well as various product extensions. Although the core product may be the main attraction for customers, it is often the product extensions that add the value and that can increase the revenue generation opportunities for sporting organisations.

*Value-based pricing* is a method of pricing products where companies attempt to first determine how much the products are worth to their customers. The goal is to set prices that are neither higher nor lower than customers would be willing to pay (Stedman 2000).

The purchase price of a ticket to a sporting event is based not only on the dollar value of that ticket, but also on the perceived value of the experience and expectations of the performance of the sports players that the person will encounter.

For many sports products a *differential pricing strategy* is common. This is where different prices are charged for different seats, or different benefits are included in the ticket price. For most professional stadium-based sports, the revenue from the ticket prices is less than the revenue expected from media rights and sales. This is not the case for smaller amateur or regional sports that often have to rely on ticket sales as the main source of their revenue. Other pricing strategies include price skimming, price penetration and price neutral strategies. These will be discussed in more detail later in the chapter.

Soccer stars command enormous transfer fees

In addition to pricing of sports products, sporting athletes and even sporting teams have prices. As we saw in the opening scene setter, David Beckham commands a large price in order to play soccer. The team he plays for at the moment (Real Madrid) not only had to pay his salary, but also a £25 million transfer fee to his old club, Manchester United, just to have him on their team. In addition he also gets a £20 000 per week image fee. How did he arrive at these prices? How would his team, Real Madrid, determine the value of this exchange? What happens if Beckham breaks his leg in the opening game of the season and doesn't kick a ball? Have they still made a good investment?

In the USA, basketball and football teams are allocated a franchise value based on how much revenue they are likely to generate from attendances at games, branding and merchandise and media rights. These franchise values are generally worth hundreds of millions of US dollars. Once again the interesting question for sports marketers is how to determine what is good value and how these prices should be set.

So let's look at the strategic pricing process in more detail.

# The strategic pricing process

As with most strategic marketing activity, pricing can be viewed as a process where a number of specific steps or decision points should be considered in order to determine a strategically viable pricing framework. The strategic pricing process is shown in Figure 8.1.

The process should begin with a review of the larger marketing and corporate objectives of the firm. This will ensure that any micro-decisions (such as what is the optimum pricing strategy) are considered in line with these bigger picture goals. Let's look at each of these stages in more detail.

**Figure 8.1:** The strategic pricing process

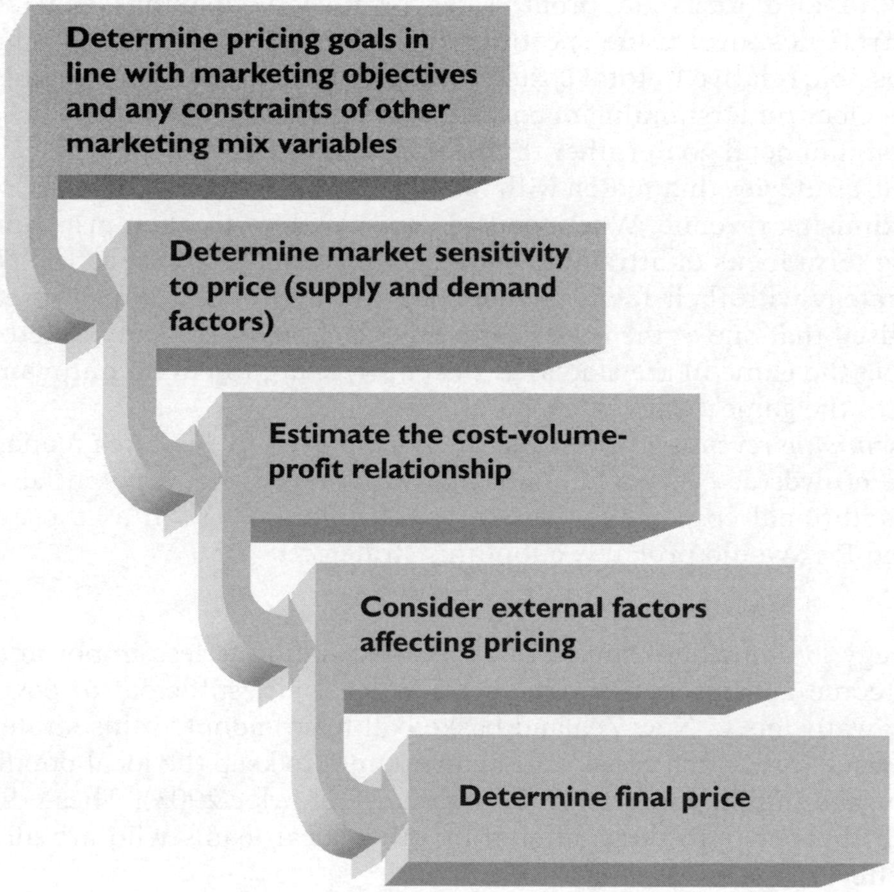


Sources: adapted from Shilbury et al. 1998, p.111; Summers et al. 2003; Kotler et al. 2003

## Determine pricing goals

Pricing goals need to be developed in line with the overall firm's mission and the larger, more general marketing goals. In addition, an intimate understanding of the customers targeted and of the marketplace are also critical in setting realistic pricing goals and objectives. It is also important to remember that pricing has a direct impact on customers' perceptions of the product and therefore on the positioning of the product.

One example of this was during 2003, when the Australian Football League had a much publicised policy that its fans and families would be their number one priority when it came to pricing of game tickets (Rucci 2003b) and particularly finals tickets. However, it was not long into the season when complaints about pricing appeared with comments that politicians, AFL officials and players were making the game elite and pricing attendance out of the reach of the 'ordinary' family (approximately $52 for a single ticket) (*The Advertiser* 2003; Rucci 2003a). Similar comments about elitism, forgetting grassroots support and lack of understanding of the pressures on family finances have also dogged many stadium sports during 2003 in relation to ticket prices (see 'Scene setter'). Thus, it is important that sports marketers not only consider the implications of their cost structures when setting prices, but also the impact of perception and positioning due to pricing.

There are a number of pricing goals or objectives that sports marketers can set in relation to pricing and each should be set in the context of the marketing goals of the firm. Marketing goals in sports organisations generally take the form of either: maximising shareholder value; survival; market-share leadership; product quality leadership; and/or community accessibility. Each will be briefly discussed next.

## Maximising shareholder value

When faced with maximising shareholder value as the overriding marketing goal, pricing strategies need to also focus on profit, sales or revenue maximisation strategies. *Profit maximisation* strategies involve the sporting organisation setting prices so that total revenue is as large as possible relative to total costs. This does not necessarily mean highest prices, but it does involve a clear understanding of costs and profit margins. This type of strategy tends to have a short-term financial goal, rather than a long-term performance or loyalty goal.

Other pricing strategies that match with maximising shareholder value are *maximising sales growth* and maximising revenue. When focusing on sales growth, then prices are usually lower and a more long-term focus of attracting a larger market share is taken. The NBA in Australia adopted this strategy with their focus for the 2003–04 year to 'Get bums on seats' (Nagy 2003, p.89). They realised that one of the issues facing the flagging interest in basketball is the lack of families watching the game in the stadia. 'If ticket prices are too high, mum and dad can't take them [the kids] to the game' (Nagy 2003, p.89).

Finally, *maximising revenue* is often a strategy employed by facilities managers who aim to encourage large crowds as every additional individual represents a potential increase in total revenue at no additional cost to the facility. Event organisers such as those working on the Australian Grand Prix would probably adopt this strategy.

## Survival

A survival strategy is one where survival of the organisation is less important than achieving a profitable outcome and prices are often set at a level just sufficient to cover most variable costs. The Manawatu Jets (a New Zealand basketball team) adopted this strategy in their 2003 season, cutting ticket prices by 38 per cent in an attempt to keep the local population interested in and to encourage families to attend their games (Knowler 2003). These discounted prices are significantly cheaper than those offered by other local teams who are all now waiting to determine the effect of such a strategy.

## Market-share leadership

When adopting this strategy, firms are generally attempting to achieve a specific market share gain in a particular planning period. Generally firms attempt to increase their market share relative to their main competitors and the most obvious method to achieve this is adopting a low-cost pricing strategy. This is also a short-term strategy that can result in price wars and heavy discounting, often bringing down the prices across the industry permanently.

## Product quality leadership

This strategy is used when the firm in question wishes to be known for the highest quality products in the market. This normally means charging a price premium or very high price in order to cover the additional costs involved in delivering products with high quality. Surfboard manufacturer BASE Boards and Surf Equipment Pty Ltd, located on Queensland's Gold Coast, have adopted just this strategy. They are competing in a tough global market for surfboards, where the world's largest manufacturer is based in Thailand, churning out 80 000 boards a year (Stolz 2003). BASE are aiming at specific markets who are looking for hand-crafted surfboards of quality that will certainly cost more than the cheaper Thailand mass-produced products, and will appeal to professional and serious surfers who recognise and are prepared to pay for quality products.

Serious surfers are prepared to pay for quality products

## Community accessibility

This pricing strategy is somewhat unique to sporting organisations and for many not-for-profit organisations, which generally have to ensure that their products are available to a diverse range of community members. When this objective is the focus, prices are set to only partially cover costs. This strategy is similar in application to survival, but is generally implemented for different reasons. Many regional and local community sporting organisations are subsidised by local or state governments in order to make their services more accessible to local community groups. National sports governing bodies also often subsidise their prices for members in order to keep total costs to a minimum and to attract more members.

An example of this type of pricing strategy was in a recent Penrith Panthers rugby league game, where children at 170 public schools throughout the Penrith region of Sydney were given free tickets to a Penrith Panthers game on a Saturday. Children had to be accompanied by an adult, and about 3000 children took up the offer. This had two benefits: first it got a number of children and families into the game that may not otherwise have come – thus increasing the potential for repeat visits; and second many of the schools who took up the offer used the tickets in a raffle or other promotion, thus raising money for the schools in the process and endearing the Panthers club to these communities (*Penrith Press* 2003).

Setting pricing goals therefore needs to be done in the context of the larger organisational and marketing goals and also needs to consider the impact of other marketing mix variables (promotion and distribution being the most common ones affected by pricing strategies). We will examine the impact of the marketing mix variables on pricing next.

## The impact of the various marketing mix variables on pricing strategy

Pricing decisions need to be coordinated with all of the other marketing mix variables. The number of intermediaries in the marketing channel, the promotional objectives and positioning of the product, the product mix and product portfolio are all elements of the marketing mix that are impacted by and can impact upon price. For example a firm that has a large number of resellers (such as a sports shoe manufacturer) may have to build a margin into their final selling price to allow these resellers to sufficiently support the product and promote it. So the price to the reseller may be low in comparison to the final selling price.

As already discussed, prices also are important in the positioning and promotional decisions of the firm. Products with high prices have to have appropriate marketing activity to support them and to communicate the added value to the final customer. Similarly the distribution strategy may be one of exclusivity, thus restricting the availability of the product, and this further supports the higher price.

The firm's total product mix also needs to be considered when setting prices. If all of the firm's products are priced at the low end of the market, it can be difficult for that firm to enter the market with a product having a premium price. The market perceptions of the brand and of the product mix may not support this strategy. Firms who face this problem often create a new brand for which they can create a new image, thus maintaining the integrity of their commercial or cheaper lines and allowing the market to consider the new product based on its value.

In conclusion then, a pricing strategy needs to be well coordinated and supported by the other marketing mix variables, otherwise consumers may be confused and this can in turn impact on the potential demand for the product. The next step in the pricing process is to determine the market sensitivity of customers to the various pricing options – that is the supply and demand factors.

## Determine market sensitivity to price

Market sensitivity is important for determining the final price range. Marketers need to know both the demand for the product and the cost to them of that product as well as the size of the potential market for that product.

Demand is the quantity of a product that will be demanded by the market at various prices for a specified period (Summers et al. 2003). In most cases the higher the price of a product the lower the quantity demanded. This relationship is traditionally shown in the form of a demand curve (see Figure 8.2). This diagram shows that as prices for tickets to a sporting event increase (P1 to P2) then demand for those tickets is likely to decrease (D1 to D2) and vice versa.

**Figure 8.2:** Demand curve for tickets to a sporting event

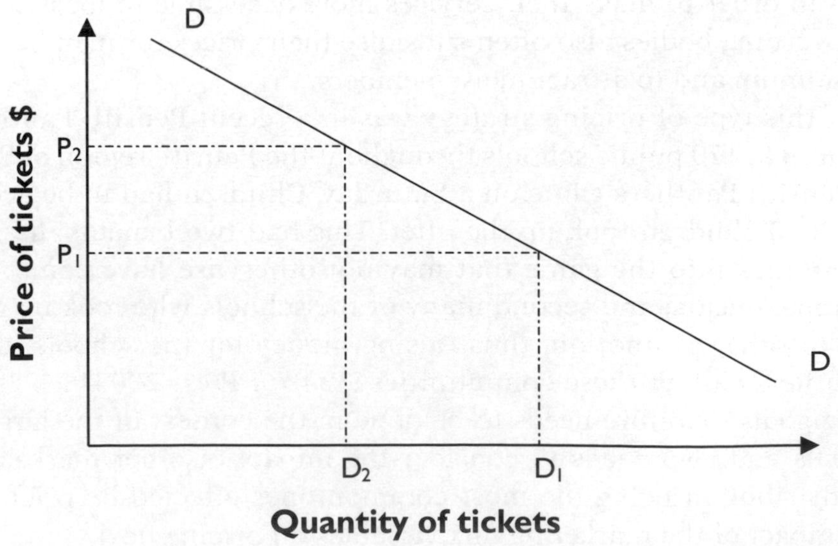

This is exactly what happened to the organisers of the 2003 Rugby World Cup. Prices for most people were far too high and as a result many games were played with partially empty stadia. New Zealand fans were particularly affected by this with ticket prices ranging from NZ$83 to NZ$648 for seats. When these prices were combined with airfares and accommodation total expenditure ranged from NZ$2995 to NZ$10 995 per person for one game. Many of the 75 000 tickets allocated to New Zealand were therefore left unsold (Bell 2003).

Consumers' responsiveness or sensitivity to price changes is known as *elasticity of demand*. When demand for a product is elastic, this means that consumers are very sensitive to changes in price and will demand correspondingly more or less of a product based on the price. When demand for a product is inelastic, then consumers are less sensitive to price fluctuations and will tolerate some level of price increases before adjusting their demand downwards. Figure 8.3 shows these relationships.

**Figure 8.3:** Elastic and inelastic demand

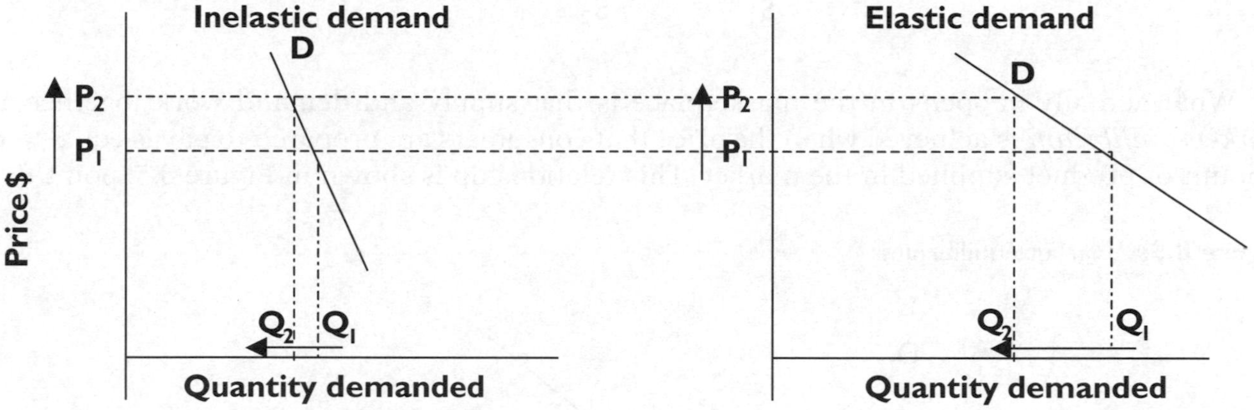


When considering customers' reactions to price changes, sports marketers also need to consider other factors that impact upon demand changes, such as substitute and complementary products. *Substitute products* are those that customers can easily and readily use in place of another product, for example tickets to either a football game or a basketball game. If consumers consider substitute products to be close, they are more likely to engage in switching behaviour and thus be more price sensitive or elastic than if substitutes are not readily available or close. A seasoned soccer fan may not consider watching an AFL game to be a good substitute for their leisure spend and may be less sensitive to increases in ticket prices to attend soccer games than someone who believes the two games are close substitutes.

*Complements* are those products that have to be used in conjunction with each other. For example most sports participation requires the purchase of particular sporting equipment and an increase in the price of equipment (netball shoes) can impact upon the demand for that sport. In addition, sports participation can also involve membership fees like gym memberships and association memberships and changes in prices of these can all impact upon participation rates.

When considering price sensitivity, marketers also need to consider the supply aspects of their product range. *Supply* is the quantity of a product that will be offered to the market by a supplier or suppliers at various prices for a specified period of time (Summers et al. 2003). When products are in demand by consumers and are providing good returns then more firms will be attracted to that market. The higher the price that can be charged for a product (P1 to P2) the more a firm is likely to want to supply that product (S1 to S2). Figure 8.4 shows the relationship between price and supply. Generally as the price that consumers are prepared to pay for sports products decreases, then the supply of them will also decrease, however if prices increase then supply will increase.

**Figure 8.4:** Supply curve for sports products

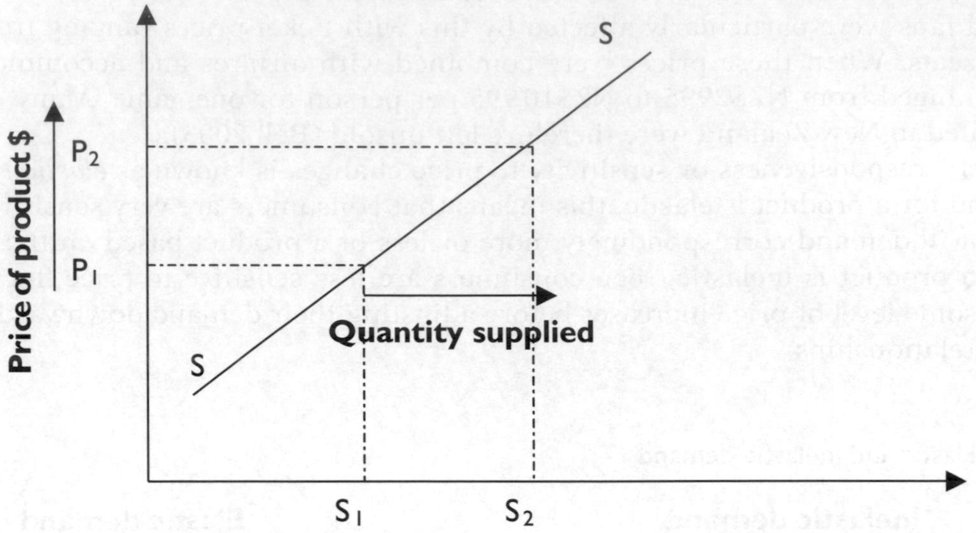


What actually happens in the marketplace is that supply and demand work together and *market equilibrium* is achieved when the price that consumers are prepared to pay is equal to the amount of product supplied in the market. This relationship is shown in Figure 8.5, point E.

**Figure 8.5:** Market equilibrium

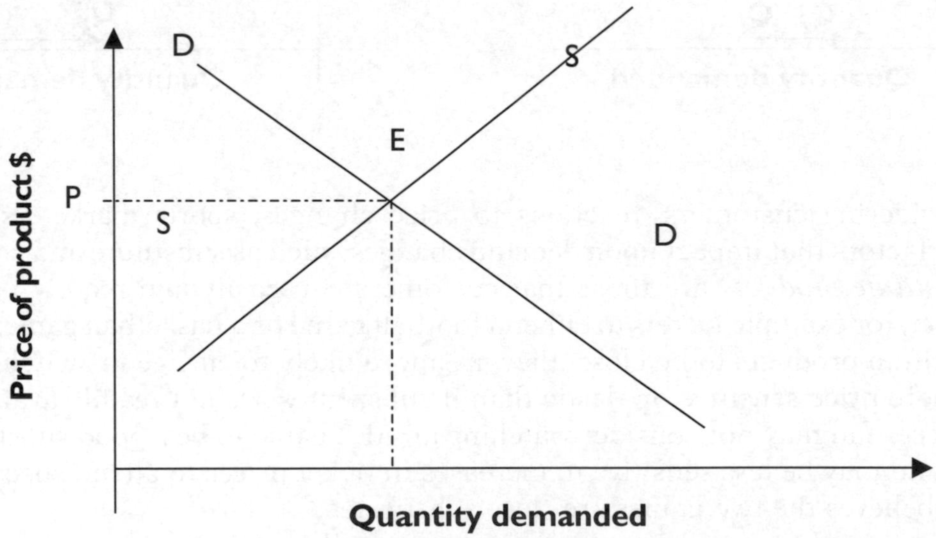


Markets will always try to reach this equilibrium point and a marketer's job is to monitor prices and price sensitivity of the customers to attempt to manipulate the price and the supply of goods and services so that equilibrium is maintained. An artificially high price will result in an oversupply and a lack of demand for products, while a price too low can cause the opposite to occur.

As an example of how supply and demand factors impact on pricing, consider a supplier of 2003 Rugby World Cup supporter's T-shirts (see Figure 8.6). This manufacturer probably had a large supply of T-shirts in the lead-up matches and prior to the start of the World Cup series (S1) and there would have also been a correspondingly high demand (D1) for this product. The price he could charge for the T-shirts at this stage would also have been high (point A) for the market to be in equilibrium. As the World Cup went on and the end of the tournament drew near, any excess stock the supplier had (which would be less than what he started with) would have been in less demand (D2) and therefore in order to reach a point where demand and supply met, the supplier would have had to reduce his price (point B).

**Figure 8.6:** Price and market equilibrium

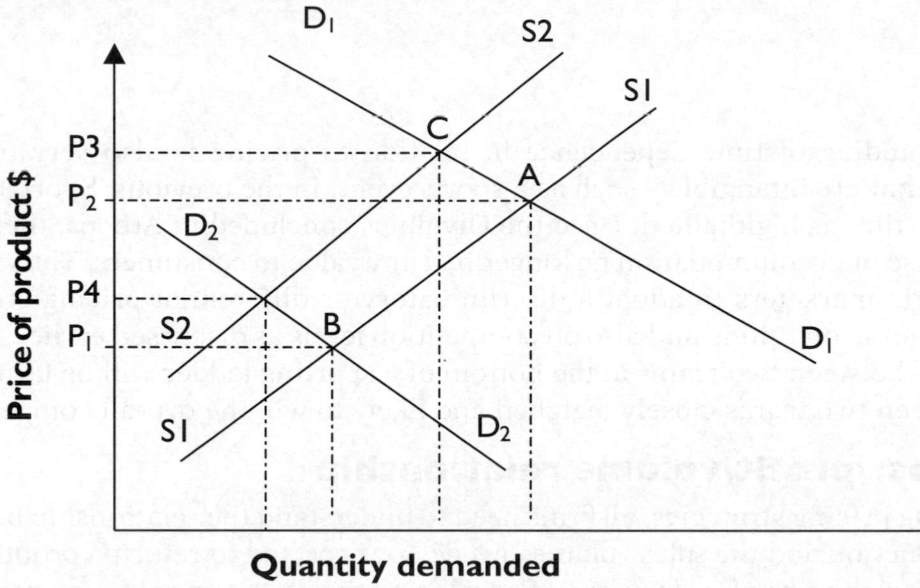


This is a case of demand driving price. Marketers can also impact price through manipulation of supply. Have a look at Figure 8.6 again and imagine what would happen if the supply curve moved up (S2) in relation to D1. This would be the same as a marketer decreasing the supply of a product in high demand. See that the price would also increase in order to achieve equilibrium (P3). Notice that in this scenario that when the demand drops for the T-shirts, the equilibrium price is also higher (P4) than in the first scenario. This is because the original price for the T-shirts (P3) was higher and thus when discounted, the final price was also higher.

Clever sports marketers use their knowledge of the relationships between supply, demand and price to ensure maximum return for their sports products. See the 'Sport spotlight' below about tickets for the Athens Olympics.

## Sport spotlight

### Olympic tickets are hot property

In spite of constant press stories about delays and other logistical problems, organisers of the 2004 Athens Games predicted that tickets would be sold out three weeks after they went on sale. Only three million tickets were available for public sale with a further 2.3 million being provided to sponsors, TV rights holders and other organisations associated with the Olympics. The opening and closing ceremonies were the most popular events with ticket requests four times the number of available seats, and the stadium holds 70 000 people. Other popular sports also had rapid ticket sales. Just over 12 months before the start of the games, organisers already exceeded their marketing targets and ticket sales by about 15 per cent and requests from the international business community and partners and sponsors had already surpassed their 2.3 million allocation. So those who wanted tickets to the Athens Olympics, needed to get in early as a combination of lower prices (20 euros less per ticket than for the Sydney Games) and smaller venues made demand for tickets skyrocket.

> Interestingly, in spite of these claims, there were many comments made about the number of empty seats at the Games during the semi-finals and less popular sports.
>
> Source: Grohmann 2003a, 2003b

This understanding of time dependence in relation to pricing is also very important for sports products that are intangible – such as a sports event. In the previous 'Sport spotlight', the critical nature of time is highlighted. Once the Olympics concluded in Athens, then any unsold seats, merchandise or accommodation no longer had any value to consumers. Thus it is common practice for sports marketers to adopt a discriminatory or differential pricing strategy where prices vary depending on timing and also on competition levels as discussed earlier. For example, tickets for games between two teams at the bottom of a sporting ladder will be far cheaper than for a game between two teams closely matched and likely to win the overall competition.

## Estimate cost/profit/volume relationship

When considering pricing strategies, all firms need to understand the relationship between price, the costs of production and the sales volumes needed or expected to return a profit. This type of analysis is also known as *break even pricing*. Focusing on the costs of production may seem like a logical way to consider pricing strategies; however for marketers of services, there are a number of complications that can make this method less desirable.

When considering costs, marketers need to understand the difference between fixed and variable costs. *Fixed costs* are those that don't change in direct proportion with increases or decreases in production activity. For the marketer of a stadium, the cost of providing that stadium in a clean and ready to operate form for a live game of sport, will be reasonably constant or fixed, regardless of whether 500 people turn up or 50 000 people arrive. The costs of cleaning the stadium afterwards however may vary directly with the number of people who attend. This type of cost is termed a *variable cost*.

When these different types of costs are calculated, they then form the *total costs* of the organisation and they represent the amount of money that needs to be made from the sales of the product in order to break even (total costs = total revenue), assuming a constant fixed cost (see Figure 8.7). When we are dealing with services, calculation of both variable and fixed costs can be quite difficult as it is hard to determine exactly what the costs are, particularly the variable costs. For example, what are the additional costs of an additional person attending a sporting event? What are the additional costs of a person joining a gym? For most sports services, the majority of costs are generally fixed and thus attracting additional revenue becomes a very profitable outcome and the focus of most marketing activity.

## Determine external factors impacting upon pricing

A number of external non-price factors also impact upon pricing in addition to the perceptions and characteristics of the consumer market already discussed. The type of market, the activity of competitors and legal and economic factors also need to be considered. We have already discussed earlier in this chapter the impact of consumer perceptions on value and pricing so now we turn our attention to these other factors.

In relation to competitors, it is important to clarify their pricing strategies to provide a framework for your own organisation's pricing. It is important to consider the price elasticity of the competitor's offer and this can in part be determined by looking at customer loyalty and market share data. Customers who are very brand loyal are more likely to be inelastic when it comes to price than those who are more fickle.

When considering competitors, it is also important to analyse whether you are in the same markets and whether you are targeting the same consumers. For example, a marketer of a sporting

**Figure 8.7:** Break even analysis

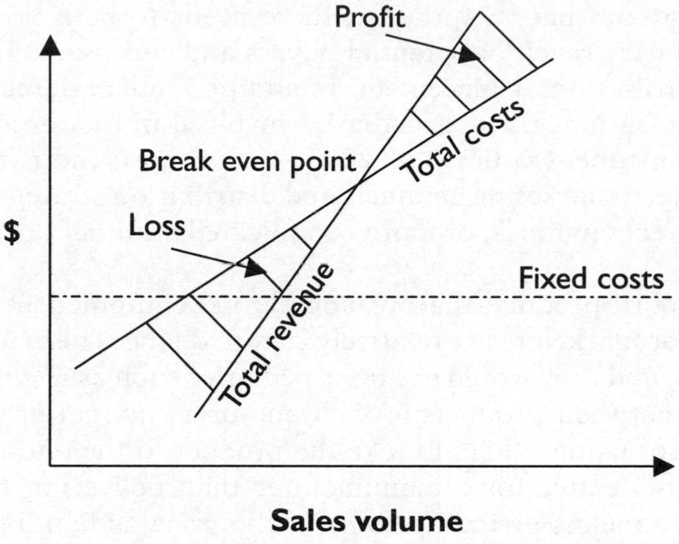


event would need to consider all other competing leisure activities for their target market when undertaking a competitive analysis. Similarly, the manufacturers of golfing equipment might consider that in addition to other manufacturers of golfing merchandise, other types of products such as school fees, holidays and other family expenditure that might be sacrificed in order to purchase a new set of clubs may also be competition.

Legal and economic constraints imposed by governments are also important when determining pricing strategies. Economic factors such as recessions, booms, interest rates and employment statistics all have an impact on how much money consumers have to spend, and in turn will impact demand and pricing of products. Most sporting products are considered as 'non-essential' or leisure products and are therefore generally the first to be dropped when financial constraints tighten.

Finally, the government has legislation to protect both consumers and other organisations from unfair or unethical pricing strategies. The Trade Practices Act clearly outlines what is legal and what is not when it comes to things like collusion (working together with other companies to set prices) and misrepresentation. You should visit the Trade Practices Act website to view how the restrictions apply to pricing: http://tpareview.treasury.gov.au/content/home.asp.

## Determine final price

Having considered all the factors that impact upon price setting, such as the organisation's overall mission, the marketing goals and marketing mix variables, the demand and supply factors, consumer sensitivities to pricing and the impact of external factors, the sports marketer is now ready to set the final price. Generally some combination of factors is considered (usually costs, competition and demand) when setting the final price, however the perceptions of consumers is also a factor that must be given sufficient attention.

As discussed earlier in the chapter, other marketing mix variables also impact on the pricing decision. One important variable is distribution. How readily available a product is and how accessible it is can both regulate and be regulated by pricing strategies. In this modern age, many sporting organisations also need to consider the role of media in making their products accessible to a wider audience and the resulting impact this has on decisions about locations of tournaments and placement of stadiums. Let's examine the issues relating to distribution of sports products in more detail.

# Distribution strategies

In any business, no matter what the product, there needs to be a way to get the product to the marketplace within easy reach of potential buyers and end-users. This process is known in marketing terms as distribution or placement. In addition, a *marketing channel* is the network of interdependent organisations or intermediaries involved in this process of taking a product or service to the final consumer (Kotler et al. 2003). In the sports industry there are a number of different ways of looking at marketing channels and distribution strategies and sports marketers can use both simple, direct channels, or more complicated, indirect ones. We will examine both in detail.

When we consider sports products that are tangible, like equipment and merchandise, then the distribution decisions for marketers are relatively easy to define. There would be a manufacturer producing the products, and they would use intermediaries such as agents, wholesalers, retailers and clearing houses to get their products to their end-users no matter where in the world they might be. This process of using others to take the product to the end-consumer is often more efficient and more cost-effective for a manufacturer than delivering the product themselves, even though it generally means giving up some of the price as handling fees to these various intermediaries.

In addition to simply getting the product to the final consumer, marketing channel members also assist in providing information to both the consumer about the product and to the manufacturer about the consumers. They can also be involved in promotional activity, finding potential customers, financing some of the channel costs and they can also help to spread the risk involved in getting the product to market (Kotler et al. 2003).

So marketing channels and intermediaries assist both the manufacturer in getting their product to a large number of end-user consumers efficiently, and they also assist the final consumer by providing a range of convenient locations for purchase of products and by increasing the potential range of products available to them for purchase. When manufacturers deal directly with end-user consumers this is known as a direct channel and when intermediaries are involved it is known as an *indirect channel*. In addition, some manufacturers use a combination strategy, dealing both directly and indirectly with consumers in an attempt to maximise their exposure to potential customers.

The emergence of the Internet and the World Wide Web has changed the distribution function slightly by making it easier for both consumers and manufacturers to make contact with each other directly without the need for intermediaries. The main disadvantage of this approach for manufacturers is that consumers understand the distribution process and often want the cost savings of by-passing intermediaries passed directly onto them, without considering that the manufacturer now has to set up systems and processes to deal with this direct distribution (e-commerce) that also have increased cost implications.

The sports product, however, is multi-faceted and in many cases has more service characteristics than characteristics of a good, particularly when we are dealing with games and participation as products. In these cases, the distribution decisions are more complex. When considering the game as a sports product, distribution considerations take into account the venue, and ways of delivering the experience of attending the game to those who cannot (or choose not to) come. This is where media becomes a critical intermediary in the sports product marketing channel. We will look at some of these aspects in a little more detail next.

## The sports facility

The sporting facility itself is a very important part of the consumption experience in sport and is one of the more tangible elements of this experience. Well-designed sports stadia can add to the physical and emotional satisfaction of sports spectators and provide a distribution role by facilitating the consumption of the sports event to a large number of people. Telstra Dome in Melbourne, Telstra Stadium in Sydney and Suncorp Stadium in Brisbane are examples of these large, high tech, multi-purpose stadia that need to consider spectator expectations, game

Well-designed sports stadia can add to the satisfaction of sports spectators

performance and support facilities in their management of sports delivery. Stadium marketing and management is actually a whole field of study in its own right and forms part of the 'servicescape' or physical environment of sports consumption.

Consumers develop allegiances and loyalty to stadia as can be seen in the case of the MCG (Melbourne Cricket Ground), SCG (Sydney Cricket Ground) and other such venues where memberships and seating allocations are sold. Stadia can also be part of the myths and legends that surround sporting achievement: 'They've never won on this ground!' or 'Welcome to the Cauldron!' Research has also shown that if consumers are satisfied with a stadium experience, they are more likely to return, which in turn can mean higher ticket sales and crowds (Wakefield & Blodgett 1994). However, not everyone can get to a stadium to watch their favourite team or game, particularly if that game is being played interstate or overseas. So sports media is also an important part of the sports product distribution system.

## The role of media in sports product distribution

Media allows sports marketers to take their products (the game) to many (sometimes millions) of people who otherwise would not be able to have that experience. Consider the Olympics for example. Many people from around the world are not able to travel to the Olympics to watch the Games live, so they rely on television, radio, the Internet and newspapers to deliver the information about the event and experience many of the tournaments from their own lounge room. The same process and considerations apply for sports marketers whose product is a team or perhaps membership and participation in a particular sport. In these cases, getting information about the product to consumers, making it relevant and interesting for them and creating opportunities for them to participate are all done through creative distribution. Manchester United's recent push into the USA is an example of this (Reuters Limited 2003).

In March 2003, Manchester United Football Club did what no other soccer team before or since has achieved (*Sports Illustrated* 2003). They had a successful pre-season tour of the United States with sell-out crowds in Seattle, New Jersey and Philadelphia. Manchester United, often touted as the only truly global sporting team, has 53 million fans worldwide and are the first foreign soccer club to make a concerted effort to crack the largely untapped American market. However, to be successful they need to maintain their presence in the highly competitive sports media market. A lucrative TV deal with YES network meant that all the premier league matches were shown on US television, which further allowed United to double its US fan base from 3.5 million to 7 million (*Sports Illustrated* 2003). Their ambition is to target the mass market of wealthy white Americans to part with their money and support the Manchester United merchandise juggernaut. Take a look at their website www.manutd.com and then browse the shop. You can buy Manchester United bedroom sets, baby wear and toys as well as jerseys, boots and leisurewear.

In summary then, delivery of the sports product to the end consumer can take a number of different approaches, depending on the type of product and the costs and benefits to both the manufacturer and the end-consumer. The longer the marketing channel the less control the marketers have over the delivery of the product, which is why in service situations it is often best to keep channels short and maintain control over the service delivery and servicescape.

Many organisations adopt multiple channels in order to best serve and attract potential customers. Figure 8.8 shows the combination of channels possible for a sports product that is an event or membership of a sporting club (intangible). You can see that there are both direct (straight to the consumer) and indirect (through intermediaries) channels possible and that some of the intermediaries also interact in order to provide the best outcome to the end consumer.

Figure 8.9 shows the combinations of marketing channels that a tangible goods sports marketer might consider. They could go directly to the consumer through the use of direct mail or direct marketing, directly to the consumer via the Internet, or they could go indirectly to the consumer by using agents, wholesalers and retailers.

**Figure 8.8:** Distribution channels for a sports event

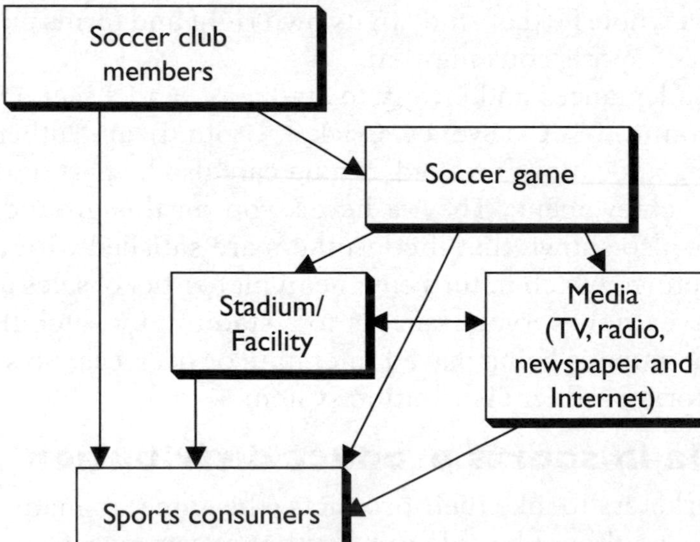


# Counterpoint

Is the TV sports boom really over? It has been noted that the Australian sports industry (and US sports industry too for that matter) is in the maturity stage of its product lifecycle and corporate sports investors and media are looking to digital broadcasting as a next possible option (Stensholt 2004). Ratings for the 2003 summer sports programs were quite good, up slightly on 2002, however much of the success of these programs depended on the performance of our Australian teams and players and this is a risky option for many media buyers. The cricket season was well supported by both spectators and television viewers due to the unexpected performance of the Indian team, making the finals an exciting and unpredictable event. However a year before, the ratings and crowd figures were well down as people had lost interest in the one-sided event.

**Figure 8.9:** Distribution channels for a sports product

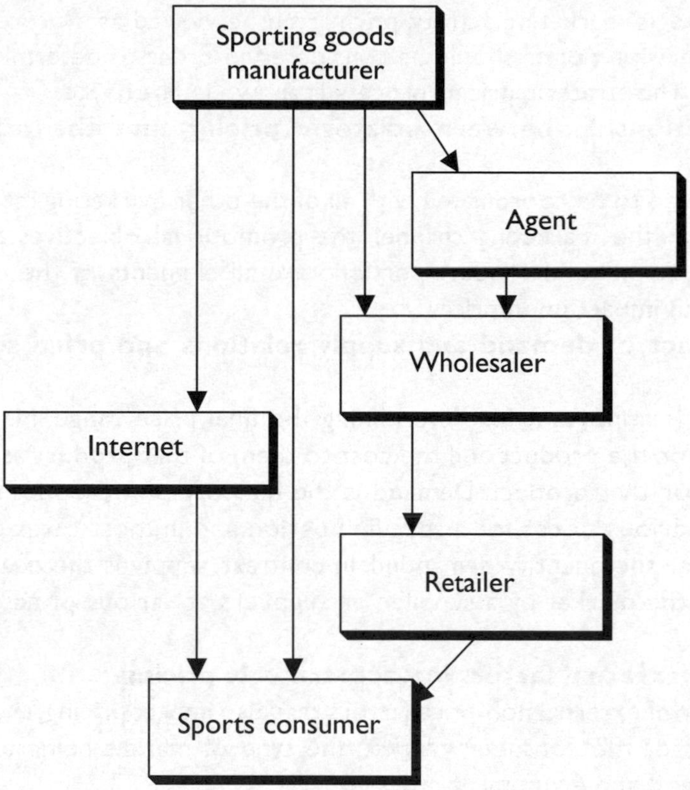


The Australian Open tennis and the Australian Open Golf Championship also had good crowds and viewership even though in the tennis neither Lleyton Hewitt nor Mark Philippoussis made the finals, and in the golf the winner was an international player with no Australians even in the top five. Channel Seven is still happily counting the profits from the 2003 Rugby World Cup and the bonus of Australia making the finals and having a semi-final match against New Zealand (3.15 million viewers).

So how can media players cushion the effect of team and player performance on their ratings? There is no way to predict or influence the final outcome and when the competition itself has a series of rounds or preliminary qualifying games then even the final contest is unknown. There is no easy answer to this question. In an attempt to partially address the problem, Tennis Australia attempt to create a festival atmosphere around the Australian Open with lots of additional entertainment and action that is not centred around the tennis. This means that even if the finals are not exciting, or if someone's favourite player doesn't make the cut, then the event and the reason to attend and to watch can still be justified by sports consumers. What do you think more grassroots regional sports can do to help buffer against surprising competition results or disappointing competition (Stensholt 2004)?

# Summary

- **explain the relationship between price, value and other psychological benefits**
  Price is part of the exchange process and is a way of quantifying the value of objects being exchanged. Value is generally the result of a mental evaluation of the perceived benefits of the exchange compared to the price (or final cost) of the exchange.

  As such, understanding customers' subliminal reactions to the perceived benefits of a sports product as well understanding the competing demands on consumer's time and monetary outlay, need to be well understood by the sports marketer.

- **explain how a sporting organisation should strategically determine their prices**
  As with most strategic marketing activity, pricing can be viewed as a process where a number of specific steps or decision points should be considered in order to determine a strategically viable pricing framework. The strategic pricing process is shown in Figure 8.1.
- **discuss the relationship between strategic pricing and the other marketing mix elements**
  Pricing decisions need to be coordinated with all of the other marketing mix variables. The number of intermediaries in the marketing channel, the promotional objectives and positioning of the product, the product mix and product portfolio are all elements of the marketing mix that are impacted by and can impact upon price.
- **discuss the impact of demand and supply relations and price sensitivity on pricing strategies**
  Market sensitivity is important for determining the final price range. Marketers need to know both the demand for the product and the cost to them of that product as well as the size of the potential market for that product. Demand is the quantity of a product that will be demanded by the market at various prices for a specified period and in most cases the higher the price of a product the lower the quantity demanded. In contrast, supply is the quantity of a product that will be offered to the market by a supplier or suppliers at various prices for a specified period of time.
- **identify how the external factors impact strategic pricing**
  There are a number of external non-price factors that also impact pricing. These are: the perceptions and characteristics of the consumer market; the type of market being targeted; the activity of competitors; and legal and economic factors.
- **identify the various channels of distribution relevant in a sports marketing context**
  In the sports industry there are a number of different ways of looking at marketing channels and distribution strategies and sports marketers can use both simple direct channels, or more complicated indirect ones.
- **discuss the core distribution concepts relevant to strategic marketing decision-making in sport**
  Marketing channels and intermediaries assist both the manufacturer in getting their product to a large number of end-user consumers efficiently, and they also assist the final consumer by providing a range of convenient locations for purchase of products and by increasing the potential range of products available to them for purchase. When manufacturers deal directly with end-user consumers this is known as a *direct channel* and when intermediaries are involved it is know as an *indirect channel*. In addition some manufacturers use a combination strategy, dealing both directly and indirectly with consumers in an attempt to maximise their exposure to potential customers.
- **identify the major issues inherent in sports facility management and how these impact sports marketing decision-making**
  The sporting facility itself is a very important part of the consumption experience in sport and is one of the more tangible elements of this experience. Well-designed sports stadia can add to the physical and emotional satisfaction of sports spectators and provide a distribution role by facilitating the consumption of the sports event to a large number of people.
- **discuss the role of media in distribution of sport to its publics**
  Media allows sports marketers to take their products (the game) to many (sometimes millions) of people who otherwise would not be able to have that experience.

## Review questions

1. What is value-based pricing?
2. Why would a sporting organisation adopt a differential pricing strategy?
3. Why might a sporting organisation consider community accessibility to be important when setting pricing goals?
4. If a sports product market is very price elastic, what happens when the price is increased?
5. What costs are important to consider when using break even pricing?
6. How has the Internet impacted on distribution decisions for sporting organisations?
7. Why is it important to consider stadium characteristics in distribution decisions relating to sports events?
8. Explain the role of the media in a sports distribution decision process.

## Applied activities

1. Name two sports products that use price-skimming strategies and two that use a penetration strategy. Comment on how the rest of the marketing mix follows the chosen pricing strategy. Do you agree with their decisions? What alterations or changes would you recommend?
2. Visit the Telstra Stadium website (www.telstrastadium.com.au) and comment on how as a facility they are considering the servicescape and experience of their audiences. What sports are played there and how do they facilitate the different needs of these different sports? How else is the ground used?
3. Compare the distribution strategies of the Manchester United website (www.manutd.com) with that of the Brisbane Lions website (www.lions.com.au). How do these sites differ and in what ways are they the same? How do they attempt to gain loyalty and direct allegiance with their customers through this distribution method?

## References

Barrnad, D. 2002, 'Near miss for World Cup Audiences', *Sports Marketing*, January, p.7.

Bell, K. 2003, 'Rugby Tries to Play Ball Over Tickets', *The Christchurch Press*, 21 August, p.5.

Grohmann, K. 2003a, 'Olympics-Athens Games Tickets are Hot Property – Organisers', *Reuters News*, 21 April.

Grohmann, K. 2003b, 'Olympics – Athens 2004 games will be sold out – ATHOC', *Reuters News*, 3 June.

Knowler, R. 2003, 'Jets Cut Ticket Prices in Bid to Score Crowd', *Evening Standard*, 25 March, p.20.

Kotler, P., Adam, S., Brown, L. & Armstrong, G. 2003, *Principles of Marketing*, 2nd edn, Prentice Hall, Sydney.

Mantanovich, T. 2003, 'Pricing Services vs Pricing Products: Don't Buy into the Duality Myth: Focus on Value to the Customer', *Marketing Management*, Jul/Aug, vol. 12, issue 4, pp.12–13.

Nagy, B. 2003, 'Full-house – That's Burton's First Goal', *The Advertiser*, 31 July, p.89.
Nimmer, D. 1971, 'Develop a Strategy for Pricing', *Innovation*, August, pp.41–3.
Penrith Press 2003, 'Free Tickets for Kids', *Penrith Press*, Penrith Football Club, 29 April, p.79.
Reid, R. 2004, 'Commercials are Big Business During Super Bowl', *Philadelphia Inquirer*, 29 January.
Reuters Limited 2003, 'Man Utd: We're on Our Way to Cracking America', http://sportsillustrated.cnn.com/soccer/news/2003/08/05/manutd_rdp, viewed 8 December 2003.
Rucci, M. 2003a, 'Time for Action on Ticket Prices', *The Advertiser*, 21 February, p.85.
___ 2003b, 'Lower Finals Ticket Prices on Way', *The Advertiser*, 4 July, p.104.
Shank, M. 2003, *Sports Marketing: A Strategic Approach*, 2nd edn, Prentice-Hall, New Jersey.
Shilbury, D., Quick, S. & Westerbreek, H. 1998, *Strategic Sport Marketing*, Allen & Unwin.
*Sports Illustrated* 2003, 'Man Utd: We're on Our Way to Cracking America', Reuters Limited.
Stedman, C. 2000, 'Value-based Pricing', *Computerworld*, March, Vol. 34, issue 11, p.58.
Stensholt, J. 2004, 'Advantage Sport', *BRW*, 29 January.
Stolz, G. 2003, 'Catching the Wave', *The Courier Mail*, 19 July, pp.69–70.
Summers, J., Gardiner, M., Lamb, C., Hair, J. & McDaniel, C. 2003, *Essentials of Marketing*, Thomson Nelson, Melbourne.
*The Advertiser* 2003, 'Only a Game, and It's Too Expensive', 6 September, p.27.
Wakefield, K.L. & Blodgett, J.G. 1994, 'The Importance of Servicescapes in Leisure Service Settings', *Journal of Services Marketing*, Vol. 8, No. 3, pp.66–76.

# Case studies for Part 3

## Twenty20 cricket bowls the maidens over!

### Dr Melissa Johnson Morgan

As 24-year-old Sarah sips champagne and watches the English summer sun slip away, 1980s pop music blares around the ground as another wicket falls. Sarah and her friends are at a Twenty20 cricket match, in fact the first game of cricket that Sarah has ever seen live. Not that she really likes cricket but Twenty20 only lasts about three hours and it is a great chance to catch up with friends and have a few drinks and a laugh. There are heaps of eligible men at the cricket and it is nice to be outside on a summer evening.

Twenty20 cricket, so named because of the 20-overs-a-side format, was launched in England in 2003 and has fast attracted the attention of spectators and players all over the world. English county cricket clubs are buzzing with excitement at the prospect of bigger crowds being drawn by the new format. The game was designed to overcome some of the 'tedium' of five-day test cricket, which is blasphemous for the cricket aficionado, but appealing to younger, time poor markets. The major attraction of the new format is that an entire game can be completed in around three hours. The cricket itself is fast and furious, with the aim of the game being to score as many runs as possible without the usual prudence of test match cricket.

The action-packed competition, which replaced the Benson & Hedges Cup in the English domestic calendar, features two weeks of group matches between the 18 counties, and a finals day in July. Each match promises non-stop big-hitting entertainment for 20 overs a side, lasting under three hours and played from 5.30 p.m. to 8.15 p.m. The duration and timing of the games makes them an ideal summer evening out for children, families and singles alike.

Each match is accompanied by an entertainment package at match venues including music, promotions, food and beverage offerings, plus a variety of interactive activities for kids. The competition is also intentionally scheduled around the longest days of the year. In addition to live spectators, the game is also seen on Sky TV and Channel 4 in England, and heard on BBC radio. The games' television appeal is heightened by gimmickry such as players being 'miked up' to commentators.

Families are certainly targeted with this new format but Twenty20 cricket has made its biggest hit with the ladies. English Cricket's marketing manager Stuart Robertson says: 'The audience profile for cricket is disastrous; middle-aged, middle-class and white. Kids think it's for oldies and women think it's for men. Twenty20 cricket is about addressing these structural barriers and the research says it is women and kids who want this sort of cricket.' Total attendance for the 45 Twenty20 matches in 2003 was 240 000 spectators, compared to only 105 000 spectators who attended 2002's 50-over competition that it replaced. This was an average of 5330 spectators per match up from 2002's 50-over competition average of 1511. In July 2004 62 per cent of Twenty20 crowds were 34 or younger. At least 23 per cent of Twenty20 crowds are women and one-third of those are first-time cricket spectators.

With a considerable female audience, there are plans by some county clubs to capitalise on this new market with speed-dating in the crowd. English county Warwickshire plans to line up would-be lovers in a speed-dating scheme in which they will have until a wicket falls to get to know each other. Worcestershire cricket club have constructed a Jacuzzi by the boundary and Hampshire have built a Bondi Beach replica to make its resident Australian spinner, Shane Warne, feel at home.

Twenty20 cricket is receiving attention in other parts of the world with the South African Cricket Board (UCBSA) set to add it to their domestic competition. Other countries including Pakistan and Sri Lanka have expressed interest in the spin-off game. Cricket Australia told the England and Wales

Cricket Board in 2004 that it was willing, in principle, to consider playing a one-off international match of 20 overs a side in the winter of 2005. There are some reservations that the English scenario, where the radical new format has breathed life into ailing county cricket, might not apply in Australia. Indeed the Australian Cricket Board has little experience with the Twenty20 format and are watching the rest of the world carefully as they uncharacteristically find themselves on the back foot. Cricket Australia emphasised that although it was open-minded about the English Cricket Board's push for a Twenty20 international, the proposal was only 'on the edge of our radar'. However, the new format seems to be gaining popularity fast and any scepticism can be likened to the introduction of one day cricket in the 1970s. When Bill Lawry's Australian team played the first one-day international in place of a rained-out Test in 1971, few could have imagined the popular, colourful and competitive spectacle it would become, nor the enlivening impact it would have on test cricket. To this end, the first international Twenty20 game for the Australian cricketers was played in early 2005 in New Zealand with players expressing cautious optimism about the future of the format.

The new format is also believed to be the game's biggest chance of inclusion as an Olympic sport. The International Cricket Council (ICC) have recognised the importance of globalising the game of cricket and their bid to introduce Twenty20 cricket in the 2012 Games is part of the global push.

As the last wicket falls, Sarah finishes her champagne and gives her phone number to a nice young man from London. It has been a great night and she makes plans with her friends to buy tickets to next week's match.

Sources:

Church, R. 2004, 'Loving the Twenty20 cricket', sportandtechnology, 23–25 September. http://www.sportandtechnology.com/features.php?pageId=0176, viewed 29 July 2004.

'Here Comes the Summer', The Twenty20 Cup, http://www.thetwenty20cup.co.uk/pages/twenty20_cricket/twenty20_cricket.htm, viewed 30 July 2004.

Saltau, C. 2004, 'Twenty-overs cricket on the way', The Age, 10 June, http://www.theage.com.au/articles/2004/06/09/1086749779396.html?oneclick=true, viewed 30 July 2004.

## Questions

1. Do you think that Twenty20 cricket will have a long-term future in the international cricket calendar?
2. Why would the ICC want cricket to be an Olympic sport? What impact would it have on the future of the game?
3. Why are young females a good target market? How could clubs add value to the game for this market?
4. Are there any disadvantages or issues in using promotions such as speed-dating as part of the Twenty20 cricket experience?

# The Maine event

**Michael Volkov**

The Australian National Rugby League competition, in quite a different configuration from the current manifestation, commenced its first round of competition on 20 April 1908 in Sydney with eight newly formed clubs (www.rl1908.com). Two of these foundation clubs were the Western Suburbs Magpies and the Balmain Tigers. These two teams, due to modern-day sporting pressures such as the corporatisation of the NRL, shrinking finances and competition rationalisation (to enable the truly national growth of the sport in Australia), merged to form the Wests Tigers team that debuted in the modern NRL competition in 2000. The Wests Tigers' brand is the most recognised brand in the NRL, the club have one of the highest fan loyalty factors in the competition and have sponsorship packages comprising of over 100 corporate partners (www.weststigers.com.au).

However, since entering the competition, the club have spent most of the three seasons since their inception embroiled in very public disputes climaxing in a player revolt in 2002. The many off-field controversies, combined with particularly poor performances on the field, culminated in the Wests Tigers being unable to attract a major sponsor until just prior to the 2003 season. The Radisson Maine Financial Group secured a 1-year deal with the club together with a further one-year option with the sponsorship agreement, mooted to be worth over $450 000 per year to the Wests Tigers. This sponsorship arrangement was greeted with excitement from both the chief executive of the Wests Tigers, Steve Noyce, and the chief executive of the NRL, David Gallop, with both stating that the deal was evidence that rugby league was still attracting the corporate dollar in Australia and that this was a healthy sign for both the club and the league.

Radisson Maine Financial Services are themselves not shy of causing controversy in the NRL. Following the sponsorship agreement entered into with Wests Tigers, Radisson Maine Financial Services lost a two-way battle to sponsor the Canberra Raiders rugby league team in the same competition. They are said to have offered the Canberra Raiders $1.9 million over three years but their bid was rejected by the club who announced their major sponsors to be the mobile phone retailer Fone Zone. Radisson Maine president Robert Bassili voiced his displeasure at the lost deal even though they already were the major sponsors of the NRL's Wests Tigers. Radisson Maine Financial Services' public relations officer Sharon Finnigan lamented the 'sad way' that the Canberra Raiders conducted business and clearly stated that Radisson Maine had 'deep pockets' and that they can now 'move on and tip our $1.9 million into something else' (Wilson 2003).

Yet the local media continued to pursue Radisson Maine Financial Services. Barely three months after the deal with Wests Tigers was brokered, *The Australian* newspaper raised claims that Radisson Maine Financial Services were not what they purported to be. Several investigative reports in the national newspaper stated that Radisson Maine Financial Services were purely masquerading as an international financial group with global shipping and aviation interests. Reports uncovered that they were nothing more than a mortgage brokerage firm set up just prior to the 2003 NRL season in a house in suburban Sydney and run by two young, Ferrari-driving salesmen. On the other hand, Radisson Maine's website claimed that the company was a global conglomerate with offices in Geneva, London, New York and Toronto, comprising a corporate structure that employed 102 executive positions.

These reported investigations led to statements by representatives of the Australian Securities and Investment Commission (ASIC – the Australian government authority that regulates companies, financial markets, financial services, organisations and individuals who deal and advise in investments, superannuation, insurance, deposit taking and credit) and the Australian Prudential Regulatory Authority (APRA – the prudential regulator of banks, insurance companies and superannuation funds, credit unions, building societies and friendly societies) that implied that Radisson Maine may not have the appropriate licences required by Australian law to conduct the business that its principles, Robert Bassili and Nick Popov, and the company's website purported to carry out.

Wests Tigers members had been courted by Radisson Maine in 'investment seminars' being held through the club and some of the players had invested heavily with the company. Yet many in the

Australian media have reported the fears of Wests Tigers' fans who say they are not convinced players would want to represent the club if the issues surrounding Radisson Maine were not resolved and that having a less than reputable sponsor does little to maintain the credibility of the club.

The New South Wales Fair Trading Minister, Reba Meagher, has instructed the NSW Office of Fair Trading (OFT – the role of the NSW OFT within the Department of Commerce is to safeguard consumer rights and to advise business and traders on fair ethical practice) to investigate claims that Radisson Maine failed to adequately respond to allegations raised regarding its 'global' business dealings. Following the OFT's lead, the Australian Securities and Investment Commission and the Australian Competition and Consumer Commission (the ACCC is an independent statutory authority that administers legislation dealing with anti-competitive and unfair market practices, mergers or acquisitions of companies, product safety/liability and third-party access to facilities of national significance) also launched investigations. The further these enquiries progressed the more scrutiny befell the Wests Tigers and the NRL with both organisations claiming that the matters being brought to light were damaging.

Following lengthy discussions with the OFT in June 2003 the Radisson Maine website now has the following message on it:

> Radisson Maine's website is currently under renovations.
> Once it returns, it will give you more informative and helpful features. We apologise for any inconvenience this may cause.
> For any enquiries, please email info@radissonmaine.com.au
> www.radissonmaine.com.au

At the time of writing this case study Radisson Maine is still listed as the major sponsor of the Wests Tigers with all investigations being closely followed by the Chief Executive of the NRL.

### *References and further information*

Australian Competition and Consumer Commission, http://www.accc.gov.au
Australian National Rugby League, http://www.nrl.com.au
Australian Prudential Regulatory Authority, http://www.apra.gov.au
Australian Securities and Investment Commission, http://www.asic.gov.au
NSW Office of Fair Trading, http://www.fairtrading.nsw.gov.au
Radisson Maine Financial Group Australia Pty Ltd, http://www.radissonmaine.com.au
*The Australian*, http://www.theaustralian.news.com.au
The History of the NRL, http://www.rl1908.com
Wests Tigers, http://www.weststigers.com.au
Wilson, Chris 2003, 'Big-Bucks Brawl over Sponsorship Rights with the Raiders', *Canberra Times*, 8 May 2003, p.32.

## Questions

1. Why was Radisson Maine so eager to sponsor a club in the NRL, even two clubs? What are the benefits for all the stakeholders in such an agreement?
2. We often discuss the damage done to a sponsor by a sponsee, yet what damage can be done in the reverse situation?
3. It is often said that any publicity is good publicity. Discuss this phrase in relation to the above case and the various stakeholders of the sponsorship deal.

# Part 4

# Marketing using sport

# Chapter 9

# Sport as a strategic marketing tool

## Learning objectives

After reading the chapter you should be able to:

- discuss the emotional power of sport when incorporated into a marketing plan
- explain how sport can enhance traditional promotional activities
- briefly discuss how organisations can use sport to develop strategic relationships
- articulate the importance of matching brand DNA when using sport as a marketing tool
- debate the advantages and disadvantages of using sport as a marketing tool.

## Scene setter

### World Cup Sponsors look to score

On 23 November 2003, the Rugby World Cup was officially over. After 48 matches over 44 days, in six capital cities and four regional venues, and in 11 stadia, it was hailed an economic and social success. An estimated 4.43 billion people watched the final game worldwide with just over 4 million of these being in Australia (one fifth of the population, making it the most watched TV program of 2003) and 14.5 million in England (Rugby World Cup 2003 IRB Report). In addition to the 400 jumbo jets full of international tourists, 1.8 million spectators and 50 000+ international visitors to Australia, the World Cup stimulated both tourism interest and general economic return for many cities and regions within Australia, with an estimated $300 million in business generated (Grigg 2002).

Companies that benefited from the World Cup in terms of their association were: Cabcharge Australia, increasing its annual revenue by 10 per cent on previous years; Vodafone reported increased phone sales; and Telstra who saw 202 000 phone calls and 226 000 SMS messages from the stadium alone during the World Cup final. In addition, 20 000 of these calls were picture messages, all a boon for the financial position of Telstra.

So why did global companies such as Visa, Heineken, Qantas, Bundaberg Rum and Coca-Cola invest millions of dollars to be associated with one sporting event? First, these global brands expected to see a short-term boost in their sales, but they also intended to generate a long-term awareness and loyalty with the people who attended and watched the World Cup events.

Marketing using sport is a powerful tool used by many organisations to leverage their brands and to create opportunities in new markets and to cement loyalties of existing customers. Brands that are associated with the positive passions and emotions that surround sport can create long-lasting images and positive attitudes with their customer bases that are almost impossible to achieve through conventional marketing. Consider this World Cup campaign: 20 countries (many European) all interested in their sport (rugby), a sport traditionally associated with professionals and highly educated people. Now imagine attempting to buy enough advertising space in these 20 countries, to achieve the same level of exposure and awareness in a 48-day period, that association with the World Cup gave these global brands. That is why sport is such a powerful addition to any organisation's marketing plan.

This chapter will give an overview on how sport can be incorporated into the marketing plan for an organisation and how to best utilise sport to create and communicate value.

## Introduction

The 2003 Rugby World Cup provided a powerful marketing platform that was used by hundreds of global and local brands as part of their marketing campaigns. The success of the Cup was a financial and marketing boon for the International Rugby Board, but also for the non-sport-related organisations that chose to align themselves with the sport and the event, including companies like Visa, Heineken and Qantas.

Up until now we have focused our discussion on the marketing of sport. This chapter is the first of two that will investigate marketing 'using' sport. That is the use of sport by organisations (whose products and services may or may not be related to sport) as part of their strategic marketing plan. We begin our discussion by looking at what makes sport a unique marketing tool and then investigate how sport should be used strategically as part of the marketing plan. It is also important that we consider how to evaluate the effectiveness of using sport in marketing. The chapter will conclude with an overview of the overall advantages and disadvantages of sport as a strategic marketing tool.

## Sport as a unique marketing tool

Sports sponsorship is the third-biggest advertising medium behind press and television with the sponsorship market in Australia worth over $1 billion dollars. This figure does not include the added leverage expenditure that companies use to maximise sponsorship dollars, and which can be as much as four times the original sponsorship expenditure.

While sponsorship has received increased attention in the last decade, most mainstream marketing textbooks still don't explicitly include sports sponsorship as part of the marketing tool kit. Some advertising and promotions texts include discussion about sport and event sponsorship as part of the promotion regime but the attributes and uses of sport specifically are rarely mentioned. Sports 'sponsorship' will be defined in more detail later in the chapter but it is important that we acknowledge upfront that the strategic use of sport in marketing extends well beyond the bounds of promotion and philanthropic corporate public relations. Sport is a unique medium through which organisations can achieve marketing objectives ranging from brand exposure to long-term loyalty programs for internal and external consumers. The next section considers the strategic use of sport in marketing but first we should investigate what it is about sport that makes it such a powerful and valuable marketing tool.

Perhaps the most powerful and unique thing about sport is the emotion that it generates and commands from participants and spectators alike. The dynamic emotional rollercoaster of sport can drag consumers through heightened senses of anticipation, joy, fear, excitement, pride, satisfaction, anger, elation, sorrow, disappointment and relief all within the timeframe of the event – a 20-second race, a two-hour game, or a month-long tournament. The inherent nature of competition provides an elevated platform of emotions that are enjoyed directly and vicariously by large groups of consumers. The wild celebrations of victory and the draining anger and sorrow of defeat are equally indulged as socially acceptable outlets of otherwise inappropriate emotions – emotions that can dissolve geographic, temporal, demographic, cultural and social boundaries.

Linking products with sport can make them seem sexy or exciting

*Harnessing the emotional power of sport* offers marketers a unique opportunity. It is difficult to make life insurance 'sexy', or stimulate wild excitement over a credit card. However, linking these product categories with sports and sporting personalities gives them access to emotions that would otherwise elude them. The pride and enjoyment elicited from fans watching their national team become the best in the world is not a feeling that can be created artificially or attributed naturally to things like clothes, beer or airlines. However, by working with that national team and that sporting code, brands in those product and service categories can form strategic alliances that let them be part of that emotional experience, and allow them to harness that pride and that happiness in the marketing of their products and services.

Sport unlocks unique qualities that other marketing tools cannot provide. Print material is one-dimensional, television is two-dimensional, events are three-dimensional but sport and sponsorship of that sport could be said to be four-dimensional (Lloyd 2001). That fourth dimension is emotion. Successful use of sport in marketing brings an emotional aspect into play that can effectively develop relationships with consumers and markets.

A related characteristic of sport as a unique marketing tool is its ability to overcome the ever-fragmenting media industry (Hancock 2003). Media tools continue to fragment and saturate the market and consumers are increasingly choosing to secure options that allow them to avoid ads altogether (pay TV, DVDs, TiVo etc.). Communicating brand and product meanings and images are no longer enough in a world where communication is becoming more logistically possible but humanly complex. Consumers need to experience brands. Using sport, marketers can present brands, products and services to consumers via a medium they have passion for, a medium that is itself experientially consumed. Consumers can experience and encounter brands in an emotional and holistic consumption environment. Sport can be a hugely effective way of cutting through the media clutter for brands and corporations (Hancock 2003, p.2). Cutting through this clutter via sport can allow marketers to target the central values and emotions of the sporting consumers.

The commitment that participants and fans make to their chosen sport also provides marketers an opportunity to foster long-term relationships and brand loyalty with these consumers. Barrelle (cited in Lloyd 2001) says that sport provides a common language that transcends geographic borders and language barriers. Fans continue to exhibit intensive loyalty to the sports, teams, players and events that they follow. Certain sports have historically attracted a particular demographic fan base that also makes for ideal target market matching and sharing within the traditional strategic boundaries of marketing activity. All of these phenomena offered by sport present a compelling brand opportunity for marketers who want not only brand recognition but brand loyalty from a specific target market.

Since ancient times, people have used sport to promote their standing and as a surrogate indicator of their power and success. The Roman aristocracy, who supported or bought gladiators, did so because it lent them a degree of loyalty, status and support that they might otherwise not have achieved on their own. Marketing powerhouse Coca-Cola must have anticipated the benefits of being associated with a mega sports event when they became the first modern-day example of sports sponsorship, placing ads in the official program of the 1896 Olympic Games.

The use of sport in marketing has been shelved by academics and many practitioners as a form of public relations or philanthropic sponsorship. However the sheer size and popularity of its use is forcing marketers to reconsider the objectives of using sport and considering its role as a much more holistic and integrated function in the overall marketing plan. The next section considers the contemporary strategic uses of sport in marketing, beginning with some clarification of what to call the use of sport in marketing.

## Strategic use of sport in marketing

The rapid growth of sports sponsorship worldwide is not justification enough for companies to jump headfirst into the Olympic-size pool of marketing using sport. Sport should be used within the context of the strategic marketing process. The strategic marketing process is the entire sequence of managerial and operational activities required to create and sustain effective and efficient marketing strategies (Van Heerden 2001).

This section covers the history and growth of sports sponsorship, and redefines the term sponsorship to reflect the greater contemporary strategic imperative of forming strategic alliances that are mutually beneficial. Finally we will outline the objectives and benefits of using sport in marketing and outline the 12-step program to sports marketing success.

### The history and growth of sports sponsorships

Corporate involvement with sport, or 'sponsorship' as we will call it for now, has moved through three distinct evolutionary phases. Beginning in the 1960s and 1970s, sponsorship agreements were largely donation-based activities with philanthropic motives on the part of the organisation. Sporting bodies, usually governed by dedicated volunteers, ex-players and the friends and family of participants, approached organisations looking for financial support and appealed to the corporate spirit of community service and goodwill. Finding a CEO who had a personal interest in the sport itself was a bonus and the corporation's donations usually secured top management good seats at the games, or maybe even a corporate box.

During the 1980s, affiliation with a particular sport, team or event was thought to be enough to justify financial involvement by the organisation. The 'rub-off' effect by this association with sport was expected to generate some positive exposure, perhaps good publicity, and show that the organisation was supporting the local or national sporting community. Again, personal sporting preferences of the CEO or top management were a big factor in agreeing to sponsor a given sport.

In the current business environment, nearly all sports sponsorships are treated as investments with an expectation that a positive return will result. No longer able to justify a donation mentality or support of a favourite team, organisations now look for leveraging opportunities that can provide a strategic advantage over traditional marketing media. The evolution of corporate financial investment in sport is finally acknowledging the imperative of matching a company's marketing objectives with the sporting proposal (LeDrew 2003).

Figure 9.1 shows the three evolutionary phases of corporate financial involvement in sport.

**Figure 9.1:** Evolutionary phases of corporate financial involvement in sport

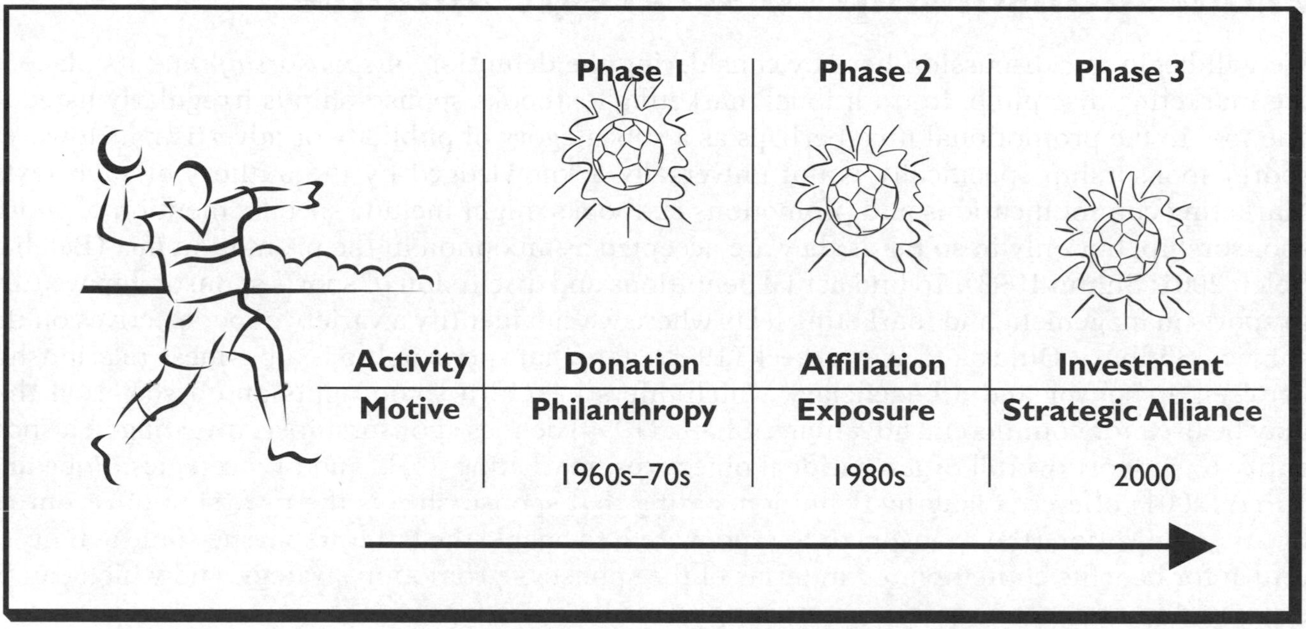


The amount spent on sponsorship has grown to an estimated US$30 billion industry worldwide, and has seen an 11 per cent compound annual growth over the last 15 years, as increasing numbers of companies recognise its value in providing meeting points with consumers (Incepta Group plc, *Annual Review* 2002). In marketing terms, sponsorship continues to grow faster than all other marketing channels (Hancock 2003). In North America, sports sponsorship accounts for over 67 per cent of all corporate sponsorship expenditure, including the arts (LeDrew 2003). Australian corporate spending on sport almost doubled between 1996 and 2000, growing from $459.4 million to $907.1 million. If we include the purchase of television rights to sport that increase is even more dramatic, from $593.4 million in 1998 to $1.25 billion in 2000 (Lloyd 2001). Commenting on the growth of sports sponsorship in Australia, Lloyd (2001, p.1) reports that 'Even without the "Olympic effect" of 2000, growth has outstripped all other mainstream media advertising in the past five years, and spending on sports sponsorship is now trailing only press advertising expenditure ($3.359 billion in 2000) and television ($2.746 billion)'.

In fact the worldwide sports sponsorship market has grown from approximately US$11 billion in 1997 to over US$21 billion in 2003 with growth projected to top approximately US$27 billion by 2005 (Li 2003). In addition to this dollar growth, sports marketing has boomed and matured into a strategic component of many companies' marketing plans (Li 2003). This growth is more than just an inevitable evolutionary phase in the business nature of sponsorship. Jobber (cited in Van Heerden 2001) believes that six factors contributed to the growth of sports sponsorship:

- restrictive government policies on tobacco and alcohol advertising
- escalating costs of media advertising
- the proven record of sponsorship

- increased leisure activities and sporting events
- greater media coverage of sponsored events
- the reduced efficiencies of traditional media advertising through clutter and switching between television programs when commercials are aired.

In addition, it might be feasible to suggest that the maturing of sporting organisations themselves, into financially accountable marketing organisations, fostered increased trust among corporate investors in the sponsorship market for some sports.

The next section will explore the redefinition of the term sponsorship to reflect the growing and maturing of sports *sponsorship* into a more comprehensive marketing platform.

## From sponsorship to strategic alliance

We will begin our discussion here by considering the definition of *sponsorship* and its place in the marketing discipline. In traditional marketing textbooks sponsorship is irregularly listed as one tool in the promotional mix, perhaps as a subcategory of publicity or advertising. However, sports sponsorship specifically is not universally acknowledged by the authors of such texts. Marketing communications and promotions textbooks might include specific mention of sports sponsorship, but only in so far as they are accepted as an option in the promotion mix (Belch & Belch 2001; Shimp 1993). To find actual definitions and discussion of sports sponsorship we turn to sports management and marketing texts where we can identify a variety of perspectives on the subject. Shilbury, Quick and Westerbeek (1998) state that sponsorship is a business relationship between a sponsor and a beneficiary, which offers in return some rights and association that may be used for commercial advantage. Shank (1999) defines sponsorship as investing in a sport entity to support overall organisational objectives, marketing goals and/or strategies. Pope and Turco (2001) offered a lengthy definition stating that sponsorship is the provision of resources by an organisation (the sponsor) to the sponsored, to enable the latter to pursue some activity in return for benefits contemplated in terms of the sponsor's promotion strategy, and which can be expressed in terms of corporate, marketing or media objectives.

A review of marketing, promotion and sports marketing literature reveals a variety of definitions about sponsorship. Some of these include statements that sponsorship is:

- a business relationship
- investment for promotional benefit
- purchase of rights and associations for commercial advantage
- payment in return for business consideration or benefit
- financial or material support in return for exposure
- deliberate financial support given to achieve brand awareness
- a form of sales promotion that creates publicity opportunities.

None of these statements adequately captures the use of sport in marketing. It is as if the term sponsorship is regrettably limited to a promotional activity and each statement has a functional quality that makes reference to a specific application or single objective. Added to this is the historic stigma of sponsorship being charitable by nature and constituting little more than philanthropy, endorsement or patronage.

Perhaps the most disappointing thing about the contemporary definitions such as those offered by Pope and Turco (2001) is that they completely fail to recognise the strategic nature of sponsorship, or the potential of this platform to satisfy the objectives of not just the sponsor but also the sponsored. In other words, the investment or association, if made with a true marketing orientation, should consider the mutual satisfaction of marketing objectives of the sporting entity and the organisation.

Sponsorship marketing should not be:

- the CEO's 'pet project'
- a stand-alone marketing tool, or
- just a simple brand exposure channel (Li 2003).

Sponsorship marketing should be embedded in corporate strategy and executed through brand value propositions.

A more strategic definition of sports sponsorship would acknowledge that the association between the sport and the sponsor should be a strategic alliance that provides marketing opportunities for both partners. In this sense: sport sponsorship is a marketing platform that may be activated and integrated into the marketing mix, and which could enhance the effectiveness and efficiency of a range of marketing activities, for both partners in the strategic alliance.

The term 'sponsorship', while convenient, does not convey the same message as a strategic alliance. The new imperative is to form a strategic alliance *through* sport. In this sense the alliance should be approached as a joint venture. In order to be considered strategic, the company must establish their objectives in seeking the alliance and also understand what their corporate identity and brand DNA are. Brand DNA is a term used to describe the unique components or configuration of a brand that give it its identity and personality. Brand DNA is defined by customers' experience and perceptions around five basic components: category, character, benefits, difference and credibility (Brandsequence, http://brandsequence.com/glossary1.html), as seen in Figure 9.2.

By approaching sports alliances strategically, the organisation can determine whether the personality and identity of the brand, based on the characteristics of the brand DNA components, are compatible with the sport entity. Each sporting organisation, national body, event and sports personality are equally responsible for determining their own brand DNA in order to ensure that they target and partner with compatible sponsors.

**Figure 9.2:** Components of brand DNA

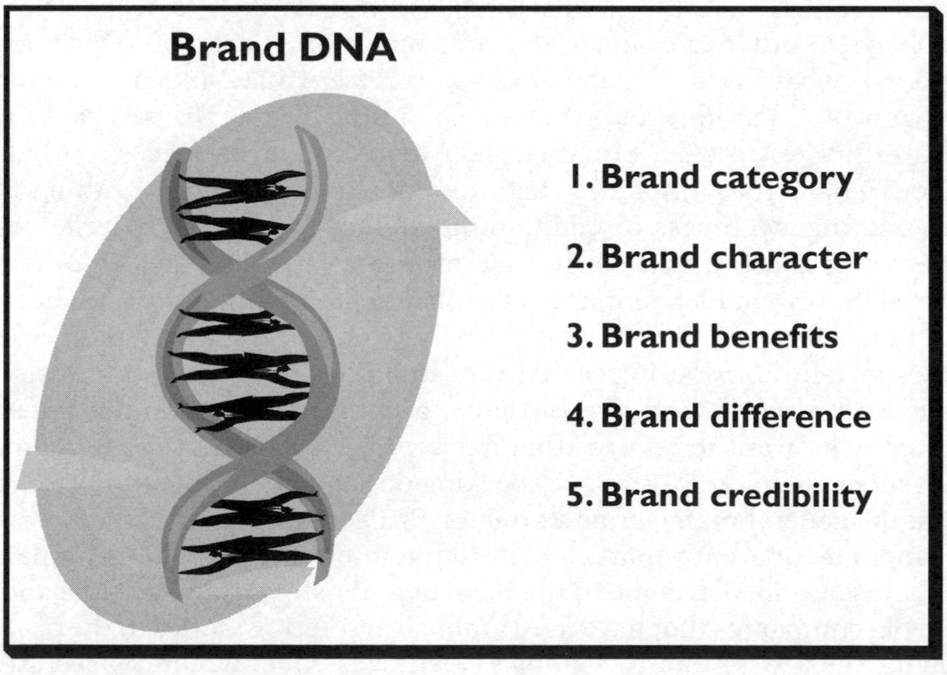


Microsoft considered the brand DNA and objectives for their Xbox brand when they formed a strategic alliance with the National Rugby League football competition in Australia. Xbox were looking for a platform to position their brand as a family product, played among families in their homes and representing 'a good set of values'. Partnering with the NRL was seen as a good fit between two major entertainment brands that generated high involvement among its consumers and a way to target Xbox's core target market of 16 to 30-year-old males, as well as widen its appeal to a broader audience (B&T 2003). At the same time, the NRL benefited from partnering with a brand that represented the new generation of sports consumers and a new era of consumption technology.

## Sport spotlight

### The science of sports marketing

SPORTS – Australians participate in it, they attend it, they watch it, they read about it and they listen to it. Therefore it's not surprising that they also value companies that sponsor it – 62 per cent of Australians say sponsorship increases their interest in using sponsors' goods and services, according to the latest Sweeney Sports Report.

So how can companies play the game and win? Unfortunately the answer isn't in textbooks or journals – even some of the companies doing it well have the occasional slip-up. 'There is no simple answer – it is both a science and an art,' Nike Pacific's brand marketing director Carl Grebert says.

That's where sponsorship comes in and due to the digital and technological revolutions in sports coverage, it is getting more and more expensive. Therefore, companies must carefully evaluate the effectiveness of sponsorship and the role it plays in a marketing strategy. 'Companies must first understand that sponsorship is not a charity and it is not advertising,' Grebert says. 'Sponsorships can do things that advertising can't, but so often it gets talked about as if it is advertising. It is amazing how many times it is bought as advertising.'

Once marketers have established the need for sports sponsorship, they must work out the perfect vehicle, whether it be an individual, a team or a sport. Grebert says in order to evaluate this a company must ask two questions. 'You need to ask what is your brand DNA – the core values and positioning that makes your brand unique and what are you trying to do?' Grebert says.

FutureBrand Australia brand strategy director Trevor Flett says that sport is a good vehicle for companies that are repositioning their brand, building a brand, creating awareness or maintaining market dominance. 'Marketers need to have a relationship with their customers and sport creates that leverage,' Flett says. 'Sport enables marketers to touch emotional parts of the heart that you wouldn't believe.' Flett says that sport is also a great way of speaking to youth, especially considering the current trend by young people to resist overt messages from marketers. '[Youth have] a culture of anti-brand,' Flett says. 'Marketers who want to address that market have to address the fundamentals of what turns them on. It is about speaking one-to-one with your customers.'

Wrights general manager and director Bridget Marcou says that in order to take ownership of events, marketers must put muscle behind their campaign. Of course, muscle can also come in the form of ambush marketing. Nike and Coke are two big companies that have used ambush marketing tactics in the past, most notably at the 1996 Atlanta Olympics. Flett says Nike, which placed strategic billboards around the city for the duration of the Olympic Games, managed the campaign successfully. 'They inherited a street credibility for doing it that way,' Flett says. However, Flett warned companies to be smart about ambush marketing, adding that Coke overdid it during the Atlanta Olympics.

Ambush marketing is also a factor companies must consider when evaluating a potential sponsorship. Brisbane Broncos general manager, marketing, Craig

Richards says companies have to be wary of the effect that ambush marketers can have on a particular event. 'If someone else can get it, you paid too much money for it,' Richards says.

Source: Plaskitt 2003

Sport can give brands credibility

Both sides of the negotiating table need to recognise the critical need for careful, structured planning and return-on-investment analysis if long-term effective partnerships are to be achieved (Hancock 2003). Before we investigate the requirements for successful sports marketing planning, we should first explore the critical pre-planning questions that need to be answered. Before embarking on actually looking for strategic sports alliances, ask the following questions to ensure that the investment develops a successful marketing platform. Some critical questions include:

- Have you created a sponsorship culture within your organisation?
  - It is important that the culture of the organisation supports the joint venture or strategic alliance theory of sports sponsorship and not the hands-off joint venture approach once followed.
- Have you changed (or do you need to change) your organisational approach to sponsorship?
  - Who makes the decisions regarding your investment in sport? Are all of the right functional and strategic personnel involved in crafting your sponsorship strategy? Who monitors and evaluates your sponsorship investment?

- Have you learnt anything from past sports investments or sponsorships?
  - It is important that you consider previous sports alliances and use the evaluation from those alliances to help you judge future investments. Did you have clear objectives and did you evaluate those objectives? Did you successfully match your brand DNA to a sporting entity and was the alliance mutually beneficial? Was the scale of your investment appropriate to your objectives and to any attributable return? It may also be necessary or desirable for you to conduct research among your target market to gauge the success of your past sponsorship programs.
- Can you learn anything from your competitors?
  - You should always monitor the marketing strategies of your competitors and if and how they are using sport in those strategies is no exception. Look particularly at why they are using sport in their marketing strategies, who are they targeting, what sporting entity are they using and why, and how successful they appear to be. It is also advisable to consider the size of the investment that they are making in order to achieve their objectives.
- Are you a market leader or follower?
  - If your company is market leader in its category then all aspects of your marketing strategy should reflect this. It is important that as a leader you don't follow the herd, that your sporting alliance is innovative and bold. Similarly, if you are a market follower or nicher, the size of your investment and the nature of your alliance should reflect this (Hirons 2002).

It is essential that marketers focus on these strategic considerations rather than on the traditional tactical focus taken with sports sponsorship. Even more alarming is that decisions regarding sports sponsorship are still made in isolation at a senior level and based on personal interest rather than strategic logic (Hancock 2003). A recent study by research company Sponsorship Insights found that CEOs and managing directors still account for 59 per cent of the final decision-makers regarding sponsorship investment in Australia. While input and commitment from senior management is essential to all strategic marketing plans, it is important that these decisions are not made without the considerable input of the marketing team and without matching the objectives of the sports alliance to overall corporate marketing strategy and plans.

## Objectives and benefits of strategic sports alliances

The overall purpose of any marketing strategy is to:

- clearly define the growth goals desired and what contribution existing products and markets can deliver
- develop a strategic platform for a new product, service and market development
- analyse competitive, market and customer positions and opportunities
- define key strategic foci to capitalise on competitive weaknesses, emerging market trends, and unmet customer needs.

In order to investigate the objectives and benefits of using sport strategically in marketing, first revise the basic stages in the marketing strategy process. The six major stages in the strategic marketing process include:

1. identifying and evaluating opportunities
2. analysing market segments and selecting target markets
3. developing a positioning statement and corresponding marketing mix strategy
4. preparing a formal marketing plan
5. executing the marketing plan
6. monitoring, controlling and evaluating the plan.

In reviewing the use of sport as a strategic marketing activity, it is important that we establish similar guidelines for the planning and evaluation of those activities. Sport has become a marketing medium, in and of itself, with the ability to target, segment, promote and cast products and services in heroic lights (Schlossberg 1996, p.6). As such it is important that we develop formal strategies for its use. As a subsequent or simultaneous activity to overall marketing strategy planning, the 12-step sports marketing strategy process outlined below should be used to plan the company's strategic alliance or joint venture with sport.

## 12-step program to sports marketing success

1. Develop a profile of brand DNA and of the target market.
2. Clarify marketing objectives of the alliance with sport in relation to overall marketing strategy.
3. Establish a budget or budgeting method.
4. Identify current opportunities in sport.
5. Establish compatibility between the sporting entities' DNA and target market(s) and those of the company.
6. Establish the mutual objectives of the strategic alliance.
7. Establish the cost of the strategic alliance.
8. Identify specific marketing activities necessary to activate the alliance and meet objectives.
9. Establish the cost of activation.
10. Establish evaluation measures.
11. Engage and activate the alliance.
12. Monitor and evaluate the alliance.

This process should be thought of as sequential, however as with all strategic planning some stages may have to be revisited and revised during the process. The process reflects a much more considered approach to investment in and/or alliance with sport than just employing sponsorship tactics. Recognition occurs at several stages that mutual development and satisfaction of goals and objectives is important to the long-term success of the alliance. You will also notice an early prompt to establish a budget for the program and then a subsequent prompt to plan for the activation or support costs, which are usually substantially higher than the initial payment made to the sport entity. Chapter 10 considers the concept of activation, or leveraging as it is more commonly known, in greater detail. It is assumed of course that you have considered the critical questions outlined previously, about the whole concept of using sport as a marketing platform for your company.

So just what do companies hope to achieve through their alliance with sporting entities? Some objectives might include local/national or even international exposure, repositioning a company or brand, highlighting a salient brand proposition, product or corporate endorsement, getting closer to trade/key decision-makers, political motives, a signpost of market leadership, communication of a specific message, and/or preventing the competition from taking advantage of the opportunity (Hirons 2002). There are other more tactical objectives such as immediate revenue generation. For Rugby World Cup sponsor, Heineken, there was immediate revenue from pourage at the venues as well as the associative benefits by leveraging the beer as a premium brand (Harty 2003). Similarly, Heineken realised immediate revenue from sales at the Australian Open tennis for which they are a major sponsor, and in addition they used the event to give them exposure to new target markets in a setting that matches their premium brand DNA.

The opportunities for using sport in marketing seem endless but the challenge is to balance the needs of your target market, marketing objectives and your budget all at the same time (Hirons 2002). Visa is a company renowned for their effective and strategic use of sport as a marketing platform. The marketing objectives of Visa's sponsorship of the 2003 Rugby World Cup centred around four areas including:

1. advertising
   a. build awareness and imagery
   b. support member acquisition and usage
2. promotion
   a. increase usage
   b. partner with strong brands
3. corporate relations
   a. enhance impact/reach of other marketing efforts
   b. strengthen corporate reputation/image
   c. use as a platform for employee programs
4. product platform
   a. showcase new technologies
   b. launch new products (Li 2003).

These objectives were set years in advance and the first activation or leveraging planning began almost three years before the Rugby World Cup even began in Australia. You can see that the objectives of the alliance with the Rugby World Cup covered a variety of marketing areas and were strategic and comprehensive in nature.

It is interesting to note that experience of sporting entities and organisations alike may offer challenges in different countries around the world. Sporting organisations in the USA for example are likely to be more skilled at creating strategic opportunities, or 'properties' as they are called, to attract corporate investment. On the other hand, large American sporting entities are also more likely to slice their properties very thinly, or be over-commercialised to a point where the value of the investment should be carefully scrutinised. Australian sporting entities are less likely to be over-sold, but have a corresponding inexperience when it comes to providing clear opportunities to facilitate the marketing platforms of corporate partners, or in providing the type of information and evaluation that is often necessary to evaluate proposals that they present. In terms of corporate investment, Australian companies place less importance on using sport to increase brand loyalty than their US counterparts, ranking it third behind building awareness and changing or reinforcing brand image. In contrast, the primary objective of US companies investing in sport is to increase brand loyalty (Sponsorship Insights 2003).

An Australian survey of sponsorship decision-makers conducted by Sponsorship Insights in 2003 revealed a range of objectives and benefits of using sport in marketing at varying levels of importance and value. From most to least important, respondents listed the following objectives for using sports sponsorship:

- to create awareness of product or brand
- to change or reinforce brand image
- to increase brand loyalty
- to showcase the company's community responsibility
- to stimulate sales/trial and/or usage
- to motivate employees
- to entertain clients and/or prospective clients (Sponsorship Insights 2003).

Respondents considered on-site signage as the most valuable sponsorship benefit to be gained in a sports partnership. Other benefits considered important included receiving category exclusivity, presence on the sport property website and cross-promotional opportunities (Sponsorship Insights 2003). The focus on exposure and brand awareness in objectives and valued benefits would seem to indicate an immaturity in the strategic nature of sports sponsorship in Australia.

In the next section we will consider why and how to evaluate the effectiveness of using sport in marketing.

# Evaluating the effectiveness of using sport in marketing

The growth of sponsorship and use of sport as a marketing platform has not been paralleled by increased sophistication in management practices. This is particularly true in the setting of objectives and subsequent measurement of those objectives. Both the sporting entity and the corporate investor need to recognise the critical need for careful, structured planning and return on investment analysis if long-term effective partnerships are to be achieved. The two most important issues are to set realistic objectives and to develop measures of those objectives in evaluation of the strategy. The increasing effectiveness of sport as a marketing platform is only defensible if a return on investment in sport can be demonstrated. As companies seek increased levels of accountability for every aspect of their marketing budgets, they will be forced to approach their investment in sport from a more analytical base (Lloyd 2001).

One of the traditional measures of 'effectiveness' in sponsorship has been measuring the equivalent media value of the publicity generated from the sporting event, or using some brand tracking measures. However, these measures don't capture the depth of information necessary to actually establish the effectiveness of the alliance. Measuring equivalent media value, for example, does not show whether or not the media generated elicited the required response. Did it convince consumers of something? Did it increase recognition of your brand? Did it position your product where you intended? Did it stimulate trial of your product or service? Simply establishing the replacement cost of equivalent media exposure doesn't answer any of these questions.

The type of evaluation carried out is completely dependent on the objectives of using sport in the first place. For example, if Qantas sponsored the Rugby World Cup to stimulate international ticket sales, then direct, behavioural and sales data should be used to evaluate this objective. How many people flew on Qantas to watch the Cup? What was the increase, if any, in ticket sales during the Cup? Compared to previous months? Compared to the same period last year? These would be useful and representative measures. However, additional objectives might have been to attract new customers and develop brand loyalty and repeat business, in which case different measures may be required, including cognitive measures such as consumers' attitudes towards the airline, and their 'intentions' regarding future flights. The reasons for their future intentions should also be determined. Purchase data such as whether or not this was the customer's first flight with Qantas should also be measured.

Westpac said that they had three objectives for the return on their investment in the Sydney 2000 Olympics: the first was business from their customer base and new customers, the second was a promotion of their brand image in the larger community, and the third was to improve staff morale. Westpac's own research, conducted just before and just after the Olympics, found that the bank's image as a good corporate citizen rose markedly during the Games, from 11th to fifth place in community perceptions; the bank has since been trying to improve and build on that. Although Westpac have never divulged the exact return on their investment in the 2000 Olympics, they insist they were ahead of target (Lloyd 2001).

An effective measure of the success of the sports marketing platform requires a deeper understanding of the relationships between a sponsor, a sport property and the target consumer. It requires a research approach based upon an understanding of the science of strategic marketing using sport. Effectiveness measures should help you answer the following questions:

- Are we aligning ourselves with the right sport property and/or the correct events to reach our desired target audience?
- Have our awareness objectives been achieved?
- Have we enhanced brand image or brand commitment?
- Have we achieved synergy between our sport property and our brand activities?
- How have our business partners perceived our use of sport or hospitality program?
- Has our relationship with sport enhanced our corporate reputation?

Agreements made between corporate investors and sporting entities should (and often do) include key measures of success. These agreements would be considered performance based agreements and use measures such as:

- sales
- brand/corporate image and/or position
- media coverage
- team or athlete performance
- event attendance.

You will note that the measures of performance are based on both parties – the corporate investor and the sporting entity. In a well-designed strategic partnership based on a sports platform, the success or effectiveness of each party's strategy should be interdependent with the other.

The success of Heineken's investment in the Australian Tennis Open may be somewhat dependent on the quality of the tournament, meaning the characteristics of the competition itself – who makes it to the finals, the quality of the tennis etc. However, the relative success of the competition may also be dependent on the leveraging of Heineken's investment and their role in improving the quality of the Open as a sporting experience.

Typical measures used to determine the effectiveness of an investment in a sport property include:

- demographics
- attendance
- psychographics
- growth trends in the property category
- competitor sponsorship activity
- fan passion and/or affinity
- television ratings
- interest levels from trade partners.

As was outlined in the 12-step program to sports marketing success, effectiveness measures must be determined from the planning stage, which includes making provision for the types of data and analysis that will be needed to determine effectiveness. Australian companies involved in sports sponsorship report that internal feedback is the most common source of analysis used when determining whether or not to change or renew sponsorships. Examining print media exposure or using clipping services is also popular, as is looking at direct sales promotion results (Sponsorship Insights 2003). Conducting primary research is relatively common also and we might expect it to become even more prevalent as sponsorship agreements become more strategic, costly and sophisticated in terms of achieving key business objectives.

The majority of the objectives and measures discussed up until now have involved business to consumer transactions, with final consumer target markets. However, another strategic use of sport in marketing is as a platform for employee motivation and reward and also as a basis of relationship building with business to business or corporate clients. Visa's sponsorship of the Rugby World Cup in 2003 was, among other things, used as a platform for an extensive employee reward and motivation scheme worldwide. Again the same rules apply to these objectives where evaluation, via appropriate measures, is imperative in determining the success of the program.

The final section in this chapter will provide an overview of the advantages and disadvantages of using sport as a strategic marketing tool.

## Advantages and disadvantages of sport as a strategic marketing tool

The power of sport as a marketing platform has been realised by sports-related and non-sports-related companies alike. Companies such as Nike and Adidas are inherently linked to sport; in fact

Nike's mission statement focuses on their mission in sport and for athletes rather than financial or commercial objectives. However, non-sports-related companies like CUB, Vodaphone, Telstra, Heineken and many others have harnessed the emotion and power of sport to provide unique opportunities in their given industries and among their target markets.

While there are many advantages in using sport in marketing there are also disadvantages to be aware of. More than just advantages and disadvantages, we should perhaps refer to them as advantages and opportunities versus the disadvantages and risks associated with using sport.

Whereas some of the advantages and opportunities may be unique to sport, many of the disadvantages are not and actually share many of the same risks inherent in promotions using uncontrollable variables like endorsement from celebrities, rock stars, movie stars etc. Table 9.1 shows a list of some of the advantages and opportunities, and the disadvantages and risks associated with using sport as a marketing platform.

**Table 9.1:** Advantages and disadvantages of sport as a marketing platform

| Advantages and opportunities | Disadvantages and risks |
|---|---|
| Highly emotionally charged interactions with consumers both internal and external | Evaluation is difficult and many measures are immature and ineffective |
| Chance to tap into extreme fan loyalty and support | Sport properties can be overpriced |
| Potential to share in large and easily identifiable target markets | Leveraging costs are high |
| Cost-effective brand and product exposure opportunities | Quality sports platforms are limited and often infrequent or seasonal |
| Increased product consumption by target consumers, including new markets | There is a risk of sponsorship confusion and/or blurring |
| Venues for product stimulation and trial | Difficult to control |
| Potential to shadow the brand personality and success of sport, teams and/or individual athletes | Subject to personality flaws and social mistakes of sporting celebrities |
| Use of expert endorsers | Clutter or overselling of some sports and/or events |
| Ever-changing supply of heroes, champions and spokespersons | Quality and excitement of competition is largely uncontrollable |

The opportunities presented by using sport as a marketing platform are based on the emotion and loyalty of the underlying competition and inherent values of sport but are limited only by the creativity and marketing prowess of the sport entities and the corporate investors who seek their platform. Many of the disadvantages and risks associated with using sport as a marketing platform can be minimised by careful planning and management on not only the part of the corporate investor, but first and foremost the sport entities themselves. One sign of business immaturity in the sports market is the lack of credible and reliable information produced by the sports themselves in determining their relative worth to potential investors. Much of the information available about sport and its value as a marketing tool remains anecdotal evidence about levels of exposure. Coupled with the continuing propensity of investors to make their sponsorship decisions largely on subjective and emotional grounds, this can only serve to hold back the success of sport as a marketing platform.

Some sport entities are slicing their properties so thinly among rights holders that they are rendered almost meaningless (Hancock 2003). There is also real concern among many major sponsors that the value of their long-term commitments to sports properties is being seriously eroded by the trend towards last-minute fire-sales by rights owners and their agents. Over-selling and over-valuing are potentially detrimental to both parties in the strategic alliance. The Australian Cricket Board have made a concerted effort to limit the number of major sponsors that they have in order to maintain the value of their sport property. In addition, they approach investors in specific industries, on the basis of building long-term, mutually beneficial relationships. Their recent search for a strategic alliance investor in the high-tech industry was in recognition of their lack of skills in this area and their desire to explore the options for electronic and digital extensions of their sport product and the changing sports consumption preferences of their target markets.

While a product's image can be enhanced by association with sport, it can also be tainted by social gaffes by sporting personalities

Finally, investment in a specific team or individual athlete carries with it all of the usual cautions and warnings associated with using celebrities. This fact is well appreciated by Nike who signed Kobe Bryant, the high-profile US basketball star in a multi-million dollar contract, just weeks before he was arrested on rape charges.

This chapter is the first of two that investigate the use of sport as a marketing platform. The unique characteristics of sport are based largely on the emotionally charged experiential platform that it represents and the often fanatical loyalty that it can be associated with. While the concept of using sport to market products and services is not new, the industry does still suffer from some business immaturity, particularly in the area of accountability and measurement of effectiveness. While sponsorship is a widely accepted concept we should be progressing to an era of strategic alliance between sport and corporate investors, with alliances seeking to achieve the mutual satisfaction of each party's objectives. While there are increasing sport properties available or opportunities for alliance, corporate investors must ensure that they are fully aware of the advantages and risks associated with such an alliance and that they fully activate and utilise the opportunity as a marketing platform and not just an opportunity for promotion.

## Counterpoint: Ambush marketing

Increasing numbers of marketers are questioning the value of high dollar sponsorships when some companies are using sport properties and sports platforms unofficially for far less investment. Using a sport property without actually contracting or paying to do so can be done legally, but many believe unethically, in a practice called *ambush marketing*. Ambush marketing is where a company advertises heavily or designs a marketing campaign to coincide with a specific sports event or season. For example many companies increased their advertising budgets during the Rugby World Cup but were not in fact official, paying partners of the IRB or the RWC. Even small, regional businesses produced ads wishing the Wallabies well or showing rugby balls and players, thereby insinuating that they were associated with the competition.

Similarly, Qantas did not successfully purchase the official airline sponsorship of the Sydney 2000 Olympics, however their presence during the Games was immense and many consumers assumed that they were in fact the official sponsor. Do you remember who was?

When asked if they thought that ambushing was a legitimate sponsorship activity, 68 per cent of sponsorship decision-makers in Australia said no, a further 18 per cent said yes and the remaining 14 per cent said they didn't know. When the same group was asked if they would ever ambush a competitor 11 per cent said they would (Sponsorship Insights 2003).

If companies are able to benefit from the sports marketing platform and openly activate alliances they aren't actually party to, it must surely devalue the sporting properties that are offered to corporate investors.

## Summary

- **discuss the emotional power of sport when incorporated into a marketing plan**
  Sport offers an almost unique platform for marketers because of the emotion that it stimulates among consumers and fans. When used strategically, marketers can try to harness this emotion and use it to stimulate interest, build relationships and motivate consumers in ways that would not be otherwise possible.
- **explain how sport can enhance traditional promotional activities**
  Sport offers much more than just cost-effective advertising exposure or novelty promotion opportunities. Sport should be used as part of the larger marketing mix as a platform for all elements and not just as a promotional medium.
- **briefly discuss how organisations can use sport to develop strategic relationships**
  The contemporary focus of sport entities and marketers alike should be on developing long-term strategic alliances to the mutual satisfaction of both partners. In this sense both partners can also use sport as a platform to enhance relationships with their business and final consumers and even their own employees and supply chain partners.
- **articulate the importance of matching brand DNA when using sport as a marketing tool**
  Brand DNA defines the identity and personality of a company's brands and in doing so offers guidelines as to the type of sport property that enhances this personality. Similarly, sports should be aware of their own DNA and seek alliances with corporate investors that enhance their brand and their overall mission.
- **debate the advantages and disadvantages of using sport as a marketing tool**
  Many of the advantages and disadvantages associated with using sport as a marketing tool can be controlled or at least minimised by careful planning and management on not only the part of the corporate investor, but first and foremost the sporting entities themselves.

## Review questions

1. What makes sport unique and attractive as a strategic marketing tool?
2. What are some of the critical questions that marketers should ask themselves before investing in a sport property?
3. What is brand DNA and why should it be considered when using sport in marketing?
4. List three advantages and three disadvantages of using sport in strategic marketing. Give examples for each.
5. Outline the challenges involved in evaluating the effectiveness of using sport in strategic marketing.

## Applied activities

1. The managing director of the insurance company you work for has asked you to evaluate a sponsorship proposal she has received from the Australian Women's Softball League. What criteria will you use to evaluate the proposal? What factors do you think are important to consider about your company and the league?
2. Visit the CUB website at www.cub.com.au and identify which sports, teams and individual athletes they use to market their products. How well do you think they have matched their brand DNA with that of the sport products they use as a marketing platform? What do you think the objectives of making these alliances are? How would you suggest they measure the effectiveness of their alliances?
3. Visit the official websites of the Olympic Games (www.olympic.org), World Cup Soccer (http://fifaworldcup.yahoo.com/) and the Rugby World Cup (www.rugbyworldcup.com). What evidence can you find that these three mega events are protecting their corporate sponsors against ambush marketers? What steps, if any, could the organisers of these events and their corporate investors take to limit the impact of ambush marketing? Whose responsibility is it to protect against ambush marketing?

## References

B&T Marketing and Media 2003, 'X Marks the Sport for the NRL', 20 March, http://www.bandt.com.au/articles/b3/0c014db3.asp, viewed 26 November 2003.

Belch, G. & Belch M. 2001, *Advertising and Promotion*, 4th edn, McGraw Hill, Boston, USA.

Belch, G. & Belch, M. 2004, *Advertising and Promotion: An Integrated Marketing Communications Perspective*, McGraw Hill, Boston, USA.

Brandsequence, 'A Glossary of Terms', http://brandsequence.com/glossary1.html, viewed 7 June 2004.

Grigg, A. 2002, 'Rugby World Cup Big Money Spinner for Australia', transcript from *Business Breakfast*, 29 November, http://www.abc.net.au/businessbreakfast/content/2002/s737256.htm, viewed 7 June 2004.

Hancock, S. 2003, 'The Status of Sponsorship', *redmandarin*, http://www.redmandarin.com/viewstatus.htm, viewed 3 November 2003.

Harty, J. 2003, 'Leveraging the RWC', *B&T Marketing and Media*, April, http://www.bandt.com.au/articles/87/0C014F87.asp, 26 November 2003.

Hirons, M. 2002, 'Swimming Takes Top Sponsorship Spot', *B&T Marketing and Media*, November, http://www.bandt.com.au/articles/11/0c011c11.asp, viewed 10 April 2003.

Incepta Group plc, *Annual Review* 2002, International Marketing and Communications, http://www.incepta.com/downloads/annualreport2002.pdf, viewed 19 July 2004.

Jobber, D. 1995, *Principles and Practice of Marketing*, McGraw-Hill, London, UK., cited in Van Heerden, C. 2001, 'Factors Affecting Decision Making in South African Sport Sponsorships', unpublished thesis, University of Pretoria, http://upetd.up.ac.za/thesis/available/etd-11072001-165433/unrestricted/01front.pdf, viewed July 14 2004.

LeDrew, J. 2003, *Sponsorship Support in Amateur Sport*, Sport Nova Scotia 2001–2003, http://www.sportnovascotia.com/contents/public_communications/Marketing/sponsorship_support.htm, viewed 3 November 2003.

Li, S. 2003, *Sports Sponsorship – A Global Business Affair*, presentation on behalf of Visa at the AFR Sports Business Summit, 16 October 2003, Sydney, Australia.

Lloyd, S. 2001, 'Sponsorship: Taking a sporting chance', *BRW*, Vol. 23, No. 26.

Plaskitt, S. 2003, *B & T*, 8 October 2003, http://www.bandt.com.au/news/53/0c01a153.asp.

Pope, N. & Turco, D. 2001, *Sport and Event Marketing*, McGraw-Hill, New South Wales, Australia.

Rugby World Cup 2003 IRB Report, http://www.rugbyfootballhistory.com/resources/RWC2003_IRB_report.pdf, viewed 10 October 2004.

Schlossberg, H. 1996, *Sports Marketing*, Blackwell Publishers, Massachusetts, USA.

Shank, M. 1999, *Sports Marketing – A Strategic Perspective*, Prentice Hall, New Jersey, USA.

Shilbury, D., Quick, S. & Westerbeek, H. 1998, *Strategic Sport Marketing*, Allen & Unwin, Australia.

Shimp, T. 1993, *Promotion Management and Marketing Communication*, Dryden Press, Harcourt Brace & Company, USA.

Sponsorship Insights 2003, Trends in Sponsorship Management: Revelations from the 2003 Australian Sponsorship Decision-making Survey, http://www.sponsorshipinsights.com.au/Docs/Australian%20Sponsorship%20Decision-makers%20Survey%202003.ppt, viewed 12 December 2003.

Van Heerden, C. 2001, *Factors Affecting Decision Making in South African Sport Sponsorship*, unpublished thesis, http://upetd.up.ac.za/thesis/available/etd-11072001-165433/, viewed 12 December 2003.

Zikmund, W. & D'Amico, M. 2001, *Marketing*, 7th edn, West Publishing, Minneapolis, USA.

# Chapter 10

# Leveraging sports marketing

**Learning objectives**

After reading the chapter you should be able to:

- recognise and explain the importance of leveraging sports marketing investments
- identify how a sport property should be chosen strategically
- understand the importance of setting objectives and matching brand DNA
- outline the two types of limitations to be considered when using sport in marketing
- identify and explain the key components in an activation and leveraging plan.

## Scene setter

### Sydney's business Olympics

The Sydney 2000 Olympics was not just a sporting feast for viewers all over the world, it also offered a unique marketing platform for local, international and global brands. The mega event offered companies the chance to indulge in corporate schmoozing, negotiate or close new deals, and in the case of Australian politicians, promote new investment in Australia.

TOP IV Partner companies, the highest level of Olympic sponsorship, paid the International Olympic Committee US$50 million and in return received a range of privileges that they used to promote and market their businesses. The initial payment to the IOC was just the beginning of what their sponsorships would eventually cost them. TOP IV companies included: IBM, Kodak, Coca-Cola, McDonald's, Samsung, UPS, *Sports Illustrated/Time* and Visa International. Some of the Australian companies with local sponsorship deals of varying value included Westpac Bank, BHP, AMP Insurance, Telstra and the now defunct Ansett Airlines.

Some of the benefits of being an Olympic partner included exclusive marketing rights, the right to use official Olympic imagery on their products, preferential access to Olympic broadcast advertising, ambush marketing protection, on-site monopolies and 'hospitality opportunities' at Olympic events. Hospitality opportunities included tickets to events and other perks, which were dispensed to regular and prospective customers, favoured employees or anyone that the organisations sought to impress or influence.

In addition to their initial US$50 million dollar investment, US sporting magazine, *Sports Illustrated*, invested a further US$30 million + to leverage their partnership via hospitality. United Parcel Service (UPS), another international Olympic sponsor, took over the Merchant Court Hotel where it accommodated the 1000 people it brought to Sydney for the Games. This included 500 clients and other corporate guests. IBM leased Crystal Harmony, a luxury liner, for 1000 of its guests and hosted parties on board every night of the Games. Every IBM guest was also given a $750 IBM palm pilot as a memento of their experience.

Selling news, soft drink, delivery services, real estate, steel, insurance, telecommunications and Australia in general, countries from all around the world identified the 2000 Olympic Games as a unique global marketing platform for business and final consumers alike. However opportunities of this magnitude don't come cheap and maximising the potential from the opportunity requires an even more substantial commitment and investment.

Source: Phillips 2000

# Introduction

While the 'Scene setter' on the Olympic Games highlighted the hospitality side of sports marketing leveraging, there are many other tools that marketers can and do use to make the most of their alliance with sport. This chapter will expand on the concepts introduced in Chapter 9 by focusing on the activation and leveraging of an investment in a sport property. Topics covered will include how to choose the right sport property to match your budget and your needs, what leveraging and activation actually mean and an introduction to the tools of sports marketing leveraging. The chapter will conclude with an extended case in point, which looks at Visa's leveraging of their 2003 Rugby World Cup sponsorship. The case examines Visa's motivations, the tools they used to leverage and their motivations for becoming involved in this mega event.

# Choosing the right sport property

A company that chooses to use sport to market themselves, their products or services, needs to carefully consider the type of sport property that will best achieve their strategic marketing objectives. There are literally thousands of sport properties on offer, from sponsorship of an individual athlete to naming rights of an entire national competition or stadium. In this section we will outline the factors that are important when choosing an actual sport property, including matching brand DNA, clarifying objectives, determining limitations, assessing company and budget size restraints, identifying leveragable benefits and establishing commitment guidelines. This section will also briefly comment on implementing formal processes and positions to perform all of these tasks.

Assuming that you have followed the 12-step Program to Sports Marketing Success, as outlined in Chapter 9 and shown in Figure 10.1, your objectives for using sport in your marketing program are now clearly determined. Similarly you should already have a profile of your brand DNA and of your target market(s).

## Matching brand DNA

You will recall that there are five components of brand DNA:

1. brand category
2. brand character
3. brand benefits

4. brand difference
5. brand credibility.

Brand DNA is a more complex concept than that of brand personality as it forces you to define the tangible and intangible, rational and emotional aspects of your brand. It also requires consideration of the competitive positioning and relevance of the brand. It is important that you understand not only your own brand DNA but the brand DNA of any potential strategic partners and that of competing brands.

**Figure 10.1:** Twelve steps to sports marketing success

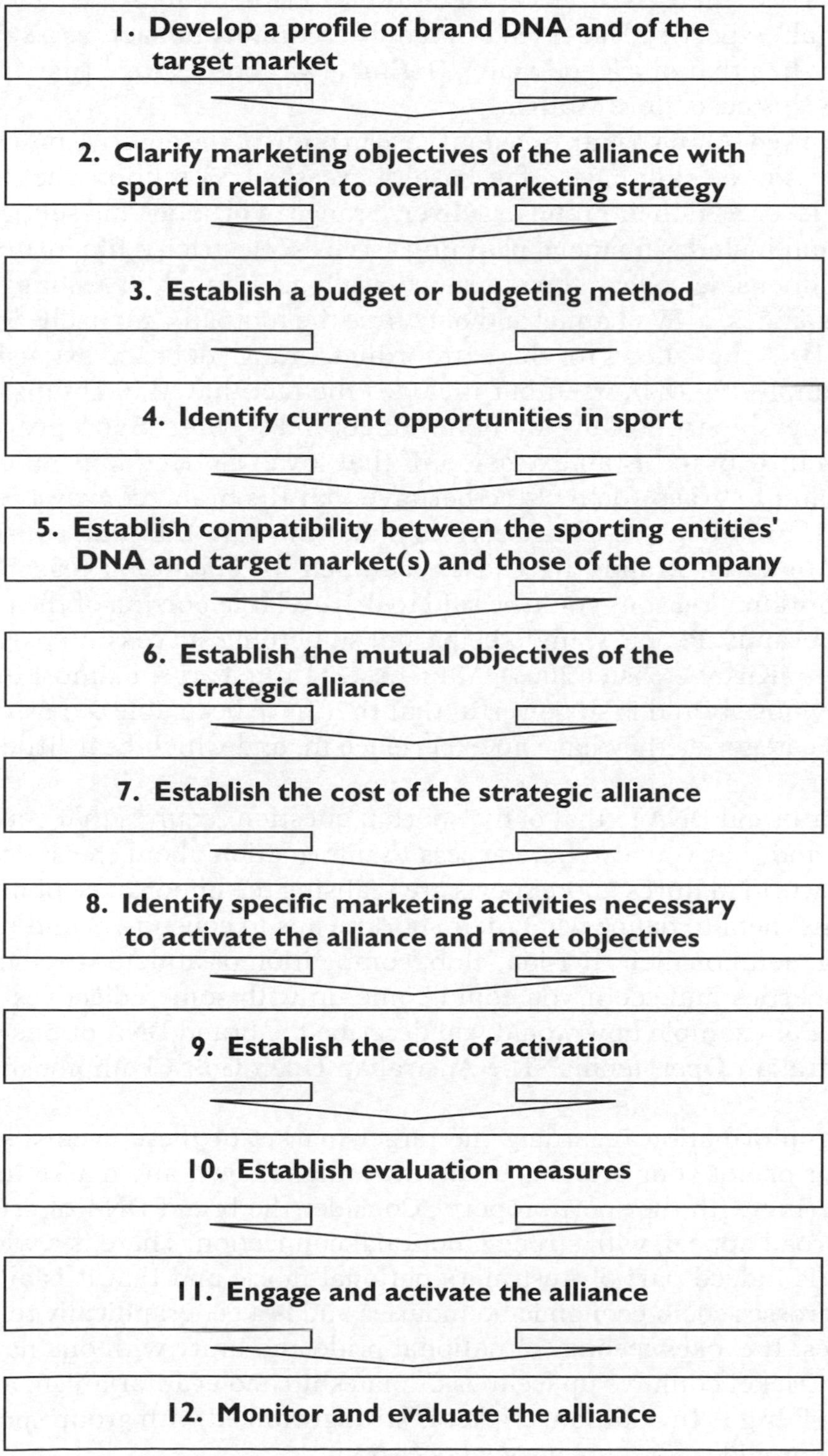
1. Develop a profile of brand DNA and of the target market
2. Clarify marketing objectives of the alliance with sport in relation to overall marketing strategy
3. Establish a budget or budgeting method
4. Identify current opportunities in sport
5. Establish compatibility between the sporting entities' DNA and target market(s) and those of the company
6. Establish the mutual objectives of the strategic alliance
7. Establish the cost of the strategic alliance
8. Identify specific marketing activities necessary to activate the alliance and meet objectives
9. Establish the cost of activation
10. Establish evaluation measures
11. Engage and activate the alliance
12. Monitor and evaluate the alliance

In selecting a sport property one should carefully scrutinise the brand DNA of the property under consideration. From a strategic sense the decision-makers will need to have established what the overall goals of the association are in order to decide on whether or not they are looking for perfect DNA alignment or perhaps finding a property whose brand DNA will lend you strength in an area that you are lacking. For example, in 2003 Steve Waugh was used by OzEmail to launch their broadbrand products. OzEmail used Waugh because his brand DNA added strength in areas that they needed help with. Waugh is not only recognisable and popular he is also perceived to be stable and trustworthy. At the time, broadband was still an untapped medium in Australia, and people weren't sure that the benefits justified adopting the new technology (Plaskitt 2003). Steve Waugh's brand DNA made him a perfect sporting personality to combat that perception. Why use a sporting entity at all? Perhaps in the absence of technical expertise there is a certain emotional element in some telecommunications decisions, and a stable sporting leader lends not only credibility but acts as a surrogate indicator of trustworthiness like that of a 'good mate'. OzEmail was borrowing 'trust' from the DNA of a sport property, in this case Steve Waugh.

Manchester United (Man U) is an excellent case in point of the emotive power of sports brand DNA. The English soccer club have a fan base in excess of 53 million people worldwide and have successfully leveraged their brand in a diverse range of product and service categories. The Man U family brand includes financial planning services, electricity, life insurance, mortgages, credit cards, bed linens, jewellery, tomato sauce, wallpaper, lunchboxes, luggage, cell phones, boxer shorts, magazines, a TV channel and of course the football club itself. So what is it about the Man U brand DNA that allows for this extraordinary range of brand extensions? The answer is probably as complex as DNA itself but includes the fact that Man U fans derive a sense of belonging and ownership from using Man U products and services. Sport provokes tremendous loyalty and the Man U brand is an extension of that loyalty, giving fans an opportunity to be part of the team and to grasp some of the heritage that the brand conveys. By being a Man U fan, buying Man U products and using services under the Man U brand, consumers show they belong to a tribe of sorts. Brands are chosen as much for emotional reasons as they are for rational ones. Emotional reasons could be said to drive a large portion of the purchase decision when it comes to brands. People want to be part of something successful, part of a legacy; they want to be winners (Kirby Webster 2003). Manchester United are an almost unique example of a sporting entity whose brand is so powerful that they have been able to leverage it themselves in industries and categories they have no experience in, and which bear little to no relation to their original sport.

Matching your brand DNA to that of the sport in question requires that you fully understand your own brand, and that you also have access to information about the sport property. As the sports marketing world matures, more sports are realising the importance of investing in market research that helps them to define what their sport means to consumers and the characteristics of their sport in general or their division, club, competition or athlete specifically. Think about certain sport properties and see if you could come up with some adjectives to describe them and their appeal. For example how would you describe the brand DNA of one-day international cricket? The Australian Open tennis? The Australian Open Golf Championship? The Ironman series?

Coupled with information regarding the target market of these events, you start to get a picture of whether or not your brand is in any way aligned or if any marketing synergy can be created by partnering with the sport property. Consider the brand DNA of cricket in Australia. Cricket offers a broad appeal, with strong emotional connection. There is a widely held cultural view that cricket is indeed part of Australia's national fabric and that it is all-embracing. As a national sport it crosses socio-economic boundaries and is a geographically relevant sport being played in all states. It evokes feelings of national pride and unity with one national team as its defining feature. Cricket conjures up feelings of mateship and egalitarianism and the Australian value of getting 'a fair go'. In addition, cricket is strongly linked with group sports consumption, family values and provides for a great social occasion.

The Australian Cricket Board are quite progressive in their 'selection' of suitable sponsors for their products and we will discuss some of their goals and objectives for the sport and how this drives their selection in the next section. For now let's focus on the brand DNA of the one-day international series as just one sport property that they have to offer. What type of product or service aligns with the characteristics outlined above and what brand in particular would find some synergy or 'fit' through an association with the series? Hindsight gives us the answer here as we consider Carlton and United Brewery's sponsorship of the one-day international series under the umbrella of its Victoria Bitter (VB) brand. Consumers see a strong fit between beer and cricket that enhances the value of this association enormously. Look at the perception map in Figure 10.2, which highlights the values, attitudes and lifestyle activities that both beer as a category, and cricket as a sport, might have in common.

**Figure 10.2:** Perceptual match between beer and cricket

Source: Keen 2003

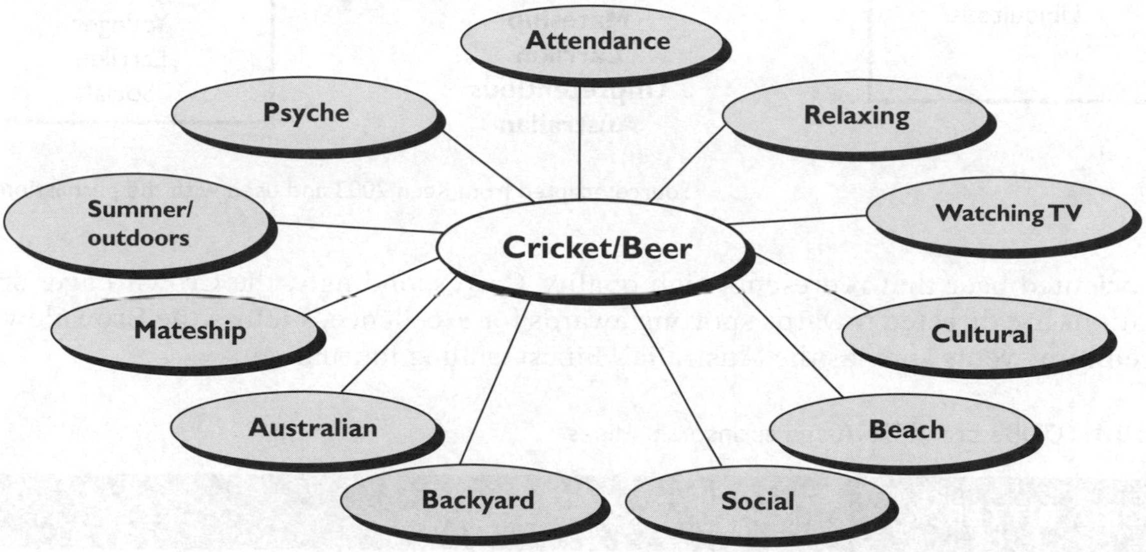


While it might appear that the fit between cricket and beer is almost obvious, you should remember that we are looking for strategic marketing opportunities here. If there was nothing more to gain from a formal association between a beer brand and a cricket property then the association would not make strategic sense. However, CUB considered that while cricket and VB were well aligned, the one-day international series specifically offered an opportunity to stretch its boundaries via its association with a more modern form of cricket. Figure 10.3 shows the brand DNA match between VB and one-day international cricket. You will see that apart from the natural alignment between beer and cricket, the relationship offered VB a vehicle to reach a larger, younger audience in an exciting and social atmosphere. In addition, the geographically labelled 'Victoria' Bitter could be seen in an international cricketing forum. Support of the national Australian team could be associated with the once state-bound VB brand.

The Foster's Group have many leading examples of carefully considered brand DNA matches with sporting properties. Under the Foster's Group, Carlton and United Breweries have built a stable of strong beer brands with deliberate and strategic links to sporting properties. Table 10.1 shows six of their beer brands with an outline of their DNA, their target markets and each brand's links to sport sponsorship properties. Notice the way in which the brands are described, first with a proposition or image, then with a tag line or slogan that encapsulates this image. The description also uses terms to depict the characteristics and strengths of the brand. It is interesting to compare the kinds of investments made under the different brands. For example, Carlton Midstrength is described as a down to earth 'real' beer that fosters feelings of mateship and has an investment in AFL and cricket. Crown Lager on the other hand is seen as a premium

**Figure 10.3:** Brand DNA match between VB and one-day international cricket

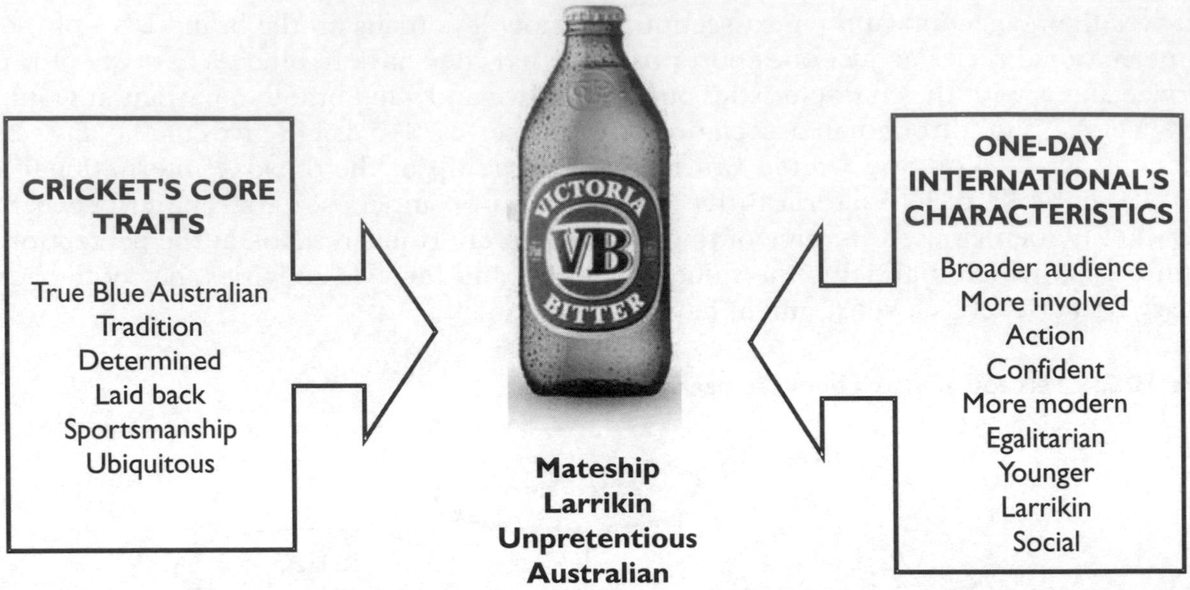


Source: adapted from Keen 2003 and used with the permission of CUB

status oriented beer that represents high quality. Correspondingly, the Crown Lager sporting associations are directed towards sporting awards for excellence, such as the Brownlow Medal and premium events such as the 'Australia's Finest' golfing tournament.

**Table 10.1:** CUB's brand DNA and sponsorship links

| | |
|---|---|
| **VICTORIA BITTER** | |
| Brand proposition (image) | A honest reward for a hard earned thirst, represented by blue collar drinking values. |
| Positioning line | 'For a hard earned thirst' |
| Primary target | All 18–54 year old males. Consuming full strength beer. |
| Brand strengths | 'Fair Dinkum', great/real beer taste. Acceptance/popularity, Aussie, ubiquitous. |
| Relevant promotional links | BBQs, camping, fishing, e.g. camping chairs, esky, car fridges etc. |
| Sponsorship link | One-day international cricket, fishing, rugby league (NSW), motor sport. |
| **CARLTON MIDSTRENGTH** | |
| Brand proposition (image) | A mid-strength beer that delivers the taste of a full strength beer. |
| Positioning line | 'Stay a little longer' |
| Primary target | Males 35+, honest, middle class, Aussie blokes. |
| Brand strengths | Traditional, down to earth, real beer credentials, taste, mateship. |
| Relevant promotional links | BBQ, camping, Aussie sports, eskies. |
| Sponsorship link | AFL – WA/QLD, Cricket – WA. |
| **CARLTON DRAUGHT** | |
| Brand proposition (image) | Australia's best draught beer. |
| Positioning line | Brewery Fresh |

| | |
|---|---|
| Primary target | 18–24 with 18–39 focus, full strength, on-premise drinking males, focus on draught beer (i.e. tap) not packaged. |
| Brand strengths | Brewery fresh, unquestionable quality, respected, straightforward, the draught beer to drink (on premise) with your mates. |
| Relevant promotional links | AFL, horse racing and properties with draught beer focus. |
| Sponsorship link | AFL, horse racing. |
| **CROWN LAGER** | |
| Brand proposition (image) | The definitive Australian Premium Beer – confident, understated and approachable. |
| Positioning line | 'Australia's Finest' |
| Primary target | All premium beer drinkers. |
| Brand strengths | 1. Unique bottle/label, Australia's #1 premium beer. 2. Restaurant heritage/premium image. 3. Consistent high quality taste. |
| Relevant promotional links | Associate the brand with special celebratory occasions (e.g. Australian Open Golf, Australian Fine Food festivals, fine dining, Father's Day, Christmas, New Year's Eve, Test Cricket, Brownlow Medal). |
| Sponsorship link | Fine Food festivals, restaurants, 'Australia's Finest' golf event, Test Cricket series, Allan Border Medal, Brownlow Medal. |
| **CASCADE PREMIUM LAGER** | |
| Brand proposition (image) | A premium beer from the oldest brewery in Australia, made from the purest ingredients. |
| Positioning line | 'Out of the Wilderness', 'Pure Enjoyment' |
| Primary target | White collar males, aged 24–35, with high socio-economic status. |
| Brand strengths | 1. Tasmanian purity and heritage. 2. Brewed at Australia's oldest brewery. 3. Premium image and consistent high quality taste. |
| Relevant promotional links | Brand is associated with the arts and lifestyle – premium Tasmanian, outdoor activities/retreats and apparel, e.g. Timberland, cultural events, i.e. performing arts, Fine Food festival, jazz events. |
| Sponsorship link | Fine Food festivals, restaurants, Australian ballet. |
| **CASCADE PREMIUM LIGHT** | |
| Brand proposition (image) | (Image) Pure, premium Cascade taste in a light beer. |
| Positioning line | 'The best light beer you'll ever taste' |
| Brand character | Contemporary, stylish, sociable, discerning. |
| Primary target | 28–35-year-old men, white/grey collar skew. Premium beer drinkers (as part of their repertoire). |
| Brand strengths | Premium packaging, pure taste, Tasmanian heritage. |
| Relevant promotional links | Golf, tennis, premium outdoor activities. |
| Sponsorship link | Golf, tennis. |

Source: Carlton and United Sponsorship Guidelines, September 2002. Used with the permission of CUB.

The Foster's beer brand is a heavily committed sponsor of Formula One Grand Prix motor racing. In 2000 the group entered into a 10-year agreement to sponsor Grand Prix worldwide, stamping their mark on the global beer market. In 2001 Fosters strengthened its commitment to Formula One by taking over the Australian Grand Prix sponsorship reins from fellow Australian brand Qantas. Ted Kunkel, President and CEO of the Foster's Group, said at the time that:

> The driving factor behind our decision to pursue the opportunity was that, unlike many national events, the Australian Grand Prix is a truly international spectacle and is part of the fastest-growing sport in the world today. It is watched by 600 million people in 212 countries around the world. What is more, we share each other's brand characteristics in both being international, aspirational, fun, exciting, youthful and glamorous ... Foster's is one of the world's fastest-growing international premium beer brands and the Australian Grand Prix, this country's premier sporting event, has great synergy with all our global marketing efforts.
>
> (Kunkel 2001)

Formula One is watched by some 600 million people worldwide

Foster's decision to invest heavily in Formula One may have even bigger rewards than they expected given China's recent investment in the sport. China has spent over a billion dollars on several motor racing facilities in Shanghai and Beijing recently, hoping to achieve global acceptance and a place on the regular sporting circuit. Foster's long-term agreement with Grand Prix worldwide may provide it with a very lucrative platform for its Chinese marketing efforts.

There are examples of brand DNA matches that are not as clear cut or indeed successful as those already discussed. In 2003, Tour De France veteran and international sporting celebrity, Lance Armstrong, was paid US$12 million to endorse Subaru automobiles. In an interesting twist, many marketing critics believe that it was Armstrong and his management team that failed to adequately assess the strategic benefit of the association and that the fit between Armstrong's brand DNA and that of Subaru were not mutually beneficial. Subaru insisted that they and Armstrong were a perfect match because they were both 'driven by what's inside'. However, critics insisted that Armstrong ran a very real risk of damaging his own personal brand by attaching to something that didn't have the same credibility that he did (Horovitz 2003).

Brand DNA is the building blocks of your brand and represents not only what the brand is but what you want it to be. In this sense it is a strategic direction and should guide your focus in shopping for a sporting property. The next section examines what your objectives are in using sport to market your brand, and establishes the importance of making sporting investments based on the fit between your objective and those of the sport property.

## Clarify and match objectives

Sport properties have value if they provide a meaningful way to build business. However, without a clear vision the use of sports in marketing can be misguided, underused, ineffective and even potentially damaging to the brand or the business as a whole. Like any marketing effort, engaging in the use of sport should be accompanied by a clear set of objectives. The objectives outline what you want to achieve and will guide all efforts surrounding the initiative including choosing a sport property and the design of leveraging programs for that property. There should also be a hierarchy of objectives so that those involved in implementing marketing programs understand which outcomes are priorities or key to the success of the program. One final reason why objectives are so important when choosing a sport property is that the 'right' property simply may not exist. However if you have a specific and strategic set of objectives in mind the good sports professional will be able to work with you to tailor a sport property to specifically meet your needs. Like any marketing effort you may not want to repeat a tried and true marketing strategy, but instead shop around for a fresh and creative approach.

As well as establishing your own objectives, you must evaluate the objectives of any potential sport properties that you consider. Similarly you need to understand the hierarchy of objectives of the sporting organisation or personality so that you can determine if there is a good 'fit' with your priorities. Remember you will be entering into a partnership, not merely purchasing exposure. Therefore, you need to decide whether or not your company will be able to contribute to the achievement of the sport's objectives, as well as considering their role in achieving your business objectives. In the interests of your long-term overall success, the sport property must also achieve their objectives. Mutual satisfaction of objectives is the ultimate goal in any sports marketing partnership.

Good objectives have five basic characteristics. They should be SMART:

1. **s**pecific
2. **m**easurable
3. **a**chievable
4. **r**ealistic
5. **t**imely.

This means that your objectives should address actual outcomes, using some quantifiable unit that can be measured, such as sales volume, percentage of target market awareness, market share or any relevant measure. The objectives should also be bound by an achievable time frame, such as 'within the next six months', or over a two-year period. You must have a time frame to work within and to use for assessment of the relative success of the program. It is also important that you do not attach unrealistic expectations to the sport property. Remember that it is only part of the overall marketing mix and objectives should reflect this.

While there may be many different factors that motivate a company to use sport in their marketing program, there are essentially four main categories of objectives for investing in a sport property. These objectives categories are:

- corporate objectives relating to the company's image, relationship building and/or employee morale
- marketing objectives of brand promotion and increased sales
- media objectives concerning cost-effectiveness and reaching target markets
- market objectives that aim to extend target markets or give access to new markets.

Objectives tied to corporate philosophy are not uncommon and are often tied to the vision of the company and their mission statement. They might include engaging a sport property because it supports the local community or to strengthen employee loyalty. Many companies have a societal statement in their vision or mission but don't have a natural link to community involvement and goodwill. Sport can give them an excellent vehicle to achieve those societal objectives.

Using sport to access new markets or penetrate existing markets is another category of objectives. Companies in the USA are using sports to mine new constituencies, including women in non-traditional markets. Women's sports in the USA have slowly been receiving better television ratings over the past five years and with these ratings have come larger sponsorship dollars. Some companies are waking up to the fact that investing in women's sports helps them reach consumers that they can't reach with men's sport properties. Research shows that women sports fans in America are 33 per cent more likely to have higher incomes than non-sports fans, 80 per cent more likely to buy a car, 44 per cent more likely to have a credit card and that women control about 75 per cent of total sports apparel dollars. Fifty-nine per cent of females also feel better about making purchases from companies that support women's sports (Roy 2003). Women's sport properties in the USA are made even more attractive by the fact that women's sports draw equal numbers of male and female fans. General Motors succeeded in reaching out to the female market by investing in one of the first WNBA sponsorship properties in America.

Women control about 75 per cent of total sports apparel dollars

Traditionally targeting male markets, General Motors harnessed the passion and inspiration that is fuelling sports participation trends to target specific models of their cars. They backed up their sponsorship with an integrated marketing program and a cause overlay dedicated to breast cancer awareness (Roy 2003). The campaign was successful in raising awareness of and opinion about GM's brands in the female target markets and GM were also successful in helping the WNBA achieve their marketing objectives of increased participation, raising player profiles and increasing exposure of the national competition.

Another common objective in using sport seems to be brand building and brand awareness. Today's marketplace is an intensely competitive environment in almost all industries. In order to make a brand stand out in the marketplace, companies will use sport to create a unique position in the mind of the consumer and use the emotive power of sport to boost the feelings towards their brand. The aim is to foster favourable recognition of the brand in the mind of the consumer so that they will be more receptive to further, more specific, marketing messages.

Other objectives may be much more specific and tangible such as those related to increases in sales and/or consumption of product as a direct result of the sport property. For a hotel chain this might mean an increase in the number of bookings at a specific venue during a specific competition. For a beer or soft drink manufacturer it might equate to increased sales before, during and after an event. This type of objective is very specific and has a definite time limit being tied to an event, or a competition or a season of play. Heineken have definite short-term sales objectives as part of their investment in the Australian Open tennis event. However they also have longer-term brand building and image objectives related to this same event. Qantas has made a very small but strategic investment in the Seniors Ping Pong Championship in the past, based on a short-term sales objective. While sponsoring the event in Australia did not provide them with any media coverage, or satisfy any broad corporate or market objectives, it did result in the sale of 2000 overseas airfares by international participants travelling to Australia for the championship. For a modest $10 000 investment by Qantas, this sport property represented good short-term value for limited commitment or leveraging effort. This leads us to the next issue in choosing a sport property, which is to determine the limitations or boundaries within which you operate.

## Determine limitations

Deciding whether or not to use sport in marketing and the subsequent choice of sport properties requires a thorough understanding of the limitations under which your company does and should operate. Limitations in our discussion will fall under two major types:

1. self-imposed limitations
2. legal limitations.

Self-imposed limitations represent those boundaries that the company decides upon strategically to protect their brands, their employees, their markets and/or society in general. Legal limitations refer to those boundaries imposed by the regulations and restrictions governing the industries and markets within which you operate. A third set of limitations, financial limitations, is also applicable but will be highlighted as a separate issue in the next section.

When choosing a sport property you should use a pre-developed list of self-imposed limitations to screen the immediate suitability of the property in question. These guidelines should be developed by upper management in direct consideration of the overall strategy of the company and/or brands involved. It is important that an effort be made to protect the integrity and positioning of your brand, protect your target markets, protect the community in general, and also the environment. While some companies seek the publicity generated from controversy, you need to understand the kind of controversy that could be appropriate, if any, and what situations are simply to be avoided at all costs.

Carlton and United Breweries (CUB) have a policy that outlines the limitations that are to be imposed when screening sport properties. These limitations include avoiding any sponsorship that could involve CUB in controversial issues or exposing the organisation to adverse criticism. CUB defines this policy further, including a list of sponsorships that are deemed as *inappropriate*:

- programs that denigrate, exclude, or offend minority community groups
- any organisation, team, group or individual sponsorship that has an under 18 years of age demographic
- personalities/celebrities under the age of 26 endorsing CUB or any CUB product (in line with the Advertising Code of Practice)
- programs that may present a hazard to the community
- programs that do not reflect community standards
- programs that could represent excessive drinking (Carlton and United Breweries 2002).

You will note that the policy includes both self-imposed regulations (for example programs that could offend minorities) and legal and industry regulations (such as those set out by the Advertising Code of Practice). The CUB policy also has clear ethical limits with regards to what is considered acceptable for a company in their industry. An evaluation must be made as to what is ethical in addition to what may actually be legal.

Legal limitations might include obvious things like not selling or promoting alcohol to minors, limitations regarding not using offensive language in promotional materials or restrictions

Tobacco companies face myriad legal restrictions regarding the use of sport for marketing purposes

like the myriad governing the tobacco industry. There are strict guidelines in many countries, Australia included, governing what tobacco companies can and cannot do with regards to all their marketing efforts. Australia has a long history of strategic association between sport and tobacco with, for example, the Benson and Hedges World Series Cricket Cup, Marlboro Motor Racing Teams and the Winfield NRL Cup. Tobacco companies using sport to market their brands face a minefield of domestic and international legal restrictions. However, in motor racing, for example, it is not only tobacco companies that have issues but also other companies that do not want to be associated with tobacco. The complex legal environment governing international broadcasting means that tobacco companies can often circumvent tobacco promotion regulations. This means that your sponsorship of a motor racing event or team could put your logo side by side with that of tobacco companies from around the world. If this association is inappropriate then so is your investment in that particular sport property. Jurisdictional issues are of concern here and you would need to be aware of the implications for your brand.

Here is an example given by Dewhirst and Hunter (2002):

> When the European Commission stipulated that tobacco sponsorships in F1 would be banned in 2006, for example, it was threatened that races might be moved out of Europe and held in alternative locations such as China, South Korea, and Indonesia (where restrictions on tobacco promotion are much less severe). Since domestic bans on tobacco sponsorship are typically not applicable to foreign media imported or transmitted into the respective country, many of F1's 300 million television viewers watching each race would remain exposed to tobacco promotions (p.149).

Open any motor car or motor bike racing magazine and you will see brands that are directly or indirectly associated with tobacco because of their association with motor sports. A Honda advertisement used in *Formula 1 Magazine* in 2001 included pictures of two Honda racing cars, one with a Lucky Strike cigarette logo on it and the other with a Benson and Hedges logo on it. *F1 Racing* magazine contained a series of Hewlett-Packard ads in 1999 that leveraged Hewlett-Packards' involvement in Grand Prix racing, showing a car covered with Benson and Hedges cigarette logos. This kind of association would be seen as totally inappropriate by other companies. For example, Microsoft's Bill Gates donates huge amounts of money to global health issues including global malaria eradication and youth diseases. Investing in a sport property that would align the company with a tobacco product would be seen as very inappropriate for their overall corporate image. Also inappropriate would be an association with a tobacco sports sponsorship by any pharmaceutical company or government body.

## Assess company and budget size restraints

When choosing a sport property you make sure you are shopping in your price range. Obviously a small regional company is not going to be able to afford or leverage a major national sporting venue naming rights agreement. Setting a realistic budget to spend on a sport property is a functional strategic step that makes up part of the overall success strategy for using sport in marketing. In addition, you need to consider the comparative size of your organisation. What level of commitment are other companies your size making to sport? Are any of your competitors involved in sport? Have a clear picture of your positioning in the marketplace and of your competitive stance.

One basic assessment is to evaluate the relative geographic scope of your target markets. As a simple rule you should choose a sport property that has the same target market coverage as you do, or that you are aiming for. If you are a small local butcher, then a local football team or local netball team might be the right match for your size business. If you are a statewide insurance company then choosing a sport property related to a state representative team or competition will be better for you. If you are a statewide insurance company looking to open interstate offices and expand to a national audience, then you might consider choosing a national sport property as a way of launching your brand nationwide. If you are a global company, then a global sport property like an Olympic sponsorship or a sport property attached to a global competition such as the Rugby World Cup, Grand Slam tennis or World Cup soccer might better suit your needs. Of course it will depend on your objectives for acquiring a sport property. Coca-Cola, a global beverage company, give their local distributors a budget for sponsorship and sport property investment to foster a grassroots, community ownership effort among their target market. Supporting the local swimming team or kid's rugby league team gives Coca-Cola a localised feel and can encourage not only positive attitude and brand preference from consumers but increased consumption of the product at local games and competitions.

Determining budget size restraints may also be a functional classification or management level division. For example, while the national marketing manager may have the power to choose a sport property worth up to $1 million, you might also give each of the state marketing managers the discretionary power to spend $30000 a year on state sport initiatives. While the budget item might belong to the state manager the decision on choosing and managing the state property should still be done in consultation with the national manager and within the overall objectives for using sport in the company's marketing program.

## Identify leveragable benefits

In sponsorship decisions of old, the CEO or marketing manager might have made decisions based on what their favourite sport was or what sports their children played. In this new strategic era of sports marketing the decision is guided by a set of objectives and the investment is leveraged for maximum impact. In choosing a sport property you must identify all potential opportunities to leverage the sport property. You should also have a pre-conceived list of preferred leveragable benefits, or those that best suit the objectives of the company.

Leveragable benefits might include:

- ticketing and hospitality
- promotions
- brand leverage
- media exposure
- merchandise presence
- signage
- advertising
- brand endorsement.

It is difficult to list all possible leveragable benefits as your own marketing creativity really provides the limits here. Like any competitive marketing effort it is advisable to look for fresh and creative opportunities and avoid recreating what has been done in the past or what is currently being done by your competitors. If you understand how the sport property can potentially be leveraged you will be able to invest leveraging dollars into the best programs and even look at leveraging other marketing initiatives in concert with the sport property.

To highlight the importance of leveragable opportunities, consider the fact that to successfully use sports in marketing your leveraging spending should equal $2 for every dollar spent on the initial acquisition of the sport property. In other words, if you pay $100 000 for signage rights at a sporting event, you should budget to spend another $200 000 in leveraging those rights.

The sporting body, organisation or individual should be able to work with you to help identify leveraging opportunities. This might be anything from joint merchandising opportunities, to client/employee entertain-ment, personal appearances or opportunities to present trophies or awards – not forgetting the leveraging possible via added media opportunities associated with these activities. There is a whole host of leveragables so make sure that you anticipate and ask for everything from the sport property you are evaluating. This includes even those small or philanthropic investments that you make. Simple acts of goodwill like sponsoring a local unknown amateur team can still have significant leveragable potential. These things include getting your business involved to build camaraderie, positioning your organisation strategically and being able to capitalise on that position. Each is a realistic goal of such programs (Roeser 2002).

In developing creative leveraging strategies you should first understand what leveraging means. Leveraging your corporate sponsorship simply means finding creative ways to create greater value for your investment in the sport property. Table 10.2 gives you some examples of leveraging ideas under seven major categories including on-site sales, traffic drivers, proof of purchase, product/trial sampling, media tie-ins, donations programs, and networking and entertainment.

We will look at more leveraging examples and tools later in this chapter. All elements of the marketing mix can be used in your leveraging strategies, depending on your objectives. Another factor that will impact upon choosing a sport property and deciding on which leveraging opportunities to take up is the level of commitment that your company is willing and/or able to make to the sport property and its use in your marketing program.

## Establish commitment guidelines

In addition to setting up financial guidelines and budgets for the use of sport in marketing, you need to be sure of the level of commitment you are prepared to make to the sport property(ies) that you invest in. This means assessing how the sport property will be managed internally, how much time and effort can the company afford to spend on fulfilling their obligations both to their marketing campaign and to their sport partner. You should not underestimate how much time and effort goes into using sport in marketing. Just because having a corporate box at the football seems like a lot more fun than managing radio commercials and print ads, doesn't mean it requires any less skill or effort to leverage effectively. Assess whether or not the sport property you are choosing requires a lot of interaction by your own senior management and employees. How much commitment will be needed from your suppliers, partners and customers? You

**Table 10.2:** Leveraging ideas and examples

| Leveraging category | Examples and ideas |
|---|---|
| **On-site sales** | Exclusive vending opportunities in sports facilities and at special events can provide your company with the opportunity to reach a large number of people in a short time frame, while at the same time keeping the competition away. Many beverage companies will look for this type of leveraging opportunity. Be careful of potential conflicts between team, sport and venue sponsors all looking for the same opportunity on game day! |
| **Traffic drivers** | Traffic drivers include any marketing vehicle that entices a person to visit your location. Traffic driver tactics include such things as product discount coupons that are distributed to event participants or spectators and redeemed at your store or website. Having the tickets to an event available exclusively at your retail outlets is another common way to drive traffic. The objective is to get the consumer to visit your location so that a product sale can be made. Fast food companies, for example, are commonly known for providing event spectators with a discount coupon on the day of the event. The end result for the fast food outlet is increased customers and enhanced sales. |
| **Proof of purchase** | Some variations of this leveraging strategy include ticket tie-ins (proof of purchase of your product(s) can be used as tickets to the event or to reduce the price of the ticket), premiums (with proof of purchase, receive an event-themed prize) or self-liquidating offer (with proof of purchase and a specified amount of money, receiving a high-valued item). All variations can be effective methods for not only leveraging your investment and enhancing product sales, but also increasing interest in the event. |
| **Product trial/ sampling** | A major strategic advantage that corporate sponsorships can provide over traditional advertising is the ability to interact directly with the consumer. Through on-site promotional displays, sampling and product testing, you are able to interact directly with consumers and to explain the benefits of your products. |
| **Media tie-ins** | Although exposure is no longer the main reason why many companies invest in sport properties it remains an important benefit. The larger the audience that you can expose your logo or message to, the more valuable your investment becomes. Look for sport properties that have developed strategic partnerships with media companies and television networks. Also don't miss any opportunity to promote your involvement with the sport through industry or sport-related media outlets. |
| **Donations program** | People have a more positive image of companies that support a program they care about. A program where money or supplies are donated for every purchase of your product or service can often lead to increased product sales. Beverage and food companies often utilise the donations program as a leveraging tool for Olympic and Paralympic sponsorships. At select times, proceeds from the purchase of your products can go to support sporting fundraisers or other community programs. The Brisbane Lions AFL team donate money to the RSPCA for every pet membership purchased by their fans. An opportunity exists there for a pet-related brand or company to purchase the pet membership as a sport property and work at leveraging this sporting and charitable RSPCA opportunity. |
| **Networking and entertainment** | If networking or client entertainment is what the company is after, using sport in marketing can be an excellent choice. Through complimentary tickets, VIP areas, receptions or cross-promotions, sponsors are able to entertain clients or engage in business-to-business marketing. Most of Australia's large brands and companies have corporate tents at Melbourne Cup Day to entertain their clients. Visa used their sponsorship of the Rugby World Cup as a worldwide employee incentive and goodwill program with great success. |

Source: LeDrew 2003

should not enter into any agreement for a sport property until you have established how you will leverage the property and whether or not you are actually willing and able to do so.

Set some guidelines about time frames also. Make sure that you have allowed a reasonable amount of time to prepare for the leveraging activities that will need to accompany your sport property purchase. Visa often purchase sport properties such as Olympic and Rugby World Cup sponsorships up to eight years in advance and start their leveraging visits and initiatives two to four years before the actual sporting event takes place. The magnitude of the sport property and your proposed leveraging activities will dictate how much lead time you will require. The important thing is to at least consider the issues when screening and choosing sport properties initially.

## Formalising processes and practices

Identifying opportunities in sport may not be as straightforward as it seems. Sure, sponsorship managers and directors are bombarded with proposals from sporting clubs and organisations offering sport properties for sale; however that does not mean all or any of them are suitable investments. In fact sporting organisations are fast realising that they need to target their sports products, not only in the hope of selling them successfully but in order to maximise the benefit of their association with the purchaser.

Rather than waiting for proposals and offers to drift in, an active marketer will shop around for sport properties that fit the profile of their brand DNA and that will help them achieve their marketing strategy objectives. Those sporting bodies and/or organisations that do bring sport properties to you for consideration should be subjected to the same analysis with regards to the fit between the brand DNAs and the potential for mutual achievement of objectives. In this sense it is important that your organisation have both people and processes in place to evaluate sport properties under consideration.

For example, who will decide whether or not a sport property should be evaluated at all? How will a decision be made as to whether or not to invest in a sport property, and who will make this decision? Once you invest in a sport property, who will manage the marketing and leveraging efforts associated with this? How will success be measured and by whom? All of these questions should be answered with a policy and set of guidelines to generally manage the use of sport in your marketing efforts.

To begin with you should require that any sport property under evaluation be accompanied by a sponsorship application and/or proposal. If you are approaching the sporting body in the hope that they can tailor a property to your needs, then a formal proposal should be developed, approved in-house and then taken to the sporting body. If the sporting body is approaching you with a proposal they should be asked to complete an application in addition to their own presentation. While many sports present polished and detailed proposals it is still advisable to have them complete an application that forces them to address critical issues such as brand fit, exposure and value, leveraging opportunities, target market profiles, existing partner information etc. Carlton and United Breweries have a simple, standard sponsorship application form that potential sport partners must complete before their property will even be considered for further screening. A copy of this application can be seen in the Appendix at the end of this chapter. This application is a very functional form largely focusing on estimated values of leveraging opportunities. Of course different companies might focus on different aspects in their own application form, depending on the nature of their industry and objectives for using sport.

It is very important that you have a process in place to deal with choosing and then managing a sport property. It may be a function of the marketing department's duties but at what level? If your company has regional, state and national managers for example, you may give each of them some power and responsibility for choosing and managing corresponding regional, state and national properties. This will only work if you also have some checks and balances in place to make sure that the overall effort is unified and synergistic. Figure 10.4 shows an example of a sponsorship proposal process map. When a proposal comes in to the company it is directed to the appropriate level of management and an initial decision is made as to whether or not the proposal represents a leveragable sponsorship opportunity or is simply a business agreement. Just because your company is being asked to sell your hot dogs at the local cricket venue doesn't mean that you are investing in a sport property. You may be entering a simple business agreement with no leveraging opportunities, rights or responsibilities. It is essential that you distinguish between the two kinds of proposals.

Your formal processes must ensure that all sport properties are held accountable for achieving quantifiable marketing and/or communication objectives and your plan to manage the property should identify who will be responsible for achieving and measuring relative success.

**Figure 10.4:** Sport property proposal process map

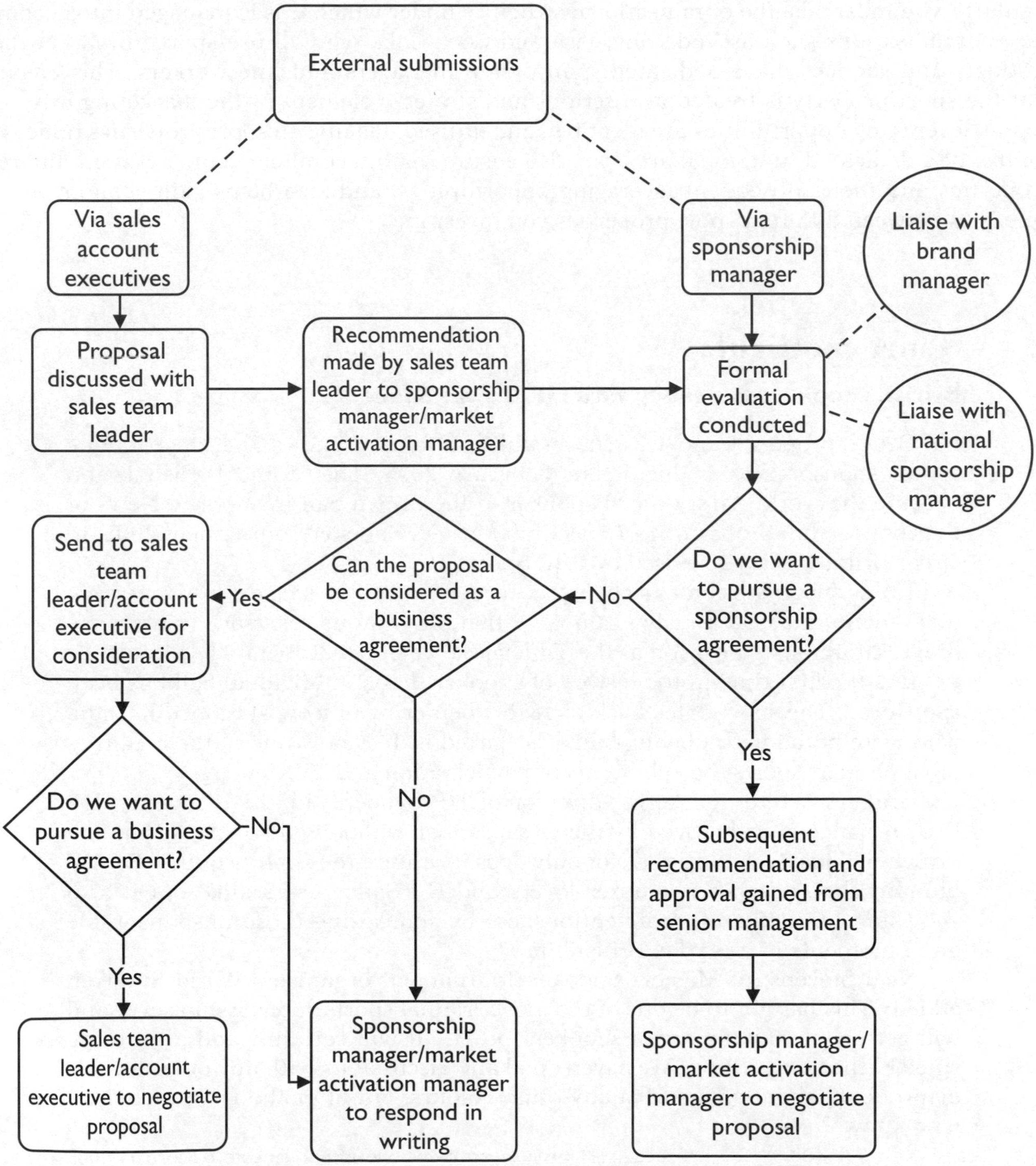


Source: Carlton and United Sponsorship Guidelines, September 2002. Used with the permission of CUB.

It may be a condition of the agreement that the sporting body supplies information of a certain kind, in a certain format at certain intervals, to assist with the evaluation of your investment. In addition there may be regular assessments made by your company and reported to the relevant people both internally and to the sporting body. Some practitioners believe that evaluation of your sport property must include an estimate of the return on your investment. This can be difficult to achieve and figures supplied by media representatives and even sporting bodies themselves are often over-inflated and exaggerated. However, one rule of thumb is that for each dollar spent, a good sport property investment should yield at least $8 (Roeser 2002). The 8:1 ROI (return on investment) rule of thumb should not be the sole basis for evaluation and again is very much dependent on the objectives of the investment in the first place.

Finally, if your company does use or is planning to use sport in their marketing program regularly, you must take the organisational structure under which this is managed into account. Large organisations such as Vodafone, Visa and Coca-Cola, who all use sport to market their products and services, have dedicated sponsorship managers and line workers. This ensures that the sport property is treated as a serious and strategic element of the marketing mix, and that all leveraging opportunities are identified and utilised. Placing all sport properties under the control of a dedicated functional area can also ensure that no conflict occurs between different properties and their subsequent leveraging opportunities, and also helps gain economies and synergies between different sport properties you invest in.

## Sport spotlight

### British snooker gets saucy with HP Brown Sauce

HP Sauce proposed and was successful in attaining one of the most unique sports sponsorships in history in February 2005. The iconic British brand became the world's first official sponsor of the brown ball in snooker. News of the sponsorship broke at the Rileys Club Masters Snooker Tournament 2005, in Great Britain, being televised by BBC Sport.

The sponsorship comes right on cue for HP Sauce. The sauce is also returning to TV with a new advertising campaign that plays on its relevance to everyday life, reinforcing its position as the 'Official Sauce of Great Britain'!

It is the first time in the history of snooker that an individual ball has been sponsored. The sport dates back to 1875 when army officers stationed in India who were bored with playing billiards started it. It is now one of the country's most popular sports: both in terms of participation and TV viewing.

Graham White, marketing director of HP Sauce, said, 'Like snooker, HP Brown Sauce is truly loved by the Great British public and so sponsoring the brown ball just feels so right. Not only does it capture the slightly quirky British humour that so typifies snooker lovers and HP Sauce users alike but it also shows an honesty and unpretentiousness by sponsoring those unsponsorable great moments in everyday British life.'

Neal Stevens, of Masters Snooker Tournament organisers World Snooker, added: 'This has got to be one of the most original sports sponsorships ever and will get people talking about snooker and HP. It will certainly add a bit more spice to the competition. We haven't had any discussions with any other brands or products about sponsoring any other colours, but after the HP Sauce deal, who knows?'

Sauce (!! ... I mean source): www.worldsnooker.com, 8 February 2005

## Leveraging the sports marketing platform

Leveraging is the art of finding creative ways to create greater value for your investment in a sport property. It requires expert knowledge and skills and is a critical element in achieving success in sports marketing. Leveraging or activation as it is also known is the real marketing work behind the initial purchase or investment in a sport property. Choosing and buying a sport property signifies the very beginning, not the end of your sports marketing campaign. An investment in the sport property often buys you the right to use the emotive power of that sport or team – how you use it depends on your leveraging skills and commitment.

It was mentioned previously that leveraging success depends on committing at least $2 for every $1 spent on the initial acquisition of the sport property. This figure can increase substantially depending on the objectives of the sports marketing program and the leveraging activities that will be used to achieve those objectives. For example the International Rugby Board (IRB) offered sport properties at all levels during the 2003 Rugby World Cup, including one they called 'Worldwide Partner Status'. Worldwide Partners, who made the biggest commitment to the event, included Visa, Telstra, Bundaberg Rum, Heineken, Qantas, British Airways and Coca-Cola. While the sport property that each partner invested in was essentially the same, the objectives of their involvement and the way in which they leveraged the event were very different.

Bundaberg Rum saw the Rugby World Cup as the jewel in the crown of their sporting involvement for 2003 and saw the Worldwide Partner Status as the perfect opportunity to escalate what it was already doing in its ongoing relationship with Australia's rugby union team, the Wallabies. Bundaberg Rum didn't leverage their partnership internationally and had very limited corporate hospitality involvement. This was a purposeful decision as the brand doesn't 'live' in the corporate world and the company was interested in the domestic marketing opportunities rather than the international potential of the brand at this point. Leveraging activities consisted largely of brand exposure, television commercials and limited edition merchandising. Heineken, on the other hand, took a very different angle on its investment as a Worldwide Partner of the Rugby World Cup. The motivation for their involvement was the strong global reach that this particular sport property could offer their brand. Heineken consider the essence of their brand's DNA to be international, in fact the 'most' international beer, so they look for sport properties that are global in reach and nature (B&T 2003a). Leveraging activities designed by Heineken included competitions to win tickets to the Cup by collecting codes from their products and entering these either via SMS or on the Heineken website. They had gifts with purchase including a ball key ring and special product labelling including the Rugby World Cup logo. They also released two specially designed commemorative products, the 1.5l magnum and the 500ml can, featuring rugby graphics and the Rugby World Cup's official branding. Heineken focused on leveraging opportunities that celebrated the fans, with advertising, merchandising and promotions all focused on their consumer target markets (Bombara 2003).

Leveraging your sport property investment is made much simpler if you have chosen the property based on your strategic objectives and with a critical understanding of your target markets. We used the example of women's sports earlier to show how GM used sport to reach new audiences. Another key target market is young people. Global statistics show that on average adults are fans of four sports, while young people are avid fans of seven. In terms of sports participation, 80 per cent of youth participate in sports compared to 41 per cent of the general population over 18 years of age. This 80 per cent also participate in more sports, averaging between seven or eight sports, compared to adults, whose average participation is in three or four sports (Roy 2003). These statistics are interesting enough on their own when thinking about using sports in marketing, but coupled with the youth market's growing buying power and strong influence on family purchase behaviours, the potential to leverage sport via youth becomes very attractive indeed.

A survey of nearly 4000 American youth online revealed that online youth aged 8 to 24 are currently spending at a projected rate of US$164 billion per year. Texaco, an American petrol company, are leveraging a NASCAR motor racing sponsorship to appeal to this growing market. Leveraging activities of Texaco's NASCAR sponsorship included youth-focused giveaways for fill-ups, with the hopes that kids would encourage parents to choose Texaco stations when filling up with petrol (Roy 2003).

Freesports appeal to people who are more interested in self-realisation than competition

When considering leveraging opportunities and factors that appeal to your consumers, you should choose marketing activities that fit well with the lifestyle and attitudes of your target markets. Just because the Olympics has phenomenal global coverage and appeal doesn't mean that it is right for your brand or your consumers. It depends on what you are trying to do, what leveraging activities might achieve this and then apply a sport that will facilitate this process with as much emotion and personal relevance as possible. Freesports (surfing, snowboarding, windsurfing, skate-boarding), despite a lack of mainstream or mass media exposure, definitely have a place in the sports marketing arsenal. The strength of freesport properties is that they attract a different audience psychographic to mainstream sports. Although many of these sports are considered extreme and youth oriented, the real strength may be that they appeal to independently minded people who are interested in self-realisation rather than competition (Fry 2001). If this image matches the brand DNA you are trying to create, or the real or inspirational values of your target market, then freesports might be a good platform for you to market your product or service. Leveraging opportunities with these sport properties won't be via mass media or mainstream media exposure but rather a flexible and uncluttered channel that is viral in nature and almost underground or cultlike in its appeal.

Sony PlayStation leveraged their support of freesports to kick off their brand-building program before they invested in and leveraged soccer properties to build mainstream awareness. Freesports also underpinned the reinvention of the downmarket Casio brand through its role in marketing the G-Shock watch brand (Fry 2001).

Leveraging activities might also include using your sport property to gain access to a 'test' audience. Global media exposure in key markets has been a key decision criterion in all of Vodafone's sport property deals including Manchester United, the Australian Rugby Union team and Ferrari racing. However, they have also leveraged their partnership with Manchester United to test mobile telephone-based services through the team's fan base by giving them the chance to listen in on the action away from the stadium (Fry 2001).

While not an exhaustive list by any means, Table 10.3 outlines a five-element marketing mix (product, price, promotion, place and people) and some of the leveraging tools that might be relevant under each element.

**Table 10.3:** Marketing mix leveraging tools

| | |
|---|---|
| **Product** | • merchandise<br>• limited editions<br>• versioning<br>• giveaways<br>• souvenirs<br>• event creation |
| **Price** | • trial pricing<br>• special offers<br>• ticket savings<br>• coupon offers<br>• loyalty pricing programs |
| **Promotion** | • mass media exposure<br>• press conferences/releases<br>• signage<br>• personal selling opportunities<br>• complimentary tickets<br>• media tie-ins |
| **Place** | • venue sales<br>• online traffic drivers<br>• mobile commerce solutions (SMS) etc.<br>• traffic drivers |
| **People** | • hospitality and networking<br>• relationship building<br>• business to consumer<br>• business to business<br>• business to employee<br>• business to supplier<br>• VIP areas |

There are many specific examples of leveraging activities and you should consider the motives and target markets of companies investing in sport properties next time you walk through the supermarket or watch television and see these activities first hand. Personal grooming products have a history of using sport to help market their products, particularly through sportsperson endorsements. Olympic athletes, national sports stars and whole teams have been seen endorsing deodorant and soap on mass media. You should be careful to distinguish investment and leveraging here as opposed to a simple business deal. Unilever hair care brand Sunsilk recently used NRL and AFL players in Australia to launch their first product and campaign targeted specifically at men. The brand, Base Elements, was not aimed at the 'metrosexual' but rather at 'real blokes' (Veldre 2003). However, Sunsilk and the Base Elements brand are not partners in the NRL and AFL in any ongoing relationship and the endorsement of the players appearing in the commercials was more likely to be a simple one-time contractual arrangement. This is different from the Colgate-Palmolive strategy in America where the company spent over $15 million in a television advertising campaign in 1993 to launch a more powerful odour-fighting deodorant formula, the Mennen Speed Stick, by teaming up with the National Football League (NFL). Their agreement constituted an actual partnership or sponsorship with Mennen Speed Stick becoming an official sponsor of NFL and antiperspirant-deodorant line of choice among players (Riddle 1993).

The important thing to remember when leveraging your sport property is that it must be embedded in corporate strategy and executed through your brand value proposition. Your investment in sport should represent a platform that could enhance the effectiveness and efficiency of a range of marketing activities and should be activated and integrated into the marketing mix. You should not think of sport as a stand-alone marketing tool. The next section showcases how Visa turned their involvement with the 2003 Rugby World Cup in Australia into an effective and impressive marketing platform.

## Visa: A leveraging case in point

Visa's involvement in the 2003 Rugby World Cup in Australia is a comprehensive example of strategic investment in a sport property and the subsequent leveraging of that investment. Visa use sport as an integral part of their global marketing strategies, being heavily involved in the Olympics, the Rugby World Cup and the NFL in America. Sport has become such a strategic component of the company's marketing mix that they regard their investment in sport as a 'door opener' to conducting business around the world. Visa's involvement in the 2008 Olympics in China will help them 'in' to that market, giving them critical contacts with government officials, exposure to the huge Chinese consumer and business markets and a business platform to work from.

The success of Visa's involvement in sports marketing could well be attributed to their strategic focus, excellent leveraging programs and the rigorous planning and evaluation of their investments. As a rule the company allow two to three times as much money to activate or leverage their investment as the cost of the sport property. They also work on leveraging sponsorships up to five to 10 years before the event. Before the announcement in July of 2003 that Vancouver would host the 2010 Winter Olympics, Visa had already started meeting with potential host countries. They have already started planning their leveraging campaign for Vancouver. Leveraging activities start long before the event while the excitement is building and extend beyond the life of the event also. Visa started tracking the ROI of the 2003 Rugby World Cup in Australia six months before the competition began. They evaluated and measured ROI globally, not just in the host country.

Let's examine the Visa brand and their sponsorship of the 2003 Rugby World Cup. Visa has a member association of 21 000 financial institutions with over a billion cardholders with spending of $2.7 trillion. They are one of the world's top 15 brands and have an ATM network with more than 800 000 ATMs in 120 countries around the word. They hold 62.9 per cent share of the global credit market in front of their closest rival, MasterCard, with 26.8 per cent (Nilson Report 2002).

In choosing to invest in a Worldwide Partner Status in the 2003 Rugby World Cup, Visa was looking to use sport as an effective marketing platform in several ways. The four major areas that they were interested in were:

- Advertising
  - Building awareness and imagery
  - Support member acquisition and usage
- Promotions
  - Increase card usage
  - Build and strengthen partnerships with strong brands
- Product platform
  - Showcase new technologies

  - Launch new products
  - Refine infrastructure
- Corporate relations
  - Enhance the impact and reach of other marketing efforts
  - Strengthen corporate reputation and image
  - Develop employee incentive, reward and motivation programs (Li 2003).

You should appreciate that the objectives of the company were diverse and ambitious, which is appropriate for a brand of this magnitude. The integrated and extensive leveraging activities they used represent an excellent marketing platform and a maximisation of their investment in the RWC property.

In activating their sponsorship Visa concentrated on five functional areas. The first was to form an *activation strategy and a taskforce* to implement that strategy. Second, a *budget* was established, based on the objectives and strategies set by senior management and the taskforce. Third, they focused on *internal sell through*, which meant gaining support and momentum for the program in-house. Fourth, they developed and acquired the *tools needed to activate and support* the program. Finally, systems to *track and evaluate* the entire program were set in place.

Visa eventually developed seven leveraging programs associated with the 2003 RWC. These included:

1. advertising
2. public relations programs
3. national promotions
4. member programs (over 80 programs in 10 markets)
5. merchant programs
6. cross-promotion with other partners
7. host market visibility programs (Li 2003).

One of the interesting and creative ways in which a company can leverage their sports platform is to create 'events' or awards associated with the event to provide for extra advertising, publicity and public relations opportunities. There were four such initiatives that Visa were involved in for the RWC and a summary of these can be seen in Figure 10.5.

One of the most impressive things about Visa's use of sport in marketing is their ability to bring together key market stakeholders in cross-promotion opportunities. This is well demonstrated in their destination marketing program from the RWC in Australia. The basic philosophy behind destination marketing for Visa is that tourists spend money. The more visitors the host country gets the more money is likely to be spent using a Visa card. Visa estimates that the destination marketing efforts during the Sydney 2000 Olympic Games resulted in a 7 per cent increase in tourism in Australia and a corresponding 23 per cent increase in Visa volume for the same period (Li 2003).

Therefore it is in Visa's best interests to make the host market for any sporting event as visible as possible. Global sporting events benefit the host market and they should leverage the events like any other sponsor or partner. Visa is well skilled at helping host countries identify common objectives and developing cross-promotion activities. Their skills in destination marketing, as a by-product of their industry, will be invaluable to developing countries like China that are embarking on a decade of major host activities including the 2010 World Expo in Shanghai and the 2008 Olympics in Beijing. Visa gave Australia excellent brand exposure before, during and after the 2003 RWC with over 500 Visa member programs in over 50 countries around the world, all of them featuring images of Australia. They actually partnered with the Australian Tourism Commission to provide joint advertising and promotions in the United Kingdom in the lead-up to the Cup. They also joined with other key stakeholders, partnering with the RWC Official Travel Operators and producing the 'Visa Guide to the RWC 2003', a guide containing over 100 merchant offers for RWC fans and visitors (Li 2003). Over 550 000 copies of the guide were distributed.

Figure 10.5: Visa's advertising and PR initiatives for the 2003 Rugby World Cup

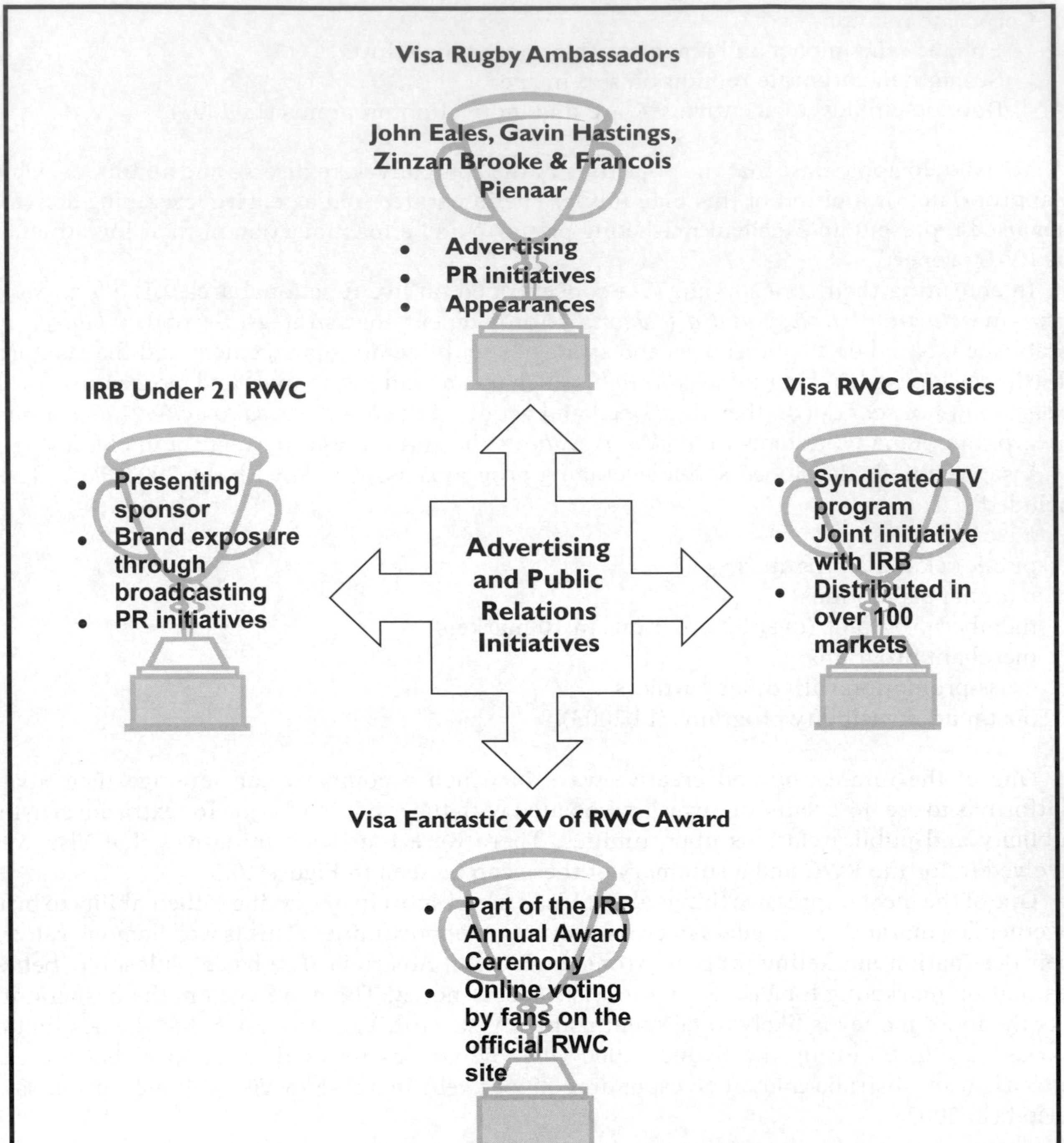


Visa can be held up as an example of best practice in using sport in marketing to both large and small companies alike. Despite the power of the Visa brand, even small companies can learn a lesson from their sports marketing leveraging activities by focusing on the creative and integrated approach taken by the company.

## Counterpoint: Leveraging 'without' investing in a sport property – Ambush marketing

If leveraging your investment in a sport property is where the real marketing benefits are, and you need to spend more money on leveraging activities than the initial acquisition price of the sport property, why buy into sport at all? Why not just carry out some leveraging activities at the same time as a major event or during a sporting season? Why not just contract with a few sporting celebrities on a one-time endorsement basis to give the illusion that you are involved with the sport?

While the ethics and legality of ambush marketing, as this practice is called, have been discussed and debated, the fact remains that major brands are making major headway by engaging in leveraging activities without buying into the related sport property.

Vodafone planned and executed a major leveraging campaign during the 2003 RWC in Australia, without being an official sponsor or partner of the event. One of the more spectacular leveraging activities they carried out was a giant floating football field. The field was constructed on a 100x20m barge using 60 tonnes of soil and almost 1000 square metres of real grass turf. It featured 10-metre high goal posts, light towers and corporate hospitality facilities for 100 people (B&T Weekly 2003b). The barge was used predominantly for brand exposure and corporate hospitality. Towed around Sydney Harbour hosting celebrity rugby games and screening the RWC action at night, the barge attracted major media attention and was a highly visible prop for the Vodafone brand. All without a single dollar being invested directly in the RWC or to the IRB.

Is it possible that sponsorship is not a good investment at all? If we can benefit from sports and sports events by clever marketing associations, why would we consider a direct investment? Leveraging a sponsorship can be very expensive and perhaps the grey area of what actually constitutes ambush marketing could save us the price of the actual sport property to begin with.

## Summary

- **recognise and explain the importance of leveraging sports marketing investments**
  Sports marketing can provide a powerful and effective marketing platform. However, choosing and investing in a sport property is only the beginning. It is the leveraging activities that surround the sport property that offer the true benefits to your brand and company. In general when budgeting leveraging activities you should allow $2 for every $1 spent on acquiring the sport in the first place.
- **identify how a sport property should be chosen strategically**
  Choosing a sport property is a strategic activity that should be based on your objectives for using sport as part of an integrated marketing program. In addition to your own objectives, you must understand those of the sport and assess whether or not you are capable of the mutual satisfaction of your objectives. Critical to the success of your investment is understanding the fit between the brand DNA of your company and the sport property. The major mistakes that companies using sport can make include: failing to establish objectives from the beginning, choosing the 'wrong' property, failing to integrate the property into the overall marketing program, not allocating a sufficient leveraging budget and failing to assess what their competition is already doing.
- **understand the importance of setting objectives and matching brand DNA**
  Before even looking for a sport property to invest in, the company must ensure that it is guided by a set of SMART objectives. SMART objectives are specific, measurable, achievable, realistic and timely. It is essential also that consideration is given to the brand DNA of both the company's product and the potential sport partner. Be sure to consider a perceptual map that shows any relationship or natural linkage between the product/service and the sport.
- **outline the two types of limitations to be considered when using sport in marketing**
  Deciding on whether or not to use sport in marketing and the choice of a sport property requires a thorough understanding of the limitations under which your company does and should operate. The two types of limitations you should consider are self-imposed limitations and legal limitations.

Self-imposed limitations are the boundaries that your company decides upon strategically to protect your brand, image, employees, your markets and even society in general. Legal limitations are all those boundaries imposed by legislation or relevant industry regulation. You should also be cognisant of financial limitations, however these considerations are more relevant in the evaluation and operationalisation of your sport investment rather than at the strategic planning level.

- **identify and explain the key components in an activation and leveraging plan**
  Once an appropriate sport property has been chosen the real work begins. Activating or leveraging your investment is a strategic marketing exercise that involves planning, implementing, executing and evaluating all activities involved. You need to make sure that your organisational structure is conducive to managing a sport property and that you have formal processes and practices in place to execute strategies.

## Review questions

1. What are the components of brand DNA and why are they important in leveraging your sport property?
2. What are the characteristics of a good objective?
3. What are the four main categories of objectives for investing in a sport property? Give examples of each.
4. What are the two types of limitations you should consider when choosing a sport property?
5. Identify at least two leveraging tools for each element of the marketing mix.

## Applied activities

1. Visit the Visa website www.visa.com and see what sports events they are currently sponsoring. What types of leveraging activities are evidenced on the website? Are there any cross-promotions with other partners? What do you think the objectives of each leveraging activity might be?
2. Visit the Vodafone (www.vodafone.com) and Manchester United (http://www.manutd.com) websites. What do you think the objectives of Vodafone's investment in Manchester United are? How are they leveraging their investment and who are the activities targeted at?
3. Your organisation, a local furniture removal business, has been given a proposal by the local university football team asking for you to be the major naming rights sponsor of the team for the next two years. How will you assess the proposal and if you decide to invest in the sport property how might you leverage your investment?

# References


B&T 2003a, 'World Cup Sponsors Look to Score', *B&T Weekly*, 23 April, http://www.bandt.com.au/articles/77/0C014F77.asp, viewed 26 November 2003.

B&T 2003b, 'Vodafone Unveils Floating Footy Field', *B&T Weekly*, 7 November, http://www.bandt.com.au/articles/88/0C01B988.asp, viewed 26 November 2003.

Bombara, P. 2003, 'Heineken Comp No Small Beer', *B&T Weekly*, July 25, p.7.

Carlton and United Breweries 2002, 'Sponsorship Guidelines', September, unpublished document.

Dewhirst, T. & Hunter, A. 2002, 'Tobacco Sponsorship of Formula One and CART Auto Racing: Tobacco Brand Exposure and Enhanced Symbolic Imagery Through Co-sponsors' Third Party Advertising', *Tobacco Control*, Vol. 11, pp.146–50.

Fry, A. 2001, 'How to Profit from Sponsoring Sport', *Marketing*, 16 August, Haymarket Publishing Ltd, London. pp.25–6.

Horovitz, B. 2003, 'Biking champ Armstrong gets $12M to peddle Subarus', *USA Today*, McLean, Virginia, 3 February, p.B.03.

IEG Sponsorship report 2003, www.sponsorship.com, viewed 10 March 2004.

Keen, M. 2003, 'Sponsorship: The Corporate Viewpoint', a presentation at Premiership Strategies 2003 Sports Marketing and Sponsorship Conference, AMI & PSI National Conference, Melbourne, 1 May.

Kirby Webster, K. 2003, 'Brand it Like Beckham', MarketingProfs.com, 10 June, http://www.marketingprofs.com/3/kwebster20.asp, accessed 13 August 2003.

Kunkel, E.T. 2001, *Address to Media on Formula One Grand Prix Sponsorship*, 23 August, http://www.fosters.com.au/corporate/news/speeches/2001/grandprixspeech010823.asp, viewed 29 January 2004.

LeDrew, J. 2003, http://www.sportnovascotia.ca/contents/public_communications/Marketing/leverage_support.htm, viewed 3 November 2003.

Li, S. 2003, *Sports Sponsorship – A Global Business Affair*, presentation on behalf of Visa at the AFR Sports Business Summit, 16 October 2003, Sydney, Australia.

Nilson Report 2002. 'Global Card Brand Results', April, Issue 762, Oxnard, California.

Phillips, R. 2000, 'The Business Olympics: Sydney's Other Games', http://www.wsws.org/articles/2000/sep2000/olym-s29_prn.shtml, viewed 29 July 2003.

Plaskitt, S. 2003, 'Waugh continues to bat for OzEmail', *B&T Weekly*, 4 April, p.2.

Riddle, J.S. 1993, 'Colgate-Palmolive Sends Speed Stick Long on NFL Sponsorship TV Drive', *Brandweek*, 2 August, Vol. 34, Issue 31, New York, pp.1–2.

Roeser, R. 2002, 'Sponsorships Don't Always Benefit Your Business', *Cincinnati Business Courier*, 11 November, http://www.bizjournals.com/cincinnati/stories/2002/11/11/smallb3.html, viewed 10 February 2004.

Roy, C. 2003, 'Corporates Mining into Sports Sponsorship', *The Economic Times Online*, 14 December, http://economictimes.indiatimes.com/articleshow/msid-357123,prtpage-1.cms, viewed 2 February 2004.

Veldre, D. 2003, 'Sunsilk gets Blokey', *B&T Weekly*, August 22, p.3.

www.worldsnooker.com/news_latest-17115, viewed 18 February 2005.

# Appendix to Chapter 10

## Carlton and United Breweries Sponsorship Application Form

**Carlton & United**
BUILDING GREAT AUSTRALIAN BRANDS

### Sponsorship Application Form

Applicants Name: ______________________

Organisation: ______________________

Address: ______________________

Phone: __________ Fax: __________ Email: __________

Event/Activity: ______________________

History of your Event/Activity: ______________________

Date/Period of Event/Activity: ______________________

Location of Event/Activity: ______________________

**To have your application evaluated you need to provide detailed information for all the listed criteria.**

**Brand**
Is there a natural fit between your event/activity property and our brand/s? Provide details of how.

**Media**
Consider the total value of media that CUB is expected to receive. I.e. naming rights, event signage, live TV coverage, paid or contra advertising promoting the event, news coverage and other mediums. Provide details of media coverage expected and its estimated value.

What is the estimated value of all exposure CUB is likely to achieve?

| | |
|---|---|
| TV | $ |
| Radio | $ |
| Press | $ |
| Signage | $ |
| Other | $ |

**Hospitality**
Do you have unique hospitality opportunities to offer? Provide details.

Sponsorship Proposal Form

**Carlton & United**
BUILDING GREAT AUSTRALIAN BRANDS

**Sales**

Will there be beverage sales opportunities? What are the estimated volumes?

______________________________

| | |
|---|---|
| Beer | litres |
| Wine | litres |
| Spirits | litres |

**Promotion**

Does your event/activity offer contain outstanding sales promotion opportunities that are aligned with our brand/s? Provide details.

**Attendance**

Will there be significant attendance or participation associated with your event/activity? Please detail expected attendance numbers and demographics.

**Corporate**

Would you envisage that your event/activity could contribute to (provide details):

- Improving CUB's image?
- Developing relationships between CUB, the community and community groups?
- Communicating key messages and/or facilitating change in community attitudes towards CUB?

**Other**

Specify confirmed sponsors and other sponsors that have been approached.

What rights and benefits are you offering and what are their estimated $ value?

| | | Est. Value $ | | | Est. Value $ |
|---|---|---|---|---|---|
| Hospitality | | | Promotional opportunities | | |
| Brand association | | | Media exposure | | |
| Merchandise presence | | | Signage | | |
| Advertising | | | Naming rights | | |
| Personalities | | | Sampling opportunities | | |
| Sales | | | Tickets | | |
| Other | | | | | |

What is the amount being sought from CUB?

| | |
|---|---|
| Cash | $ |
| Product | $ |
| Other | $ |
| **Total** | $ |

Sponsorship Proposal Form

Carlton & United
BUILDING GREAT AUSTRALIAN BRANDS

**Other Comments/Details**

# Case studies for Part 4

## Bigger does not necessarily mean better

### Amy Boyle

In real estate the mantra is *location, location, location*. In sponsorship marketing, the mantra should be *strategic, strategic, strategic*.

Contrary to popular belief, it's not about how much money a company spends or how big a company is that makes it successful at sponsorship marketing. On the surface it may seem like the more money a company is willing to invest, the more exposure it will receive from a sponsorship. One only has to look at the big national brands like Coca-Cola, Miller Lite, Nike and others to see the evidence, right?

Well, one study tells a different story. Results of a 2001 study that tested recognition levels of sponsors after a season of AAA Minor League New Orleans Zephyrs baseball games showed that a small, local car wash earned recognition levels as high as some of the big national brands.

Let's look at how the small car wash retailer did it. Approximately 600 questionnaires were distributed over a series of three baseball games at the end of the 2001 Zephyrs season to test the effectiveness of sponsorships at the ballpark. The questionnaire provided a list of 18 brands (12 Zephyrs sponsors and six foil items) from which participants were asked to pick those they recognised as Zephyrs sponsors. Of the 600 surveys distributed, the study garnered 179 usable responses for analysis.

Data were assessed for frequencies and percentages of recognition of each sponsor. Table 1 shows recognition levels of each of the Zephyrs sponsors tested, as well as the foil items.

To ascertain whether there was a difference in recognition levels due to sponsor involvement (i.e., whether major sponsors were recognised more frequently than mid-level sponsors and whether mid-level sponsors were recognised more than minor sponsors), the mean recognition scores of the three different groups of sponsors were compared. Miller Lite and Coca-Cola are classified as major Zephyrs sponsors with investment levels of more than $100 000 per season. Ochsner and Louisiana Office Supply are categorised as mid-level sponsors with investments that average $15 000 per season and Safari Car Wash and 5 Minute Oil Change are considered minor sponsors with investments of less than $5000 per season.

As would be expected, major sponsors achieved a much higher level of recognition than mid-level and minor level sponsors on average. However, Safari Car Wash (f = 119), despite being considered a minor level sponsor, scored particularly high recognition scores for its category. With an investment of less than $5000, Safari earned recognition scores just as high as established brands like Miller Lite and Coca-Cola, which were spending more than $100 000 during the season. This bucks the traditional philosophy that how much money a company spends dictates the level of sponsor recognition it can expect to achieve.

#### *What did Safari Car Wash do right?*

Safari came up with a novel idea and executed it in a way that caught people's attention. The company created a promotion called the 'Dirtiest Car in the Parking Lot'. In between the fifth and sixth innings, the announcer would make a public address announcement that sounded quite serious (like the tone used when a PA announcer informs an audience that someone has left their lights on) saying, 'Attention fans: the owner of a Gray Volkswagen Jetta, license plate number XJW 154 …' Then his voice would boom, 'YOU HAVE THE DIRTIEST CAR IN THE PARKING LOT!'

Fans would go nuts and cheer in response. The promotion was a huge hit.

Safari ensured that the promotion was done consistently throughout the season. It's well-known that frequency is important in any type of advertising medium. The same holds true for sponsorships. Safari Car Wash's promotion was done at every home game over the season. Fans came to expect it over time.

Safari was careful to choose a sponsor property, a minor league baseball team, which allowed them to have a novel promotion with high degree of frequency. If the company had tried to execute the same idea with the National Football League New Orleans Saints, a major league sports franchise, it would have had to pay a lot more money. So choosing a property in which a small company can be a significant player for the amount of dollars it has to spend is important.

There's a lesson or two in these findings that can help companies in their own sponsorship marketing efforts. I'm convinced that the companies that pay attention to their sponsorship marketing efforts, the ones that make a true investment of not only money but time and resources and creativity, the ones who do not treat it as an afterthought to their advertising efforts – those are the companies that have success.

Some guidelines about improving a sponsorship marketing program:

1. Be strategic about your approach to sponsorship marketing. Make it part of your annual plan and integrate it into your other marketing efforts – advertising, public relations, community relations and the like. Equally as important, be strategic about each individual deal that you negotiate.
2. Choose opportunities that are appropriate for your budget, where you can have a dominant role in some part of the event.
3. Be creative about your approach. It takes more than just signage and an announcement to make an impact. Think of ways to incorporate your brand in a way that interests people and grabs their attention. The signage and announcements can help but they can't stand alone.

**Table 1: Summary of Frequencies & Percentages for Sponsorship Recognition**

| Sponsor | Frequency of Recognition | f % |
|---|---|---|
| Miller Lite | 146 | 81.6% |
| Coca-Cola | 144 | 80.4% |
| Pizza Hut | 143 | 79.9% |
| Cingular Wireless | 123 | 68.7% |
| Safari Car Wash | 119 | 66.5% |
| Ochsner | 106 | 59.2% |
| Baby Ruth | 105 | 58.7% |
| Coors Light | 93 | 51.9% |
| Academy Sports & Outdoors | 71 | 40.0% |
| Chevron | 66 | 36.9% |
| Louisiana Office Products | 56 | 31.3% |
| 5 Minute Oil Change | 55 | 30.7% |
| Ace Hardware (Foil) | 38 | 21.2% |
| Shell (Foil) | 24 | 13.4% |
| Office Depot (Foil) | 22 | 12.3% |
| St. Charles Hospital (Foil) | 19 | 10.6% |
| Digital Consulting | 17 | 9.5% |
| Tropicana (Foil Item) | 13 | 7.3% |

## Questions

1. What did Safari Car Wash do right in managing their sponsorship?
2. What principles from media planning can you apply to sponsorship planning?
3. What else can this case study teach you about sponsorship marketing?

# 2000 Olympics: Carrying a torch for Shell

## Bridget Marcou

### *Background*

Australian public relations (PR) firm Wrights were faced with a challenge of Olympian proportions when their client Shell Australia became an official supporter of the Sydney 2000 Olympic Torch Relay.

With limited time to leverage sponsorship in a period of highly competitive sponsor activity, Shell had to act swiftly to design and implement a comprehensive marketing campaign that maximised awareness of their Olympic involvement.

The Olympic Torch Relay was primarily sponsored by AMP, with Shell in a supporting role as the Sydney 2000 Olympic Games Official Fuel and Oils Supplier. Consequently, whatever was done to highlight Shell's participation had to involve an additional element that would generate publicity and opportunities to build community relations in 145 towns and cities over the 100 days of the torch relay.

### *Solution*

The solution was found in Shell's 15-year association with Questacon, established in 1980 as Australia's first interactive science centre where visitors are encouraged to get hands, minds and bodies on the exhibits. Based in Canberra, the Shell Questacon Science Circus is part of an outreach program run by Questacon, which travels to regional, remote and Aboriginal communities across the nation to present a mix of science and entertainment.

Shell designed and constructed a purpose-built Shell Questacon trailer that would accompany the torch relay around Australia in the 100 days leading up to the opening of the Games at Homebush on 15 September 2000.

The PR firm was in charge of the logistical management of the road show, managing a rotating staff roster, mapping the journey and ensuring accommodation at each point, as well as the planning and coordination of large-scale media and community relations campaigns at each of the 145 sites visited.

### *Objectives*

The purpose of sponsoring the Torch Relay and involving the Shell Questacon Science Circus was to encourage positive interaction between Shell and local communities. In the 100 days of the Torch Relay, more than one million people had the opportunity to interact with Shell.

### *Highlights of the event*

From the arrival of the Sydney 2000 Olympic Torch in Australia on 7 June, the Shell Questacon Science Circus proved a huge hit with each local community it visited on its epic journey.

This was made possible through the use of a purpose-built Shell-branded trailer/stage, which was towed by a Shell-branded Holden motor vehicle. Negotiations with Holden resulted in supply of the vehicle to Shell free of charge for the duration of the Torch Relay.

The Shell Questacon Science Circus included a show about the science behind sport and was performed to an audience ranging from primary school-aged children to adults. A highlight of the performance proved to be the technology behind the Olympic Torch, with the Shell Questacon Science Circus being the only sponsor on-site with a replica torch that the public could touch.

The scholars who travelled with the Circus were young science graduates undertaking a Diploma of Scientific Communication at the Australian National University in Canberra. The scholars are provided with media training during their studies and were therefore well equipped to deal with the media during the Torch Relay road show.

The Shell Questacon Science Circus Torch Relay exhibition completed its journey in Sydney on Thursday 14 September, the day before the Opening Ceremony, where it moved into Homebush for the Sydney 2000 Olympic Games celebrations.

A Shell Olympics database was developed that was designed to incorporate the names of the Olympic Torch committees, distributors, accommodation and media in each town the Shell Questacon Science Circus visited. The database proved to be an invaluable communications tool and was highly beneficial while the Circus was on the road, enabling organisers to have instant access to contacts in each town. This was particularly evident when re-confirming or amending accommodation bookings for the scholars, providing easy access to information even when out of the office.

### *Feedback*

Feedback from the scholars indicated that the Shell Questacon Science Circus performed to capacity crowds at each of the celebration sites, with the public continuing to wait in line to touch the replica torch and learn about how it works.

The presence of the only replica torch at each of the Circus performances was reported to be the envy of other Torch Relay sponsors, with the initiative proving a resounding success.

While the Shell Questacon Science Circus had to focus its performance on the technology behind the Olympic Torch, it did not take away from the impact the Circus had at each of the celebration sites. The ability of the Circus to adapt to meet the needs of each of the communities was reflected in the continued positive feedback received from local councils, SOCOG (the Sydney Organising Committee for the Olympic Games) and Shell Distributors.

Free Olympic merchandise was also distributed to schoolchildren at each of the celebration sites. As a result of the interest in the merchandise, Shell received an additional request for order forms to purchase Shell Olympic clothing and memorabilia, which were provided to the on-the-road team.

### *Media*

Shell undertook a targeted media program for the Torch Relay, including the syndication to national print and electronic media of an announcement media release, state by state media kits and progressive targeted regional media releases.

Interviews were coordinated with more than 10 children's television programs and more than 15 radio stations around the nation. Exceptional coverage for Shell's involvement in the Torch Relay was secured on 10 national television programs, including the main news bulletins on all networks in both Victoria and New South Wales. Melbourne's *Herald Sun*, Australia's highest circulation daily newspaper, printed two full-page stories on the Shell Questacon Science Circus.

Taking into consideration the circulation of all publications and electronic media up until Friday, 15 September 2000, there had been over 12 801 231 opportunities for Australians to read or hear about Shell's involvement with the Sydney 2000 Olympics.

### *MCG event*

Special media coverage was in place for the Olympic Torch's arrival at the MCG – scene of the last Olympics in Australia, the 1956 Melbourne Games.

An outstanding promotional opportunity arose for the Shell Questacon Science Circus at the MCG on Sunday, 30 July 2000. This consisted of a three-minute live interview with one of the scholars on the big screen before the main AFL match of the day, and featured Shell branding.

This live-to-air segment also took place just prior to the historic return of the Olympic Flame to the MCG, with Shell being the only Olympic sponsor to initiate a promotion on the day. Taking into consideration that the total crowd figure at the MCG for the day was over 75 000 it proved an extremely effective method of increasing awareness of Shell's involvement in the Sydney 2000 Olympic Torch Relay.

### *Overall results*

The number of people who attended Shell Questacon Science Circus events nationwide and the volume of media coverage for the involvement of Shell in the Torch Relay and in the Olympics as an Official Supporter, far exceeded Shell's original objective for the project.

The overwhelming ground-level community support and positive reception received for the Shell Questacon Science Circus from each of the towns and cities it visited highlights the benefit and value for Shell from its decision to participate in the Torch Relay.

## Questions

1. What needs to be done to lift the profile of a supporting sponsor for a high-profile event?
2. How did Shell ensure its mainstream business was highlighted through this sponsorship?
3. Suggest ways that Shell could build on its involvement in the Olympics to generate ongoing corporate reputation benefits.

# Part 5

# Contemporary issues

# Chapter 11

# Globalisation of sport

## Learning objectives

After reading the chapter you should be able to:

- explain what is meant by an organisation having a global marketing strategy
- discuss the advantages and disadvantages of operating globally
- identify the main drivers for globalisation
- outline the globalisation process and explain how a sports organisation can implement a globalisation strategy
- discuss the issues facing sports organisations considering globalisation.

## Scene setter

### Going to extremes

Is extreme ironing to be the next global sport? It is currently touted as the fastest growing 'White-goods extreme sport'. So what is it, I hear you ask? Extreme ironing is where people around the globe combine their love of extreme sports such as rock climbing, skiing, snowboarding, canoeing and trampolining with ironing. The 2004 Guinness Book of Records defines it as a global sport that combines a household chore with an extreme sport. There are an estimated 500 to 1000 extreme ironing enthusiasts in Germany, South Africa, Australia, Austria and New Zealand and it is starting to catch on in the USA, with reports of extreme ironers appearing in California and Colorado (extremeironing.com 2003). Some teams of extreme ironer even have corporate sponsorship. But does this sport really have what it takes to be known as a global sport? And just what does it mean to be a global sport?

The sport began seven years ago when a young man from England decided he'd rather be rock climbing than doing his ironing, so he took his ironing with him and hence the sport was born. With the official launch of extreme ironing in the USA this year, the aim of the originators is to make it an Olympic sport! South African Anton Van De Venter seems to be hooked on the sport, having broken the high-altitude record in August 2003 by ironing his national flag at the 20 000 ft summit of Mount Kilimanjaro, nude in freezing temperatures (apparently clothing is optional in this sport). Agreeing with him would be Britain's Geoff Reiss and Ian Mitchell, one of whom claimed the land speed record of 125 mph while ironing a shirt in the back of a BMW on a raceway in Yorkshire, and the other having sawed through ice in Wisconsin in March to iron underwater. So it is definitely not a sport for the faint of heart and there are numerous new challenges every day being thrown at new extreme ironing enthusiasts, such as the man who just recently jumped from a sheer rock face in Melbourne with his ironing board. It also seems that pseudonyms are also popular such as 'Steam' and 'Cool Silk'.

Interestingly the actual quality of the ironing completed under these bizarre circumstances does count in competition ironing, with pressing quality accounting for 60 points, style for 40 points and speed for 20 points (120 points total is possible). Maybe you should visit their website and see for yourself? http://extremeironing.com

Sources: Fox 2003, p.103; Belluck 2004; http://extremeironing.com

# Introduction

This chapter examines the issue of globalisation of sport and begins with an overview of just what is meant by a global marketing strategy. It then looks at the costs and benefits of adopting a global strategy before moving on to a discussion of the key drivers of globalisation and the process of globalisation. The last part of the chapter deals with the issues facing sporting organisations attempting to implement a global strategy.

When sports marketers are dealing with a relatively small and mature sports market, such as found in Australia and New Zealand, looking to markets abroad is really their only option for growth. Operating globally however is a stiff challenge for marketers who need to consider a strategy of globalisation in an integrated manner. Globalisation is quite different to internationalisation, and even to operating in a global market. Let's see what it is really all about.

Extreme ironing – the next Olympic must-watch sport?

## What is globalisation?

Globalisation is really a particular type of international strategy that an organisation can adopt. A global company is one that has the capacity to do business in all hemispheres of the earth (north, south, east and west) even though they may not actually operate in all of them (Yip 2003). A global organisation has a diverse range of languages, currencies, cultures, legal and political systems, time zones, educational backgrounds of managers and employees, and different climates and different levels of national economic development to deal with. This makes global organisations complex and sometimes slow to change.

Global organisations do not use a standardised approach to either their product development or their marketing, rather they tend to absorb and then capitalise on the strengths and peculiarities of the various countries in which they do business (Yip 2003; Keegan & Green 2000). Very few of the world's top 500 multinationals have a genuinely global presence, with most restricting their activities to North America, Europe and Japan (Walker 2002). Genuinely global corporations such as Nestlé, Unilever, Coca-Cola, IBM and Sony not only have global sales efforts but also global production operations.

So to recap, an organisation that does business outside its domestic market would have an international strategy. If that organisation was to only deal with one country, or a few specific countries, then it would not be a global organisation, rather it would be an international organisation. Global organisations like Coca-Cola consider the entire world to be a potential market and they use a different approach in each country they enter to match that country's specific market needs.

Eight countries lined up for the inaugural Polocrosse World Cup

For many sporting organisations a truly global strategy is not possible, due to the specialised and often regional or parochial nature of the particular sport. For example, how big can the global appeal of polocrosse be? Polocrosse has been referred to as rugby on horseback and at the inaugural World Cup game in April 2003 there were eight countries represented: Zimbabwe; New Zealand; England; Ireland; Canada; South Africa; the USA; and Australia (Targett 2003).

This international representation was actually pretty good considering the limited appeal the sport has both domestically and internationally (less than 1 per cent of the Australian population participate in horse sports [Sweeney Sports 2003]). The sport was invented in 1938 and approximately 5500 people play polocrosse internationally in 12 countries (3500 of these from Australia). Although the sport is growing in popularity, in many of these countries only about 100 players in total play the sport (see more about polocrosse at http://www.polocrosse.net or http://www.nzpolocrosse.com/).

In comparison, soccer is played in more than 100 countries and has approximately 200 million active players worldwide. There are just over 1.5 million teams and the sport has been around in one form or another in many parts of the globe for about 500 years, though modern soccer as we know it, was really invented in 1863 (http://www.fifa.com/en/index.html). So as a sport, soccer really has much more potential than polocrosse to appeal to a global market. In addition, soccer has serious economic clout globally. For example, in the 2002 Soccer World Cup, the 32 nations that competed accounted for 84 per cent of the world GDP. In addition, the two countries that hosted the event, South Korea and Japan, both received an increase of $6.9 and $23.8 billion dollars to their respective economies. Soccer also has a social role in many countries with people feeling a passionate association with the game. This was particularly evident in the absenteeism rate in Britain due to the World Cup. During 2002 absenteeism due to people staying home to watch games cost the British economy $4.7 billion (about 0.3 per cent of GDP) and was forecast to cost the 10 largest European economies up to $8.1 billion in lost economic output – all for a four-week sporting festival. Now, that's global power!

In addition to sport as a game, sporting goods manufacturers can, and often do, have an international focus. Sporting apparel manufacturers tend to have their production activities located in countries with low labour costs and their marketing activities located in high-tech countries with strong economies. Sports clothing and merchandise is a fast growing global business with nearly half of all global sponsorship coming from sportswear industries and Nike is the biggest spender of the lot (Marqusee 2000). However, if one uses the earlier definition of global versus international organisations, then many of these sporting goods companies would not be considered as truly global.

So if having a global strategy means a highly complex and flexible organisation, wouldn't this be more expensive than just operating in a domestic or limited international setting? To answer this question we need to examine the disadvantages and advantages of globalisation further.

## The disadvantages of globalisation

There are essentially five main costs or disadvantages to adopting a globalisation strategy. These are: increased management costs; commitment to early market entry; lack of market responsiveness; loss of competitive flexibility and responsiveness; and hindrance of profit performance in some markets due to competitive positioning in others. Each of these will be examined in more detail.

### Increased management costs

Globalisation can incur considerable manage-ment costs through increased coordination, reporting requirements and possibly even additional staff. The complexity of managing across a wide range of cultures and currencies can increase organisational reporting requirements considerably and these additional management functions can also necessitate additional staff. Further, local country requirements for management reporting, taxation and employment can also increase costs and therefore need to be carefully considered.

The Fédération Internationale de Football Association (FIFA; the international soccer federation) has experienced just this occurrence. Founded in 1904 with just seven country members it now comprises 204 member associations from nearly every country in the world (more members than the United Nations) and the complexity and increased management commitments have meant a very different and more complex management structure for FIFA than was possible in 1904.

Another cost for sporting goods companies considering globalisation can be the poor public image that moving production and factories to Third World countries can bring. Nike have seen this problem in the last few years and other sporting companies such as Adidas, Reebok and Mitre have also had to deal with negative public opinion and domestic blacklisting of their products due to this problem. In spite of this, sporting goods manufacturers have not succeeded in eliminating child-labour in many of their factories, and in many cases women earn, on average, one-third less than their male counterparts in these operations.

One of the main culprits for this problem is soccer-ball stitchers in India. In 1998 it was estimated that about 10 000 children were employed in the production of sporting goods in India and today that figure is not estimated to be much different, in spite of many efforts by humanitarian groups to change the system (Global March 2002). The problem for these populations is that these sporting goods companies offer secure employment and even though the wages are low they are reliable. Thus for many families living below the poverty line, there are few other legal or ethical options.

## Early commitment to market entry

Adopting a global strategy can also result in an earlier commitment to a market than would otherwise be warranted if that market entry were considered on its own merits. The move for China to join the Asian Cricket Council is one such example of this. Cricket has, at best, a marginal following in China and the returns for the cricketing associations from there will be low if anything at all. However, the international cricketing community is committed to a global strategy for their game and this combined with the long-term potential of China as a market and the possibility of future rewards, by virtue of the enormous population and increasing wealth, have enough attraction for the international cricketing community to accept their nomination.

## Lack of market responsiveness

Another disadvantage of globalisation is that companies can be tempted to adopt standardised product and promotional policies that can have the disadvantage of alienating customers who see no relevance to advertising messages that are obviously from another country. The most extreme result of this action is that companies can end up with a strategy that doesn't satisfy customers anywhere.

Coca-Cola is one of the very few global organisations that have managed to deliver a relatively standard product and very similar promotional strategies around the world. Even the famous McDonald's have a different product range in different countries and they adopt localised promotional strategies to target different cultural and ethnic groups in different countries. With the increased emphasis on digital technologies and digital broadcasting, global audiences are becoming more fragmented and segmented, which has further decreased the attractiveness of a standardised global product (Marqusee 2002).

## Loss of competitive flexibility and responsiveness

Increasing the spread of international operations can also result in the organisation losing flexibility and responsiveness to market changes and conditions. Companies that have offices and activities far from their customers can lose touch with the needs and wants of those customers and this can also increase the chances of smaller, more flexible local organisations taking market share. In the case of sporting organisations, most international governing bodies also have strong national and then regional subgroups that help to maintain grassroots contact with customers and, in turn, ensure that they manage the day-to-day issues in a timely manner.

In spite of this, many regional and local sports lovers often feel removed from the decision-making and political manoeuvrings that can preoccupy national sporting bodies. When a sporting organisation hears calls from media and customers to 'get back to their roots' and 'time to get back to basics', then they know that they have lost contact.

### Hindrance of profit performance

Finally, the level of competitive integration required for a truly global organisation can mean sacrificing profits or competitive position in individual countries. For a global organisation to be successful there must be integration in the business function across the entire organisation. This can increase currency risks by incurring costs and revenues in different countries and it can also mean hindrance in terms of local competition due to a larger global strategy. This is partially the case for the International Cricket Council in their move into China (example given earlier). The cricket council will not be expecting to make a profit from this decision for some time and the costs of setting up a competition and the layers of competition required to be able to perform at an international level will be considerable. However, they are looking for long-term returns and they believe that this strategy will be a sound investment in the global future of cricket.

In spite of these disadvantages, there are in fact many advantages for organisations to adopt a global strategy. Let's review these.

## Advantages of globalisation

There are generally four major benefits for an organisation to adopt a global strategy. These are: cost reductions; improved quality of products and programs; enhanced customer preferences; and increased competitive leverage. Let's examine these in more detail.

### Cost reductions

An integrated global strategy can save costs through economies of scale (pooling production for one or more countries), through lower production costs (attained by moving production to countries with low labour costs), through focusing production from many local plants to a few global ones, by taking advantage of flexibility in production costs across the globe and moving production to take advantage of those savings and through enhancing the bargaining power for purchase of production items.

In the case of sports events these sorts of cost savings are usually seen in terms of media investment and sponsorship. Many media companies are keen to expand their potential audiences and the larger and more global the sport the better the potential return and lower the incremental costs. The same is true for global sponsors of sport. They can achieve considerable cost savings and potential market increases if they back a global sport.

This was the case with many of the sponsors of the 2003 Rugby World Cup. Companies like Vodafone, Heineken and Visa have signed on as global sponsors for a number of World Cups. All these countries see the benefits of being aligned with a sport that is followed and watched in many countries around the world. Investing in two or three World Cups means that these companies are gaining promotion and marketing exposure for World Cups being played in the future at today's dollar value and this can mean millions of dollars in cost savings.

Heineken in particular have been associated with this sport for a long time and when Heineken became a worldwide partner for the Rugby World Cup in 1995, rugby was hardly a global sport and sales of the beer in many rugby countries (particularly Australia and New Zealand) were tiny. At the 2003 World Cup, Heineken were able to show that 30 per cent of their sales worldwide were from eight of the top 10 rugby playing nations (Reuters 2003) and their sponsorship considerably expanded their reach into Africa and Eastern Europe at little additional marketing cost. In fact their ad, shot in New Zealand for the Rugby World Cup, was shown in several other countries without any negative market reaction. Their slogan for the World Cup was '20 nations, 48 matches, one beer'.

Further, sport is commanding an increasing proportion of the global public discourse in advertising, politics, newspapers, television and the Internet, and global sports media organisations like Rupert Murdoch's Fox, Sky and Star TV have major sports broadcasting investments in Australia, North America, Asia, Europe and now South America. These types of global investments in sports products are a good example of the cost efficiencies of a global operation. Another such venture is the company Global Sports, an online sporting goods broker.

This company plans to become the world's largest online sporting goods retailer, bringing together some of the largest names in sports stores and manufacturers all in one place (Green 2000).

## Improved quality of products and programs

Globalisation often means that firms can focus on a smaller number of products and programs rather than on a wide range as many domestically focused organisations need to do, because the sales volume for those products will generally be so much greater (Yip 2003). For example Toyota have a far smaller number of models around the world than do General Motors and many of Toyota's models are globally accepted (Yip 2003). The International Rugby Board are planning to spend much of their well-documented $45 million profit from the 2003 World Cup on improving opportunities for grassroots rugby in a number of different countries. They also plan to constantly evaluate the game to make sure it stays exciting and crowd friendly. These strategies are directly aimed at an attempt to increase the popularity of the sport globally and thus increase the global market for both the sport and for its global sponsors.

## Enhanced customer preferences

Global availability and recognition can enhance customer preferences and brand loyalty. Suppliers that can not only supply products and services globally, but can also service and maintain customer expectations are often highly sought after.

This particular advantage of globalisation is often the main motivation for food, beverage and leisure organisations to consider global expansion. McDonald's has taken advantage of this particular aspect in its marketing programs globally, claiming that service standards, product taste and quality are consistent throughout the world. McDonald's latest involvement in the Olympic movement is therefore an interesting one. While McDonald's have been associated with various Olympics, this is the first time they have signed a long-term deal to cover four consecutive Games from 2004 onwards. McDonald's will be the official restaurant for all these games and will have access not only to spectators, but athletes and officials as well (Dow Jones International News 2004).

For sporting events, brands and images are valuable properties. American tattooists report that the Nike Swoosh is their single most requested design (Marqusee 2002) and all because people associate something of value with this particular brand symbol. Sport is a symbolic good and carries many symbolic values, thus branding and marketing can account for a large proportion of global value for sports products. Having global recognition of that value is a powerful attraction for global expansion.

## Increased competitive leverage

Organisations that adopt a global strategy are able to insulate themselves against competition by providing more points to attack and counterattack than companies that are more concentrated in their operation. In addition, competitive leverage is also increased as having a global reach means that organisations are able to affect markets more quickly, using local markets in a global sense.

The main factor for sporting organisations considering a global strategy then, is to find the balance between over-globalising and under-globalising and to maximise the advantages that can accrue to the firm with this strategy (Yip 2003). For some organisations however globalisation will not be an option.

The AFL in Australia is one good example of this as already discussed in Chapter 7. The AFL is the most profitable sporting code in Australia with just over 3 million people watching the 2003 grand final (Davis 2003). However, in spite of the game's popularity here, it has little attraction or relevance in many overseas countries, not the least reason for which is its name – Australian Football League. As Chapter 7 mentioned, the closest any other country gets to the game is Gaelic football and even then the rules are slightly different. In a mature sports market that is becoming increasingly saturated with sports product and choices, it will be more and more difficult for the AFL to enter the global marketplace.

In spite of this the AFL is being driven to seriously consider how it can adopt a global strategy. There has been a serious push to increase the number of international teams with 30 countries now boasting an AFL team (the Copenhagen Crocodiles, the Tokyo Goannas and the Nashville Kangaroos). The games played are about equivalent to schoolboy football in Australia, but there is a definite marketing strategy to expand both the global interest and global talent pool of the sport. Exhibition games, coaching clinics and linking with Australian ex-patriots is the starting point of their strategy (Smith 2001). Another example in this area is the V8 Supercar and Nascar series, which has recently taken its tour global in an attempt to generate new audiences and to take on stadium sports head-on for market and wallet share. This move has taken the bold step into China, looking to capatilise on the large market potential there. See the 'Sport spotlight'. To understand the factors that stimulate a global strategy, we need to look more closely at the drivers for globalisation.

V8 has recently taken its tour global

## Sport spotlight

### The global strategy for V8 Supercar

V8 Supercar is a category of touring racing that evolved in Australia in the early 1990s. Originally the series was battled out between the Australian-built Fords and Holdens, although now the series sees many international companies competing. In its early days the series ran in opposition to the 'official' super-touring category, which had international regulations and international representation. However the increased power of sponsorship, driver talent and fan attention that was moving to the V8 series has resulted in this being the main international series and the original super-touring series being the amateur category (V8 Supercar 2004).

In July 2004 the Australian Vee Eight Supercar Company (AVESCO) became Australia's largest sports exporter, by signing an agreement with the Shanghai Greenland Group. This agreement will see the V8 Supercar Championships raced at the new multi-million dollar Shanghai international circuit each year for the next five years (V8X 2004). Currently 60 million people in Asia watch the sport and this deal will increase the television coverage of the series to 70 countries or more than 500 million homes globally. When the first event is launched in June 2005 it will be the biggest contingent ever of people and equipment to fly out of Australia for a single sporting event (Alternative News Network 2004). So the sport that is one of the most popular in Australia and in New Zealand is set to become a truly global sport with an audience base in the hundreds of millions.

# Drivers of globalisation

Drivers for globalisation can be considered from four different perspectives. These are: market drivers; competitive drivers; government drivers; and cost drivers (see Figure 11.1). Drivers are factors that can give rise to the need to consider a global strategy and while we consider them under these four main groupings, in reality firms deal with combinations of these occurring simultaneously. Let's review them in more detail.

## Market drivers

Market drivers are based on consumer behaviour, the structure of distribution channels and the nature of marketing in the particular industry under review. Changes in consumer lifestyles and consumption patterns, establishment of world brands, the spread of global media and the growth of global consumerism are all factors that can prompt an organisation to consider a global strategy. These market drivers are causing many sporting organisations to look globally for increased markets and increased fan bases. Remember the story in Chapter 8 about Manchester United? They have a global fan base of 53 million people with more fans in Japan than in the UK. Many other sporting franchises are looking at their success and considering how to enter the global marketplace.

**Figure 11.1:** Drivers of globalisation

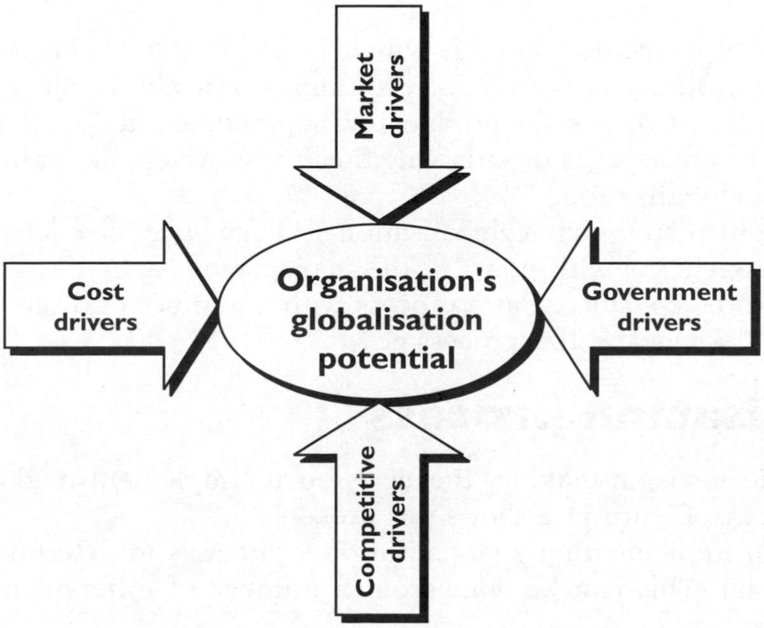


Source: Yip 2003, p.10

### Competitive drivers

These drivers depend on the actions of competitors. Factors such as increasing world trade, new global economies, the growth of global networks and the increasing number of global competitors all contribute to this driver prompting consideration of globalisation.

Increasing competition for the hearts and minds of sports fans and changes to the consumption preferences of the Generation X and Y sports consumers are prompting considerable changes and the adoption of a global view by many sporting organisations. Decreased leisure time and an increase in the use of electronic entertainment has meant that sport is now competing with video games, computer games and other electronic devices for the next generation of sports fan.

These electronic forms of entertainment are truly global in nature and are increasing in popularity and appeal. Marketers of extreme sports have accepted this challenge far better than traditional stadium-bound sports, pioneering interactive games portraying the latest extreme heroes. Soccer and golf have begun to enter the market, but they struggle with how to make full use of the virtual playing field that can ultimately make their games more exciting than the real thing.

Even horse racing has entered the digital realm. Virtual horse racing (http://www.racing-index.com/virtual_horse_racing.html) allows you to own racehorses, feed, stable and train them and then even race and bet on them to win real money all from the comfort of your own computer. You can even race on international tracks against other horse owners and trainers and when the horses get too boring, you can also add greyhounds to your racing stable.

### Government drivers

Government globalisation drivers are essentially founded on the rules and economics of the businesses in the marketplace. Reduction of tariffs, creation of traditional blocs, strengthening of world trade institutions, privatisation of state-dominated economies and a shift to a more open market approach by many closed systems are all factors that might encourage an organisation to consider globalisation.

In the case of sporting goods manufacturers, tariffs, government trade incentives and labour regulations are all considered when decisions are made about locating activities in other countries. Even governments use sport as a globalisation driver. Take for example the latest push by Britain's Prime Minister, Tony Blair, to bid for the 2012 Olympics. The bid cost Britain £2.5 billion despite fears that London could never really successfully house, transport or run such a large event. However the support and involvement of the government in the bid, has increased investor confidence in the British economy and resulted in a stronger currency all because of the potential benefits of hosting the Games (Beard et al. 2004).

### Cost drivers

The final driver for globalisation is cost, which is largely dependent on the economics of the organisation. Continuing pressures for economies of scale, advances in technology and transportation and increasing costs of product development are factors that are relevant in this grouping. Many of the advantages of satisfying these cost drivers have already been addressed under advantages of globalisation.

So how should a firm approach a globalisation strategy once they determine that this is the best marketing approach? As with many of the management activities discussed in this text, globalisation can also be considered as a process with a number of discrete steps or stages for marketers to follow. Let's look at this process now.

## The globalisation process

As with all strategic decision-making, the decision to implement a global strategy can be considered as a process. Figure 11.2 shows this process.

The first stage in implementing a globalisation strategy is to determine the organisation's globalisation potential. This can be done from a number of different perspectives, but you

**Figure 11.2:** The globalisation process

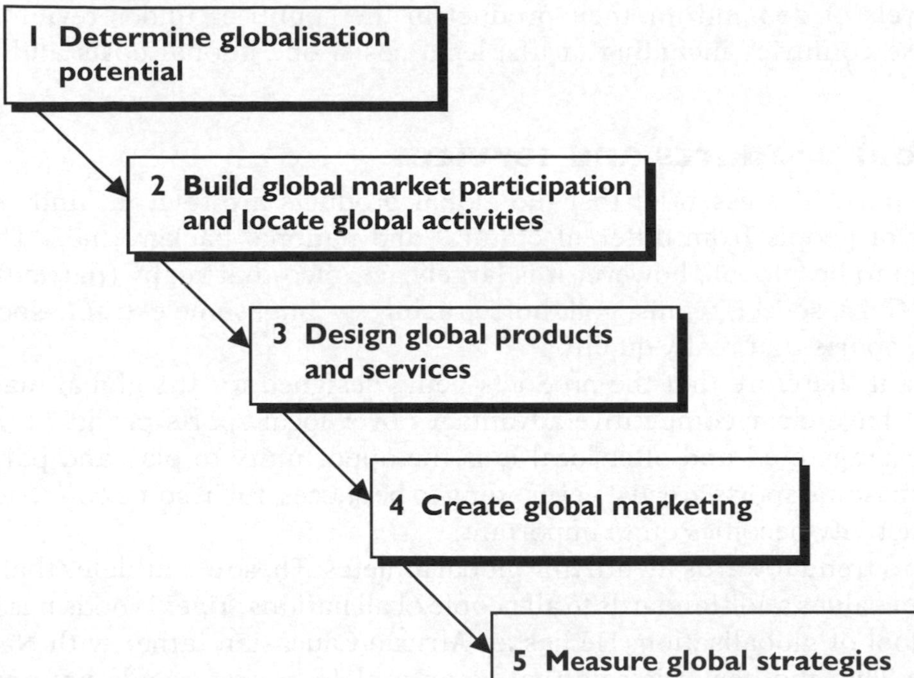
1 Determine globalisation potential
2 Build global market participation and locate global activities
3 Design global products and services
4 Create global marketing
5 Measure global strategies

should first consider the organisation's culture (see Table 11.1 for desired organisational features for globalisation) as well as the four drivers for globalisation discussed previously. In addition, it is important to remember that drivers can operate in different directions (positive or negative) depending on the situation, timing and countries being considered and that the level of globalisation potential will therefore change over time as these drivers change.

**Table 11.1:** Desired organisational features for globalisation

| Culture | Organisational structure | Management processes | People |
|---|---|---|---|
| Global identity and interdependence | Centralised global authority, no domestic international split | Extensive coordination of processes<br>Global sharing of technology | Multi-country careers<br>Foreign nationals in home and third countries |
| | Strong geographic dimension relative to business and function | Global strategy information system<br>Global strategic planning, budgets, performance reviews and compensation | Extensive travel |

Source: Yip 2003, p.185

## Build global market participation and locate activities

When considering globalisation, the organisation also needs to look at the transferability of its business models and the level of competition and potential demand for its products and services. It is also important to look at the ease of market entry and other economic factors that might be relevant when considering where to locate activities and how to best participate in the local markets.

As an example, a sporting goods manufacturer may be considering expanding their operations and sales globally. When reviewing this stage of the globalisation process they would need to consider the levels of demand for their product in the countries under review and the costs of entering those countries including tariffs, legal costs, operational costs and exchange rate fluctuations.

### Design global products and services

In the case of sport, it is essential that the global products are relevant and recognisable to a large number of people from different cultural and national backgrounds. There are many sports that claim to be 'global', however it is largely accepted that rugby (particularly following the 2003 World Cup), soccer, tennis, golf, horse racing, cycling, some extreme sports and motor racing are a few sports that really qualify.

It is important therefore that the products being designed for the global market are easily understandable, have clear competitive advantages over local sports products (more exciting, better media coverage etc.) and offer local fans the opportunity to play and participate in the sport. In addition, some sports are just never going to be successful in some countries, so choosing the location of activity becomes quite important.

There is also a trend towards identifying global athletes. These are athletes that communicate a particular set of values and standards to all people of all nations. Tiger Woods has been classified as the best symbol of globalisation. He has an African/Caucasian father with Native American ancestors and a Thai mother. It is said that as an athlete he transcends nationality, race and culture. Not only ethnically is he a global figure, but his chosen sport was traditionally seen as an elite sport and Tiger's success and mastery of the game has turned it into a game for the people, making it attractive for a broader and younger population (*The Globalist* 2002). Unlike Michael Jordan and David Beckham, who are recognised internationally but known to be American and English, Tiger is considered to be a global citizen.

### Create global marketing

Global marketing means taking account of local variation where needed, but adopting a global positioning and branding strategy to ensure the product or service is immediately recognisable and that the core values of the brand are translated regardless of the country being targeted. Obviously consideration needs to be given to translation issues of brand names and legal issues with terminology and positioning strategies. When considering the web as a marketing tool, consideration also needs to be given to languages used and images presented.

Some areas of marketing are more difficult to standardise, such as packaging (due often to local regulations and labelling laws), pricing (due to currency fluctuations and market economies) and advertising (due to legal requirements and local cultural customs). Distribution strategies can often be standardised, though some minor local variation may be needed at times.

### Measure global strategies

As with all strategic initiatives it is important to be able to measure the success of the strategy and to build in the ability to modify or alter tactics to account for market activity. Measurement of the success of global marketing strategies can be more complex than measurement of local marketing strategies due to time differences, differences in local cultures and customs, and requirements to vary the strategy as necessitated by local anomalies.

## Issues facing sporting organisations considering globalisation

Many global commentators have noted that even though our worldwide population is approximately 6 billion people and counting, we are now closer than ever to our international neighbours. Electronic communications and 24-hour media access to any part of the world have meant that everyone is under the global spotlight and that entry to all global marketplaces is possible.

As we have already seen in this chapter, globalisation refers to the processes of change at political, economic, social and cultural levels that are producing a more interdependent and interconnected world. Sport is increasingly contoured by the global flows of people, ideas, technology, finance and media products and has been described as a universal language. Current issues in relation to globalisation of sport focus on two main aspects of the global sports process – the migration of elite sports men and women and the media/sport/advertising nexus. In the former area of work the thrust of the discussion suggests that player migration is the result of multi-causal factors and cannot be reduced to the economic issue. Players have become sports products in their own right and high profile players like David Beckham, Tiger Woods and Ian Thorpe are seen as global icons. Those who see this move as negative for the sports industry suggest that these 'larger-than-life' icons represent the antithesis of sport ideals – that they are no longer participating and playing the sport due to a love of the game or due to an allegiance to a club or country, rather they are mercenaries who will go where the highest bidder takes them regardless of the sport.

In contrast the commentary regarding media and sport has focused on the relationship between global local issues as part of the wider evidence that greater interconnectedness produces local consequences and forms of resistance. In this, once again, the argument that global media empires are attempting to shape and change sport to meet their own needs, regardless of the grassroots support and demand for the sport, is one that needs to be considered.

While the globalisation of sport has created wealth for many people and institutions in the sports and media worlds, wider public interests are not particularly well served by media coverage. The merging of media companies, sports organisations and sponsors has led to a serious dilemma for many sports journalists, who find themselves squeezed between the demands of an industry and a loyalty to serve the public interest. The first step should be to get some distance between the sports journalists and the groups on whom they're reporting. The media and the world of sports are converging into one profit-making entity. For example, why are resources expended on match reports only, and not diversified enough to cover all aspects of an industry becoming increasingly political, commercial and having a social impact?

Another issue of concern in relation to sport and media is that very few women occupy high profile positions in international sports management. This discriminatory view of women's capabilities is combined with marketing campaigns suggesting that sport and men are synonymous. These have led to the undervalued role of women in international sports management. To this end the appointment of Gianna Angelopoulos as the first woman President of an Olympic Games Organising Committee was momentous.

In addition, although global sport has never been bigger, a host of sporting scandals – from Olympic bidding scandals to cricket corruption, from footballers' treatment of women in football to drugs in the Tour de France – have shaken major sports to their foundations. Sport is now a major global industry, but can it handle the pressures of the age of accountability?

On this issue global sporting organisations also have to consider equality and justice, particularly in the use of child labour in production of sports products across world markets. Many international organisations are attempting to bring the Olympic values of ethics and fair play to the sportswear industry as a means of addressing these issues. The huge irony is that ethics and fair play are at the centre of the Olympic ideal, and yet the global industry profiting from the global popularity of sport is making those profits by exploiting and abusing huge numbers of workers (International Federation of Journalists 2004).

## Counterpoint

In spite of the benefits of globalisation to many large organisations, there is also a dark side that needs to be considered. Deregulated money markets and the increasing sophistication of information technology have meant that money can now flow from one account to another without any regard for national boundaries or legal niceties. In this environment, illegal bookmaking syndicates have flourished and they seek to exploit sport's huge popular base.

Corporate sponsors, advertising and marketing agencies, media empires, governments and politicians all have an investment in the sports product and all seek to shape it to their own ends. Match fixing allegations, controversies with drugs and other issues have plagued sport from grassroots levels to the highest puritan ideal – the Olympics. In addition the global media investment in sport is really, for the most part, in direct conflict with the very nature and essence of sport – expectation, excitement and unpredictability. Multinational media giants buying and selling sport are continually striving to reduce it to a commodity status where control and certainty can prevail. The bigger the investment, the greater the temptation to exercise hands-on management and control and to change the shape of sport as we know it.

In addition the increasingly growing amount of money invested in global sport is concentrating wealth and power between sports and among nations. Scores of traditional and indigenous pastimes as well as once vital modern sporting subcultures are being pushed to the margins and threatened with extinction. In Asia, hockey is being overwhelmed by cricket and in England cricket is being overwhelmed by soccer. Increased investment has also meant that disparities in wealth exist between sporting organisations (Manchester United is a classic example), resulting in changes to the game to make it more appealing and 'televisable' and changing the whole spirit of competition.

Amid all this money and hype it is important to remember that sport began as play, that all sport emerges from human exertion, and that in our childhood we would interact with balls, sticks and other naturally occurring features – do we really want to change all that (Marqusee 2002)?

## Summary

- **explain what is meant by an organisation having a global marketing strategy**
  Globalisation is really a particular type of international strategy. A global company is one that has the capacity to do business in all hemispheres of the earth (north, south, east and west) even though they may not actually operate in all of them. A global organisation has a diverse range of languages, currencies, cultures, legal and political systems, time zones, educational backgrounds of managers and employees and different climates and levels of national economic development to deal with.
- **discuss the costs and benefits of operating globally**
  There are five main costs or disadvantages to adopting a globalisation strategy. These are: increased management costs, early market entry, lack of market responsiveness, loss of competitive flexibility and hindrance of performance in some markets due to competitive positioning in others.

  There are four major benefits for an organisation to adopt a global strategy. These are: cost reductions, improved quality of products and programs, enhanced customer preferences and increased competitive leverage.
- **identify the main drivers for globalisation**
  Drivers for globalisation can be considered from four different perspectives. These are: market drivers, competitive drivers, government drivers and cost drivers (see Figure 11.1 for more information). Drivers are factors that can give rise to the need to consider a global strategy, and while we consider them under these four main groupings, in reality firms deal with combinations of these occurring simultaneously.
- **outline the globalisation process and explain how a sports organisation can implement a globalisation strategy**
  The globalisation process discussed in this chapter has five stages: determine globalisation potential; build global market participation and local global activity; design global products and services; create global marketing; and measure global strategies. Sporting organisations can use this process to construct and advise their globalisation strategy.

- **discuss the issues facing sporting organisations considering a globalisation strategy**
  As with all strategic decision-making, the decision to implement a global strategy needs to be considered in the context of both the internal and external environments. Sporting organisations have a number of issues that particularly affect them in this decision. The first is the migration of players, the second is the involvement of media and the third are issues relating to ethics, fair play, sexism and morality. Sporting organisations are more than ever under the global spotlight and these issues need careful consideration and a commitment to transparency and honesty to ensure continued public support.

## Review questions

1. How does globalisation differ from internationalisation?
2. How are costs sometimes increased through adopting a globalisation strategy?
3. What is meant by the term market drivers?
4. How would a global marketing strategy differ from a domestic one?
5. Why would it be important to measure the success of a global strategy?

## Applied activities

1. Consider your favourite sport. Is it or could it be globalised? Write a brief report either explaining why this sport is a success globally or how the sport could be globalised.
2. Interview five people to determine their recall of the major global Olympic sponsors (McDonald's, Coca-Cola, Atos Origin, General Electric, John Hancock, Kodak, Panasonic, Samsung, Swatch and Visa). See how many people were aware of these before and then after the 2004 Olympics. What conclusions can you draw for these global organisations about the success of their investment?
3. How does the increased use of and access to the Internet impact upon the ability and likely success of a sporting organisation considering a global strategy? What would some of the hindrances to using the Internet as the foundation for a globalisation strategy be?

## References

Alternative News Network 2004, http://us.altnews.com.au/drop/node/view/237, viewed 13 October 2004.

Beard, B., Clement, B. & Rowbotham, M. 2004, 'Blair goes for Olympic Glory', *The Independent*, London, 16 January, p.1.

Belluck, P. 2004, 'Get Out Your Boards: Extreme Ironing May Soon Be Hot', *New York Times*, 28 May 2004.

Davis, M. 2003, 'AFL to Ruck Against Rugby', *The Australian*, 26 November, p.20.

Dow Jones International News 2004, 'McDonald's Renews Olympic Sponsorship through 2012', 26 February 2004.

Fox, B. 2003, 'Advocates of Newest Sport are Extreme and Wrinkle Free', *Of the Patriot-News*, 24 October 2003, p.103.

Global March 2002a, 'Play Fair in the Sporting Goods Industry', *Global March Newsletter*, Vol. 4, No. 2, October 2002, www.globalmarch.org/newsletter/october-02_page5.php3, viewed 14 October 2004.

Global March 2002b, 'Labour Standards in the Sporting Goods Industry', *Global March Newsletter,* Vol. 4, No. 2, October 2002, www.globalmarch.org/newsletter/october-02_page5.php3, viewed 14 October 2004.

Green, H. 2000, 'Can Michael Rubin Take Global Sports Across the Goal Line?', *Business Week Online* <www.businessweek.com:/ebiz/0011/em1115.htm?scriptFramed>.

International Federation of Journalists 2004, 'Media and Sport: Time for Fair Play and Journalism that Makes Public Winners', IFJ, http://www.ifj.org/default.asp?Index=2512&Language=EN, viewed 14 October 2004.

Keegan, W.J. & Green, M.S. 2000, *Global Marketing*, 2nd edn, Prentice Hall, New Jersey.

Kotler, P., Adam, S., Brown, L. & Armstrong, G. 2003, *Principles of Marketing*, 2nd edn, Prentice Hall, Sydney.

Marqusee, M. 2002, 'Sport as Apocalypse', *Frontline*, Vol. 17, Issue 16, 5–18 August.

Reuters 2003, 'How Heineken Fell to a Kiwi Marketer's Spell', *National Business Review*, 21 November.

Smith, A. 2001, 'Aussie Rules Global Gaze', *Radio National: The Sports Factor*, 6 July.

Sweeney Sports 2003, *The Sweeney Sports Report 2002/2003*, Sweeney Research Pty Ltd, South Melbourne.

Targett, T. 2003, 'Horseback Rugby', *The Courier Mail*, 15 February.

The Globalist 2002, 'The Global Tiger', Sunday 28 July 2002.

V8 Supercar 2004, www.fact-index.com/v/v8/v8_supercar.html, viewed 13 October 2004.

V8X 2004, www.v8x.com.au/cms/A_102073/printArticle.html, viewed 13 October 2004.

Walker, A. 2002, 'Multinationals 'not truly global', *BBC News*, Monday 2 September, http://news.bbc.co.uk/1/hi/business/2229974.stm, viewed 14 October 2004.

www.fifa.com/en/index.html (accessed 29 February 2004).

Yip, G. 2003, *Total Global Strategy II*, Prentice Hall, New Jersey.

# Chapter 12

# The future of sports marketing

## Learning objectives

After reading the chapter you should be able to:

- define forecasting
- understand basic forecasting techniques
- understand the importance and process of long-range planning
- identify some future trends in the marketing of sport
- identify some future trends in marketing using sport.

## Scene setter

### The World Wide Web of sports

Whether it's to view real-time Webcasts or to run their own fantasy team, fans are flocking to the Net – and paying – to get their fix.

On 31 March, half a million fans jammed a dozen stadiums from San Diego to Cincinnati to kick off the American rite of spring called Major League Baseball. Bob Bowman wasn't one of them. The CEO of MLB.com, a wholly owned subsidiary of MLB, instead watched seven live video streams of different opening day contests on the computer at his office in New York City.

True, the quality of PC video didn't rival big-screen TV. But what the computer did offer was unparalleled access: At the click of a mouse, fans around the globe could get live baseball on demand, plus searchable highlights, condensed game footage of key plays, and replays of classic games. 'Even those of us who love the game can't watch it every day on TV,' says Bowman. 'You can on the Net. It was made for baseball.'

Fans seem to agree. Despite a stiff charge of $79.95 for the season or $14.95 per month, 20 000 people have signed up for the fledgling MLB.TV service in just its first two weeks – only 5000 shy of the total Bowman had forecast for the entire season. It's a nifty addition to the 1 million subscribers who pay to access live streaming-audio broadcasts either through Real.com or MLB.com. Add to that the $20 million that Seattle media company RealNetworks (REAL) have coughed up to nab exclusive online audio and video rights to MLB content, and a raft of top-drawer online advertisers, and Bowman's 170-member team is earning an operating profit.

**WALLET-OPENERS**. Fantasy-sports enthusiasts are relatively insensitive about price, paying anywhere from a few dollars for simple statistics to $100 a season to play in a league. Adds John Bruel of sports-marketing and research consultancy Avila Partners: 'Sports-fantasy leagues have had better than 20 conversion rates from free users to paying customers over the past couple of years. Normally, when a site goes from free to paid it falls off the cliff. But today, millions of people are paying $20 or more for the right to have a team in the league for any one of these sports.'

Sports fans are proving far more willing than the overall Internet populace to open their wallets. More than twice as many visitors to NASCAR.com buy tickets and retail goods as compared to visitors to non-sports sites.

Source: Salkever 2003

# Introduction

Technology, particularly the Internet, has changed the way consumers do many things in contemporary society. Everything from paying bills to sending presents can be done from your desktop or mobile Internet service. It seems that sports spectating is no different, and while technology like the Internet and mobile communication devices may not replace actual live spectating, they may become a large part of the global sports diet.

This chapter examines the concept of forecasting as it relates to planning in sports marketing. The world is in constant motion with markets, technology, society, economies etc. constantly changing. It is important therefore that we think about what 'might' happen in the future or better still what the likely possibilities are in relation to our sport or industry, and develop appropriate plans to capitalise on the future. There is also a discussion about the difference between corporate strategy and robust strategy provided by long-range planning.

Finally, in conclusion of this chapter and of this textbook we will outline some of the trends in the marketing of sport and in marketing using sport. Some of these trends are beginning and some are mere speculation. The important thing is that you consider your role as a marketer in a dynamic and undulating sportscape. One thing for sure is that sport will continue to be a part of our social fabric and still has vast potential as a business discipline.

# Predicting the future: Forecasting and long-range planning

Predicting or speculating on the future is a global business pastime. In every industry around the world business analysts try to forecast what will happen to prices, markets, technologies, demand, supply and many other critical business factors. This section defines what forecasting actually means and identifies some basic forecasting techniques. In particular, a very simple model of 'plausible' forecasting is presented that anyone can undertake easily, cheaply and quickly. We will also introduce the concept of long-range planning and discuss how to integrate short-term strategies while accommodating the changes and alternatives that may be necessary for long-term success.

Whether you are marketing sport or marketing using sport, the concept of 'the future' is an important one. There are many sophisticated computer modelling and marketing simulation tools available to assist business decision-makers with their questions about the future. However, roughly 80 per cent of all technological forecasts turn out to be wrong (Golden, Milewicz & Herbig 1994). This doesn't mean that we should give up on forecasting or throw technological forecasts out of the window. The truth remains that the future is rarely certain and so some system of forecasting is necessary. The key is to balance your forecasting tools. Don't over-rely on technology-based forecasting tools while ignoring social and economic changes that are not reflected in their decision schemes. Another common mistake by forecasters seems to be the favouring of dramatic predictions of change over the reality of incremental change. It is easy for analysts in a particular industry to get caught up in the innovations of the moment and magnify and project these innovations via an industry 'group-think' approach to the future.

The message here is for you to be balanced and realistic in your approach to forecasting and planning for the future. This does not limit your creative strategy or your ability to be innovative in the marketplace. Rather, it will give you a more realistic or 'plausible' set of guidelines to develop real working strategies for the future.

## Forecasting

What is forecasting? Forecasting is predicting, projecting or estimating some future event or condition that is outside an organisation's control and provides a basis for managerial planning (Golden, Milewicz & Herbig 1994).

Understanding the concept of forecasting is important as it is the basis for many of the 'predictions' in business-based reports and forms part of the basis on which many decisions are made. Whether you are involved in the sports industry directly, or you are using sport in the marketing of your product or service, you must understand how to facilitate strategic planning and how to evaluate plans that are presented to you. Quite often these plans will be based on the prediction of certain changes in the future or alternatively on certain variables not changing in the future. A basic understanding of forecasting will allow you to decide whether or not these predictions (or lack thereof) are reasonable for a given sport or business situation.

Some of the common mistakes made in the forecasts of products, growth markets and business trends are based on:

- over-reliance on the underlying technologies of the forecast, ignoring customer needs
- excessive optimism
- failure to conduct simple cost/benefit comparisons
- inadequate definition of markets, users, comparability from year to year
- failure to adjust for historical experience, and
- marketers and forecasting technicians becoming caught up in the spirit of the times (Golden, Milewicz & Herbig 1994).

There are four basic categories of forecasting models:

1. Judgemental models
2. Technological forecasting models
3. Time series models
4. Causal models.

Judgemental models rely on intuitive judgements, opinions and probabilities. We discuss one such method in this section that we call 'plausible forecasting'. Technological forecasting methods also rely on judgement and are particularly appropriate for very new technologies and very long-range forecasting. Time series models are based only on past data with the focus on using patterns, changes, disturbances and trends in the data to forecast the future. The final category of forecasting, causal models, is based on the relationship between predictable factors and outcomes.

In choosing the most appropriate forecasting technique you should evaluate a number of critical factors:

- **Time horizons**. Most managers will want the forecast result to extend as far into the future as possible. But a manager must choose the right technique for the period of time desired.
- **Technical sophistication**. Match the sophistication of your organisation and the skills of the people who will be doing the forecasting to the technique to be used. Forecasting requirements should also be factored into database and information network designs within the organisation.

- **Cost**. Greater accuracy has its price. How precise do you need to be? How much is the information worth and how much is the company willing to commit?
- **Data availability**. Before choosing a technique, the forecaster must consider the extensiveness, currency, accuracy and representativeness of the available data. More data tend to improve accuracy, and detailed data are more valuable than those presented in the aggregate. Because a technique's ability to handle fluctuations is important to a forecast's success, the manager must match the sensitivity and stability of a technique to the random and systematic variability components of a data series.
- **Variability and consistency of data**. Beyond changes that might occur in the company's structure or its environment, the manager must look at the kinds of stable relationship assumed among a model's independent variables (represented by the 'external stability' dimension).
- **Amount of detail necessary**. While aggregate forecasts are easy to prepare, the manager will need specific information (including individual product classes, time periods, geographic area or product-market groupings, for example) to determine quotas or allocate resources. How much information is available? How much is necessary to provide excellent results?
- **Accuracy**. Is it satisfactory to be 95 per cent, 99 per cent or 99.9 per cent accurate? Why do you need the forecast? Accuracy and cost are often traded off. The degree to which this is possible depends on the importance of the forecast and the decisions that will rely on the information.
- **Timing**. When will the forecast be used? Timing issues may involve the frequency or intervals of forecasting required, and/or the cyclical nature of a specific business/industry.
- **Form**. Who will use the data? All information collection, manipulation and dissemination should consider the users of that information. Forecasting should produce information in such a form that best facilitates decision-making (Golden, Milewicz & Herbig 1994, pp.35–6).

It is very difficult to forecast the 'future of sport' in light of turbulent times and complex factors that characterise the modern sports business environment. However, there should be no excuse for not at least contemplating the future of sport and coming up with possible or 'plausible' scenarios and stories to describe what is likely to happen in your sport or industry using sport in the future.

## Plausible forecasting

This section gives a brief overview of a very simplistic forecasting model that you can use in the classroom, a sporting organisation or a business. It could be best categorised as a type of judgemental forecasting and for our purposes we will refer to it as 'plausible forecasting'.

Plausible forecasting is a way to lead discussion about what might happen in the future of your sport or other business and to identify those factors or events that are critical or central to your sporting business success. We can summarise the process in three basic steps:

### Step 1: Identifying critical factors

You should begin by gathering together a group of 'relevant' participants that might include employees, board members, industry experts, academics, partners, athletes, coaches and anyone else that is affected by or will affect the future of your sporting business. Invite this group to a discussion forum about 'the future' where you will brief them about your ideas and concerns for the future and provide them with any relevant planning, industry, market or environmental information. Then at the forum ask each of them to write about four areas on a poster:

1. positive comments (optimistic)
2. negative comments (pessimistic)
3. different ideas/opinions
4. questions about the unknown.

Have people place their Post-it notes in four areas around the room. Then collate the comments for discussion with the facilitator and the group. Identify the key areas of uncertainty and those factors that appear to be central to the success and/or failure of the sport business in the future.

### Step 2: Plotting critical factors – The four futures model

Figure 12.1 shows the basic concept of the four futures model. From the discussion with your group of key stakeholders, select two variables at a time that affect your sport but for which the future is unknown. When you plot these factors you are essentially outlining four possible futures for your sports business on the basis of those particular factors (shown as futures 1 to 4 in Figure 12.1). The two possible outcomes for each variable are also obtained from the judgement-based discussions held with key stakeholders.

**Figure 12.1:** The four futures model

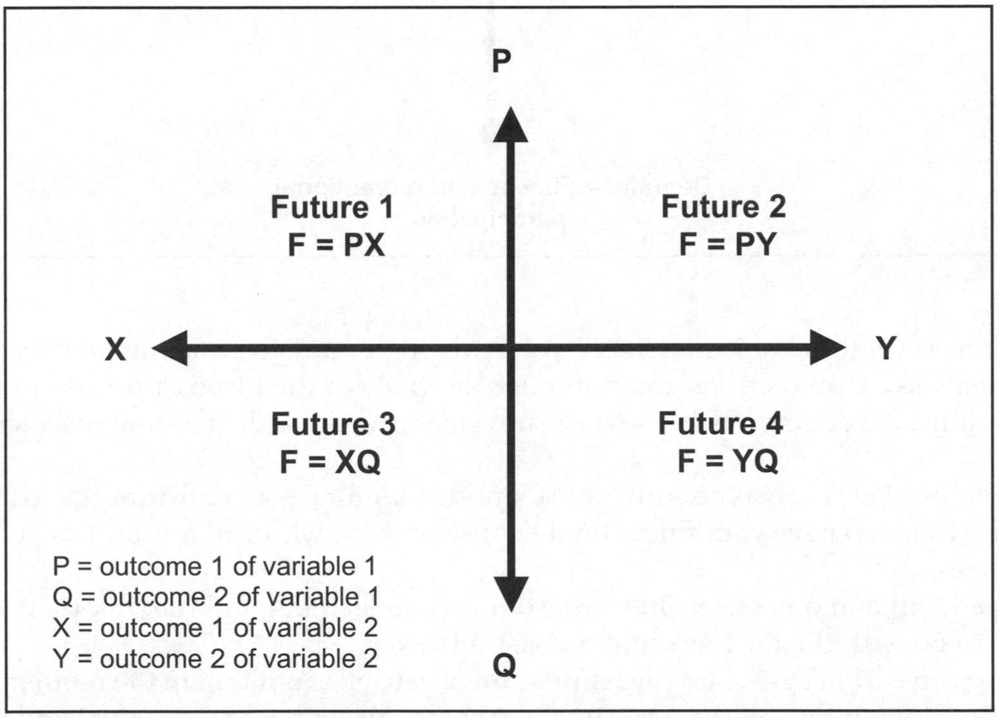


### Step 3: Planning for the future

For each of the four possible futures you should draft some preliminary strategic plans and contingencies to take to the planning committee or to be used by key decision-makers. Further investigation of each possible future may be warranted, including some secondary data collection and possibly even the application of further forecasting techniques where the cost vs benefit ratio warrants it. For example, the government may be concerned about the future allocation of public funds to sport. How can they be sure that they will be spending money in the right areas in the future? What will the future trends of sports participation be at the community, state and national levels? If discussions show that supply and demand of sporting facilities are two critical factors for the government they might consider a four futures model that looks something like the one in Figure 12.2. In this model the supply factor has two possible outcomes, one where the government focuses on facilitating the growth and commercialisation of large sports, and the other where the government focuses on grassroots spending on community, exercise-based sports participation. The demand factor has similar outcomes, one being that the demand is for competition and elite sports spectating, while the other demand outcome is demand for community-based fitness facilities. Based on those factors and the combination of their possible outcomes, the government can now further investigate and plan for four possible contingencies with regards to directing sports funding.

**Figure 12.2:** Possible four futures model for the supply and demand of sports facilities

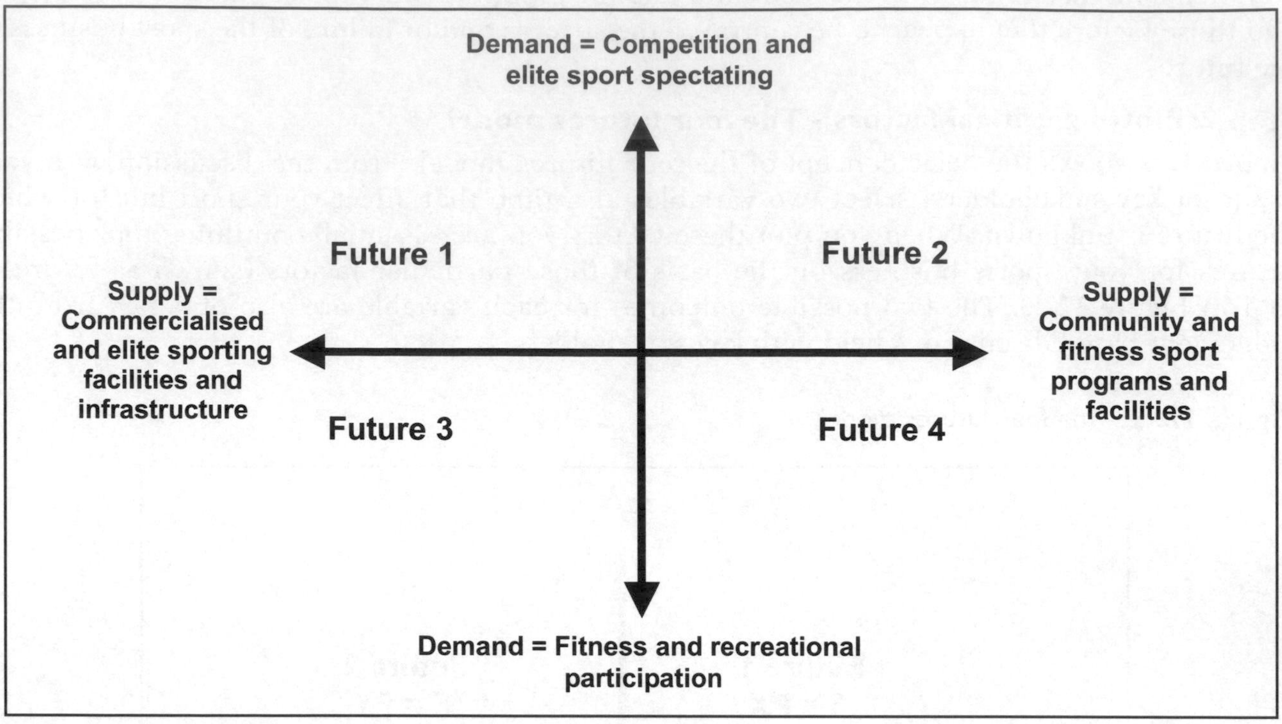


Remember to try to be objective when participating in any forecasting activity. Forecasting biases can easily skew predictions and minimise the value of the forecast for use in planning. In order to minimise the effects of biases on the forecasting process decision-makers should ensure that they:

- Know their market. There is no substitute for understanding your consumers and stakeholders. Make sure that you have your finger on the pulse of those who will buy and use your products and services.
- Be independent and objective. Question your own judgement and that of others and don't be tempted to go with the flow or build on past mistakes.
- Be conservative. Don't give into the temptation of getting caught up in the moment, promising or expecting 'big things' all the time. Realise that many changes are gradual and incremental. Deflate forecasts for margins of safety also.

The next section will examine the concept of long-range planning and developing robust strategies.

## Long-range planning

Forecasting models and predictions of the future are of little value if your organisation concentrates on the development and implementation of short-term strategies. In fact an even greater problem is the conflicting nature of what is needed for short-term success and what is needed for long-term survival and success.

Much of modern-day corporate strategy can be classified as short-term. In practice, corporate strategy is about optimising current performance, matching the organisation's activities to the environment and to its resource capabilities (Mercer 1998).

Long-range planning, on the other hand, should be concerned with 'robust strategy', which above all else concerns itself with the long-term survival and maximisation of the business and its stakeholders. Robust strategies are the operationalisation of those activities that will ensure that all potential threats are covered. These long-range or robust strategies are designed to exploit any potential that might emerge from changes in the external environment, and guard against the whole range of threats that might endanger survival in the long-term (Mercer 1998). The major

**Table 12.1:** Differences between 'corporate' and 'robust' strategies

| | Corporate strategy | Robust strategies |
|---|---|---|
| **Objectives** | Optimising performance | Ensuring survival |
| **Characteristics** | Short-term, single focus | Long-term, divergent coverage |
| **Outcomes** | Effective commitment | Comprehensive understanding |
| **Beneficiaries** | Individual profiteers | Community stakeholders |

Source: Mercer 1998, p.176

difference between these types of strategies and shorter-term corporate-based strategies is that robust strategies focus on critical developments in the external environment, not just the marketing environment but the wider social, political, economic and global environments. Corporate strategies tend to make themselves ultimately dependent on the manipulation of internal resources and accountability rather than deliberate long-term success and survival in the marketplace. Table 12.1 highlights the differences between 'corporate' strategy and 'robust strategies'.

So how does the process of long-range planning fit in with the development of shorter-term strategic plans and objectives? Ideally long-range planning would precede the setting of shorter-term corporate strategy and the satisfaction of one would lead to the satisfaction of the other. However, as we mentioned earlier it is possible that long-range plans may actually conflict with the maximisation of opportunities in the short-term business environment. Therefore you need to be able to carry out forecasting and future planning, develop your robust long-range strategies and then compare these with shorter-term corporate strategies to plot the best possible course of action. Figure 12.3 shows the possible stages involved in developing a long-range marketing plan. You will note that the last three stages are about reconciling your long-range robust strategies with your shorter-term corporate strategy. This might mean changing or altering one or both strategies in some way.

By treating long-range planning and short-term corporate strategy development as separate tasks, organisations should be better able to take account of future changes. This may involve some tweaking and steering of

**Figure 12.3:** Stages in the development of a long-range marketing plan

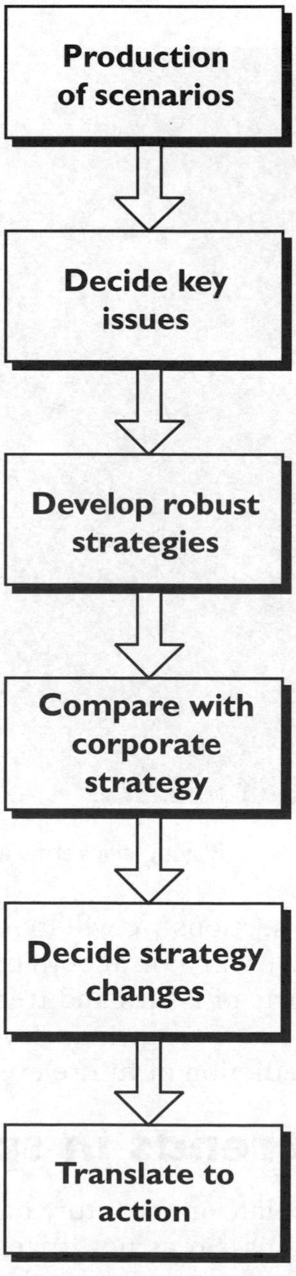


Source: Mercer 1998, p.178

short-term strategies and objectives but will provide a better overall strategic direction for the future. As sporting organisations struggle with the creation of strategic and business-oriented structures, they must consider their approaches to strategic planning and implementation very carefully. Some sporting clubs, including the seemingly market-oriented UK rugby clubs, have been accused of short-termism that impedes their ability to generate and implement strategic marketing plans (Harris & Jenkins 2001). UK soccer clubs and indeed many European soccer clubs on the other hand seem to have mastered the integration of long-range and short-term strategies. The Australian Cricket Board is similarly committed to long-range planning and short-term strategies, which is evident in the strategic plan they released in 2002 titled 'From Backyard to Baggy Green: A Strategic Plan for Australian Cricket 2002–2004'. The document covers four strategic priorities of the organisation, which are to:

1. strengthen and protect the spirit of cricket
2. thrive at the elite level
3. attract, develop and keep people in the game
4. ensure cricket has a strong and sustainable financial base (Australian Cricket Board 2002).

Playing cricket as a kid can lead to a lifelong interest in the game

In the next sections we will look at some changes that have or are taking place in the sports industry now. We will look at both trends in the marketing of sport and trends in marketing using sport. These sorts of issues and trends are important for both forecasting and future planning. Keeping up to date in your industry is imperative if you are going to be able to add any intuitive value to the prediction of future events in your business.

## Future trends in sport

Before we speculate on the future of sport we should preface our discussion with a warning about future predictions. So as not to get 'caught up' in the spirit of our topic we should remember that many past prognosticators have been wrong about innovations that they vowed would most certainly change our lives. Video phones were going to revolutionise our communications; colonies on the moon would be flourishing by now, as would the practice of eating our food via

**Table 12.2:** The future that wasn't

| | |
|---|---|
| **Videophones** | Unveiled at the 1964 World's Fair, engineers said they would replace standard phones by 2000. Available but vastly unpopular and expensive. |
| **Moon colonies** | *New York Times* in 1960 predicted a 'flourishing civilisation on the moon twenty or thirty years hence'. |
| **Food in pills** | The Jetsons' preferred diet was said to have been an imminent reality. |
| **Cars that drive themselves** | Sensors in the car and on the road were behind the 1950s idea of an 'automatic vehicle'. They never moved past prototype. |
| **Jet packs** | A 1969 prototype, test piloted for *Popular Science* magazine, was predicted to revolutionise short distance travel. A mass-market model never managed to fly. |
| **Moving sidewalks** | Part of the 1964 World's Fair exhibit 'City of the Future'; a better exhibit might have included scooters and rollerblades. |

capsules. Cars should be driving themselves by now and rocket-propelled backpacks should be our kids' preferred mode of transport – that or the moving sidewalks that should be lining our futuristic city streets. Alas, none of these things have come to pass. Table 12.2 outlines these predictions and when they were made.

It is fair to say that some futuristic proposals have also been sadly underestimated by businesses of their time. Take a look at some of the quotes below and think about any modern-day equivalents that you might have difficulty conceptualising. Is it possible that you are missing the next big thing?

- 'This "telephone" has too many shortcomings to be seriously considered as a means of communication. The device is inherently of no value to us.' *Western Union internal memo 1876*
- 'Everything that can be invented has been invented.' *Charles H. Duell, U.S. Commissioner of Patents 1899*
- 'The wireless music box has no imaginable commercial value. Who would pay for a message sent to nobody in particular?' *David Sarnoff's associates in response to his urgings for investments in radio in the 1920s*
- 'Who the … wants to hear actors talk?' *H.M. Warner, Warner Brothers 1927*

Sports marketers have also been known to fail in the prediction of 'winning new concepts' and market needs. Rugby League's Super League fiasco and American XFL (extreme football league – rock and roll wrestling meets gridiron) are examples of two very costly mistakes. Super League administrators grossly underestimated the loyalty and grassroots support for the traditional competition and club structure that already existed. Their attempt to create new clubs was met with much resistance from both players and supporters alike. Despite the increased salaries of the players, the league eventually failed due to the lack of support from fans and therefore sponsors. The XFL failed to capture the imagination of either wrestling or football fans in America as it fell short of the expectations and traditions of both markets.

Some of the current and future trends in sport are 'back to the future' in nature. In the 1950s, officials in developed countries limited sport in schools and warned people to stay away from large gatherings in a desperate attempt to limit the spread of polio. The outbreak of fear caused by terrorist attacks around the world threatens to have a similar effect on modern sporting events. The minor league baseball league in America recorded its lowest crowds in history in 2002 due in part, franchisors speculated, to the fear of terrorist attacks at public events (Facer 2002). Pre-Games sales for the Athens 2004 Olympics were abnormally low as terrorist bombings in the lead-up to the games fuelled a growing concern that they would be the target of attacks that Greek security forces were not prepared for.

The social accountability and morality of sports teams and celebrities is also heading back to the future. Sport should be an inherently healthy and wholesome pursuit and generalities are often made that this should also be true of sports stars as role models. The high paying heyday of the 1980s and 1990s in high-profile sports such as football, basketball and baseball seemed to forgive a range of immoralities and legal and social violations among sports stars. However, as sport becomes even bigger business sporting teams and celebrities are being held more accountable for their actions as immoral and/or illegal behaviour is translated into lost revenue and the breakdown of hard-won sponsorships. Elite athletes will be held increasingly accountable for their on- and off-field behaviour.

What you really need is a balanced perspective when forecasting or interpreting future changes. Make sure that you analyse a multitude of factors including environmental, technological, social, political and legal factors when contemplating the likelihood or impact of any one future change. The next sections take a brief look at some of the more interesting and/or significant trends in sports marketing.

## Trends in the marketing of sport

**New product development** is not new in sport, with indoor cricket and touch football just two examples of sports products that were developed to target new and different markets. Rule changes, equipment changes, venue modifications are all possible when looking to repackage or retarget an existing sport. Beach volleyball began as a variation on the traditional game, utilising a different venue and a smaller number of players. The sport grew from a trendy sports variant into a serious international competition featured in the Olympic Games line-up. English cricket recently repackaged and revamped traditional cricket into a competition called Twenty20 cricket. The shortened game has just 20 overs per side and can be completed in around three hours. The game targets a young professional audience who don't have the time or the inclination to spend all day or indeed several days watching one-day or test cricket matches. Twenty20 cricket is often scheduled at night to allow spectators to go to the game after work in place of other social activities such as going out to dinner or the pub. The competition has enjoyed great success with young English professionals who have flocked to Twenty20 cricket and made the competition a part of their social calendar. In 2003 the English Twenty20 Cup attracted 255 000 spectators and surpassed that figure in 2004 by the middle of the game schedule (Twenty20 Cup 2004). Time-poor spectators will no doubt continue to support sports that cater to the limited amount of time dedicated to leisure activities and entertainment.

No doubt all sports will consider game and competition variations in the future in order to target new markets and/or grow existing markets. Trends such as the growth of recreational and leisure-oriented sports activities and a drift away from competitive team sports participation could also give rise to some interesting new variations of traditional sports.

**Volunteerism** is a $42 billion a year activity in Australia. Hundreds of thousands of people give up their time and energy to the value of $42 billion each year in Australia to keep both grassroots and professional sporting programs, charities, religious and social programs running (Volunteering Australia 2004). In both the present and increasingly in the future, the work and life balancing act will make volunteering either unattractive or impossible for many adults. Many people are simply not prepared to give up their dwindling leisure hours in this way. This creates an obvious problem in that many sports rely on volunteers in both an administrative and an active coaching/refereeing capacity. Many sporting bodies and clubs cannot afford to pay for their traditional volunteer roles to be filled by paid employees and professionals. However, on the flipside there is an increase in the willingness to consider capital involvement – 'how much can I pay as a substitute for involvement' – and this could be one area that sporting organisations could exploit. The danger however remains that volunteerism drives not only the functional aspects of sport but many of the social, emotional and communal ties to games and clubs that help keep sports alive and viable at both the grassroots and elite levels.

The decline in volunteerism can also be attributed to an ageing of the global population, an increase in the use of technology to consumer sport and perhaps even the drift of professional sports away from community-based programs.

**Technology** is impacting on almost every aspect of every sport in the world. From the clothes that athletes wear to the surfaces they play on, technology is changing the face of sport. The changes are apparent for the way in which people consume sport also. More and more people choose to consume sport via the Internet, mobile devices and even substitute sports spectating for virtual participation via games and simulators. Rather than looming like some cataclysmic event, these changes are incremental and invasive and involve technical, social and economic factors. Consider some of the changes that we have perhaps already seen and by now find quite underwhelming. In May 2003 the final of a FIFA tournament was played on a new technology-advanced artificial turf for the first time. So what, you might ask? Well, the quality of the pitch can dramatically affect the outcome of a game and artificial turf has the potential to increase the speed of play and make matches more exciting, thereby increasing audiences and revenues (Prism 2003). At the same time, artificial turf can change the game and sometimes increase the risk of injury. Swimming is another sport that has attempted to harness technology to improve the performance of athletes. For example, Speedo's Sharkskin swimsuits were designed to emulate a shark. They sought a design that decreases drag, boosts performance by compressing the muscles, and minimises discomfort and rubbing (Wagner 2004). The suit's fabric is treated with a coating of Teflon or a similar substance, resulting in water sliding off the suit and an interesting side-effect where air is trapped between the suit and the swimmer's skin making the swimmer more buoyant (Zempel 2001). This caused a number of swimmers at the 2004 Olympics to go to the blocks dry since they were afraid of losing some of the suit's buoyancy by warming up. Therefore it would seem that the suit has the potential to affect behaviour as well as performance.

Other technological trends include the increasing popularity of mobile technologies and wireless Internet applications. In 2002 Bill Gates showed us Microsoft's new 'wrist communicator', a watch that can deliver the news headlines, local weather, stock prices, and of course sports news headlines and eventually real time stats. The watches are now beginning to appear and while they still have more gadget value than true information value, it is the potential of such a device that should interest sports marketers.

Mobile technology along with the ever increasing interest in online sports betting makes a powerful combination. Interactive gambling channels are springing up in Europe; those such as iSports TV interactive gambling are quickly gathering momentum in the UK. Sports betting online is growing in popularity in Switzerland, Austria and Germany with the Scientific Games Oddset system catering to over 100 million customers. Peer-to-peer technology is also being used to establish person-to-person betting exchanges all over the world. System provider TradingSports Exchange have plans to continue business development in Europe,

Technology is constantly changing sport

North America and Asia in the future. An interactive TV sports service has been launched by pay-TV operator Sky Television in New Zealand, hoping to attract its 350 000 subscribers to a range of betting features (*Sport and Technology News* 2003).

## Sport spotlight

### Finger sports

As people use computers and the Net much more in the future, there will be exploration of niche sports as people become more aware of the diverse possibilities open to them. Computers will greatly enhance many sports. We will see significant overlap of computer games and sports, as a range of force feedback technology makes for computer games that are increasingly physical. Such equipment may also be used in training, guiding the student in exactly the optimal movements, eliminating bad habits as soon as they start. Artificial intelligence will enable sports personalities to be emulated so that anyone can play against top level players via their games machine.

Glasses with head-up displays, active contact lenses or wall-sized screens will all provide a superb visual environment in which to participate or spectate. Sports heroes might make more money from recording their behaviours on DVD and competing with every Tom, Dick or Harriet virtually thereafter than from actually playing in the real world. We can expect that such developments would increase the overall skill levels in every field.

Many computer games are networked today, and a big surprise when this trend started was just how many people want to be spectators in computer games. Having been trashed by a competitor, they want to see someone else fall victim later. Most people logged onto networked games platforms are just watching rather than playing. It can't be long before we see major TV events at the top levels of some popular games (there have already been a few minor series based on computer games). These 'finger sports' may take a significant proportion of sports revenue, though there will doubtless be fierce debate as to where the boundaries of 'real' sport lie when nerds start taking some top sports prizes.

Technology is making itself known in all facets of sport at all levels from the live online streaming of women's college basketball games in America to mobile phone accessible instant images of horses before, during and after European racing events. Organisers of the Athens Olympics pinned their hopes on Internet ticket sales as a solution to their distribution problems for the 2004 Games, while individual sporting clubs all over the world place more and more reliance on technological solutions like the Internet as part of their marketing mix. Manchester United relies heavily on their agreement with Vodafone to provide supporters with a wide range of mobile services including results, news, still and video images, ringtones and even Man U computer games. As wireless Internet access becomes the norm in coffee shops and airports, sporting stadia are investigating the need for and possibilities of such access on their home turf. Sports broadcasting is a hotbed of technological innovation with new improved visuals accompanying cricket, tennis and football broadcasts. ESPN also showcased a number of innovative new technologies at the X Games in August 2003 and continues to push the limits of broadcasting technologies, giving spectators a simulated experience of what the athletes actually do.

Many national league bodies such as America's NFL and Australia's ACB have deliberately and actively sought hi-tech partners to help them face the future challenges and demands of a growing techno-fan base. Technology is allowing fans and spectators to become more 'actively' involved whether it is through simulations, real time data viewing, or even voting via SMS text messaging systems for MVPs (most valuable player) and favourite athletes.

New products and services are being created for some sports via technology. Major League Baseball, the NFL and even some college-level sports are selling live or delayed broadcasts of games online for subscription or pay-per-view rates. Cricket fans in Australia can also subscribe to enhanced information services via SMS technology on their mobile phones where they can receive game highlights, commentary and regular interval updates etc. about matches in progress.

Technology also impacts upon the administration of clubs and sports. The French Football Federation have partnered with software supplier Oracle-Manapps to supply their 130 leagues and districts with a secure intranet system to deal with the flow of information from 5000 competitions, 1 million matches per year, 2.3 million licensees, and 27 000 referees who can now supply match reports via their new generation mobile phones (Sport and Technology, June 2003).

Source: Pearson 2003

**Emerging markets** like China are hot topics in almost every industry and sport is no exception. As domestic markets are conquered, Australian, American and European sporting bodies are looking at the mega populations of countries like China, India and even South America as potential new fan bases for their sports. This can have various impacts including the development of particular games in those countries, the relocation of events to these markets or inclusion of these countries in international tours, and more recently the recruiting of players from emerging markets. Recruiting players from emerging markets serves two purposes. First, it can serve as a novelty for domestic fans and uncover talents with little to no competition for their signing. Second, it can emotionally link an entire nation to a sport that they otherwise are unfamiliar with. This has been the case with two giant Chinese basketball players, Yao Ming and Yi Jianlian. Latest rookie talent Yi Jianlian from China stands 6ft 11in tall and is believed to be only 15 years of age. Before even being recruited to an American junior league, Adidas and Nike began battling over this giant boy, Adidas eager to loosen Nike's hold on Chinese basketball. Nike eventually won out signing Yi to a six-figure multi-year deal worth far more than the boy's actual salary and more than even Yao Ming's original Nike contract (Larmer 2003). Sporting franchises, sponsors and broadcasters alike are all vying for the attention of potential new market stars like Yi Jianlian because of the more than 1.3 billion home country supporters that he might bring with him.

Sports giant ESPN also forecasts that the NBA and Major League Basketball in America will experience exponential international growth because of the dramatic numbers of international recruits. With 67 new international players on the NBA roster in 2002 and the continued success of Japanese starts Hideki Matsui and Ichiro in baseball, the sports merchandising opportunities alone are staggering.

In their top 10 list of forecasts for the future of sports business, ESPN included:

1. The NBA and Major League Baseball will experience exponential growth.
2. More teams will institute variable ticket pricing.
3. Sports apparel and merchandise will go retro.

4. More athletes will buy interest in sports teams.
5. Action sports will continue to garner attention.
6. Stadium naming rights will continue to rise.
7. More teams will rely on ethnic marketing.
8. Insurance coverage will dictate the size and length of players guaranteed contracts.
9. Interest and following of high school level sports will rise as recruiting ages lower.
10. Technology will compete with live action sports.

Source: Rovell 2002

## Trends in marketing using sport

We mentioned a variety of ways to use sport in marketing in Chapters 9 and 10 and some of the advantages and pitfalls that accompany sports strategies. In this section we will briefly look at several issues that are worth watching when marketing using sport. They are by no means the only contemporary challenges for marketers and they may represent both opportunities and threats depending on the stakeholder in question.

**Retro appeal**. In the wake of the fall of mega sporting personalities like Kobe Bryant, companies have become nervous about signing athletes to long-term multi-million dollar endorsement contracts. One fallout has been a rise in the popularity of past legends, those who have already experienced sporting success and managed to maintain a squeaky clean image into retirement. Obvious living legends like Michael Jordan continue to attract huge dollars but even long dead athletes like Walter Payton of Chicago Bears fame are hot property for companies like IBM and apparel merchandiser Next. Next signed with Payton's Trust to license his name, image, photograph and signature on a line of retro jerseys and hats, because it believed he had proven his integrity and popularity (Janoff 2004). New mega signings still occur with Nike's mid-2003 signing of child star LeBron James to a seven-year, $90 million deal a case in point. However, in many cases the new endorser faces may be veteran, retired or deceased players with unsullied reputations.

Other retro moves include Nike's Air Jordan and Air Force One revivals with the latter receiving major airtime when rapper Nelly sang about the shoes on his 2002 multi-platinum album *Nellyville*. Retro has also helped to put retired players back in the public eye and increased the value of former stars like NFL players John Elway, Joe Montana and Howie Long, ex-baseball star Cal Ripken, cricket legends Allan Border and Steve Waugh, ex-rugby league great Wally Lewis and enduring tennis legends like Pete Sampras and Martina Navratilova.

Another interesting backlash from the personal shortcomings of individual sporting celebrities might be the increase in interest in groups of athletes or whole clubs. This will help organisations avoid situations where the fate of one athlete can make or break an entire marketing campaign.

Squeaky-clean sporting legends could well become more marketable than their contemporary counterparts

**Overpricing**. As mega sports and mega events are continually carved up and sold off, companies are becoming increasingly wary about whether or not they are getting value for money from their sports investments. This might have several impacts. For example, some analysts believe that grassroots sports sponsorship is on the rise and that this trend can be attributed to a number of factors including:

1. Increasing clutter in sports sponsorship (Olympic, collegiate and professional)
2. Escalating big-time sports sponsorship costs
3. Increasing integration of sponsorships
4. Increasing consumer-market fragmentation
5. New trends in sport (extreme and fringe sport popularity) (Greenwald & Fernandez-Balboa 1998).

All of which have the potential to push companies to look elsewhere for sports marketing opportunities, particularly in previously undervalued markets. Analysts see more companies looking beyond traditional pro sports towards niche sports, such as snowboarding, skiing and extreme sports events, and also more towards tennis, golf, soccer, bowling (the most popular participation sports in many developed countries) and even fishing. Even something as niche as paintball could have marketing impact as participation there has increased 47.5 per cent from 1998 to 8.7 million in 2002 in the USA (Janoff 2004).

Overpricing is also an issue to finals consumers. As discussed in Chapter 8, ever increasing ticket and merchandise prices have the potential to alienate even the most loyal of fans.

## Counterpoint

Sport is a huge part of the Australian culture and in several decades it has also become more professional and more organised than ever before. More Australians watch sport now than in any other time in the country's history and there are more sporting facilities at every level than most Australians could have ever dreamed of. The sporting future of Australia should be very rosy indeed. Why then in 2004 has the Australian Government declared that childhood obesity has reached epidemic proportions and Australia is second only to the United States on the dubious honour roll of having the most deaths due to obesity in the world?

Government and private sector funding alike is poured into sporting facilities and competitions in Australia but it seems that spectating rather than participation will define the nation's sports obsession in the future. 'Fast food' sports and alternative consumption such as sporting video games and interactive television may actually be cannibalising the sports participation market. Is it possible that the biggest challenge in the future of sport will be to design and offer sports, games and fitness activities that cater to a time-poor market and at the same time offer an exciting and competitive experience? Will sports spectating grow at the expense of sports participation?

## Summary

- **define forecasting**
  Forecasting is predicting, projecting or estimating some future event or condition that is outside an organisation's control and provides a basis for managerial planning.
- **understand basic forecasting techniques**
  There are four basic categories of forecasting models:
  1 Judgemental models
  2 Technological forecasting models

3 Time series models
4 Causal models.

What is important is that the right technique is chosen for the right situation and that any method used is balanced with intuitive insight and realism with regards to predictions.

- **understand the importance and process of long-range planning**
  Long-range planning and the development of robust strategies is important if the impact of future events is going to be maximised or minimised depending on the degree to which those events represent opportunities or threats. The process of long-range planning and the resultant development and implementation of robust strategies can guard against short-termism in managerial perspective. Long-range planning must be reconciled with corporate strategy so that the two don't work in conflict.
- **identify some future trends in the marketing of sport**
  The impact of technology may dominate many of the future trends in sport. Changing everything from the sports product itself to the way it is delivered and consumed, technology will continue to offer challenges and opportunities for sports at all levels. Other trends include a decrease in volunteerism and an increase in the importance of emerging markets like China and India.
- **identify some future trends in marketing using sport**
  Marketing using sport might take a look at many of the retro opportunities in the future to avoid the unpredictable nature of individual athletes and appeal to the nostalgic emotion of fans and spectators. Marketers might also look to grassroots and fringe sports to provide value for money opportunities in highly targeted markets.

## Review questions

1. What is forecasting?
2. What are some of the common reasons why forecasts of business trends fail?
3. How can decision-makers minimise the effects of biases on the forecasting process?
4. What is a 'robust' strategy and how is it different from corporate strategy?
5. What are the typical stages in developing a long-range marketing plan?

## Applied activities

1. Do a search on the Internet about *rule changes in cricket*. Have there been any changes in the rules of international cricket in the last decade? If so, what were they and why were they made? Is there any debate about proposed changes? If so, what are the arguments for change and why are or aren't they necessary? What impact will any such rule changes have on the 'business of cricket'?
2. Read ESPN's 'Forecasting the sports business future' http://espn.go.com/sportsbusiness/s/2002/1230/1484284.html and read what was considered the

top 10 trends to watch for in 2003–2004. How many of those issues were actually hot topics? What evidence is there that those forecasts had an impact on the relevant sports and industries? If you had to write the list for this year, what would you include?

3. You are the marketing manager of a large national insurance company. Your company invests heavily in sport, using it for their national marketing campaigns. It is time for your two-yearly review of your sports marketing programs and you need to make some recommendations to the committee on what you should do in the future with regards to using sport in marketing. What process will you use to forecast and plan for the future? What are some of the key issues that you will bring to the committee's attention?

# References

Australian Cricket Board 2002, 'From Backyard to Baggy Green: A Strategic Plan for Australian Cricket 2002–2004', pp.1–21.

Facer, D. 2002, 'Minor-league Baseball Searching for Crowds', *Deseret News*, 21 May, http://deseretnews.com/dn/view/0,1249,400009755,00.html, viewed 12 July 2004.

Golden, J., Milewicz, J. & Herbig, P. 1994, 'Forecasting: Trials and Tribulations', *Management Decision*, Vol. 32, No. 1, MCB University Press Limited, pp.33–6.

Greenwald, L. & Fernandez-Balboa, J. 1998, 'Trends in the Sport Marketing Industry and in the Demographics of the United States: Their Effect on the Strategic Role of Grassroots Sport Sponsorship in Corporate America', *Sport Marketing Quarterly*, Vol. 7, No. 4, pp.35–47.

Harris, L. & Jenkins, H. 2001, 'Planning the Future of Rugby Union: A Study of the Planning Activities of UK Rugby Clubs', *Marketing Intelligence and Planning*, Vol. 19, No. 2, pp.112–24.

Janoff, B. 2004, 'The World Not According to Kobe', *Adweek Magazines Newswire*, BPI Communications, 12 January.

Larmer, B. 2003, 'The Next Yao Ming?', *Time Magazine: What's Next*, August 24, http://www.time.com/time/covers/1101030908/xyi.html, viewed 27 February 2004.

Mercer, D. 1998, 'Long-Range Marketing', *Journal of Marketing Practice: Applied Marketing Science*, Vol. 4, No. 6, pp.174–84.

Miller, M. 2004, 'Forward Thinking', *PC Magazine*, 17 February, p.5.

Pearson, I. 2003, 'The Future of Sport', Sphere, BT Group, http://www.btplc.com/pda/Innovationandtechnology/Insights/IanPearson/sport.htm, viewed 12 February 2004.

*Prism* 2003, 'Testing the Future of Sport', June-July, No. 197, The University of Strathclyde, pp.1–3, http://www.strath.ac.uk/news/prism/.

Rovell, D. 2002, 'Forecasting the Sports Business Future', ESPN Sports Business, December, http://espn.go.com/sportsbusiness/s/2002/1230/1484284.html, viewed 12 February 2004.

Salkever, A. 2003, 'Sports Score Big Online', *Business Week Online*, 15 April, http://www.businessweek.com:/print/technology/content/apr2003/tc20030415_9738_tc109.htm?tc, viewed 29 February 2004.

*Sport and Technology News*, June 2003, http://www.sportandtechnology.com/news, viewed 12 February 2004.

Twenty20 Cup 2004, http://www.thetwenty20cup.co.uk/, viewed 14 May 2004.

Volunteering Australia 2004, *A National Agenda on Volunteering: Beyond the International Year of Volunteers*, http://www.volunteeringaustralia.org/publications/nat_agenda.html, viewed 3 July 2004.

Wagner, C. 2004, *The New Bodysuit: Is it Equipment or Costumer?*, http://www.crosslink.net/~cherylw/bodysuit.htm, viewed 15 October 2004.

Zempel, C. 2001, 'The Emperor's New Swimsuit', *Swimmer Magazine*, Jan-Feb, as cited in Wagner, C. 2004, *'The New Bodysuit: Is it Equipment or Costumer?'* http://www.crosslink.net/~cherylw/bodysuit.htm, viewed 15 October 2004.

# Case studies for Part 5

## ING runs into sports marketing success

### Dr Melissa Johnson Morgan

ING, a global financial institution of Dutch origin, operate in 65 countries offering banking, insurance and asset management to over 60 million private, corporate and institutional clients. ING have a diverse workforce of over 115 000 people.

In 2002 the company conducted research probing the world of sponsorships. The company wanted to partner with 'something' but it had to be the right 'something'. Strategists at ING's global headquarters analysed more than 100 types of sponsorships, investigating and surveying both internally and externally, to find the right fit. Eventually they decided that sport offered some unique marketing opportunities and that running in particular was a good 'fit' with their organisation.

Distance running was seen to fit well with ING values such as challenging limits, long-term vision and the drive to do more. In addition, running attracts a diverse field of participants and spectators in terms of gender, age and nationality, which matches the diverse and international character of ING's clients. Running is a true global sport, unhindered by cultural or language differences and is also surprisingly upscale with running being a common passion among business leaders (385 CEOs ran the New York City Marathon in 2004).

ING instigated a comprehensive and strategic plan to sponsor running and running events and to actually become involved in the sport in such a way that it added value to participants and to the organisation itself. One of the first sport properties it acquired was the title sponsorship of the New York City Marathon. This was followed by the acquisition of title sponsorships of races in Amsterdam, Brussels, Ottawa and Taipei.

The ING New York City Marathon, with more than 35 000 finishers, two million spectators, and an international television audience of 243 million, is the largest one-day sporting event in the world. The New York City Marathon website http://www.ingnycmarathon.org/ received 26 million hits and 153 781 unique visits on race day in 2004. It is a blue-chip sport property and the cornerstone of ING's foray into the sport of running.

Obtaining the title sponsorship of the New York City Marathon was no easy task as the organisers of the event had resisted having a title sponsor for 35 years. However, ING put forward a proposal to not only be a financial sponsor of the event but to work to make the event and the sport of running in general even better. ING built an enhancement element into the contract for the New York City Marathon deal, which dedicates a portion of the annual activation dollars to improving the race.

ING have stated that they want to 'own' the sport of running. They have taken their sport sponsorship very seriously and are embracing the marketing opportunities associated with their investment at every level of the company. One of the key components of their strategy is the leveraging activities associated with individual running events like the New York City Marathon. At the 2004 event, ING leveraged their investment by saturating the New York area with their brand and products. They used a balance of marketing and community service to create a strategic plan that proved a winner.

Leveraging activities could be divided into three categories, those held in the New York area prior to the event, those held in the New York area on the day of the event, and those held outside the New York area. At the heart of the strategy to leverage the event prior to the day was the 'Run For Something Better' campaign. ING worked with the city parks department to 'adopt' four public parks in New York (Thomas Jefferson Park in Manhattan, Astoria Park in Queens, and McCarren Park and Red Hook Park in Brooklyn). ING then selected four female marathon contenders and paired each with one of the parks. The women ran to raise capital improvement funding for 'their' parks.

Another pre-event leveraging activity was held at the annual Health and Fitness Expo in New York where ING showcased more than static messages. ING's marketing team put a camera on top of a police cruiser and videotaped the entire 26.2 mile route, then played the fly-through video at the exhibit in fast motion which lasted about seven minutes. Thousands came to get a look at the course while ING staffers talked up the company and its offerings and handed out custom ING Pace Wristbands that would later let runners know if they were ahead or behind at each marker during the race. Also prior to the event, street teams went door-to-door in all five boroughs of New York handing out fliers that folded into megaphones to get the public jazzed up about the race.

On the day of the race, ING set up 'Cheering Zones' throughout the race course to generate awareness. These tented zones provided a rallying point for communities to cheer their runners on and extend the reach of the event beyond traditional locations. The Cheering Zones featured wireless devices that consumers could use to check real-time progress of runners, two large monitors broadcasting live coverage, snacks and a local DJ. Spectators were also given pompoms, balloons, kazoos, and 'Go!' signs that they could customise with their favourite runner's name. New York was a sea of orange, ING's corporate colour.

To stretch the equity of the event and their investment in running around the world generally, ING also held 47 marathon themed events in other ING locations around the world prior to the race weekend.

ING executives believe that their first New York City Marathon was a huge success and they are pleased with their decision to use running as the foundation of their strategic marketing plan around the world. Post-event research to evaluate the campaign showed a big boost in awareness of the brand and its offerings, a huge jump in perceived attributes, an increase in intention to purchase, and a dramatic increase in favourability. The benefits were not only for the company however. In the true spirit of sport sponsorship leveraging, ING actually enhanced the property it was leveraging, complemented the city it was invading, and created a better experience for everyone involved.

As part of their ongoing commitment to the sport ING also developed the ING World Marathon Ranking, the first-ever elite, global points system to determine the best marathoner in the world, which culminates at the 2005 ING New York City Marathon with a $1 million prize. For the first time, the rankings put men and women in one pool to determine the world's overall best marathoner. The athlete's points are calculated on the basis of their performance in the best of three marathons over a two-year period. The performance in one race will be related to the world record, the course record and the field for that particular race – with a position bonus for top 10 runners (male and female).

With innovative leveraging design, strong strategic direction and an ongoing financial commitment, ING will continue to grow the sport of running and marathon eventing and their own corporate identity well into the future.

### *References*

'Best Activation of a Sports Sponsorship', Event Marketer, http://www.eventmarketermag.com/BEST_ACTIVATION_OF_A_SPORTS_SPONSORSHIP.917.0.html, viewed 16 February 2005.

'ING becomes first title sponsor of New York City Marathon', ING, http://www.ing.com/group/showdoc.jsp?docid=074733_EN&menopt=, viewed 16 February 2005.

Our Sponsors, http://www.ingnycmarathon.org/generalinfo/sponsors.html, viewed 16 February 2005.

## Questions

1. Why did ING choose to sponsor a sport instead of something else like the arts or a charity? Were running and the New York City Marathon in particular good choices?
2. How did ING leverage its investment in running? What do you think the objectives behind these leveraging activities were?
3. What lessons could other companies learn from ING's investment and leveraging of running as a strategic marketing tool?
4. One problem that global companies sometimes face is not having a 'local' identity. What could ING do in the future to 'localise' itself using its running sport property in your country?

# Fanatics: A new breed of super fan?

## Dr Melissa Johnson Morgan

Meaning an ardent devotee or an enthusiast, the term *fan* is short for fanatic (*The American Heritage Dictionary of the English Language*). Being a 'fan' of a particular sport or team or individual seems to infer that you are more involved and emotional than someone who might be considered just a spectator. Fans feel some emotional attachment and/or team identification and affiliation with the sport or players of that sport. Since the beginning of sporting times people have hero-worshipped sports people. Romans chanted the names of their favourite gladiators at the Coliseum and wealthy citizens bestowed favours on their favourite chariot riders. It is not uncommon in modern times to find families who have followed the same football team for over three generations and to see people dressed in team colours from head to toe on game day. In the modern world of sports tourism we also see great hordes of devoted fans following their favourite cricket, rugby or soccer teams around the world to show their support in international competitions.

A 'fanatical' fan is a fan that perhaps engages in behaviour that is beyond the normal devoted fan. A devoted fan might go to every game, but a fanatical fan might go to every game spray-painted green wearing a yellow wig and screaming rehearsed chants of support during play. England's Barmy Army, a group of vocal and boisterous cricket supporters who follow the English side around the world, have evolved from a loosely bound group of fellow fans to a highly organised group of fanatics who are afforded cult status and whose name is a registered trademark sold on merchandise around the world. The Barmy Army have a distinctly non-cricket image and have certainly gained initial recognition because of their much more football-fan-like behaviour, and therefore their distinctly different image to the average cricket spectator. Studies into the membership and behaviour of the Barmy Army have found that apart from a love of and loyalty to English cricket, the apparent power, masculinity and nationalism afforded the group are huge drawcards for those involved.

Much of the research on 'fanatical' fans has assumed that the fan is dedicated to a particular sport, team or sporting person, for example fans of Australian swimming, Lleyton Hewitt, Manchester United or the Brisbane Lions. Each of these is an individual and definable sporting entity that can be marketed and merchandised accordingly. Fans of these sporting entities usually identify with it, and are motivated by the achievement, aesthetics, drama, skill, knowledge, social opportunities and even escapism that come with being a fan of that particular entity.

Members of the recently formed Bundy Good Timers rugby union supporters are a group of highly organised and even professionally sponsored fans of the Wallabies, Australia's representative rugby union team. What started out as a few mates who were fanatical fans of the Wallabies has developed into a 1500-strong club of Wallabies fans that are sponsored by Bundaberg Rum and have their own management company. Upwards of 200 Bundy Good Timers can be seen sporting their green and gold Bundaberg Rum Bundy Good Timers shirts at games all over Australia during the representative season. This level of organisation, support and professionalism among the fans rather than the actual sport participants seems to have heralded a new era in sport spectating.

Perhaps even more interesting however is the emergence of a new breed of 'super fan'. Super fans appear to be using the group itself as the basis of identification and motivation and not concentrating their membership around a particular team or even a particular sport. They are in essence fans of being fans! The best example of this is a group who call themselves The Fanatics. The Australian-based group, founded in 1997, began as an informal group of 'mates' who followed the 1992 and 1996 Olympic Games, the 1996 Cricket World Cup and the 1996 Rugby Union Wallaby Tour. The mates shared a love of sport and frequently dressed in patriotic colours and sang patriotic songs or spruced rehearsed chants in support of their country's team or individual athlete. The group made a name for themselves at tennis tournaments where, similar to the Barmy Army, they broke the mould of the quiet tennis spectator with their coloured wigs, banners and between-service songs. Formalisation of the group first began after they were approached by Tennis Australia to participate more formally and actively in motivating crowds to support Australian tennis players. Tennis Australia, after strong accounts by Tony Roach and John Newcombe, believed that the support of this vocal and patriotic group could actually turn the tide for Australian tennis stars in tough matches both at home and overseas. The association helped them organise group seating and encouraged the players to socialise with them after matches and recognise and socialise with them during and after events.

Since their formalisation as a 'fan group', The Fanatics have worked with Australian national rugby, tennis, cricket, SOCOG, the Australian Olympic Committee and the National Football League. The band of a few mates has expanded to include the participation of over 2900 different members and 17 000 tour participants since 1997, all aged between 18 and 35. The age limit is intended to ensure that the group is motivated largely by the social benefits of being involved and to keep the activities of the group young and slightly outrageous. Despite the outrageous nature of their appearance however, The Fanatics have a code of conduct that they impose to ensure that sporting behaviour is displayed at all events. They are very careful, for example, that their chants at tennis tournaments are short and end well before players ready themselves for the next point. This extract from their website about an upcoming tour of the Davis Cup Tennis tournament is a good example of that sentiment:

> ...remember you are representing Australia & the good name of the Fanatics & the 17 000 Fanatics who have been on tour with us before so if you see someone acting like an idiot please remind them of that & tell them to pull their head in.

The Fanatics have a formal website offering information and discussion boards about a wide range of sports and sports-related issues, including AFL, basketball, cricket, golf, rugby league, soccer, tennis, rugby union, general sports and stadium information and reviews. The site also includes member news, press clippings, member spotlights, a photo gallery, sports news, tour reviews, upcoming tours and a merchandise shop.

The Fanatics are an opportunistic group that find and/or create sports opportunities on which to base their activities. Not all of these activities are sports-based, for example other supported events include an annual trip to Gallipoli to celebrate Anzac Day and tours to Oktoberfest, St Patrick's Day in Dublin and the running of the bulls in Pamplona. The Fanatics are surely a new breed of super fan that transcend the boundaries of one sport and are motivated by group affiliation, celebrity, power and patriotism. Super fans appear to be celebrities in their own right and identify with the role as a 'fan' as much as if not more so than with the sport or the team involved.

This new breed of super fan should be watched carefully by sporting administrators, sports sponsors and sport marketers as they represent a new tool and indeed a new property in the increasingly complex sport market.

### *References*

Bundaberg Rum, Bundy Good Timers, http://www.bundabergrum.com.au/flash/index.php, viewed 3 February 2005.

Parry, M. & Malcolm, D. 2004, 'England's Barmy Army: Commercialization, Masculinity and Nationalism', *International Review for the Sociology of Sport*, Vol. 39, No. 1, pp.75–94.

*The American Heritage Dictionary of the English Language*, 4th edn, 2000, Houghton Mifflin Company.

The Fanatics, http://www.thefanatics.com/, viewed 3 February 2005.

## Questions

1. What opportunities can you see for using a super fan group like The Fanatics in your marketing program? You should take the perspective of marketing using sport here.
2. Why is it important that The Fanatics are not attached to one particular sport? What are the implications for the future of sport spectating?
3. The Fanatics grew from the informal gathering of a few mates at some sporting events to a highly recognisable and commercial group that has already had over 17 000 people involved in domestic and overseas sporting tours. Do you see any potential problems with organising and managing the group in the future?
4. Visit The Fanatics website, http://www.thefanatics.com and do a review of all the ways in which you can become involved with the group. What needs and motivations do you think are being addressed by these offerings?

# Index

## H



## I



## K



## L



## M



## N

## T



## U



## V



## W



## X



## Z